FROMMER'S
Easy TO
LONDON

By
Jason Cochran

EasyGuides are ✦ Quick To Read ✦ Light To Carry
✦ For Expert Advice ✦ In All Price Ranges

FrommerMedia LLC

Published by
FROMMER MEDIA LLC

ISBN 978-1-62887-015-2 (paper), 978-1-62887-045-9 (e-book)

Editorial Director: Pauline Frommer
Editor: Craig Nelson
Production Editor: Lindsay Conner
Cartographer: Roberta Stockwell
Cover Design: Howard Grossman

For information on our other products or services, see www.frommers.com.

FrommerMedia LLC also publishes its books in a variety of electronic formats. Some content that appears in print may not be available in electronic formats.

Manufactured in the United States of America

5 4 3 2 1

CONTENTS

ABOUT THE AUTHOR

Jason Cochran was awarded Guide Book of the Year by the Society of American Travel Writers' Lowell Thomas Travel Journalism Competition and by the North American Travel Journalists Association. He is the author of *Frommer's EasyGuide to Walt Disney World and Orlando*, and he wrote the London, Orlando, and San Francisco guides for the Pauline Frommer series. He has written for publications including the *New York Post*, *Travel + Leisure*, *USA Today*, and *Scanorama* (Sweden) and been on staff at *Entertainment Weekly*, *Budget Travel*, and AOL Travel (Executive Editor). He devised questions for the first American prime-time season of *Who Wants to Be a Millionaire* (ABC) and produced and hosted *AfterShark*, the AOL post-show for Mark Burnett's *Shark Tank* (ABC). He has appeared as a commentator on, among others, *CBS This Morning*, *The Early Show* (CBS), *BBC World*, *Good Morning America*, CNN, BBC World, and the CBC, and he is a video host on AOL. He is an alumnus of Northwestern University's Medill School of Journalism and New York University's Graduate Music Theatre Writing Program. He is editor of Frommers.com.

I have received lots of invaluable help over my wonderful years in London, but for this edition, special gratitude must go to a few people in particular: Jodie Byford at London & Partners, Emma De Vadder at Visit England, Steve and Hillary Bowsher, Martin Lowe and Joel Fram, Jennifer Jellicorse, and Yhago Maia. Thank you.

ABOUT THE FROMMER TRAVEL GUIDES

For most of the past 50 years, Frommer's has been the leading series of travel guides in North America, accounting for as many as 24% of all guidebooks sold. I think I know why.

Though we hope our books are entertaining, we nevertheless deal with travel in a serious fashion. Our guidebooks have never looked on such journeys as a mere recreation, but as a far more important human function, a time of learning and introspection, an essential part of a civilized life. We stress the culture, lifestyle, history and beliefs of the destinations we cover, and urge our readers to seek out people and new ideas as the chief rewards of travel.

We have never shied from controversy. We have, from the beginning, encouraged our authors to be intensely judgmental, critical—both pro and con—in their comments, and wholly independent. Our only clients are our readers, and we have triggered the ire of countless prominent sorts, from a tourist newspaper we called "practically worthless" (it unsuccessfully sued us) to the many rip-offs we've condemned.

And because we believe that travel should be available to everyone regardless of their incomes, we have always been cost-conscious at every level of expenditure. Though we have broadened our recommendations beyond the budget category, we insist that every lodging we include be sensibly priced. We use every form of media to assist our readers, and are particularly proud of our feisty daily website, the award-winning Frommers.com.

I have high hopes for the future of Frommer's. May these guidebooks, in all the years ahead, continue to reflect the joy of travel and the freedom that travel represents. May they always pursue a cost-conscious path, so that people of all incomes can enjoy the rewards of travel. And may they create, for both the traveler and the persons among whom we travel, a community of friends, where all human beings live in harmony and peace.

Arthur Frommer

THE BEST OF LONDON

Whether you realize it or not, London shaped your destiny. There's hardly a quarter of the globe that it hasn't changed. The United States was founded in reaction to London's edicts. Australia was first peopled with London's criminals. Modern Canada, South Africa, and New Zealand were cultivated from London. India's course was irrevocably changed by the aspirations of London businessmen, as were the lives of millions of Africans who were shipped around the world while Londoners lined their pockets with profits. You're holding proof in your hands of London's pull: that you bought this book, written in English somewhere other than in England, is evidence of London's reach across time and distance.

London is inexhaustible. You could tour it for months and barely get to know it. Few cities support such a variety of people living in remarkable harmony. That diversity makes London like a cut diamond; approach it from a different angle each day, and it presents an entirely fresh shape and color. From famous stories to high style, London is many things in every moment.

LONDON's best ATTRACTIONS

- **British Museum** (p. 89): Some of the most astounding treasures of the classical world are housed in one overwhelmingly glorious neoclassical building.
- **British Library** (p. 87): The finest and rarest books on the planet, plus the Magna Carta, are laid open for your eyes.
- **Churchill War Rooms** (p. 99): A time capsule of the tense days of World War Two and the most advanced biographical museum in existence.
- **Museum of London** (p. 118): Beside a remnant of a Roman wall, the city's spectacular story is retold with the non-stop dazzle of precious finds.
- **National Gallery** (p. 93): Some 2,000 masterpieces, the cream of every genre, reside at what may be the best fine art collection in the world.
- **Natural History Museum** (p. 106): For kids it's all about the dinosaurs, but this "cathedral of nature" has major chops as a research facility.

o **St. Paul's Cathedral** (p. 120): Sir Christopher Wren's masterpiece is the icon of London and a shrine to historic events and people.

o **Tate Modern** (p. 114): Bankside's hymn to the "shock of the new," a former power station, makes for an unforgettable riverside afternoon.

o **Tower of London** (p. 122): Britain's gruesome underbelly and its glittering Crown Jewels coexist in one sprawling city castle of stone.

o **Victoria and Albert Museum** (p. 108): Always evolving and growing, this is probably the world's finest collection of decorative arts.

o **Westminster Abbey** (p. 101): Be awed by Britain's ancient spiritual heart, where nearly 1,000 years of monarchs have been crowned and many are buried.

LONDON'S essential
EXPERIENCES

o **Climbing the Dome of St. Paul's Cathedral:** Wren's baroque masterpiece, **St. Paul's Cathedral**, stirs emotion in everyone who lays eyes on its lead-coated wooden dome. But it's the climb to the Golden Gallery for a 360° panorama that will stay with you forever. As for Wren, he was forced to add the balustrade for Queen Anne. "Ladies think nothing well without an edging," he complained. See p. 120.

o **Surveying the City from Southbank:** In 1957, the Thames was declared "biologically dead." Today, it flows with life. Alongside it, as restaurants, bars, and creative developments continue to pop up, a walk along the South Bank from Westminster Bridge to Tower Bridge has become one of the world's great promenades. The ever-changing perspective from Parliament to the Tower is ceaselessly inspiring.

o **Following in Royal Footsteps:** London is where some of the most famous characters in history played their scenes. Nearly every British monarch since 1066 was crowned in **Westminster Abbey** (p. 101). Henry VIII strutted around **Hampton Court Palace** (p. 132), Charles I lost his head at **The Banqueting House** (p. 103), and Queen Elizabeth resides at **Buckingham Palace** (p. 98). And the story goes on: The future King George VII is probably being diapered elsewhere in **Kensington Palace** (p. 105) even as you explore it.

o **Flying High on the London Eye:** Ride to the top of our generation's contribution to London's beloved landmarks for a far-reaching shot of the cityscape. Time your trip for early evening as the sun starts to sink and the lights come on across the metropolis. See p. 113.

o **Honoring the struggles of World War Two:** More than 70 years later, the Blitz isn't far from many Londoners' minds. Dig into the power of their resistance at the superlative time capsule of the **Churchill War Rooms** (p. 99), the immersive **Museum of London Docklands** (p. 127), the floating military museum *HMS Belfast*, and by seeing original bomb scars on the side of the **V&A** See p. 108.

o **Taking Afternoon Tea:** Look smart at **Brown's** (p. 34), **Fortnum & Mason** (p. 149), or the **Langham** (p. 35), where the traditional tea ritual carries on as it did in Britain's colonial heyday.

o **Spending an Evening at a West End Theatre:** London is the theatrical capital of the world. The live stages of **Theatreland** around Covent Garden and Soho offer a unique combination of variety, accessibility, and economy—but the shows of the Fringe are where the future can be found. See p. 165.

LONDON'S best FOOD

- **Tucking into Honest British Ingredients:** After many lost years of too much boiled cabbage and bread, the English have fallen back in love with farm-fresh ingredients. The gastropub movement, epitomized by its still-potent pioneer, **The Eagle** (p. 73), is just the beginning. Delectable English traditional cooking can be found from the oldest establishments (**Rules**, p. 64) to the neighborhoody holes in the wall (**Duck-soup**, p. 59; **10 Greek Street**, p. 58).

- **Sinking a Pint in a Traditional Pub:** From Tudor coaching inns to riverside taverns, London's pub culture spans the centuries. Raise a pint where Shakespeare did at **The George**, immerse yourself in an ale at Dr. Samuel Johnson's local **Ye Ole Cheshire Cheese** (p. 81), or down a microbrew inside a UNESCO World Heritage site at **Meantime** in Greenwich (p. 130). Then repeat. See "Pubs" on p. 77.

- **Mining the Stalls at Borough Market:** The top weekend port of call for London foodies is the Thursday-to-Saturday produce market under the railway by London Bridge station—not least for the free samples dished out by vendors keen to market their wares. You'll find stalls selling everything from wild mushrooms and white port to pastries and homemade sweets: It's food heaven. See p. 71.

- **Enjoying Food from Asia:** London's first Indian restaurant opened in 1810, and Asian food of every origin is now the capital's most popular cuisine. Try the range of modern bites at **Imli Street** (p. 60); take in a traditional meal under the gold silk wallpaper at Covent Garden's **Punjab Restaurant** (p. 66), opened by an Indian wrestler back in 1947 (p. 67); or see how Londoners put a sociable twist on the noodle hall by meeting some new friends at the communal tables of **Wagamama** (p. 70) or **Busaba Eathai** (p. 68).

- **Chowing Down on English Cheese:** England produces hundreds of artisan cheeses. Check out the West Country cheddars, red Leicester, and goat's cheeses at cheese-mongers like **Neal's Yard Dairy** (p. 72) or eat a gloppy, gooey plate of raclette at **Kappacasein** (p. 71). But get your fill while you're here: You can't get it back through Customs.

- **Tasting Britain's Fading Traditions:** As young English diners insist on flashier fare, the older ways of cooking become rarer. Whether it's jellied eels in the protected interior of **M. Manze** (p. 72), the deep-fried goodness at the linoleum-lined "chip-pie" **Fryer's Delight** (p. 74), or the traditional "caff" of the **Regency Café** (p. 69), mid-century Britain is still steaming along—affordably.

LONDON'S best HOTELS

By 2014, London will have 130,000 hotel rooms—some better than others.

- **Meet the Locals at a Family-run B&B:** Mom-and-pop inns have taken a hit because of the dominance of corporate hotels, which are often run by people who are as unfamiliar with the city as you are. But you can still find some stellar homegrown hospitality where owners put you first, including the Valotis and Cabrals of the **Alhambra Hotel** in St Pancras (p. 24), the Beynons of Bloomsbury's **Jesmond Hotel** (p. 25), and the Callises of **22 York Street** in Marylebone (p. 35).

- **Lose Yourself in a Grande Dame:** The first all-service grand hotel in Europe, the **Langham**, was built in 1865 and it's still extending top-flight hospitality to guests with taste—and cash (p. 35). **Brown's** has attracted royalty and creative misadventures since the mid-1800s and now blends old-style class with style (p. 34), while the world-famous **Savoy** still stands atop her field for luxury, legends, and Thames views (p. 28). Best of all, you can visit them without a key.

o **Pay Less Than $50:** You may not think it's possible, but with advance planning, you can get a new, impeccably maintained private room in the center of town for only £29 a night. Book ahead with the British chains **Premier Inn**, **Travelodge**, or **easy-Hotel**, or with the imported budget brands **Ibis** or **Tune**, and London is yours, cheap. See p. 41.

o **Sleep Where History Happened:** Rather than tear it down, Londoners would rather revitalize it. There's no more luscious restoration than that of the swoony spires of Gilbert Scott's neo-Gothic **St Pancras Renaissance Hotel** (p. 23). Have a chlorine-free swim where printing presses once printed the morning news at **One Aldwych** (p. 28), or take a room with a four-post bed where the great thinker William Hazlitt breathed his last at the dusky **Hazlitt's** in Soho (p. 27).

o **Enjoy Style for Less:** "Boutique" hotels are encroaching deeper into budget territory than ever before. At **Z Hotel Soho** (p. 30), surrender a little space but none of the chic at a berth in the heart of Soho. In Southwark, buzzy Dutch boutique **CitizenM** (p. 37) has huge beds and a loopy personality, but a small price. And the newly built **Nadler Soho** (p. 29), where faux fur covers your bedspread, rooms have everything you need, including a mini-kitchen, for democratic prices.

LONDON'S best FOR FAMILIES

o **Cruising London's Waterways:** In addition to the grand River Thames, London has a working canal system that once kept goods flowing to and from the city's docks. The best value trip is aboard the **Thames Clipper** from Westminster to Greenwich, passing under Tower Bridge. See p. 234.

o **Losing Your Way in the World's Most Famous Hedge Maze:** The green labyrinth at **Hampton Court** twists and turns for almost half a mile. When you manage to extricate yourselves, stroll through centuries of architectural styles at this stunning palace, home of many an English monarch. Don't forget to pick up a kids' activity trail. See p. 132.

o **Seeing Peter Pan in Kensington Gardens:** You'll feel like a character from a Victorian novel as you see Sir George Frampton's beloved 1902 statue of the boy who played the panpipe there. There's no better way to admire and enjoy the "green lung"—central London's largest and most popular open space in a city that holds the record for the most green space for a city of its size. See p. 140.

o **Going Botanic in Royal Kew:** The **Royal Botanic Gardens,** Kew, house more than 50,000 plants from across the planet, including Arctic and tropical varieties. Youngsters will love the 200m (656-ft.) high Treetop Walkway, up in the Garden's deciduous canopy. After all that greenery, head across the Thames for hands-on engineering displays at the **Kew Bridge Steam Museum.** See p. 133.

o **Asking How, Where, and Why:** Inside South Kensington's **Science Museum,** the Atmosphere and Lauchpad galleries use interactive exhibits to keep inquisitive minds occupied. Or pilot a simulated ship at the kid-centric **National Maritime Museum**. See p. 107 and p. 129.

o **Learn the Panto Lingo:** From November to early January, join one of Britain's most delightful holiday experience: Pantomime, which are slapstick musical romps through famous stories, usually starring D-list celebrities (such as David Hasselhoff or Henry Winkler as Captain Hook—both played him here since 2010). Hiss villains, shout instructions for heroes, and giggle at good-natured drag. Try the **Theatre Royal Stratford** (www.stratfordeast.com), the **New Wimbledon** (www.atgtickets.com), the **Hackney Empire** (p. 169), or **The Richmond Theatre** (www.richmondtheatre.net).

LONDON'S best FREE & DIRT CHEAP EXPERIENCES

o **Visiting the Great Museums:** London's state museums and galleries—including most of the big names—show off their permanent collections for free. Locals need the break—the average monthly rent here is £1,106, a high. They include the **British Museum, National Gallery, National Portrait Gallery, Tate Britain, Tate Modern, Natural History Museum, Science Museum, V&A,** the two **Museums of London,** and the **British Library.** See Chapter 5.

o **Taking in Fresh Air and a City View:** North of the River Thames, **Hampstead Heath** offers miles of woodland trails, historic pubs, and sumptuous mansions. To the south, the heights of **Greenwich Park** enjoy a panoramic sweep that takes in the royal borough's 18th-century maritime architecture and the steel-and-glass of Canary Wharf. See p. 140 and p. 141.

o **Dining on the Cheap:** Away from the main tourist drag and the Michelin-starred hotspots, London is surprisingly well equipped with affordable, tasty places to enjoy a full meal for under £10. Among the best are two of the West End's most venerable budget pit stops, **Cafe in the Crypt** at St Martin-in-the-Fields and the **Stockpot.** See p. 62 and 63.

o **Going to the Library:** The best and most easily accessible of London's specialist (and free) libraries is the **Wellcome Collection,** which houses a grisly cornucopia of medical materials, paintings, and drawings (p. 91). Staff offer free tours and workshops to help guide you through the collection. The **British Library**'s free exhibitions include priceless manuscripts (p. 89) And don't forget **Jeremy Bentham** at University College London! He himself is stuffed and on display. See p. 90.

o **Catching a Free Event in the Center of the City:** From the Lord Mayor's Show to the Notting Hill Carnival, almost every major public event in the capital costs nothing to attend. See "London Calendar of Events," p. 236.

THE best HISTORIC EXPERIENCES

o **Meeting the Heroes and Villains of History:** Get face-to-face with a rogue's gallery from the past at the **National Portrait Gallery**, where faces seem to watch you across time with a sparkle in their eye. The gang's all here, from a supercilious Henry VIII to a pugnacious Hogarth to a kind-eyed Princess Diana, already becoming a memory. See p. 94.

o **Taking a Tour of Royal London:** From palaces and parks to the royal art collections, history, geography, and culture has been shaped—or owned—by centuries of aristocratic rule. You can see the best of it in a day, including the Queen's favorite grocer, **Fortnum & Mason** (p. 149), plus any one of 800 other Royal Warrant holders (p. 154).

o **Peering into a Time Capsule:** Some museums preserve scenes that were frozen in time. No reconstructions or fakery here: You'll gaze upon truly authentic World War Two military operations at the **Churchill War Rooms** (p. 99), admire the graves of great artists and the location of epic rituals as **Westminster Abbey** (p. 101), and roam the very rooms used in daily life by kings and queens at **Buckingham Palace** (p. 98), **Hampton Court** Palace (p. 132), **Kensington Palace** (p. 105), and **Windsor Castle** (p. 210).

o **Shopping in the Grandest Department Stores of Them All:** And, no, it isn't Harrods. **Liberty of London** was founded in 1875 and moved to its current half-timbered, mock-Tudor home in 1924, and **Selfridges** (p. 151), both designed and built by Americans, redefined sales methods and played crucial roles in world history. See p. 150.

o **Imagining Domestic Life Through the Ages:** At the **Geffrye Museum** (p. 126) period re-creations of interiors from the Spartan 1630s to the flashy 1990s allow visitors to understand how home life has changed. But nothing immerses you in the past quite like the brain-bending role-playing of a night visit to **Dennis Severs' House** (p. 125).

o **Staying at a Classic Hotel:** From the Art Deco interiors of **The Savoy** (p. 28) to the liveried door attendants of the **Goring** (p. 31), nothing epitomizes historic London quite like its upscale hotels. Discretion has never gone out of style here.

SUGGESTED ITINERARIES & NEIGHBOR- HOODS

Few great modern cities are as multilayered, intricate, and yes, *messy* as London, Western Europe's most populous city (8.3 million in 2013), and that's because history was knitted into its very layout. London is mostly the haphazard product of blind evolution, which piled up over successive generations to produce a complicated metropolis. One could say that London simply happened.

As recently as the early 1800s, London—and by London, I mean what we now call The City, between St. Paul's and the Tower—was a compact, teeming monster where many lives, birth to death, were carried out within the same few blocks. Within that frenzied cluster, districts developed out of logic or bias—the smoke of industry was banished downwind, for example, and kings lived near the Thames for easy transportation. All around The City were dozens of villages, many of which retain their names as modern neighborhoods and a whiff of their original personalities.

Quickly, London swelled to swallow its current territory. Yet because of ancient echoes, neighborhoods remain surprisingly small—many are just minutes across by foot, and all but the most crucial streets can change names several times. It's still possible to stroll along and sense sudden shifts in energy and character. In many ways, London is still a complex system of hamlets. It's one of the many delights that makes it so surprising. It also means it can take a lifetime to scratch its surface.

Addresses sometimes reflect this improvisation; a building numbered 75 may face one that's numbered 32, just across the street. Despite this, it's immensely difficult to get lost. In 2012, the city installed some 1,200 Legible London map **"Finger Posts"** throughout town. Wherever you are, a map is near.

If you want your own map, forgo the oversimplified one your hotel might offer. The most cherished one is the *London A-Z* (www.az.co.uk), first compiled by the indefatigable Phyllis Pearsall, who walked every mile of the city for the 1936 debut edition and commanded the resulting cartography empire until her death 60 years later. Its *London Mini A-Z Street Atlas* (£5.50) fits into a jacket pocket. (Don't buy the app, which drains batteries quickly.) Just be sure to call it the "A to Zed" or you'll get a funny look; in England, the last letter in the alphabet is, quite sensibly, pronounced to not rhyme with eight others.

LONDON IN 1 DAY

First of all, what were you thinking? If you're in town on a layover, didn't you know that most airlines will allow you to stick around for a few days at no charge? Never mind. What's done is done. Eat a huge breakfast and make your way to Tower Hill.

1 The Tower of London ★★★

Start here (p. 122) because it usually opens an hour earlier (9am) than most attractions. Spend about 2 hours making stops at the **Crown Jewels** and the **White Tower,** and snap that requisite photo of the **Tower Bridge** (p. 122) from the quay. Grab a triangle sandwich (the quintessential London lunch).

Tube it west on the Circle or District lines to Westminster.

2 Westminster Abbey ★★★

Allot a rushed 2 hours to see the effigies of kings and queens (p. 101). Of the **Chapel of Henry VII**, Washington Irving wrote: "Stone seems, by the cunning labor of the chisel, to have been robbed of its weight and density, suspended aloft as if by magic, and the fretted roof achieved with the wonderful minuteness and airy security of a cobweb." Outside, take in the **Houses of Parliament** (p. 99) and **Big Ben's Elizabeth Tower** from across the street.

Walk up Whitehall, passing No. 10 Downing Street (the Walking Tour on p. 187 will guide you).

3 The National Gallery ★★★

At **Trafalgar Square**, a symbolic heart of the city, you can finally see some of the world's most famous paintings in person (p. 93). Park guards also turn a blind eye to tourists climbing alongside those famous bronze couchant lions, each of them 20 feet long. But don't mount them—they're cracking.

From the Strand, head to the back of Charing Cross station and cross the Thames.

4 London Eye ★★

There's time for a revolution on London's favorite contemporary icon and the new focal point of national celebrations. (p. 113), In the colder months, you'll be there to watch the sun go down slowly as **Big Ben** gongs.

Finish just north of the Gallery, around Leicester Square.

5 West End Show ★★★

Curtains go up around 7:30pm (p. 165). Enjoy an ice cream during interval—it's a custom here. Afterward, head to a **pub** and raise a pint to a city where you've barely scratched the surface (see p. 77 for ideas).

LONDON ON A 2ND DAY

You're going to have to move fast, but you'll be able to see some highlights. Take the Tube to Mansion House, Blackfriars, or St Paul's.

1 St. Paul's Cathedral ★★★

As you appreciate the underside of her dome, also appreciate the grave fact that before the 1940s, you could barely see her flanks, but bombings devastated the buildings that once hemmed her in.

Cross the Thames on the Millennium Bridge (the Walking Tour on p. 191 will help).

2 Tate Modern ★★★

Here's a museum (p. 114) in a colossal structure that can be more memorable than what's on display inside it—although Rothko's Four Seasons paintings can't fail to put you in a restive mood. If it's summer, catch a matinee at **Shakespeare's Globe** (p. 114), just a few yards east; in summer, an afternoon pint at the wooden-galleried **George Inn** (p. 79), noted by Dickens and Shakespeare alike, will recharge you.

Take the Jubilee line from Southwark to Green Park.

3 Green Park ★★

Walk south through Green Park (p. 140) to behold the front of **Buckingham Palace** (p. 98); if you're here in March, you may be lucky enough to see fields of daffodils in bloom. Return to Piccadilly to browse the classy shops lining it, including **Fortnum & Mason** (p. 149).

Take the Tube's Piccadilly Line (notice the century-old tilework) to Russell Square.

4 The British Museum ★★★

You'll spend the afternoon roaming it (p. 87), but you'll scarcely grasp the import and craftsmanship of what you see. The aesthetic exertions may induce cravings for cream tea at its Court Restaurant—it's only £8.50.

Catch Bus 55 toward Oxford Circus. Sit on the top level for the views!

5 Oxford Circus ★★

Wind up the afternoon with a dive into the bustling fitting rooms of the shops on **Oxford Street, Regent Street,** and **Carnaby Street** (p. 147), where you'll find a huge selection of cool clothes at what Londoners call "High Street" prices—meaning they're sane. Walk southeast for a few minutes to Frith Street in Soho and have dinner at **Arbutus**, a Michelin-starred neighborhood gem that charges prices far below its rank, and afterward, stroll past the lights of **Piccadilly Circus.** If you still have juice left, walk down Haymarket, turn left on Cockspur, and follow it down Strand to Aldwych.

6 Radio Rooftop Bar ★★

The haute, polished architecture of the ME London hotel is a flashy counterpoint to the antiquities you've been absorbing all day, and the breathtaking panorama of the city from the terrace of its glassy tenth floor bar more than justifies the luxury price of its cocktails (© **020/7395-3440**; Mon-Wed to 1am, Thurs-Sat to 3am, Sun to 10:30pm; Tube: Temple or Covent Garden). You're standing on the site of the old Gaiety Theatre, where 100 years ago the famous "Stage Door Johnnys" came shopping for wives among the chorus girls. History is in every footprint here.

LONDON ON A 3RD DAY

Follow the itinerary for 2 days in London, but add in one of the city's South Kensington museums, preferably the **Victoria & Albert** (p. 108), and follow that with a walk through **Hyde Park** (p. 140), possibly to see the **Diana, Princess of Wales Fountain**, and to tour the public areas of her son and grandson's home, **Kensington Palace** (p. 105), in adjoining **Kensington Gardens**. Take the Tube or a bus to Westminster, and dive into the time capsule of the **Churchill War Rooms** (p. 99). Follow that with a stroll along South Bank from Westminster to London Bridge, taking your pick among the pubs and restaurants you find along the path.

AN ITINERARY FOR FAMILIES

There's no bad neighborhood to stay in if you've got kids, because London is low-rise and manageable. But make sure they're ready to climb stairs if you're taking the Tube. On paper, some of London's museums sound as if they'd be too dry, but in reality, they bend over backward to cater to children—sometimes even at the expense of adult minds. Every major museum, no exceptions, has an on-site café for lunch.

Day 1: Double-Deckers and Thames Clippers

Forget expensive open-top tours: Start your day seeing Piccadilly Circus, Trafalgar Square, St. Paul's Cathedral, the Tower of London, and much more for the price of bus fare on an antique, double-decker **Routemaster bus** with an old-style staircase on the back end. Take route 15. After the Tower, head to the ferry dock outside and see the city from the river on a **Thames Clipper** (p. 234). Disembark at **Tate Modern** (p. 114), which comes fully loaded for young exploration with family trails, a learning zone on Level 5, and some very cool video tablets for interpreting the art. Take the Tube to Leicester Square for a **West End musical** (p. 165).

Day 2: Covent Garden and Coram's Fields

Make your way to Covent Garden's **London Transport Museum** (p. 92) where kids can pretend to drive a bus and explore other eye-level exhibits. Then bring your brood a 15-minute walk north to the **British Museum** (p. 87) and hook them up with crayons and pads, exploration backpacks, and the special 12-object collections tour geared to young minds. If they're the daring types, the mummies never fail to impress. Just east you'll find a city park just for children: the 7-acre **Coram's Fields** (www.coramsfields.org) was set aside in 1739 for an orphanage at a time when 75% of London kids died before the age of five. Its southern stone gate is where mothers once abandoned their babies in desperation. Today, no adult may enter without a child and it's the scene of daily joy between parents and children; there's a petting zoo, two playgrounds for all ages, sand pits, and a paddling pool.

USE the code

London is chopped into geographic parcels, and you'll see those postcodes on street signs. The heart of the city, in postcode terms, is near the Chancery Lane Tube stop. From there, areas are given a compass direction (N for north, SW for southwest, etc.) and a number (but ignore that, since a number greater than 1 doesn't mean the area is in the boonies). In the very heart of town, addresses get an extra C for "centre," as in WC1, which is where Covent Garden is located. Every address in this book includes its postcode, which corresponds to the neighborhood in which you'll find it. Don't worry—you won't need to memorize these because each listing also includes the nearest Tube stop to help you quickly place locations on a map. Here are some of the most common postcodes:

WC1 Bloomsbury
WC2 Covent Garden, Holborn, Strand

W1 Fitzrovia, Marylebone, Mayfair, Soho
W2 Bayswater
W6 Hammersmith
W8 Kensington
W11 Notting Hill
SW1 Belgravia, St. James's, Westminster
SW3 Chelsea
SW5 Earl's Court
SW7 Knightsbridge, South Kensington
SE1 Southwark
SE10 Greenwich
EC1 Clerkenwell
EC2 Bank, Barbican, Liverpool Street
EC3 Tower Hill
EC4 Fleet Street, St. Paul's
E1 Spitalfields, Whitechapel
E2 Bethnal Green
E14 Canary Wharf/Isle of Dogs
N1 Islington
NW1 Camden Town
NW3 Hampstead

Day 3: The Brompton Road Museums

Today is devoted to exploration of the Brompton Road museums, a trio of world's-bests for kids: Take the Piccadilly Line to South Kensington, where the **V&A** (p. 108) has hundreds of hands-on exhibits for kids (look for the hand symbol on the maps), such as trying on Victorian costumes to trying on armor gauntlets. Next door, the plain-speaking signs and robotic dinosaurs of the **Natural History Museum** (p. 106) impress kids as much as the airplanes and space capsules over their heads at the **Science Museum** (p. 107)—both institutions furnish even more kids' trails and activities for free. Go east on the Circle or District lines to Temple, and you're at the dancing water jets of the **Somerset House** courtyard (home of the Courtauld Gallery, p. 91). But if the weather doesn't suit that, the **London Eye**'s capsules are safe, climate-controlled, and move imperceptibly, and the view of the city they've just criss-crossed will stimulate and inspire kids.

A DISCOVERY WEEKEND

The *Frommer's Easy Guides* are designed to give you a firm introduction to the sights, hotels, and restaurants that speak most to a visitor about what's going on in each destination. But authentic London doesn't begin and end with what we cover in these pages, and if you dip into the way that London locals live every day, your visit will be immeasurably richer.

From Arthur Frommer's *Europe on $5 a Day* (1957)

"All you've heard to the contrary, Londoners are among the warmest people of Europe, and London is a friendly and inviting city. It has charm and a politeness of attitude that belie its big-city status. You'll want to extend your stay . . . Can you live in London on $5 a day? There's nothing to it."

Day 1: Brixton and Bollywood

When Victoria was Queen, families flocked to live near the incandescent lights of Brixton's Electric Avenue, which in 1888 became one of London's first shopping streets lit by electricity. Today, it's a boisterous immigrant community. By day, explore the glazed awnings of its markets, where to inhale the aroma of meat and exotic spices is to walk through a portal to Jamaica, India, or China, and to be reminded that London, like few others, is a truly worldly city. In the evening, experience London's huge South Asian population—Indians are nearly 2 percent of the population, and the richest man in Britain, Lakshmi Mittal, is Indian-born— by attending a Bollywood film at the Boleyn Cinema (www.boleyncinema.com; Tube: Upton Park), a historic 1938 Art Deco building and the second-largest Bollywood screen in the country that loves the genre.

Day 2: Go Football Mad or Cricket Crazy

London hosts 13 professional football (soccer) teams, more than any other city on Earth. From mid-August to mid-May, catch matches at some of the best Premier League teams: **Chelsea** (www.chealseafc.com), **Arsenal** (London's first club; www.arsenal.com), **Fulham** (www.fulhamfc.com), or **West Ham United** (www.whufc.com), which in 2016 takes up residence in the former Olympic Stadium at Stratford. Filling the gap from April to September, and less likely to pelt you in the skull with a beer bottle, is cricket. Attend "test matches" at Marylebone's **MCC Lord's Cricket Ground** (www.lords.org) or Oval's **Surrey County Cricket Club** (www.surreycricket.com). If you figure out how the game works, fill me in, won't you? It's a little like baseball—and a lot like watching grass grow.

Day 3: Ale, Yorkshire Pudding & Tough Questions

On Sunday afternoons, find a pub with an inviting garden for **Sunday Roast**, a spread of meats with the trimmings, Yorkshire pudding (a pastrylike shell), and gravy, washed down with copious amounts of beer. It's the more leisurely equivalent of brunch: After a long week of working for the Man, Londoners hang out until they're ready for Monday. On Sundays, some pubs also hold **pub quizzes**, another staple of British life. Form teams and answer trivia for lame prizes, but be warned: Foreigners always go down on the sports and politics questions.

Neighborhoods in Brief

London's neighborhoods were laid out during a period of wagon and foot traffic, when districts were defined in narrower terms than we define them today; indeed, for centuries people often lived complete lives without seeing the other side of town. Ironically, in our times, the Tube has done much to divide these districts from each other. Visitors are likely to hop a train between them and don't often realize how remarkably close together they really are.

Are these the only areas of interest? Not even close. Literally hundreds of fascinating village clusters abound, many with names as cherishable as Ponders End, Tooting, and The Wrythe. But visitors are likely to spend time here:

BLOOMSBURY & FITZROVIA

Best for: Museums, affordable inns, residential streets, universities, and homewares and electronics shops on Tottenham Court Road

What you won't find: Evening entertainment, nightclubs

Bloomsbury's dark-brick, white-sashed residential buildings and leafy squares date mostly from the Georgian period, when the district became the first in a chaotic city to be developed. The refined air attracted the intelligentsia nearly from the start, and its two universities are both 19th-century institutions. The British Museum settled here, too. Bloomsbury became a place of remembrance on July 7, 2005; of the 52 who died that day, 26 perished underground on a bombed Piccadilly Line train between King's Cross and Russell Square stations, and 13 were killed on a double-decker bus passing through Tavistock Square. Bloomsbury's cozier sister Fitzrovia, similar in character but devoid of major attractions, lies on the western side of Tottenham Court Road. Famous residents include George Bernard Shaw and Virginia Woolf, who both lived (at different times) at 29 Fitzroy Square.

KING'S CROSS

Best for: Budget hotels, trains heading north (and south to Paris), alternative/down-and-dirty nightlife, student housing, takeaway counters

What you won't find: Top-notch restaurants, parks, shopping

Recently, the area around King's Cross station was an unsavory tenderloin of porn stores and warehouses. Its turnaround, currently in play, has been just as dramatic, as millions of pounds are poured into its derelict industrial infrastructure. Legend (surely apocryphal) says the Celtic queen Boudica rests somewhere near Platform 8. Fans of Harry Potter know that the young wizard boards the Hogwarts Express at the (fictitious) Platform 9¾; the movie versions have shot at Platforms 4 and 5 but used prettier St. Pancras station, next door, as a stand-in facade. Change came, as it often has in English history, from France. The Channel Tunnel Rail Link is the starting point for Eurostar train trips to France and beyond.

MARYLEBONE & MAYFAIR

Best for: Shopping, hotels, restaurants, small museums, strolling, access to Regent's Park and Hyde Park, embassies

What you won't find: Historic sights

The middle-class hubbub of Oxford Street west of Regent Street divides high-hat Marylebone from its snobbish southern neighbor, Mayfair. Both play host to upscale shopping and several fascinating, if overlooked, museums, but there the similarities end. World-famous Mayfair, typified by hyperluxe bauble shops and blue-blood heritage (the present Queen was born on Bruton St.), has a high opinion of itself as a starchy enclave of wealth and it has less to offer the casual tourist. The title of the musical *My Fair Lady* is witty wordplay on how its Cockney heroine, Eliza, would have pronounced "Mayfair lady.") Marylebone (MAR-le-bun), on the other hand, benefits from convenient Tube and bus connections and lively sidewalks crowded with evening celebrants, particularly around James Street. Also, thanks to a territorial local authority, its main shopping drag (Marylebone High St.) remains one of the last important streets in London that isn't awash with the ubiquitous corporate chain stores.

SOHO, COVENT GARDEN & CENTRAL WEST END

Best for: Shopping, restaurants, theater, cinema, nightlife, opera, free art (National Gallery and National Portrait Gallery), star sightings

What you won't find: Elbow room, hotel values, silence

London's undisputed center of nightlife, restaurants, and theater, the West End seethes with tourists and merry-makers. After work, Old Compton Street and Covent Garden overflow with people catching up with friends; by 7:30pm, the theaters and opera houses are pulsing; by midnight, the action has moved into the dance halls of Leicester Square and lounges of Soho; and in the wee hours, you might find groups of partiers trawling Gerrard Street, in teeny Chinatown, hunting for snacks. Oxford Street is the city's premier shopping corridor; the western half between Oxford Circus and Marble Arch is the classier end, with marquee department stores such as Selfridges and Marks & Spencer. Prim Trafalgar Square, dominated by the peerless National Gallery, has often been called London's focal point. On a sunny day, you'll find few places that exude such well being.

WESTMINSTER, INCLUDING ST. JAMES'S

Best for: Historic and government sights, river strolls, St. James's Park

What you won't find: Affordable hotels, a wide choice of restaurants

This is near the central West End, but its energy is different. It's a district tourists mostly see by day. South of Trafalgar Square, you'll find regiments of robust government buildings but little in the way of hotels or food. Whitehall's severity doesn't spread far. Just a block east, its impenetrable character gives way to the proud riverside promenade of Victoria Embankment, overlooking the London Eye, and just a block west, to the greenery of St. James's Park, which is, in effect, the Queen's front yard. North of the park, the staid streets of St. James's are even more exclusive than Mayfair's, if that's possible.

THE CITY

Best for: Old streets, the Tower of London, St. Paul's, financial concerns

What you won't find: Nightlife or weekend life, affordable hotels

Technically, this is the only part of London that's London. Other bits, including the West End, are under the jurisdiction of different local governments, such as Westminster or Camden. Shocking as it is to realize that the Queen herself lives in SE1, the soothing reality is that the greater city is still considered to be London. The City, as it's called, is where most of London's history happened. It's where Romans cheered gladiators. It's where London Bridge—at least 12 of them—touched shore. It's where the Great Fire raged. And, more recently, it's where the Deutsche Luftwaffe focused many of its nocturnal bombing raids, which is why you'll find so little evidence of the aforementioned events. Eager to put the war behind it, the city threw up blocks of undistinguished office fortress towers. Outside of working hours, the main thing you'll see in The City is your own reflection in the facade of corporate offices on lockdown. Although this is where you'll find such priceless relics as the Tower of London, St. Paul's Cathedral, the Tower Bridge, the Bank of England, and the Monument, many remnants are underfoot, since much of the spider-web of lanes and streets dates back to the Roman period. Buildings have come and gone, but the veins of the city have pumped in-situ for thousands of years.

THE SOUTH BANK, SOUTHWARK & BOROUGH

Best for: Museums, memorable pubs, strolls, gourmet foods and wines

What you won't find: Shopping, parks

During Southwark's recent rehabilitation from a crumbling industrial district, a blighted power station became one of the world's greatest museums (the Tate Modern), a master playwright's theater was re-created (the Globe), and a sublime riverfront path replaced the coal lightermen's rotting piers. A dramatic showpiece (the National Theatre) anchors them. Now, the South Bank, which stretches from the London Eye east to Tower Bridge, has reclaimed its status as a pleasure garden, and its once-dank railway viaducts are filled with cafés and reasonable restaurants. A new skyscraper, The Shard, lords over it all, but it's gratifying to see that some things never change;

Borough Market, which attracts gourmet foodies from around the world, is the descendant of a market that fed the denizens of that medieval skyscraper over the water, London Bridge.

VICTORIA & CHELSEA

Best for: Boutiques, low-cost lodging, town homes, wealthy neighbors

What you won't find: Transit options, street life, museums

Victoria doesn't technically apply to the neighborhood around the eponymous train station—Belgravia (to the west) and Pimlico (south and east) take those honors—but generations of tourists have learned that some of the city's most affordable hotels are found within walking distance of Victoria station, and the shorthand stuck. Most of the area, which is residential, was developed starting in the 1820s in consistent patterns of white stucco terraced homes. Then, as now, it's a lovely place to spend the night, but it doesn't wake up much during the day. Chelsea, though, has a history of well-heeled bohemianism—Oscar Wilde, James McNeill Whistler, and the Beatles all lived here—although it's known more as one of the city's most exclusive communities, and a stroll past boutiques and pocket-squared residents on the King's Road (turning ever-more corporate and indistinct) leaves little doubt about the prestige of living here.

KENSINGTON, KNIGHTSBRIDGE & EARL'S COURT

Best for: Museums, shopping, French pastries, hotels, celebrities

What you won't find: Historic sights

Here, one expensive neighborhood bleeds into another. South Kensington and Brompton draw the most visitors to their grand museums; and Knightsbridge is where moneyed foreigners spend and brag—London has the third-highest number of billionaires in the world, after New York and Moscow. Privilege has long had an address in Kensington—that's a reason those edifying institutions were located here to begin with, away from the grubby paws of the peasants. Kensington Palace, at the Gardens' western

end, is where Prince William and Kate are raising George. The orphan among this opulence is Earl's Court, the only area deprived of a contingency to the park, and consequently a frumpy zone good for cheap eats and sleeps, although the hotel scene is shifting east.

BAYSWATER & PADDINGTON

Best for: Cheap inns, ethnic food, well-preserved Victorian thoroughfares

What you won't find: Attractions, non-chain stores, street life

Its whitewashed, terraced houses were briefly the most fashionable in the city (Churchill and Dickens were residents), yet today, the sizable transient population, including tourists, deprives it of sustained energy. One exception to the muddle is Queensway, a popular shopping street crowned by Whiteleys, a 1911 department store edifice converted into a mall. Although Paddington station is one of London's most beautiful train hubs (it was built by the legendary architect Isambard Kingdom Brunel in 1838), it's also the most inconvenient—although Heathrow fast trains go from it.

DOCKLANDS

Best for: Developments, ancient warehouses, super-cheap chain hotels

What you won't find: Street life, nightlife

Most of East London along the north side of the Thames is ignobly called by a single, sweeping name: Docklands. Yet Captain Cook set off on his explorations from here, and its hand-dug basins once teemed with ships bearing goods from around the planet. Docklands made colonial Britain successful—and thus America, Canada, Australia, and South Africa, too. Adolf Hitler swept most of that away, and after a fallow generation, East London's hand-dug pools have been resettled by corporations in stacks of fluorescent-lit office cubes, and the Olympics settled here in 2012. Away from the river, in salt-of-the-earth neighborhoods like Bethnal Green, Stratford, and West Ham, the city's Pakistani and Indian populations flourish, with marvelous food and shops.

Other Great London Neighborhoods

Mostly because of iffy transit connections (for example, service by a single Tube line that, should it go on the blink, would derail your vacation), This book doesn't focus on them as prime places to stay, but there's no doubt that hanging out here will be worth the time.

ISLINGTON

Best for: Antiques, gastropubs, theater, street markets, cafes, strolls
What you won't find: Museums, hotels

Few neighborhoods retain such a healthy balance between feisty bohemianism and groomed prosperity, and almost none retain streetscapes as defiantly mid-century as Chapel Market. Islington's leafy byways are dotted with antiques dealers, hoary pubs with backroom theater spaces, beer gardens, and most pleasingly on a sunny day, pedestrian towpaths overlooking Regent's Canal. Why more tourists don't flood Islington is a mystery—and a blessing.

CAMDEN

Best for: Alternative music, massive clothing markets, punks, pubs
What you won't find: Refined company, hotels, upscale restaurants

Name a British tune that got under your skin, and chances are it received its first airing in the beer-soaked concert halls of Camden Town. London's analogue to San Francisco's Haight-Ashbury District, it was big in the countercultured '60s and '70s and is still grotty enough for Amy Winehouse to have expired in. The area's margin-pushing markets, which hawk touristy hokum in the former warehouses and stables serving Regent's Canal, are so thronged with weekend sightseers that the inadequate Tube station only serves one-way traffic on Sunday afternoons.

GREENWICH

Best for: Museums, antiques and food markets, river views, strolls, pubs
What you won't find: Hotels, bustle

Greenwich, on the south bank across from the Canary Wharf developments, retains the tranquility of an untouched village. Such lovely insularity exists because the Tube (well, the DLR) didn't connect it to the greater city until 1999—all the more remarkable when you consider the town's illustrious pedigree as a royal getaway (it's got the oldest royal park in London), as a scientific capital, and as one of the world's most crucial command centers. If it all sounds like a living museum, it is: On top of being a UNESCO World Heritage Site (Maritime Greenwich), the village is literally the center of time and space, since it inhabits the exact location of Greenwich Mean Time, and of longitude 0° 0′ 0″. Set away from town there's the colossal O_2 dome, the city's iconic concert venue.

WHITECHAPEL & SPITALFIELDS

Best for: Nightclubs, music, South Asian food, galleries, clothing
What you won't find: High-end restaurants, hotels

If Mayfair is London's champagne, Spitalfields has been its hangover. For centuries it was an impoverished, squalid slum. Jack the Ripper slashing and The Elephant Man suffering jibes—it happened here. That's in the history books now. The gallery-clogged area (which blends seamlessly with edgy Spitalfields [SPIT-all-fields], just north, and Dalston past that) settled into anonymity as a refuge for immigrants. Now prostitutes and orphans are replaced by hipsters and scenesters, which may not be an improvement. The Whitechapel Gallery is among Europe's best fringe modern art exhibition spaces; and Old Truman Brewery, once a mire of industrial gloom, is now a complex of cafes and stages. You may have heard that Camden was the place to be, but the cool kids are here now.

NOTTING HILL

Best for: Markets, village vibes, restaurants, pubs, touristy strolls, antiques
What you won't find: Well-priced shopping, museums, Hugh Grant

Thanks partly to Hollywood, this westerly nook of London, once known for its race riots, appears high on many visitors' checklists. Its Saturday Portobello Road market, the principal draw, is fiendishly crowded but not revolutionary.

HAMPSTEAD

Best for: Cafes, parks, pubs, historic homes, high-end shopping

What you won't find: Unique shops, hotels

In hilly North London, the little houses and hidden mews are adorable, but it all feels like a very wealthy, very insulated bubble, or at least like a party to which you weren't invited. Fortunately, Hampstead's wooded green space, the Heath, is enough to make anyone forget the slight, and its stately brick homes impress.

LONDON'S HOTELS

From nineteenth-century grand hotels to modern style boutique inns, from eccentric quarters above pubs to family-run townhouse B&Bs, London's range of accommodation is as diverse as the city it serves. Lodging is likely to be the single biggest expense of your trip, so you should take pains to make sure the place you choose spotlights the city at its best. Fortunately, there is superlative value to be found in all the neighborhoods you are most likely to be.

In case you were leaning against family-run B&Bs, be assured that they're more private than you might think. You'll feel like you're staying at an inn, not crashing a home. There's also this: If you stay at one, you'll be privy to the owners' counsel about what's worth doing and what's not. These days, most hotel desk clerks are actually from continental Europe, and many of them know London only barely better than you do. But people who run family inns are on top of the scene.

When it comes to researching prospective hotels, don't get caught up in star ratings (or for guesthouses, the diamond ratings) claimed on websites. In Britain, the difference between no stars and one star has nothing to do with the quality of the linens or the size of the bathroom. The extra star comes because the establishment will serve you food. Distinctions like that aren't important to tourists who are in town to see the sights. In fact, the more stars a place has, the more likely it is to charge for using its amenities, so focus instead on the location and the price of the rooms.

In many of the hotel write-ups, you'll read a range of prices. London's non-corporate hotels are pretty good about sticking to their posted rates; in fact, every property is required by law to post them in the lobby. Hotels may charge more if there's a major event happening, such as the London Marathon (April) or in the month of July.

Accommodations are subject to a Value Added Tax (VAT) of 20%. Happily, almost all small B&Bs include taxes in their rates, so you don't have to think about it for the lowest-priced places below, although you may be charged 3% to 5% more to use a credit card. However, more expensive hotels (those around £150 or more) tend to leave taxes off their tariffs, which can result in a nasty surprise at checkout. It never hurts to ask if the rate "excludes VAT."

HOTELS BY PRICE

EXPENSIVE

The Ampersand Hotel ★★, p. 30
Brown's Hotel ★★★, p. 34
Charing Cross Hotel ★★, p. 27
The Goring ★, p. 31
Hazlitt's ★★★, p. 27
The Langham ★★, p. 35
Malmaison ★, p. 39
The Mandeville Hotel ★, p. 35
No. 10 Manchester Street ★★, p. 34
Number Sixteen ★★★, p. 31
One Aldwych ★★★, p. 28
The Rookery Hotel ★★★, p. 39
Park Plaza Westminster Bridge ★,
  p. 28
Radisson Blu Edwardian Mercer Street
  ★★, p. 28
St Pancras Renaissance Hotel ★★,
  p. 23
The Savoy ★, p. 28
South Place Hotel, p. 39
Staunton Hotel ★, p. 23

MODERATE

22 York Street ★★, p. 35
Alhambra Hotel ★★★, p. 24
Apex City of London ★★★, p. 40

CitizenM London Bankside ★★★,
  p. 37
The Fielding Hotel ★★, p. 29
The Fox & Anchor ★, p. 40
Harlingford Hotel ★, p. 24
Hart House Hotel ★★, p. 35
The Hoxton ★, p. 40
Jesmond Hotel ★★★, p. 25
Lime Tree Hotel ★★, p. 31
London Bridge Hotel ★★, p. 37
Luna Simone Hotel ★, p. 32
Mad Hatter Hotel ★★, p. 37
The Nadler Kensington ★, p. 32
The Nadler Soho ★★★, p. 29

INEXPENSIVE

B+B Belgravia ★★, p. 32
Celtic Hotel ★★, p. 26
Crestfield Hotel ★★, p. 26
Hotel Meridiana ★, p. 26
Lincoln House Hotel ★, p. 36
Morgan Guest House ★, p. 33
Oakley Hotel ★, p. 33
Seven Dials Hotel ★, p. 29
The Wardonia Hotel ★, p. 27
Z Hotel Soho ★★★, p. 30

KING'S CROSS & BLOOMSBURY

The 2007 opening of St Pancras International terminal for Eurostar's high-speed trains to continental Europe made the neighborhood prime, and junky B&B catastrophes favored by construction workers instantly brightened into inns you could send your mom to. Even better, many guests only stay a night before catching a train, so owners are likely to cut a deal with you if you stay longer. The area is also better situated than Earl's Court or Bayswater, given that it's served by six important Tube lines and from here, the attractions of the West End and Soho are just a 20-minute walk away. Bloomsbury's chocolate-colored Georgian townhouses lie within a 20-minute walk of Soho and Covent Garden, and they're near the Piccadilly Line to

London Hotel Price Categories	
At the smaller family-owned hotels, breakfast is often included, while it comes as extra at the top end of the scale. Hotels are categorized by the lowest en suite double rate.	
Inexpensive	Under £95
Moderate	£96–£150
Expensive	£151 and up

London-Wide Hotels

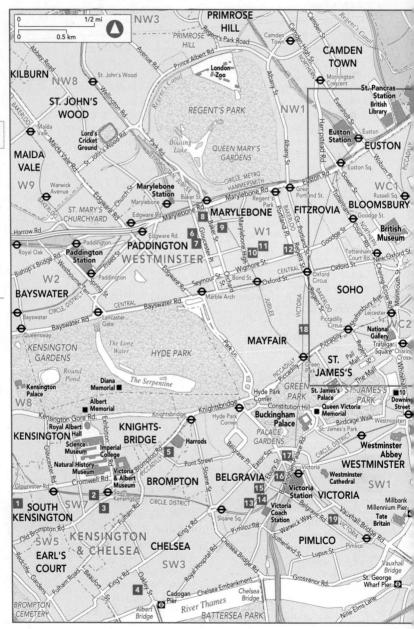

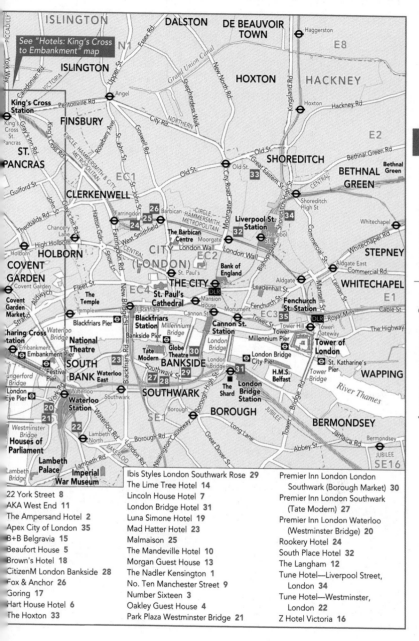

See "Hotels: King's Cross to Embankment" map

King's Cross Station

King's Cross St. Pancras

22 York Street **8**
AKA West End **11**
The Ampersand Hotel **2**
Apex City of London **35**
B+B Belgravia **15**
Beaufort House **5**
Brown's Hotel **18**
CitizenM London Bankside **28**
Fox & Anchor **26**
Goring **17**
Hart House Hotel **6**
The Hoxton **33**

Ibis Styles London Southwark Rose **29**
The Lime Tree Hotel **14**
Lincoln House Hotel **7**
London Bridge Hotel **31**
Luna Simone Hotel **19**
Mad Hatter Hotel **23**
Malmaison **25**
The Mandeville Hotel **10**
Morgan Guest House **13**
The Nadler Kensington **1**
No. Ten Manchester Street **9**
Number Sixteen **3**
Oakley Guest House **4**
Park Plaza Westminster Bridge **21**

Premier Inn London London
 Southwark (Borough Market) **30**
Premier Inn London Southwark
 (Tate Modern) **27**
Premier Inn London Waterloo
 (Westminster Bridge) **20**
Rookery Hotel **24**
South Place Hotel **32**
The Langham **12**
Tune Hotel—Liverpool Street,
 London **34**
Tune Hotel—Westminster,
 London **22**
Z Hotel Victoria **16**

King's Cross to Embankment Hotels

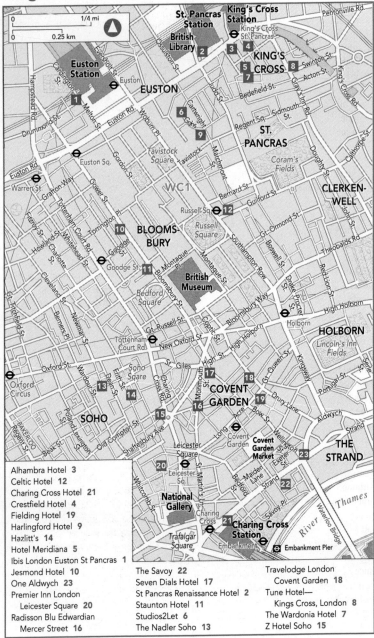

Alhambra Hotel **3**
Celtic Hotel **12**
Charing Cross Hotel **21**
Crestfield Hotel **4**
Fielding Hotel **19**
Harlingford Hotel **9**
Hazlitt's **14**
Hotel Meridiana **5**
Ibis London Euston St Pancras **1**
Jesmond Hotel **10**
One Aldwych **23**
Premier Inn London
    Leicester Square **20**
Radisson Blu Edwardian
    Mercer Street **16**

The Savoy **22**
Seven Dials Hotel **17**
St Pancras Renaissance Hotel **2**
Staunton Hotel **11**
Studios2Let **6**
The Nadler Soho **13**

Travelodge London
    Covent Garden **18**
Tune Hotel—
    Kings Cross, London **8**
The Wardonia Hotel **7**
Z Hotel Soho **15**

Heathrow. To be honest—and let's spill a dirty secret here—these places are better located than many of London's most expensive hotels. That's why faceless investment firms have spent the last few years snapping up B&Bs that were previously run by the same families for generations. There is now a real risk of booking into a property where you're processed like a number; the family-run hotels in this book are holdouts where you can rely on personalized treatment. Gower Street is busy but lined with affordable guesthouses, while Russell Square, just east of the British Museum, tends toward machinelike tourist hotels. Beware the 1,600-room Royal National Hotel, a beastly concrete colossus brimming with noisy school groups but little charm. Because it's so big, it often appears as a budget hotel option in packages, but you can do better. So does the nearby Imperial Hotel, which won't tuck you in with the warm-and-fuzzies.

Expensive

St Pancras Renaissance Hotel ★★ This Gothic red brick palace, built in the 1870s as a lavish terminal hotel for a railway line, is one of London's most distinctive buildings, and its 2011 restoration, overseen with exactitude by English Heritage, not only rescued a Victorian icon but also created one of the city's most distinctive properties. Premium rooms look out at the ribbed, cast-iron cavern of the train shed, where Eurostar arrives and departs for Paris. The most expensive Chambers rooms have 18-foot ceilings and details such as (now non-working) fireplaces, arched windows, and substantial wooden doors, but rooms in the newly built Barlow wing are spacious, modern, and suit those with corporate hotel tastes. The public spaces are a gilt-and-tile parade of self-important Victorian excess, from the winged Grand Staircase to the lushly carved The Gilbert Scott brasserie (named for the architect; local star Marcus Wareing is the chef) and the old wooden Booking Hall, now a bistro where old English punch cocktails are revived. His building was "too good for its purpose," lamented Scott, whose own son went mad and died in one of the rooms. To think this narrowly avoided being pulled down, saved only by a private developer—and to dream of the astonishing private apartments that are now in the upper floors, in the rafters of the clock tower. The hotel is worth a wander even if you're not staying here—management knows it's a jewel, and it welcomes visitors.

Euston Rd., London, NW1. www.stpancrasrenaissance.co.uk. ℂ **020/7841-3540.** 245 units. Doubles from £255–450. Tube: King's Cross St Pancras. Amenities: Restaurant, two bars, pool, gym, spa, free Wi-Fi in Chambers rooms, otherwise £15/day.

Staunton Hotel ★ The Staunton is an admirable, welcoming, small B&B. Although it's situated in a pair of 230-year-old town houses on the corner of two loud streets (Store and Gower), windows have been double-glazed and adorned with treatments, which tamps down a bit on aural clutter. Well-appointed rooms also have safes, and AC, which is uncommon in Georgian-era buildings like these, but no lift, which is. We imagine the owners charge more than the B&B average because rooms are ever slightly larger-than-usual, as well as for the formidable location within walking distance of the entire West End.

13-15 Gower St., WC1. www.stauntonhotel.com. ℂ **020/7580-2740**. 17 rooms. £160 to £215 doubles, £20 less for 60-day advance purchase. Tube: Goodge Street. Amenities: Full breakfast, free Wi-Fi.

WHAT TO EXPECT AT town house hotels

Many B&Bs owners proudly boast that they occupy "listed" buildings. What does that mean? It means that it has historical or architectural importance—it's a surviving example of a fine Georgian town house, for example, or it occupies a stately Victorian terrace. To keep unsentimental developers from knocking down a gem, "listed" buildings are protected. Changing anything, down to the color of the paint, requires permission, and that is tough to come by. American tourists who are unused to London's listed buildings tend to post huffy online reviews complaining about the very things that define them, penalizing properties for a broad cultural truth that makes London history what it is. That hotel is not a dump! It's carrying the torch of English hospitality.

Rooms are small by American standards. Often, interior walls were added to subdivide rooms after the house was built, but don't blame the current owners for it. Most subdivision was done in the mid–20th century to fill a housing gap after many of the city's big hotels were destroyed in the war, and now, even removing those slapped-up walls requires civic approval, which is nigh impossible. You are unlikely to have a closet and in some rooms suitcases can be hard to open without using the bed. The largest rooms in such B&Bs usually face the front.

Bathrooms are even smaller. In the old days, all guests shared bathrooms, but to suit changing tastes, landlords have slotted booths containing the staples (toilet, shower, sink) into rooms that weren't designed to have them (remember,

Moderate

Alhambra Hotel ★★★   A well-kept, family-run spot, the comforting Alhambra is an inn with heart, and a top value. Its proprietors, whose family has owned the land for decades and isn't at risk of being elbowed out, take pride in the family business, and they keep the prices low. Picture simple but dignified rooms (LCD TVs but no phones, always spotless) squeezed into old spaces and freshened up with bright bedspreads; cream pinstripe wallpaper; inviting royal blue carpeting; and built-in desks with chairs. Frank Valoti, the patriarch, does the cooking, and he dabbles in art, too; in the basement breakfast area, check out the pastel still life he drew to show Europeans what's included in his generous full English breakfast. Bruno Cabral, his attentive son-in-law, handles the hotel's modernization, such as the addition of free Wi-Fi and in-room safes, a rarity for this price point. If you share a bathroom, there are plenty to go around. The same family runs an annex across the street that has the same high standards. In winter, it's easy to negotiate rates down by as much as 30 percent.

17-19 Argyle St., WC1. ✆ **020/7837-9575**. www.alhambrahotel.com. 52 rooms. Singles £69–97, doubles £80–111. Tube: King's Cross St. Pancras **Amenities:** Full breakfast, lobby computer, free Wi-Fi.

Harlingford Hotel ★   Among the standard B&Bs on the tranquil crescent of Cartwright Gardens, it rises above with a design that takes a cue from its logo: an easy chair with a pillow emblazoned with an H. All beds are piled with just such a pillow, and bedspreads match curtains in an array of purples, golds, and creams. It doesn't hit you over the head; it's simply all-around nice, as are the newly spruced-up bathrooms they're not allowed to bash down plaster), which cuts down on floor space. Adding bath cubicles makes for smaller rooms, but it's one of the reasons why town house B&Bs are so much more affordable than standard hotels.

Don't expect an elevator, or "lift." It takes years of begging and a small fortune to convince the council to permit the destruction that elevator installation wreaks, so few hotels have them. Assume you're going to have to use the stairs. They may be narrower than you're used to, especially the ones leading to the cellar, but on the bright side, the banisters are pretty. Rooms on higher floors receive more light, less noise, and fewer patrons.

Ceilings get lower as you go higher. Until the 20th century, the floors of fashionable town houses served distinct functions. The cellar was for kitchens and coal storage. The ground floor was usually used for living rooms. The first and second floors were reserved for bedrooms, and the top floor was for servants and for the children's nursery, which accounts for the slightly lower ceilings there. If you book a top-floor room, you won't feel like Alice in Wonderland—ceilings are 2.1m or 2.4m (7 or 8 ft.) tall.

Not all windows are double glazed. You think you hear traffic now? Imagine how it sounded when horses and carriages were clattering up the cobbles at all hours. If you're a light sleeper and your chosen B&B doesn't have double glazing, simply ask for a room at the back. Rooms on back stairway landings often don't adjoin other rooms, either, which takes care of more ambient noise.

with seafoam-green tile work, slender spigots, and designer sinks. All of this tastefulness is imposed on typically small-ish London town house–hotel quarters. The staff, which serves a free full English breakfast in the ground-floor breakfast room, loans keys to the semicircular park out front, where tennis and giant trees beckon. The owner's family has run this place for three generations (their pets, Zizi the black cat and Chiyo the pup, live on the premises) and it is attentive in a way many rivals no longer are. Around the corner is the Lord John Russell, a true local pub whose landlord refuses to extend the hours and make it a nightspot. "We're a pub," he sniffs. "We don't serve past 11."

61-63 Cartwright Gardens, WC1. © **020/7387-1551**. www.harlingfordhotel.com. 43 rooms. £88 singles, £120 doubles. Tube: Russell Square. **Amenities:** Cooked or continental breakfast, lounge, free Wi-Fi.

Jesmond Hotel ★★★ I have a soft spot for this place. I stayed here often when I was a backpacker (in number 3, a cozy single on the rear landing—still there, still snug). Back then, the Beynon Family, who took over the Jesmond in 1979, had a young son, Glyn. Today, Glyn is a grown family man and he's in charge—and he's doing a solid job of updating the family B&B in a historic Georgian townhouse (ask to read the history he wrote of it) far beyond the expectations of its tariff range. He installed new bathrooms with all-new piping, accounting for the larger-than-average showers, he soundproofed the front windows to keep out the roar of Gower Street's bus traffic, and he converted the house's 18th-century coal chute into a kitchen where full English breakfasts are served in a cellar breakfast room that doubles as a day lounge. The back garden provides welcome respite and is cultivated with flowers and wooden chairs. He also converted the former parlor, with its antique (non-working) fireplace, into room 2, a spacious double. It's simple, it's friendly, and it's still one of London's last "they're charging *how* much?" values. Pay for 6 nights from October to March, and you can stay for 7. Don't confuse this place with the Jesmond Dene, a B&B on Argyle Square in King's Cross—it's very good, too, but not as central as the Jesmond.

63 Gower St., WC1. ℂ **020/7636-3199**. www.jesmondhotel.org.uk. 15 rooms. Singles £50–60, doubles £85–110. Tube: Goodge Street. **Amenities:** Full breakfast, free Wi-Fi.

Inexpensive

Celtic Hotel ★★   In 2007, the Duke of Bedford evicted the beloved St. Margaret's budget hotel after a residence of half a century. As its devotees howled, the premises were swiftly converted to an expensive boutique hotel. The St. Margaret's operators, the eccentric but dedicated Marazzi family ("We were swindled!" one exclaimed to me), decamped nearby to the Celtic, transforming a bleak guest house (near the British Museum and the Tube to Heathrow) into their new, charismatic budget citadel. Few other budget hoteliers put as much heart into making sure guests are acclimated to London by answering questions, obliging special dietary requests, and filling bellies with a cooked breakfast that's so enormous (try the banana yogurt) that lunch might become optional. To keep attracting longtime regulars, many of whom know staffers by name, the Celtic retains the features that made Maggie's a quirky stalwart: rooms do not have TVs or phones, furniture is endearingly mismatched, and the lounge is a hub for socializing with fellow guests. Add £6 to £22 if you don't want to share shower or toilet. You must book directly.

61-63 Guilford St., WC1. ℂ **020/7837-6737**. www.celtichotel.com. 30 rooms. Singles from £58, doubles from £79, Tube: Russell Square. **Amenities:** Cooked breakfast, two lounges, free Wi-Fi.

Crestfield Hotel ★★   Every city needs a few basic, secure choices that aren't grim. Rooms are tiny, freshly painted in canary yellow and done up with lace curtains, and there are generous touches such as baskets of potpourri. Rooms also boast TVs (albeit teeny ones), but no phones. Bathrooms (most rooms have their own, with toilet) are essentially tiled cubicles with drains in the floor, but the £100 family room for four is a true steal. Room 9, a double, is located on a landing facing the back, so it's even quieter than most. If you're only staying on weekdays, ask for a special deal, because the hotel sees a lot of weekend trade. Private bathrooms cost £10 to £15 more. Seriously, what more do you require?

2-4 Crestfield St., WC1. ℂ **020/7837-0500**. www.crestfieldhotel.com. 52 rooms. £40 singles, £50 doubles. Tube: King's Cross St. Pancras. **Amenities:** Bar, continental breakfast, free Wi-Fi.

Hotel Meridiana ★   This is what a value hotel should be: not lavish, but you happily get what you pay for. The walls can be thin, the rooms truly teeny, many rooms share bathrooms, but everything is spotless and breakfast (served in a room so small that sometimes you have to wait your turn) is a proper cooked one. Heating and hot water are reliable, too, which isn't always the case in buildings of this age, and some rooms have drawers, another relative curiosity. If you just want a place to sleep where you'll have no regrets about hygiene or price, this no-frills B&B is a decent choice. You're unlikely to get as much value for the price elsewhere.

43-44 Argyle Sq., WC1. ✆ **020/7713-0144**. www.hotelmeridiana.co.uk. 27 rooms. Singles from £43, doubles from £62. Tube: King's Cross St Pancras. **Amenities:** Full breakfast, free Wi-Fi.

The Wardonia Hotel ★ The Wardonia has a fresher look than many of its neighbors. The inn posts floor plans of its rooms online (spoiler alert: they're wee), and its TVs offer more than 30 channels, both of which are unusual for the city. The rooms' style is less unusual—very simple in blue and white fabrics and plain brown wainscoting, bathrooms with showers but not tubs—although the crazy low rates, which haven't gone up in half a decade, are something to astound. Everything's en suite, so it doesn't seem like the owners have cut many corners to deliver low rates apart from not serving breakfast. The Wardonia is plainly a value contender. Prices may dip about £10 lower in winter.

46-54 Argyle St., WC1. ✆ **020/7837-3944.** www.wardoniahotel.com. 65 rooms. £40 singles, £55 doubles, £70 triples. Tube: King's Cross St Pancras. **Amenities:** Free Wi-Fi.

SOHO, COVENT GARDEN & WEST END

This is the middle of London. The part of town that offers everything you need outside your door. The area that also offers streets crawling with inebriated 20-year-olds singing drinking shanties in full voice after midnight. You may not care, because staying centrally can save on Tube fare more than it costs in shoe leather.

Expensive

Charing Cross Hotel ★★ The railway terminal hotel above Charing Cross Station was opened in 1865 and underwent many lives (and Blitz damage) before coming under the recent control of Guoman Hotels, a capable British hospitality company that's rising in global stature. Now the Charing Cross is a well-run, upper-moderate hotel that dips its toes into luxury trimmings (heated bathroom floors, illuminated wardrobes, walk-in showers, and so forth) without going over-the-top on price. The location is spectacular and could command higher rates: steps from Trafalgar Square in one direction and morning strolls on the Thames in the other. Breakfast (crowded) is taken with a view toward St Martin-in-the-Fields, and at night, some 350 candles are placed throughout the hallways and up the sweeping grand staircase that once signified the privilege of a more genteel age.

The Strand, WC2. ✆ **0871/376-9012.** www.guoman.com/charingcross. Rooms £169–239. Tube: Charing Cross or Embankment.

Hazlitt's ★★★ A stay here is like a slumber in a time machine. Each room is its own individual historic universe, the centerpiece of which is a deep oak or carved four-poster bed. Around you is a bathroom with antique fixtures and heavy silk curtains that, when pulled closed after a long day, make you feel as if you are the master of your own Georgian townhouse—plus, of course, modern expectations such as AC, flat-screen TV, and safes. Breakfast including fresh-baked croissants arrives on a tray every morning, delivered by miraculously discreet staff. When you step out your front door, you're in the thick of the West End, completing the opulent fantasy. "Dandyism is a variety of genius," wrote William Hazlitt, a great thinker and writer of his age. He died here when it was a rooming house, in a small bedroom at the back of the third floor, in 1830 at age 52.

6 Frith Street, W1. ✆ **020/7434-1771**. www.hazlittshotel.com. 30 rooms. Rooms £215–330. Tube: Tottenham Court Road. **Amenities:** Room service, free Wi-Fi.

One Aldwych ★★★   The pie-shaped, onetime headquarters of the *Morning Post*, built in 1907 and not too sprawling, contains a consistently high-quality boutique with two restaurants, a double-tall, sculpture-filled lobby lounge, and a theatrically lit, chlorine-free underground swimming pool where the printing presses used to be. Rooms are contemporary and designed with environmentalism in mind, have beds to sink into, and some even sneak a view of the Thames. The staff is truly five-star in that it tries to meet needs without being asked, and its location feels impossibly considerate, too: steps from Covent Garden and Trafalgar, a walk down Strand to St Paul's, and a quick and gorgeous stroll over the Waterloo Bridge to the glories of Southbank. Deals on Lastminute.com save up to £100, and booking more than 90 days ahead can knock 20% off the rate.

1 Aldwych, WC2. ✆ **020/7300-1000**. www.onealdwych.com. 105 rooms. Doubles from £264–312. **Amenities:** Two restaurants, cocktail bar, pool, gym, free Wi-Fi.

Park Plaza Westminster Bridge ★   You won't believe the view some rooms have: straight down Westminster Bridge at the Houses of Parliament and Big Ben's tower, like a floor-to-ceiling fantasy. Although rooms, suited to business travelers, are plenty big and have all the latest gadgets, that view won't be accompanied by a boutique experience; this modern, glassy full-service machine is dominated by a central atrium that feels more like a convention hotel (the "Internal Facing" rooms get that booby prize; the "Iconic View" rooms get the goods), but that means there are lots of rooms which are in turn more likely to be discounted in low season. Studio rooms have microwaves and fridges, plus pullout beds, which is a boon for families, and there's a dark and soothing indoor pool, which is a boon for warding off the stress of battling other tourists all day.

200 Westminster Bridge Road, London SE1. ✆ **0844/415-6780**. www.parkplaza.com/westminster. 1,019 units. Doubles £175–339. Tube: Waterloo or Westminster. **Amenities:** 2 restaurants, bar, pool, fitness center, spa, free Wi-Fi.

Radisson Blu Edwardian Mercer Street ★★   This funky luxury hotel is packed into one of the oddly-shaped points on the Seven Dials intersection, and the resulting jigsaw leads to some to fun and surprising room configurations. It also means you're delightfully close to the city's best shopping, dining and entertainment. There's a real boutique hotel feel, from the sassy art and richly draping, velvety soft goods to the fact your HD screen runs off Apple TV technology. Deluxe rooms come with free movie, Wi-Fi, and a daily cocktail, but often the Standard rooms, £50 cheaper, are priced incredibly well for the area.

20 Mercer Street, WC2. ✆ **020/7836-4300**. www.radissonblu-edwardian.com. 137 rooms. Rooms £149–263. Tube: Covent Garden **Amenities:** Bar/restaurant, fitness center.

The Savoy ★   Few cities can claim hotels as iconic as The Savoy, a name that is synonymous with exclusivity and merits a visit even if you, like most people, cannot afford to stay there. From the shimmering gleam of its Art Deco porte cochere to its antique revolving doors to the palatial receiving rooms off the lobby, the Savoy has vibrated with high history, half Edwardian and half Jazz Age, since 1889. Off to the left, past the restaurant run by Gordon Ramsay, the American Bar has been a hushed laboratory for upscale cocktails for a century. A small museum about the Savoy's history, open to anyone, reminds you how much happened here: Churchill puffing, Chaplin mugging, Wilde and Bosie dallying, Gilbert and Sullivan pattering in its theatre, Monet and Whistler painting the river from their windows. It would be redundant to say that rooms, each unique, are the pinnacle of luxury and that your every need, from floral to gourmet, will be attended to with abject elegance and for a dear price, but would you be surprised to learn that the hotel, run by Fairmont and owned by the nephew of the King of Saudi Arabia, now subtly exploits its Hollywood past by hanging paintings of movie stars in its Thames Foyer and placing photos of them on nightstands? Good night, Burt Lancaster.

Strand, WC2. ✆ **800/257-7544** (U.S.) or 020/7836-4343 (London). www.fairmont.com/savoy-london. 268 rooms. Rooms from £390 Amenities: Swimming pool, gym, spa, two bars, three restaurants, business center.

Moderate

The Fielding Hotel ★★
It's nearly impossible to beat the location, just steps from Covent Garden food and shopping, which is why you overlook the size of the rooms at this well-run family-owned hotel. In this early 19th-century warren of tight staircases and fire doors, appealingly cramped, attractively decorated, and sometimes slightly airless tiny rooms snuggle you with a certain throwaway charisma. Room 10 is a double with a sitting area that catches lots of afternoon light thanks to its corner position and copious windows. Everything's en suite (but mostly shower only). Trivia: Oscar Wilde was convicted of gross indecency in the Bow Street Magistrates' Court next door.

4 Broad Court, Bow St., WC2. ✆ **020/7836-8305**. www.thefieldinghotel.co.uk. 24 rooms. Rooms £140–180. Tube: Covent Garden or Holborn.

The Nadler Soho ★★★
This summer 2013 arrival, a custom build announced by an Art Nouveau sculpture of the Greek goddess of the moon, gets moderate lodging right by providing style without pretension or henpecking guests with extra fees. Quiet, high-design rooms are compact but nonetheless kitted out with twists such as wide beds, mini-kitchens with a third tap for filtered water, a microwave, big glassy bathrooms with rain showers, plenty of power points plus a loaner plug adapter, a half-hour of free national calls a day, and HD TVs that double as music players. Deluxe rooms, at the top of the middle rate scale, sleep up to four. There's no restaurant, but that's no problem since you're in the very heart of Soho—which alone would be reason to book here, even if the product weren't such strong value.

10 Carlisle Street, W1. ✆ **020/3697-3697**. www.thenadler.com. 78 rooms. Rooms £155–255. Tube: Tottenham Court Road. **Amenities**: Free Wi-Fi.

Inexpensive

Seven Dials Hotel ★
There are nearly no budget hotels near Covent Garden. If you're this central, you can charge more. Here, though, everything is little: the stairway, the rooms—and correspondingly, the rates. Furniture and bathroom doors appear to be duking it out for supremacy, still, there's usually enough storage space, a TV mounted on an armature, a basic writing desk, teeny clean bathrooms, and firm beds, albeit ones covered with dowdy bedspreads. Forget the lack of a lift and all the ways it's average. Its situation on Monmouth Street, steps from a rainbow of pubs, shops,

and bars clustering around Covent Garden, is without compare. Dump your bags and go play, because the price is right.

7 Monmouth St., WC2. ☏ **020/7681-0791**. www.sevendialshotellondon.com. 18 rooms. Singles £95 doubles £105. Tube: Covent Garden **Amenities:** Full breakfast, free Wi-Fi.

The Z Hotel Soho ★★★   Here's the formula: extremely compact rooms, glassy sleek style, thrilling location, and since extras such as breakfast are pre-paid when you book, the staff leaves you alone, keeping costs down. The formula, devised by career hotel professionals in 2011, works because it's done with design smarts: they poured a lot of cash into the bedding and the 42-inch TVs (the better to drown out Soho noise) but did without cupboards. Quarters are close, but quirky, with a zig-zaggy internal courtyard and a roof deck with a nifty view of the Palace Theatre. If you share a room with a platonic friend, note bathrooms, though stocked with Thierry Mugler toiletries, are enclosed by panels of fogged glass. The lowest price is for a single; add £20 for a double bed and another £10 for a queen; doubles without windows cost the same as a single room. Just be sure to pronounce it "zed." Rhymes with bed—what it's good for. There is a second location in much less desirable Victoria, a block west of the station (5 Lower Belgrave Street, SW1. Same phone. 106 rooms, 60% of them windowless.)

17 Moor Street, W1. ☏ **020/3551-3700**. www.thezhotels.com. 85 rooms. Rooms £75–160. **Amenities:** Café, free Wi-Fi.

SOUTH KENSINGTON, VICTORIA & EARL'S COURT

Reaching the energy of Piccadilly Circus takes about 20 minutes on the Underground from here, and that remove from the action has traditionally fueled low-priced competition. Unfortunately, things are changing. As rents rise, fewer family-run hotels can afford to stay open and many food options have gone corporate. As more affordable hotels develop in the West End and points east, increasingly it makes less sense to put up with the inconveniences of staying here, South Ken and Victoria have slipped a few notches in desirability for tourists. As the tides of tourism swirl out of this area, many dried-up B&Bs thoughtlessly slap pillows down for undiscriminating online bookers, so buyer beware.

Expensive

The Ampersand Hotel ★★   In August of 2012, this grand hotel from 1888 was given a fresh makeover that's both sassy and reverently British, and now it's got its cool back for the first time since Victoria. Cleverly, rooms, set over seven floors, are gently themed to poke the disciplines mastered at the museums on nearby Brompton Road: astronomy for singles and doubles, music for superior rooms, ornithology for deluxe rooms, and so on. They don't skimp on goodies, from the quality of the towels to the free soft drinks in the minibar, and ceilings are high. The basement bar, the Mediterranean-themed Apero, is cheerfully snazzy, while the Modern English-style Drawing Rooms do double duty as tea room and champagne bar. All in all, the frisky interior is a stylish counterpoint to the nineteenth-century pomp of the exterior, and it's literally steps from the Tube.

10 Harrington Road, SW7. ℗ **020/7589-5895**. www.theampersandhotel.com. 111 rooms. Doubles from £174–286. Tube: South Kensington. **Amenities:** Bar, restaurant, gym, free Wi-Fi.

The Goring ★ Only one five-star hotel has the Royal Warrant from the Queen for Hospitality Services. Only one has been run by the same family since 1910. Only one hosted Kate Middleton, the wife of a future king and mother of another, in her final night as a single girl before she walked down the aisle of Westminster Abbey. This is the Goring, exclusive and classic, assiduously appropriate in style and rich in expensive fabrics, down to the Gainsborough silk on the walls. Peter the Doorman has been wearing his bowler hat in the foyer for nearly half a century, and the statue of the founder gets a new flower in its lapel every day. The effect is something like an English country house, especially as you look our your oversize windows at the back gardens, kept lush for your personal enclave. You just can't get more blue-blood English than this.

Beeston Place, SW1. ℗ **020/7396-9000**. www.thegoring.com. 69 rooms. Rooms £370–840. **Amenities:** Gym access, restaurant, bar, paid Wi-Fi.

Number Sixteen ★★★ The Firmdale Hotels group is a fixture on the city scene. Mostly it operates boldfaced-name hotels in the West End—the kinds of memorable places where cocktail-swilling scenesters loiter and fashion magazines shoot. Here, though, husband/wife designer/owners Tim and Kit Kemp create one of the loveliest B&B experiences in the city. Expect all the trappings of a luxury hotel, only in a series of very well refurbished town houses in an updated English country style. Every available space is adorned with displays of forward-thinking British art from the Kemps' considerable collection, and all rooms, which are individually designed and truly beautiful (Kit even published an interior design coffee table book, *A Living Space*), come with huge, come-hither beds laid with more pillows, skirting, and spreads than most people have at home. On the ground floor, a library and a drawing room with an honor bar are at your disposal. In the morning, sunlight pours across the verdant back garden (accented by a soothing ornamental pond) into the conservatory where afternoon tea is served. The location off restaurant-rich Old Brompton Road, near the banner museums, ranks high for quiet.

16 Sumner Place, SW7. ℗ **020/7589-5232**. www.numbersixteenhotel.com. 41 rooms. Rooms £180–375. Tube: South Kensington. **Amenities:** Conservatory, free Wi-Fi.

Moderate

Lime Tree Hotel ★★ Some owners freeze their B&Bs in time. Not Matt and Charlotte Davies, who brightened a once-frumpy guesthouse into a place that feels as current as it is friendly, and who keep guests just as up-to-date with daily suggestions. The brick townhouse is historic, so no lift is permitted, but rooms are updated with fresh curtains, cupboards, and touches such as bedside reading lights. If you have a room on the front, you'll have a small balcony over busy Ebury Street; in the back, you'll overlook the cute flower garden. Some rooms have only a shower, but others have a tub, too.

135–137 Ebury St., London SW1W 9QU. www.limetreehotel.co.uk. ☎ **020/7730-8191**. 25 units. £155–180 double. No children 4 or under. Tube: Victoria or Sloane Sq. **Amenities:** Full breakfast, free Wi-Fi.

Luna Simone Hotel ★   Because this prototypical townhouse B&B began as two hotels that were conjoined in the 1990s, you'll sometimes see it called the Luna & Simone. Although it's a protected building with old metalwork on the banisters and oddly sized guest rooms, the owners have taken pains to modernize with fresh, inexpensive furniture and modernist prints by Rothko and Miró. Its two large morning rooms, done up like a diner, have a weird undulating blue ceiling that makes scooping your cereal feel a bit like doing the backstroke (and eat quickly—breakfast ends early, at 8:30am). Everything is in excellent condition, which is a bit of a surprise when you consider that the owners have been at it since 1970. Prices for rooms rise based on availability.

47-49 Belgrave Rd., SW1. ☎ **020/7834-5897**. www.lunasimonehotel.com. Doubles £100–140. Tube: Victoria or Pimlico. **Amenities:** Free Wi-Fi.

The Nadler Kensington ★   What may look from the outside like another stucco town house is actually a intelligently designed and carefully serviced oasis (charcoals, woods, gentle stripes) that aims to deliver low prices without sacrificing a sophisticated atmosphere. The founder calls the concept "affordable luxury." That's not just hooey. You get flat screen TVs; free Internet; a free music library; air-conditioning; some oversized showers; safes; lots of outlets; plenty of storage space; and, most helpfully, mini-kitchens with fridges, microwaves, and a kettle, so you can prepare simple meals. The westerly location is offset by plenty of grocery options, and the genuinely interested staff is truly helpful. When this place was called Base2Stay, it proved so successful that the owner built and opened The Nadler Soho (p. 29) based on the same concept and now both properties share a name, too. Pay a week in advance and you'll get 10 percent off.

25 Courtfield Gardens, SW5. ☎ **020/7244-2255**. www.thenadler.com. 67 rooms. Singles £99–118, doubles £129–195. Tube: Earl's Court.

Inexpensive

B+B Belgravia ★★   Although it follows the form of a typical town house hotel (rooms of various sizes, mostly small; stairs instead of lifts), it dares to have a strong sense of style and doesn't stint on hospitality. An ocean of white paint has been applied to every surface, and a futuristic glass-floored bridge was constructed, no doubt at great expense, to link the ground-floor sitting area (stop by the free espresso machine) with the light-drenched kitchen and dining area. The bathrooms, with cylinder sinks and pleasingly detailed tilework, bear little resemblance to the dated closets on offer at the competition. You won't spot a yard of chintz, although Ikea is well represented. Each night on your pillow, instead of chocolate, you may find a slice of "rock," a traditional British seaside treat. Down the street at 82 Ebury, it rents a few more "Studio" rooms with compact self-catering kitchens that can be slightly cheaper.

64-66 Ebury St., SW1. ☎ **020/7259-8570**. www.bb-belgravia.com. 26 rooms. £89–130 www. bb-belgravia.com. Tube: Victoria **Amenities:** Full breakfast, free Wi-Fi.

SHOULD I pack IT?

Mind the culture gap! Don't let these quirks take you by surprise:

○ Although all hotels include towels and linens, you'll find for the most part that travelers are expected to bring their own washcloths. Don't ask me why.

○ Many beds have duvets but not top sheets. It's just a European style; locals would probably explain that the duvet cover *is* the top sheet.

○ You may find that your bed is made each day but your sheets aren't changed. This, too, is normal, and it saves on water, electricity, and detergent. If you want them changed, simply request it.

○ Nearly all rooms in the budget category have TVs these days, but not cable, so expect only four or five broadcast (or "terrestrial") channels.

○ Ask for a loaner hair dryer or curling iron because your non-British one probably can't handle the increased voltage. New non-British hair curlers fare better, although they may get hotter than they do back home.

○ Not every small hotel stocks irons, sometimes for safety reasons.

○ Your family-run B&B probably can't employ a porter but rare is the place that doesn't have at least one strong person to tote your baggage upstairs.

○ Many places don't have air-conditioning because during a normal summer London doesn't get that hot. If there's a heat wave, though, you'll be glad to have it.

Morgan Guest House ★ Every time I visit, I'm amazed by how chirpy the guests look. They treat this cramped Georgian B&B like home, lingering over breakfast to swap travel tales, or hanging out on the staircase in the foyer to warn each other of the bad plays seen the night before. There must be something extra special about this place, or its owners, Ian Berry and Rachel Joplin, for it to attract such friendly devotees. I suspect the low prices keep frugal people in high spirits. They're so low only because not every room has its own bathroom, and nothing has been overly modernized, but standards are otherwise high, with orthopedic mattresses and a peaceful communal garden with white iron furniture. The family room has a double, a bunk bed, and a bathroom for £148, which is a good deal. Over a stay, you almost get the sense of what it must have been like to live in a mid-20th-century boardinghouse.

120 Ebury St., SW1. ℭ **020/7730-2384**. www.morganhouse.co.uk. 9 rooms. Doubles £84–108. Tube: Victoria.

Oakley Hotel ★ An unheard-of value. The rates, like the homey vibe, channel a bygone era: £45 for singles and £59 for doubles or twins without bathrooms, £85 with. But there's a trade-off: It's a 20-minute walk to the Tube or a 10-minute bus ride from Victoria Station, rooms have no phones or Wi-Fi (only in the lounge) and shampoo isn't provided. Although half the rooms share bathrooms, there are so many WCs that you won't have to wait even if everyone else has just consumed a pork vindaloo. Since the mid-'80s owner Brian Millen has kept the 1850s house in fine condition and he's got some gorgeous furniture, much of it older than the house itself. The double with a four-poster bed was a favorite of the late, dissolute football superstar George Best, who regularly stayed here, presumably on his London binges. About 90m (295 ft.) outside the front door on busy Oakley Street, you'll find the tranquility of the Thames River and, across the cast-iron Albert Bridge, soothing Battersea Park. Repeat: It's not for luxury. It's for astonishing value that, for some, may make a trip affordable.

73 Oakley St., SW3. ℗ 020/7352-5599. www.oakleyhotel.com. 12 rooms. Tube: Sloane Square or South Kensington. **Amenities:** Full breakfast, full shared kitchen, free Wi-Fi in lounge.

MARYLEBONE, MAYFAIR & KNIGHTSBRIDGE

For visitors who want a balance of central location and private residential vibe, Marylebone's the place. A 10-minute walk takes you to the "smart" end of Oxford Street and Mayfair to the south, the wide-open fields of Regent's Park to the north, and the shops and cafes of Soho to the southeast. Add to that one of the most attractive shopping thoroughfares in the city (Marylebone High St.) and a cluster of affordable restaurants (on James St.), and you've got the makings for an ideal tourist stomping ground—hence the higher prices.

Expensive

No. 10 Manchester Street ★★ There's previous little to pick apart in this very good red brick hotel located on a quiet street behind the Wallace Collection (p. 111) and near Oxford Street. Rooms are relatively large and the big beds and rain showers may tempt you away from exploring the city. For all its surface Edwardian style, it's modernized: On the ground floor, there's a dedicated cigar smoking terrace and humidor room—some of its guests are businessmen from moneyed Muslim countries and they can't drink alcohol in the bar. Americans can finally get a legal taste of Cuban cigars there. This solid, perfectly sized hotel could charge a lot more than it does, and it delivers a distinctly London cultural experience.

10 Manchester Street, W1. ℗ 020/7317-5900. www.tenmanchesterstreethotel.com. 45 rooms. Doubles from £160–264. **Amenities:** Restaurant, bar, cigar lounge, free Wi-Fi.

Brown's Hotel ★★★ The classic, rambling Mayfair hotel (est. 1837) is epitomized, but updated with bright, offbeat interiors that won't make commoners feel out-of-place. That is, if they can afford to get in to begin with. History is in every creak: The first-ever phone call was placed from its ground floor, and in 1907, Mark Twain scandalized the press by appearing in its lobby in his blue bathrobe. "Mark Twain exhibited himself as an eccentric today," tittered the *Times* on the front page, "and every staid Londoner who witnessed the exhibition fairly gasped." While staying here, Lord Kelvin elected to harness Niagara Falls, Rudyard Kipling finished *The Jungle Book*, and Stephen King started *Misery*. I myself swear I saw the ghost of a maid in the Kipling Suite one morning, but I can't afford to double-check. Of course, you can simply satisfy yourself with the servile atmosphere at its afternoon tea, probably London's finest, for £40. Even at that price, you may do well to remind yourself it's all-you-can-eat. Fill up, because everything at Brown's is a memory worth cherishing.

30 Albemarle St., W1. ℗ 020/7493-6020. www.brownshotel.com. £395–555 Tube: Green Park. **Amenities:** Restaurant, tea room, bar, spa, free Wi-Fi with online booking.

The Langham ★★ In 1863, while Americans were shooting each other in farmyards, London was assembling the first and most celebrated grandee dame hotel in Europe. She survives, but it was touch and go during the 20th century. The polished lobby is perfumed, the lifts swathed in leather, the rooms each a private cocoon of ordered wainscoting, enveloping beds, and bathrooms with toiletries in pink paper cartons kept in a box by the sink. Its Palm Court has been serving high tea (£40) since 1865. One cocktail in its Artesian bar is served with a paper panda head that has been filled with the wafting scent of aromatic bitters—you crush the panda before enjoying it. That sort of whimsy is favored by moneyed tourists from the Far East, and for service and discretion, along with that long history, there are few peers. The tariff is also something for the record books, but that's the price you pay to be in the company of Lady Di, Wallis Simpson, and Winston Churchill, who rightly favored it, and Arthur Conan Doyle, who sent Sherlock Holmes here in several stories. It's a few short blocks from Oxford Street's best shopping.

1c Portland Place, Regent Street, W1. ℂ **020/7636-1000**. www.langhamhotels.com. 380 rooms. £312–444. **Amenities:** Two restaurants, two bars, spa, business center, swimming pool, 512kb free Wi-Fi.

The Mandeville Hotel ★ Although it has gone off the boil from a few years ago, when its autumnal hues and metallic flourishes brought buzzy contemporary flair to a once-staid Marylebone inn, the Mandeville is still worthy. Yes, the rooms vary wildly in size, but they're spotless, designed thoughtfully, and the amenities are generous. The bar and restaurant, Reform Social & Grill, is chill enough to attract locals, although it's also so sopping with exaggerated Englishness it feels a touch Dignified—I mean, a marmalade martini? Still, it's fun, and the many restaurants of St Christopher's Place are a 3-minute walk south, as is Oxford Street.

Mandeville Place, W1. ℂ **020/7935-5599**. www.mandeville.co.uk. 142 rooms. Doubles from £165–205. **Amenities:** Restaurant, bar, cigar lounge, paid Wi-Fi.

Moderate

22 York Street ★★ You might wonder at first if you have knocked on the door of a private home of some bohemian doctor or lawyer. Inside, Michael and Liz Callis are going for a farmhouse feel, with warm wooden floorboards, plenty of antiques and oriental rugs, and large bathrooms, almost all of which have tub/shower combinations. Guests get their own keys and are let loose to treat the five-level premises as their own, which includes plenty of tea, coffee, and biscuits for munching. Adding to the home-away-from-home feel, breakfasts are served in the kitchen at a communal country table where you meet your fellow guests. The food includes some fantastic pain au chocolate. Although they're not explicitly banned, kids may not feel comfortable.

22 York St., W1. ℂ **020/7224-2990**. www.22yorkstreet.co.uk. 10 rooms. Single from £90, double from £129. Tube: Baker Street **Amenities:** Continental breakfast, free Wi-Fi.

Hart House Hotel ★★ Andrew Bowden has been a part of this place since he was 6 years old and his family took it over, so he knows it, and the city, very well. He and his staff run this cute B&B with the consistency you'd expect of a posher place. He outfits chambermaids in dark blue frocks, and stocks rooms with top-quality furniture, built to last. He even thought to install power outlets near the desk, a telling consideration that too often escapes even the loftiest hoteliers. Showers tend to be on the small side (it's an old building, so what else is new?), but rooms are cared for,

FINDING HOTELS online

You may be used to booking through sites such as Expedia.com or Travelocity.com for the best prices, but when it comes to London, think again. Many London hotels, particularly the most affordable ones, are privately owned, and many of them are represented on the Web by third-party travel agents and booking engines that pad the price with a few extra bucks, which they'll skim off for themselves as commission. So if you call the hotel directly for your bookings, you'll not only get the lowest price, but you'll also have the power of negotiation.

Another danger of making an online reservation: There are heaps of lousy budget hotels in London, particularly around Paddington and Earl's Court, that post misleading images on the Web, and it's easy to end up in a seedy one. **Mobissimo.com, Momondo.com,** and **Kayak.com** are three "aggregator" sites that scan dozens of sites for deals and pull them all together. If you hit them, you don't need to hit Travelocity or the like, because it includes them in the search.

Visit London, the city's official tourism office, also has an area on its website (www.visitlondon.com) for discounted hotel bookings, although it's maintained by Expedia. At Heathrow, St Pancras, and Victoria, plus at 17-19 Cockspur Street near the southwest corner of Trafalgar Square, stop by the **British Hotel Reservation Centre** (© 020/7592-3055. www.bhrc.co.uk), which also books for free online. **Lastminute.co.uk** is one of the most popular booking sites in the U.K., but always double-check that its rates actually represent savings, and the apps **Hotel Tonight** and **Hotels Now** sometimes bear cheap fruit. Other popular offshore hotel sites include **Booking.com, Eurocheapo.com, HotelsCombined.com, Laterooms.com.** and **Venere.com.** And **Priceline.co.uk** works just like its American counterpart; most of its hotels are corporate-owned. As with all bid-for-travel sites, you could end up with a deal, but remember that as hotels add star levels, they also add extra charges for you.

embellished with little sculptures, and outfitted with other functional touches such as bedside reading lamps. Room 9, on the back, comes with an enormous bathroom located in its own nook, and the family-ready quad is a mere £180. Always ask it for a better price than what's posted; Bowden often grants it.

51 Gloucester Place, W1. © **020/7935-2288**. www.harthouse.co.uk. 16 rooms. Singles from £79, doubles from £140. **Amenities:** Full breakfast, free Wi-Fi.

Inexpensive

Lincoln House Hotel ★ As affordable inns go, it's in extraordinarily good condition—or, as Londoners might say, "in good nick"——and it's the only property on its street that cares to put out flowers. Each of the 24 rooms has a private bathroom, so that's easy, but the rates are byzantine, subcategorized by bed size. For example, a single "small" is £69 because it has a twin bed, but there's a "single plus" with a 4-foot-wide bed that goes for £95. Forget all those prices now because the owners regularly lop off as much as 50% if it's not busy. Half the fun of Lincoln House, which has been in the same family for more than 30 years, is the nautical theme, which recurs in unexpected ways (portholes as mirrors, antique barometers as art). Handmade paneling in the hallways adds warmth. The one bummer is that the bathrooms are prefabricated fiberglass units, but if you've ever been on a cruise ship, you'll cope.

33 Gloucester Place, W1. ✆ **020/7486-7630**. www.lincoln-house-hotel.com. 24 rooms. Singles from £69, doubles from £105. Tube: Marble Arch. **Amenities:** Continental breakfast, free Wi-Fi.

THE SOUTH BANK, SOUTHWARK & BOROUGH

Since medieval times until about 15 years ago, "respectable" Londoners wanted nothing to do with this once-industrial area. They wish they'd bought property now. It's actually a terrific place to dwell in good weather, when the area comes alive with walkers, booksellers, pub-goers, and playgoers reveling in the nearby re-creation of Shakespeare's *Globe*. And moderate hotels are proliferating.

Moderate

CitizenM London Bankside ★★★   It takes about 10 seconds for the hip factor to rejuvenate your self-esteem in this affordable luxury concept, a top value in town. The hyper lobby, a super-Scandinavian playpen for some interior designer with ADD, seems to hum day and night with people getting cocktails, telecommuting, or reading one of the hundreds of orange-and-white Penguin classic paperbacks—a retro icon for British readers, but the only thing that's old-fashioned here. Check-in is self-guided by kiosk, and rooms are compact but arranged with genius. The platform beds are massive and piled with body pillows, the bathrooms slotted into the space with calculated aplomb, and you control everything from the blinds to mood lighting with the bedside "MoodPad" tablet. When the wake-up alarm goes off, computers gently dial up your lights, then chimes, then tunes your TV to the morning news. The brand began in the Netherlands in 2008, hence the funky grammar on the signage and the cheeky Mario Testino portrait of pop star Robbie Williams showing his sequined Union Jack thong to everyone waiting for the lift.

20 Lavington St., SE1. ✆ **020/3519-1680**. www.citizenm.com/london-bankside. 192 rooms. Doubles £99–£189. Tube: Southwark or London Bridge. **Amenities:** Free movies, free Wi-Fi.

London Bridge Hotel ★★   A 1916 telephone exchange building near the base of the Shard has been gussied with current flourishes such as walnut floors and red suede furniture, making for a casually distinguished mid-level hotel. Deluxe rooms come with a few blessings you don't find in many other London hotels, including walk-in closets and DVD players. Not a chain, its independence results in an attentive management, which is why it attracts repeat guests. On weekends, rates plummet, and it often lays out cheap discounts on its website, such as staying 3 nights for the price of 2. This is not the same property as the Mercure with the same name.

8–18 London Bridge Street, SE1. ✆ **020/7855-2200**. www.londonbridgehotel.com. 138 rooms. Doubles from £99–276. Tube: London Bridge. **Amenities:** Restaurant, bar, gym, free Wi-Fi.

Mad Hatter Hotel ★★   Decent pub hotels, which are hotels above pubs, are a dying breed in London. A pub hotel that bills itself more as a borderline mainstream hotel, it could easily seduce guests into lingering in its gorgeous Victorian-styled bar, part of the sizable Fuller's chain. But upstairs, soundproofed from the typically English frolic but close enough for a quick pint, the sizable, good-value rooms feel like they were lifted from a business hotel. Think decent-size bathrooms with tub/showers,

HOW TO GET YOUR HOTEL FOR free

What if I told you that you could spend 6 nights in London, airfare and hotel included, for $1,049 in the summer? Or for around $1,200 over the American Thanksgiving holiday weekend? Even in summer, when airfare alone costs $1,200, air-hotel packages can cost about the same—except they come with hotel, breakfast, and often a tour or two thrown in. With math like that, it's as if the hotel stay is free. How do they do it? Contracted rates and bulk buying.

I love air-hotel packages. There's often no cheaper way to get to London. And unlike escorted tours, with air-hotel packages you don't have experience the city on a bus—you get your air ticket and your hotel voucher, and off you go to explore. The lowest prices are from eastern American cities such as New York and Boston, but for a few dozen dollars more, you can leave from just about any other American city. You can also often extend the return airfare by as much as a month without having to buy more hotel nights (although you can do that, too).

The catch with package deals is this: Many of the least expensive hotel options are pillow mills that have seen better days. Still, the money you save could make or break your trip, and besides, even at the worst hotels, most of the time you'll either be touring or unconscious. For a little more peace of mind, you could also upgrade to a slightly more expensive property.

The king of affordable air-hotel deals is **Go-Today.com** (✆ 800/227-3235; www.go-today.com), which usually offers 4-, and 6-night packages to London, sometimes paired with other European destinations such as Paris or Rome, including local flights between the cities (as low as $1,300 for 6 nights—that's a touch over $200 a day). Other big brokers can share the same inventory, so options might be similar among them: **Virgin Vacations** (✆ 888/937-8474; www.virgin-vacations.com), the air-hotel wing of funky Virgin Atlantic Airways, does 4-, and 6-night deals. Sometimes you can score with **British Airways Holidays** (✆ 877/428-2228; www.baholidays.com) but some of its packages are priced higher than others on the air-hotel market. Also beware of its airline sales that come with hotel rooms, because sometimes, other companies beat those prices. **Gate 1 Travel** (✆ 800/682-3333; www.gate1travel.com) most often offers "Independent Vacation" packages that include London and one other European city. **E.E.I. Travel** (✆ 800/927-3876; www.eeitravel.com) can be similar to Go-Today at its lowest end.

rose-colored bedspreads matching painted accent walls, a lift, and ice machines—rare as diamonds in the U.K. The rack rate for its 30 rooms with breakfast is £205 for singles or doubles, a bit high, but in reality, you'll pay around £150 for advance bookings Just 5 minutes from the Tate Modern or the National Theatre on the Thames, the location may be its best feature. Some rooms can be conjoined for families.

3-7 Stamford St., SE1 ✆ 020/7401-9222. www.madhatterhotel.co.uk. 30 rooms. Doubles from £149. Tube: Southwark or Blackfriars. **Amenities:** Full breakfast, pub, free Wi-Fi.

THE CITY

Things get more expensive in the City, where expense accounts reign beside HM the Queen. You'll get more style, and you'll be in historic quarters, but you'll be farther from the big attractions, and at night, there are not many choices for food. If your goal is spending the wee hours in the clubs of Smithfield and Spitalfields, though, you'll be within foot range. There are many corporate hotel choices east of the City in the Canary Wharf and Docklands region, however, they're designed more for people doing business in those areas. From the ExCeL, a major convention center in far East London with lots of hotels for attendees, it will take you 45 minutes to reach Trafalgar Square; the Jubilee Line from Canary Wharf is faster, but the prices are geared toward business travelers.

Expensive

Malmaison ★   Malmaison is the sole London branch of a burgeoning British design chain. Rooms are hyperbolic in their mid-'00s design (slender art lamps, dark earth tones and metallics, lurid lighting like a game show set from a decade ago, and machinelike lever handles on everything from the sinks to the doors), but the beds don't suffer from the same preening. They're giant, just soft enough, and inviting, and the bathrooms have both showers and tubs along with sinks like oversize noodle bowls. There's a buzzing brasserie and bar in the basement, but you'll find plenty of nightlife right out the door around Smithfield Market. The hotel routinely cuts deals, especially on weekends. Because it's not snooty, this full-service hotel has the right level of *Zoolander*-esque posturing. The brand was recently purchased, and a through freshening-up has been announced.

18-21 Charterhouse Square, EC1. ☏ **0844/6930-656**. www.malmaison-london.com. 97 rooms. Doubles £205–275. Tube: Barbican. **Amenities**: Restaurant, bar, gym, free Wi-Fi.

The Rookery Hotel ★★★   In the 1990s, three derelict houses and shops were converted into a hotel, and using the same formula as their Hazlitt's in Soho—charactered antiques and era wood paneling blended with top-line attention and discretion—the owners fashioned this creaking, tucked-away realm of open fireplaces and polite staff that give a sense of what it must have been like to live with money in the 19th century. It's elegant, but not like a stuffy blue-blooded dowager—more like a well-read bachelor uncle. Each huge room is a unique, rambling surprise, filled with four-poster beds, Persian rugs, gilt-framed mirrors, and oil paintings like a professor's study, but not neglectful of modern necessities such as flat-screens and iPod docks. The result is one of London's most unique and repeatable hotel experiences, romantic beyond measure, yet also one that feels the most authentically London. There's no restaurant or anything like that, but you can get food brought to your room, as your breakfast will be. Also note that some rooms have pull-chain toilets and tubs with European-style hand-held shower nozzles. The location near Smithfield Market is calm and off the main.

Peter's Lane, Cowcross St., London EC1. ☏ **020/7336-0931**. www.rookeryhotel.com. 33 units. £282–£306. Tube: Farringdon or Barbican. **Amenities:** Free Wi-Fi.

South Place Hotel ★★★   Plugged-in, stylish, and sexy: That's the crowd this hotel goes for, and you'll feel that way, too. The first hotel to be built from the ground up in the Square Mile for a century, every inch was run through the design filter, and much of the art was commissioned by celebrated contemporary artists. Rooms, charcoal-grey with wool carpets, large, and hushed, are fully up-to-date with luxury expectations, so you'll find plenty of outlets, AV connections, blackout blinds closed from a bedside panel, and big a bed you can flop around in. By evening, the two restaurants,

Angler and a 3 South Place Bar & Grill, have lured both named chefs and some of the liveliest professionals from the City before they head just east to the party grounds at Spitalfields. This newcomer pumps on all cylinders—there's nearly nothing wrong with it—yet despite the hot scene, it never ignores the relaxation of its guests. On weekends, rates can dip to £170.

3 South Place, EC2. © **020/3503-0000**. www.southplacehotel.com. 80 rooms. Doubles from £213. Tube: Moorgate or Liverpool Street. **Amenities**: Two restaurants, three bars, guests' lounge, gym, spa, business center, free Wi-Fi.

Moderate

Apex City of London ★★★ A superb contemporary boutique brand that many foreigners don't know about and yet appeals to their standards for space and style, Apex is a friendly and peaceful urban retreat that actually looks like its pictures. You'll find it literally steps from Tower of London, and a few rooms glimpse the Tower Bridge—along with the balcony, worth the upgrade of £15–30. During the weekend, when The City is deader than Old Marley, it can be steal—I have seen £99 then, although its regular pricing is still a better value than most of its competition. It's handsomely designed by chic Scots, with huge rooms done in hardwood and walnut, Nespresso pods instead of awful instant coffee, and bathrooms larger than many B&Bs' guest rooms, including walk-in power showers. The **Apex London Wall**, just as good, is in the side streets north of Bank station, and the **Apex Temple Court**, off Fleet Street, is also tops, but for the views and its affordable proximity to the river, it's a solid choice.

No. 1 Seething Ln., London EC3. © **020/7977-9500**. www.apexhotels.co.uk. 179 units. Doubles £140–340. Tube: Tower Hill. **Amenities:** Restaurant, bar, gym, free local calls, free Wi-Fi.

The Fox & Anchor ★ We all claim to want an old-fashioned English inn, but do you really want the chintz, the lace curtains, and the blank walls? In the thick of Smithfield's nightlife (so bring earplugs if you require them), this fun little find took a tiny old-fashioned pub hotel and upgraded it so it only *looks* old—brass saddle-bowl sinks, mullioned windows, wooden floors, and in the case of the Smithfield room, a freestanding tub in the room (that fills fast), yet they're also current with sound systems and flat-screen TVs. This is a case of making a leap forward by looking back. Downstairs, of course, there's a Victorian-era pub of mahogany, brass, and etched glass. It was also upgraded from the authentic original.

115 Charterhouse St., London EC1. © **020/7550-1000**. www.foxandanchor.com. 6 units. Doubles from £120. Tube: Barbican or Farringdon. **Amenities:** Full breakfast, restaurant, bar, free Wi-Fi.

Inexpensive

The Hoxton ★ It was a revelation when it opened in 2006, but now everyone's doing cheap luxury this way. Self-consciously quirky rooms brag exposed brick walls, rain showers, and industrial-chic set pieces like dim lighting, metal, and stained wood. Continental breakfast is delivered teach morning via a bag you hang on the door, which can make you feel like an monkey at the world's hippest zoo, and there's free water and milk for your little fridge. The public spaces, including grill styled after an American diner, supply hangouts in their own right. As a testament to its local pride, "concept" rooms are decorated with arty things that came from within a 3-minute walk of the hotel, in Shoreditch. Keep an eye on its website for sensational discounts, such as its legendary £1 sale events. For trips 6 months in the future, you stand a fair chance of reserving a place in for £49 to £99. Most times, though, you will be unlikely to pay less than £159, although weekends are dramatically cheaper.

81 Great Eastern St., EC2. ✆ **020/7550-1000**. www.hoxtonhotels.com. 208 rooms. Doubles £99–169. Tube: Old Street. **Amenities:** Restaurant; bar; 1 hr. of free phone calls daily to UK, US, and Europe; free Wi-Fi.

THE BUDGET HOTEL CHAINS, CITYWIDE

The biggest tourism headline in the past decade has been the proliferation of giant hotel chains that lure bookings with predictable standards, decently sized rooms, and unbeatable lead-in rates for people who can pay many months ahead of time. Increasingly, family-run B&Bs cannot compete with the brand recognition of these companies, and indeed, these well-funded chains often operate in neighborhoods and in converted buildings where private inns cannot. If you find the hotel brands you know are too full, poorly located, or too expensive, try these, but be warned—so many people habitually turn to them that their prices frequently rise past the point of value, particularly close to the dates of stay.

easyHotel ★ This is how you do London super-cheaply while avoiding hostels. Its founder, Stelios Haji-Ioannou, has made himself a minor celebrity by creating budget brands (easyJet, most famously) that cost less when you book early and more if you reserve at the last minute. So it goes here, where reservations are accepted only over the Web, but typically cost £25 for double rooms if you book 6 months ahead, and £49 to £65 if you procrastinate. Stelios' other revelation is, to others, a curse: prefabricated room units that differ only in how little floor space you're given. Beds are double-size with white duvets, with rarely an inch of space between mattress and wall. No phone, no hair dryer, no frills at all. You may find a long ledge on which to pop a travel alarm clock, but bathrooms aren't more than plastic cubicles combining a shower, toilet, and sink in one water-splashed closet. The cheapest rooms don't even have windows. Want to watch TV? You'll pay £5 for 24 hours. Want housekeeping? £10. Now you know what easyHotel is good for: no-nonsense sleep. Even the location choices are cheap. They're big in parts of town that are passing their prime.

www.easyhotel.com. No phone reservations.

easyHotel Earl's Court 44-48 West Cromwell Rd., SW5. Tube: Earl's Court.

easyHotel Old Street/Barbican 80 Old Street, EC1. Tends of be the least expensive easyHotel in central London. Tube: Barbican or Old Street.

easyHotel Paddington 10 Norfolk Place, W2. Tube: Paddington.

easyHotel South Kensington 14 Lexham Gardens, W8. Tube: Earl's Court or Gloucester Road.

easyHotel Victoria 36-40 Belgrave Rd., SW1. Tube: Victoria or Pimlico.

Ibis Hotels ★★ This 600-strong French chain by the Accor hotel giant is distinguished by its trademark 3-foot-square windows, its just-off-the-margins locations, and its simple but cheerful decor. You'll get a double bed, bathroom with shower, climate control, a 24-hour kitchen, TV, phone, free Wi-Fi, at least one outlet, and a built-in desk. The breakfast charge varies per property (£7.50 is typical), but food is usually served from 4am, making this a smart choice if you need to catch an early flight or train. The fresh-baked breakfast baguettes are delicious—hey, it's French. But let's be frank: You'd have to be mad to think these rooms are worth the price once they go above £170, so book as far ahead as possible. There's also **Ibis Styles**, the "all-inclusive" brand that is slightly more upscale and includes breakfast and Wi-Fi, and **Ibis Budget,** a bare-bones, shower-only crash pad once known as Etap or Formule 1; rooms there have style but are very simple, sleep up to three people, and have free Wi-Fi and TV, but practically nothing else frilly.

No English-reservations hotline. www.ibishotel.com.

Ibis Budget London Whitechapel 100 Whitechapel Road, E1. ☎ **020/7655-4620**. 169 rooms. Rooms from £60–81. Lots of Indian restaurants in the area, £5 breakfast. Tube: Whitechapel or Aldgate East.

Ibis London Blackfriars 49 Blackfriars Road, SE1. ☎ **020/7633-2720**. 297 rooms. Rooms from £132–294. Around the corner from Tate Modern. Tube: Southwark or Blackfriars.

Ibis London City 5 Commercial Street, E1. ☎ **020/7422-8400**. 348 rooms. Rooms from £112–259. Close to Whitechapel and Spitalfields. Tube: Aldgate East.

Ibis London Earl's Court 47 Lillie Road, SW6. ☎ **020/610-0880**. 504 rooms. Rooms from £105–179. Quite far west, but lots of rooms. Tube: West Brompton.

Ibis London Euston St Pancras 3 Cardington Street, NW1. ☎ **020/7388-7777**. 380 rooms. A very convenient location. Rooms from £138–241. Tube: Euston or Euston Square.

Ibis Styles London Southwark Rose 43-47 Southwark Bridge Rd., SE1. www.southwarkrosehotel.co.uk. ☎ **020/7015-1480**. 114 rooms. Rooms £111–£235. Higher-level than a typical Ibis, with motorized curtains, a top-floor bar with a sunny western exposure, and, behind a curved wall, smartly designed bathrooms. Brilliant location near Borough Market and Shakespeare's Globe, and rooms near the top have a great view of the Shard. Tube: London Bridge or Southwark.

Premier Inn ★★★ This is many British travelers' favorite economy brand hotels, not just because its rooms feel the most upbeat, but also because it adapts properties to their surroundings. At 47,000 bedrooms and growing, it's the largest hotel chain in the United Kingdom, and rooms (maximum of two adults) offer a king-size bed, bathtub and shower with all-purpose shower gel, tea- and coffee-making facilities, TV, phone, iron, AC (sometimes), at least three outlets, and a desk. Increasingly, it require you to check in at a kiosk, eliminating the chance to talk to staff about recommendations, but that tells you about the tourist churn that this company is going for—it's owned by the same group that owns the Costa Coffee chain, which sometimes appears in the lobby, as does a mass-appeal bar/café, Thyme. Unlike Travelodge, there are in-room phones and hair dryers. Its prices start as low as Travelodge's (£19 nearly a year ahead), and the final prices end up much the same. Like airline tickets, prices rise as availability dwindles, and in busy times, prices soar higher than where they should be, so book ahead or look elsewhere. Take the prices below and clip £10 off for booking ahead online with a nonrefundable reservation. If you go farther out from city to other Premier Inn locations (there are less convenient properties besides what's on this list), you may save £25 but you will spent a lot of time and money on the Tube. The brand will begin opening an even cheaper and more compact concept, Hub by Premier Inn, in London starting in August 2014.

☎ **0845/099-0095**. www.premierinn.com. **Amenities:** Bar/café, 30 min. free Wi-Fi daily, then £3 for 24 hr.

Premier Inn London Angel Islington 18 Parkfield Street, N1. *℮* **0871/527-8558**. 95 rooms. Rooms £79–170. Contemporary building near antiques shops of Islington. Tube: Angel.

Premier Inn London Blackfriars (Fleet Street) 1–2 Dorset Rise, EC4. *℮* **0871/527-9362**. Underrated location but limited evening food options. 256 rooms. Rooms £110–159. Tube: Blackfriars.

Premier Inn London City (Monument) 20 St Mary at Hill, EC3. *℮* **0871/527-9452**. 184 rooms. Soon to open after conversion from an office building, there will be few food options nights and weekends. Tube: Monument or Tower Hill.

Premier Inn London City (Old Street) Corsham Street, N1. *℮* **0871/527-9312**. 251 rooms. Rooms £80–115. Quick walk to Shoreditch nightlife. Tube: Old Street.

Premier Inn London City (Tower Hill) 24 Prescot Street, E1. *℮* **0871/527-8646**. 196 rooms. Rooms £49–175. Near nightlife of Whitechapel and Shoreditch. Tube: Tower Gateway DLR or Aldgate.

Premier Inn London County Hall County Hall, Belvedere Road, SE1. *℮* **0871/527-8648**. 324 rooms. Rooms £107–169. Sells out often; beside London Eye (no view). Tube: Waterloo or Westminster.

Premier Inn London Euston 1 Dukes Road, WC1. *℮* **0871/527-8656**. 266 rooms. Rooms £79–139. North Bloomsbury, near railway station and many Tube lines. Tube: Euston.

Premier Inn London Kensington (Earl's Court) 11 Knaresborough Place, SW5. *℮* **0871/527-8666**. 184 rooms. Rooms £89–115. A bit far west, ample windows, southern rooms face gentle rumble of Tube stop. Tube: Earl's Court.

Premier Inn London Kensington (Olympia) 22–32 West Cromwell Road, SW5. *℮* **0871/527-8668**. 90 rooms. Rooms £49–107. A bit far west; Earl's Court is slightly better located. Tube: Earl's Court.

Premier Inn London Kings Cross 26–30 York Way, N1. *℮* **0871/527-8672**. 276 rooms. Rooms £79–145. A new build east of the railway station, near many Tube lines. Tube: King's Cross St Pancras.

Premier Inn London Leicester Square 1 Leicester Place, WC2. *℮* **0871/527-9334**. 85 rooms. Rooms £99–150. Unbeatable central location opened 2012, often noisy outside but rooms are sound-insulated with neoprene. Tube: Leicester Square.

Premier Inn London Southwark (Borough Market) 34 Park Street, SE1. *℮* **0871/527-8676**. The best one. 59 rooms on three floors in quiet courtyard off river. Rooms £89–156. Off the river, breakfast facing St Paul's. Tube: London Bridge.

Premier Inn London Southwark (Tate Modern) 15A Great Suffolk Street, SE1. *℮* **0871/517-9332**. 230 rooms. Rooms £114–161. Newly built hotel tower, underrated location. Tube: Southwark.

Premier Inn London St Pancras 88 Euston Road, NW1. *℮* **0871/527-9492**. Rooms £145. Soon to open. Near many Tube lines, opposite British Library. Tube: King's Cross St Pancras or Euston Square.

Premier Inn London Tower Bridge 159 Tower Bridge Road, SE1. *℮* **0871/527-8678**. 195 rooms. Rooms £104–161. A touch far from the Tube. Tube: Bermondsey or London Bridge.

Premier Inn London Victoria 82–83 Eccleston Square, off 55 Gillingham Street, SW1. *℮* **0871/527-8680**. 110 rooms. Rooms £89–142. In a former budget travelers' neighborhood. Tube: Victoria.

Premier Inn London Waterloo (Westminster Bridge) 85 York Road, SE1. ✆ **0871/527-9412**. 234 rooms. Rooms £128–159. Opened 2013 on the West side of Waterloo station in the onetime General Lying-In maternity hospital. Tube: Waterloo.

Travelodge ★ Go online right now, because rates start at a head-slapping £19 if you book 11 months ahead. That more than makes up for having the thinnest amenities of the newly built economy brands, with some 500 locations in the UK and nearly two dozen in the Greater London area. It's nicer than the American Travelodge brand, which is a separate beast entirely. Expect king-size beds, bathtub and shower, TV (but no phone, hair dryer, or toiletries), paid in-room movies, a wardrobe, at least one power point, and a desk. Breakfast, if your property offers it, is about £7 more. "Family rooms" have a pullout couch for two kids but cost the same as a double. Searching on its site delivers a grid of the available London hotels and prices. The £19 is the non-refundable "Saver" rate, but if you want a rate that you can get out of, get a "Flexible" rate, which start at £46—still incredible. There are more locations in town, but these are the ones within easy walking distance. Prices below are *typical* rates and go down to £25 if you're first in and pop up at peak.

✆ **08719/848484**. www.travelodge.co.uk. **Amenities**: Bar/café (often), Wi-Fi £10 a day.

Travelodge London Central Bank 19-23 St. Swithin's Lane, EC4. ✆ **0871/984-6485**. Tube: Bank. Rooms £80. Showers but not bath, quiet on weekends. Tube: Cannon Street.

Travelodge London Central Euston 1-11 Grafton Place, NW1. ✆ **0871/984-6332**. Rooms £89–119. North Bloomsbury location, near many Tube stops, opposite railway station. Tube: Euston.

Travelodge London Central City Road 1-23 City Road, EC1. ✆ **0871-984-6333**. Rooms £73–88. Farther from the West End. Tube: Moorgate.

Travelodge London Central Kings Cross Willings House, 356-364 Grays Inn Road, WC1. ✆ **0871/984-6256**. Rooms £65–87. Quick walk to Tube stop. Tube: Kings Cross St Pancras.

Travelodge London Central Marylebone Harewood Rose, NW1. ✆ **0871/984-6311**. Rooms £68–89. Ten minutes' walk from Regent's Park. Tube: Marylebone or Edgware Road.

Travelodge London Central Southwark 202-206 Union Street, SE1. ✆ **0871/984-6352**. Rooms £70–108. Underrated location 5 minutes' walk from Tate Modern. Tube: Southwark.

Travelodge London Central Tower Bridge Lloyds Court Business Centre, 1 Goodmans Yard, E1. ✆ **0871/984-6388**. Rooms £70–92. Tube: Tower Hill.

Travelodge London Central Waterloo 195-203 Waterloo Road, SE1. ✆ **0871/984-6291**. Rooms £69–116. Ten minutes' walk south of Waterloo. Tube: Waterloo or Lambeth North.

Travelodge London Covent Garden 10 Drury Lane, WC2. ✆ **0871/984-6245**. Rooms £64–109. The best one. Coldly brutalist but very well-located. Tube: Holborn or Covent Garden.

Travelodge London Farringdon 10-42 Kings Cross Road, WC1. ✆ **0871/984-6274**. Rooms £64–86. Quiet neighborhood. Tube: Kings Cross St Pancras.

Travelodge London Kings Cross Royal Scot 100 Kings Cross Road, WC1. ✆ **0871/984-6272**. Rooms £63–74. Ten minutes' walk from Tube. Tube: Kings Cross St Pancras.

Travelodge London Vauxhall 3 Bondway, SW8. ✆ **0871/559-1860**. Rooms £72. Tube: Vauxhall.

Tune Hotels ★★ This recent Malaysian brand import provides everything you need in a modern crash pad but nothing else: en-suite power shower, round-the-clock reception, air conditioning, but not even a closet—you get hangers. If you want more, you pay a few pounds more at a time: towel rental, TV, Wi-Fi, safe, hair dryer, and even windows come at a price. The a la carte model a great way to keep costs down but not a path to luxury, yet the facilities are clean to a corporate standard and designed with modern/minimalist zip. And don't write off a windowless room's power to help you overcome jet lag. Prices are as low as £35 for an online booking months in advance and go to £125 or so last-minute. Windows cost about £15 more.

No phone. www.tunehotels.com.

Tune Hotel—Liverpool Street, London 13-15 Folgate Street, E1. 183 rooms. About a third of the rooms lack windows, so there are more deals. Tube: Liverpool Street.

Tune Hotel—Westminster, London 118-120 Westminster Bridge Road, SE1. 83 rooms. An easy walk to the London Eye and Big Ben. Tube: Lambeth North.

Tune Hotel—Kings Cross, London 324 Gray's Inn Road, WC1. 218 rooms. Tube: Kings Cross/St Pancras.

Tune Hotel—London Paddington 41 Praed Street, W2. 137 Rooms. Handy for catching early-morning Heathrow Express trains. Tube: Paddington.

RENTING A ROOM

English hosted accommodation has long been one of the world's great travel bargains, but they are being supplanted by corporate hotels. Americans in particular seem to forget there are plenty of locals eager to make a few pounds by welcoming you into their homes, and as they vie for your business, they make for some great places to find cheap deals. One potential hidden advantage of this sort of stay comes if you've got a car—for example, if you're stopping in London during a drive round the island. Staying with a family in zone 3 or 4 may enable you to park your car cheaply. What's included? At the minimum, a bed and breakfast. Everything else depends, since homestays are as unique as the hosts themselves. Your hosts may offer to show you the town or they may leave you in peace. They may have searingly fast Wi-Fi or they may think toaster ovens are the cutting edge of technology. Armed with your wish list, these brokers should be able to pair you with suitable options.

Maggie Dobson has personally selected the homes that make it into the stable of **At Home in London** (✆ **020/8748-1943;** www.athomeinlondon.co.uk) since 1986. Her properties are in the tourist areas of West London, near the Tube, and are priced accordingly: mid-£80s (central London) to scarcely £30 a night (Zones 2 & 3). **The Bed and Breakfast Club** (✆ **020/7371-3202;** www.bulldogclub.com; stay@bulldog-club.com), around since 1988, aims to provide a luxury experience in the kind of home you might see spotlighted in a decorators' magazine. Rates hover around £80 to £120, all units are nonsmoking, and they come with a full English breakfast.

London Bed and Breakfast Agency (✆ **020/7586-2768;** www.londonbb.com) pays extra attention to listing trustworthy hosts for single female travelers, with rates generally between £60 and £100. No kids under 5 are allowed (a good rule of thumb for any homestay, I'd say).

The following agencies see things the old way. That is, their main concern is placing you in a home at the price you can afford. I can't promise that your hosts will bend over backward to show you the city (which may actually suit more private travelers), but I can promise low prices:

London Homestead Services (℡ 020/7286-5115; www.lhslondon.co.uk), in business since 1985, is incredibly cheap (£22 to £35 for both doubles and singles), because they're located in commuter neighborhoods a good half-hour train ride from town, within small, traditional homes. Remember that you will have to pay a little more for trains to reach those neighborhoods.

Established in 1992, **Happy Homes** (℡ 020/7352-5121; www.happy-homes.com) specializes in rooms in southwest London, about a 25-minute commute to the West End. Unfortunately, its clunky website means you have to call to hash out where you're going to stay. For less than 2 weeks, single rooms are £25, doubles £40, plus a one-time fee of £25 per person. If you pay with a credit card, you'll incur a surcharge of 3 percent—still legal here.

If you're scraping the linty depths of your wallet, try **Annscott Accommodation Service** (℡ 020/8540-7942; www.holidayhosts.free-online.co.uk). The price of a single room with shared bath arranged by Annscott (in business under one name or another since the early 1990s) goes as low as £17, topping out at £40. Doubles are £34 to £65. Why? Most are 30 minutes by train from town, but it's otherwise perfectly acceptable and established.

RENTING A FLAT

The British love renting full homes or apartments when they go on vacation and, culturally speaking, that's important, because it means they have lots of them available back home, and you have a long, long list of potential places to pick through. When you arrive, you'll often find a folder that schools you in the best local shops and restaurants, and you may encounter neighbors keeping an eye on the place and on your welfare (at one property I know of, the owner herself pops round and pretends to be a helpful neighbor), which is an advantage if you want to learn more of the city's secrets. Many properties have minimum stays of 5 to 7 nights, but that varies by property. Beyond the rental-by-owner matchmaker sites **Airbnb.com**, TripAdvisor's **FlipKey. com, Housetrip.com**, and **VRBO.com**, try these established London specialists.

Dealing in U.K. flats from a convenient, licensed U.S. office since 2002, **New York Habitat** (℡ 212/255-8018 in U.S.; www.nyhabitat.com) reps some 440 furnished rentals. Units for two range £80 to £250, but they come larger.

For a good range of homes from mid-range to fantasy, the well-established **Coach House Rentals** (℡ 020/8133-8332; www.rentals.chslondon.com) shines brightest in West London and Westminster. After a £90 administrative fee, large, well-appointed units go from £150 to £300 a night—as much as many hotels, but for rambling spaces that sleep up to nine people.

The operators of **Loving London Apartments** (℡ 800/961-8138 from the U.S.; www.lovinglondonapartments.com), a clearinghouse for hundreds of flats in a wide range, visit every property themselves. What began in 2003 as a booker for Spanish vacation villas spread to London in 2005, run by Brits. You can find late-breaking "hot deals" on its site; using those, I've found rooms in getting around Zone 1 for £29 a night, but £100 more than that is an advance-booking standard.

Set up in 1995, **Outlet 4 Holidays** (www.outlet4holidays.com) has flats better located for tourists than perhaps any other firm's. The Outlet's locations are around Soho cafe-and-club scene, smack in the West End. £125 a night is the norm, but there are extra fees for checking in outside of business hours. Should trouble arise, the company's office is in Soho, so you won't have far to go for assistance.

A higher-end renter, **One Fine Stay** (☏ **917/383-2182;** www.onefinestay.com), shoots its flats as if they're photographing a fashion spread, which tells you something about both its owners and its clientele. Central London digs are well over £200 a night, with impeccable design and customer service to match.

A variety of properties exist for the sole purpose of renting flats to visitors. Flats are renovated with complete current fittings, including Wi-Fi, AC, full kitchens and washer/dryers, and yet there's a staff on property to respond to your needs. **Studios-2Let** (Cartwright Gardens, Bloomsbury, WC1. ☏ **020/7486-9020;** www.studios2let. com. Two-person studios from £340/week. Kitchens but no washer/dryers; Tube: Euston) is one of the more affordable. One of the most gorgeous is **AKA West End** (5 Bentinck Street, Marylebone, W1. ☏ **020/7467-5930;** www.stayaka.com; from £370 Tube: Bond Street), in the former London offices of Russia's notorious KGB; the surviving circular lift is a treasure. Another, in Knightsbridge, is the 21-unit **Beaufort House** (45 Beaufort Gardens, SW3; ☏ **020/7584-2600;** www.beauforthouse.co.uk. from £306; Tube: Knightsbridge), converted from a few conjoined townhouses 2 minutes' walk west of Harrods. It attracts a discreet Middle Eastern clientele.

The French-owned **Citadines** (☏ **011-33-141-/05-79-05** (France); www.citadines. com) runs corporate-style private, apartment-like quarters, and it has five locations citywide. In order of centrality: Trafalgar Square, Holborn, South Kensington (priciest, from £200), Barbican (cheapest, from £87), and Islington.

HOME EXCHANGES

You'd be surprised how many Londoners are dying to visit your own stomping grounds, and if you make contact with the right people, you can swap houses at an agreed-upon time (sometimes simultaneously). It sounds strange, but nothing tends to get stolen because swappers often become good friends. Not just that, but their neighbors will often pop by to check up on you, so you have a built-in social circle (and source of insider advice). You can truly live like a local when you swap homes, and quite a few people end up doing it year after year.

Plenty of exchange clubs exist, and because London's an interesting place, it's pretty well represented in all of them. Which club should you choose? Well, since almost all of them are pitched to specific clientele, that's for you to decide. Here are the biggies, in alphabetical order:

Digsville.com (☏ **877/795-1019**): For $45 a year, this popular and well-designed site allows users to see photos of their prospective swap and even read feedback from others who have traded with its owner.

HomeExchange.com (☏ **800/877-8723**): When *The Holiday* came out, this club's listings shot from 6,000 to more than 20,000. Now there are 46,000. This is important because the more members, the more potential swaps. It breaks searches down by interest, including for seniors and long-term stays. It costs $10 a month to list.

Homelink.org (☏ **800/638-3841**): Popular with British and Australian travelers (with members in 80 countries), this service, around since 1953, costs $89 per year.

Intervac (☏ **800/756-4663**; www.intervacus.com): Intervac has been around for half a century, but its old catalog system has migrated to the Web. Its claim to fame is that some 80% of its listings are international (30,000 families are represented), which means (as it puts it), "you compete with fewer Americans for overseas properties." Access to all international listings is $100 a year.

There are additional exchange sites for special interest groups, designed to provide safe haven for travelers with particular needs. **SabbaticalHomes.com** caters to academics; **Independent Living Institute** (www.independentliving.org) is a free database maintained by a Sweden-based advocacy group for people with disabilities; **HomeAroundtheWorld.com** (☏ **020/7564-3739**) is for gays and lesbians and costs £45 for a year.

Or you could roll the dice with a website like **CouchSurfing.com,** on which folks (generally younger) offer spare space to visitors. That's free, but there is no vetting system, so consider the risks that might come with accepting an offer.

CHEAP DORM ROOMS

Wait, don't skip this section yet! Staying in an empty college room in the summertime is actually an ideal budget saver. After all, given the size of London's hotel rooms—even the pricey ones—you're not going to get much more space than a college student, anyway. There are 24 universities and colleges in town with 350,000 students, and schools nurture a lucrative sideline by renting rooms during holiday periods. For summer, reservations are accepted starting in March or April. At all of them, you should expect a wood-frame bed with linen, a desk, a dresser, an in-room sink, the possibility of an equipped kitchen (although it might be shared), an en suite bathroom (usually), laundry facilities, breakfast (often at a reasonable charge), Wi-Fi, and phones in the room or in the hall. A few even have TV lounges. If you're still stuck after plowing through this list, try contacting **Venuemasters** (☏ 0114/249-3090; www.venuemasterslondon.co.uk), an organization that helps tourists locate and book academic accommodations in the U.K. for free.

London School of Economics (☏ **020/7955-7575**; www.lsevacations.co.uk). Check these rooms out first. They're in terrific condition, with modern furnishings and the dignity that you'd expect of a school that trains the world's future power players in business. Generally, rooms rent cheaply (£42 to £70) for July, August, and the first chunk of September. A few rooms may be available at Christmas or Easter, too. There are seven locations around town. In order of centrality to Trafalgar Square: Northumberland House, Grosvenor House Studios, High Holborn, Carr-Saunders Hall, Passfield Hall, Bankside House, Rosebery Hall.

Some single rooms at **City University London** (☏ **020/7040-7040**; www.city.ac.uk/accommodation) are open from early July to early September. Prices are £35 a night and £210 a week.

University College London (☏ **020/7631-8310**; www.ucl.ac.uk/residences). Its dorms are less prestigious than LSE's, but they still fit the bill and aren't depressing. From late June to mid-September, 14 residences are available for public use at £33 to £49, but only five properties have private bathrooms. One hall in Fitzrovia, Ramsay, comes with breakfast.

King's College (℃ **020/7848-1700;** www.kingsvenues.com): Open late June through mid-September. Three residences (Stamford Street, Great Dover Street, Hampstead) are in central London. The candidates have kitchens but not utensils and cost £55 to £65.

International Students House (229 Great Portland St., W1; ℃ **020/7631-8300;** www.ish.org.uk; Tube: Great Portland Street): Part dorm, part subdued hostel, in two buildings close to each other. Rates are £21 to £26 in a gender-separated dorm, £50 singles, £33 twin, £104 quad. Bathrooms are shared, and some are co-ed but partitioned. Rooms are notably clean, but other academic rooms are cheaper and more private. Continental breakfast is included.

LONDON'S RESTAURANTS

n 1957, Arthur Frommer visited London for his seminal *Europe on $5 a Day*. Although London merited the very first destination chapter in the book, his report was gloomy: "With great despair, this book recommends that you . . . save your money for the better meals available in France and Italy. Cooking is a lost art in Great Britain; your meat pie with cabbage will turn out just as tasteless for 40¢ in a chain restaurant as it will for $2 in a posh hotel." The report for 2014 is a little different: Prepare to be wowed.

4

Thankfully, the English palette has caught up with the rest of the world, and the residents of London now rightfully pride themselves on their advanced and multicultural cuisine. Your food will almost certainly not be tasteless, and cabbage has been banished from most menus.

Now that the floodgates of E.U. bureaucracy have broken and the city is swarming with working people from all over the world, it's possible to find nearly every imaginable style of international cuisine, things the British of 40 years ago were reticent to try. Fish and chips, which was for a time relegated to the suburbs, is making something of a comeback, although instead of slinging it for £4, pubs are charging more than twice that for the nostalgia fix. Indian restaurants, or "curry shops," were huge a decade ago but have largely flamed out, to be replaced by the city's latest go-to casual cuisine: Thai. You'll find that everywhere.

Don't like meat? London's greenie culture is far more entrenched than in nearly any other Western city, and virtually every menu will have at least three or four—usually more—items for vegetarians to eat. The situation for vegans isn't quite as obvious, but most servers understand vegan dietary requirements and are likely to know which dishes comply. The news is just as good for people with food allergies: A majority of potentially irritating ingredients is marked when you buy it pre-made at the major shops.

But eating in London inventively can still be a problem because the options are now dominated by chain restaurants—albeit chains that will be new to you because they often don't exist far outside of London. When a moderate establishment proves its salt, it multiplies across the city. I have included a few of the better-quality ones simply to widen the net and to make your touring easier. Beware of relying on Yelp or Google or Apple maps to find places on the ground. Their inventory is vastly incomplete and

Restaurant Prices

Price categories are based on a typical main course.

○ **Expensive** (£££) = £17 +
○ **Moderate** (££) = £10 to £17;
○ **Inexpensive** (£) = under £10.

Doggy bags are frowned upon, and most restaurants will expect you to give up your table after 90 minutes to 2 hours.

results favor chains, so you'll miss a lot of good things. You'll also discover that London reviewers, perhaps still unconditioned to so many choices, may be less appraising and descriptive than you or I might be. However, you can find some good deals on restaurant sites such as **TopTable.co.uk** and **SquareMeal.co.uk**.

Every place in this chapter has one thing in common: One way or another, low price or high, multiple locations or a single hole in the wall, every place on this list says something about London of the moment, and eating at one of them will help you understand what it's like to be a Londoner.

RESTAURANTS BY CUISINE

AMERICAN
Hard Rock Café ★, p. 68
Muriel's Kitchen ★★, p. 69

ASIAN
Busaba Eathai ★★, p. 68
Mr. Kong ★★, p. 62
Ping Pong ★, p. 68
Wagamama ★★★, p. 70

BAKERY
Beigel Bake ★★, p. 76

CONTEMPORARY EUROPEAN
10 Greek Street ★★★, p. 58
Arbutus ★★★, p. 58
The Wolseley ★★★, p. 67

FILIPINO
Josephine's Restaurant ★★, p. 53

FRENCH
Le Troiseme ★, p. 61

INDIAN
Indian Veg Bhelpoori House ★, p. 57
Imli Street ★★, p. 60
Punjab Restaurant ★★★, p. 66
Woodlands ★★, p. 63

INTERNATIONAL
Bill's ★★, p. 65
Café in the Crypt ★, p. 62
Caravan ★★★, p. 53
Dabbous ★★★, p. 52
The Delauney ★★, p. 63
Camera Café ★, p. 57
Ducksoup ★★, p. 59
Giraffe ★★, p. 75
Gordon's Wine Bar ★, p. 62
Hix ★★, p. 58
Leon ★★★, p. 69
Little Bay ★★, p. 74
Oxo Tower ★★, p. 70
The Stockpot ★, p. 63

ITALIAN
Bar Italia ★★, p. 61
Carluccio's ★★, p. 68
Jamie's Italian ★, p. 66
Pizza Express ★, p. 53
Ristorante Olivelli Paradiso ★★, p. 57

JAPANESE
Inamo ★, p. 60
Koya ★★, p. 61

MEDITERRANEAN
Sarastro ★, p. 64

MEXICAN
Wahaca ★★, p. 71

MODERN BRITISH
Fifteen ★★, p. 73
One Leicester Street ★★, p. 59
Story ★★★, p. 70

PERUVIAN
Ceviche ★★★, p. 59
Coya ★★, p. 67

PUBS
The Anchor Pub ★★, p. 78
The Argyll Arms ★★, p. 78
The Chandos ★, p. 78
The Coach and Horses ★, p. 79
The Coal Hole ★, p. 79
The Dove ★, p. 79
The George Inn ★★★, p. 79
The Grenadier ★★★, p. 79
The Lamb and Flag ★★, p. 80
McGlynn's Public House ★, p. 80
The Narrow Boat ★★, p. 80
The Salisbury ★, p. 80
The Ship & Shovell ★★, p. 81
The Ten Bells ★, p. 81

Ye Olde Cheshire ★★★, p. 81
Ye Olde Mitre ★★★, p. 81

SEAFOOD
J. Sheekey ★★, p. 64
North Sea Fish ★★, p. 53
Poppies ★★, p. 76

TAKE-AWAY
Borough Market ★★★, p. 71
Dinner Jackets ★, p. 66

TRADITIONAL BRITISH
Browns ★, p. 65
E. Pellicci ★★, p. 76
The Eagle ★★★, p. 73
Fryer's Delight ★★, p. 74
Great Queen Street ★★★, p. 65
The Ivy ★, p. 59
M. Manze ★★, p. 72
The Narrow ★, p. 75
Regency Café ★★★, p. 69
Rules ★★, p. 64
St. John Bread & Wine ★★, p. 75
Tramshed ★, p. 73

VEGETARIAN
Food For Though ★, p. 66
Mildreds ★, p. 61

BLOOMSBURY, FITZROVIA & KING'S CROSS

Expensive

Dabbous ★★★ INTERNATIONAL A white-hot table, Dabbous (the S is silent) shines through arty, crisp dishes using local and seasonal ingredients. The setting is kind of ugly, all concrete and exposed ducts, and the menu gives no hint of the inventiveness to follow, so the fun is putting yourself in Chef Ollie Dabbous' hands and seeing what inventions he's come up with: Coddled egg with smoked butter, then returned audaciously to the shell? Hot hazelnut-crusted bread? Barbecued Iberico pork with savory acorn praline? Rather than over-salt or heavily spice, he'll lightly char something or create a suspended emulsion of another thing, and that's why this is one of the most in-demand restaurants in town. Downstairs in Oskar's Bar, cocktails are made with homemade infusions, there's a shortened menu of barbecued meat, plus cheeses you may never have heard of—Lancashire bomber? More, please.

39 Whitfield St., W1. ⓒ **020/7323-1544**. www.dabbous.co.uk. Tues–Fri noon–3pm, 5:30–11:30pm, Sat noon–3pm, 6:30–11:30pm. Set four-course lunch menu £28, four-course dinner menu £42. Reservations required. Tube: Goodge Street.

Moderate

Caravan ★★ INTERNATIONAL The redevelopment of the 67-acre industrial wasteland north of King's Cross station will take a decade, but construction is cooking along now, and even from square one, Caravan, in the old Granary building, made the changes cool. So basic and industrial-feeling (long blonde tables, canvaslike sheets for window shades, plain metal racks for bar shelves) that it feels like could be converted to a ceramics shop overnight, Caravan roasts its own coffee, bakes its own goods—the jalapeno cornbread is moist and kicky—and pushes its tapas-size dishes into fun flavor realms like salt beef terrine and chipotle ricotta stuffed into an edible zucchini flower and garnished with fried capers. After dinner, kick back in its front yard, in an amphitheatre overlooking the Regent's Canal. Its first location in the City (11–13 Exmouth Market, EC1; © 020/7833-8115) has a similar vibe, but with less open space and other menu twists (blue cheese and peanut wontons).

1 Granary Square, N1. © **020/7101-7661**. www.caravankingscross.co.uk. Mon–Tues 8am–10:30pm, Wed–Thurs 8am–11pm, Fri 8am–midnight, Sat 10am–midnight, Sun 10am–4pm. Small plates £5–6.50, pizzas £7–9. Tube: King's Cross St Pancras.

Josephine's Restaurant ★★ FILIPINO Local Filipinos favor it, which is somewhat surprising when you take a gander at the schticky trappings (bamboo chairs, a slatted ceiling, basic canteen plates). The hearty food arrives via dumbwaiter from the cellar; eschew the Chinese dishes (which aren't terrific) for the more challenging Filipino choices (which are), such as *rellenong pusit* (whole squid stuffed with seafood, chestnuts, and spice), chicken adobo (tangy chicken with garlic; the Philippines' national dish), and crispy *pata* (oven-baked pork leg). Try the cassava cake for dessert; it tastes like sweet potato with yam cream.

4 Charlotte St., W1. © **020/7580-6551**. www.josephinesrestaurant.co.uk. Mon–Sat noon–3pm and 6–11pm, Sun 12:30–10:30pm. Mains £8–£11. Tube: Goodge Street or Tottenham Court Road.

North Sea Fish ★★ SEAFOOD Don't expect a linoleum-lined chippie, but a classy fish market-cum-restaurant, hidden on a lost-in-time side street. Every hotel manager within a walkable radius recommends it. Portions are huge, and there's always a selection of fresh fish (sole, salmon, halibut, and so on). If you need a healthier option, you can also get your fish grilled, and keep in mind that sitting down to eat will cost nearly double what using the take-away desk does. Try the terrific homemade tartar sauce, or, for fans of little fishies, sample grilled sardines with salad.

7–8 Leigh St., WC1. © **020/7387-5892**. www.northseafishrestaurant.co.uk. Mon–Sat noon–2:30pm and 5:30–11pm. Mains £10–20. Tube: King's Cross St. Pancras or Russell Square.

Pizza Express ★ ITALIAN This chain is so ubiquitous—some 400 outlets in the U.K., more than 70 in London—you could call it a modern British institution. In fact, since its rise, which began in 1965 (9 years before McDonald's first stuck its flag in English soil), it seems like half the casual restaurants in town have added knife-and-fork, thin-crust pizzas-for-one to their bills of fare. Two dozen varieties—not too bready, well topped, plus gluten-free versions—and pastas and salads rightfully keep the traffic flowing. You can't swing a pepperoni without hitting a location, which makes it a fair fallback for families. The location at 10 Dean St. in Soho is probably the best for evenings because it sometimes books concerts by important names like Van Morrison and Jamie Cullum (Reservations: © 020/7437-9595; www.pizza expresslive.com; Tube: Tottenham Court Road).

London-Wide Restaurants

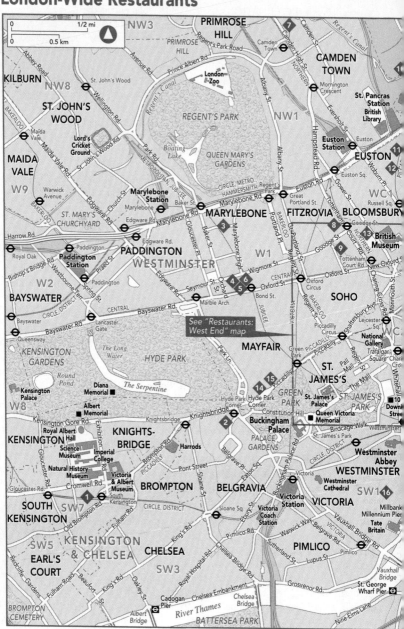

See "Restaurants: West End" map

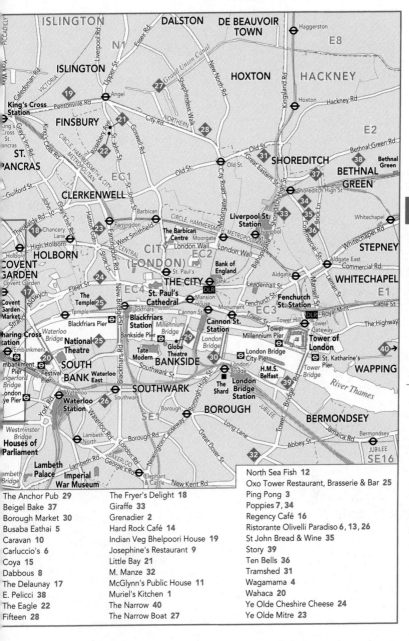

The Anchor Pub **29**

Beigel Bake **37**

Borough Market **30**

Busaba Eathai **5**

Caravan **10**

Carluccio's **6**

Coya **15**

Dabbous **8**

The Delaunay **17**

E. Pelicci **38**

The Eagle **22**

Fifteen **28**

The Fryer's Delight **18**

Giraffe **33**

Grenadier **2**

Hard Rock Café **14**

Indian Veg Bhelpoori House **19**

Josephine's Restaurant **9**

Little Bay **21**

M. Manze **32**

McGlynn's Public House **11**

Muriel's Kitchen **1**

The Narrow **40**

The Narrow Boat **27**

North Sea Fish **12**

Oxo Tower Restaurant, Brasserie & Bar **25**

Ping Pong **3**

Poppies **7, 34**

Regency Café **16**

Ristorante Olivelli Paradiso **6, 13, 26**

St John Bread & Wine **35**

Story **39**

Ten Bells **36**

Tramshed **31**

Wagamama **4**

Wahaca **20**

Ye Olde Cheshire Cheese **24**

Ye Olde Mitre **23**

West End Restaurants

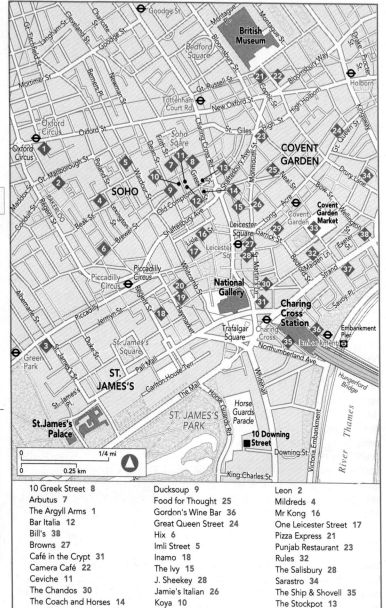

10 Greek Street **8**
Arbutus **7**
The Argyll Arms **1**
Bar Italia **12**
Bill's **38**
Browns **27**
Café in the Crypt **31**
Camera Café **22**
Ceviche **11**
The Chandos **30**
The Coach and Horses **14**
The Coal Hole **37**
Dinner Jackets **33**

Ducksoup **9**
Food for Thought **25**
Gordon's Wine Bar **36**
Great Queen Street **24**
Hix **6**
Imli Street **5**
Inamo **18**
The Ivy **15**
J. Sheekey **28**
Jamie's Italian **26**
Koya **10**
The Lamb and Flag **29**
Le Troisième **19**

Leon **2**
Mildreds **4**
Mr Kong **16**
One Leicester Street **17**
Pizza Express **21**
Punjab Restaurant **23**
Rules **32**
The Salisbury **28**
Sarastro **34**
The Ship & Shovell **35**
The Stockpot **13**
The Wolseley **3**
Woodlands **20**

30 Coptic St., WC1. ✆ **020/7636-3232**. www.pizzaexpress.com. Chain-wide hours generally Mon–Sat 11:30am–midnight, Sun 11:30am–11pm. Mains £8–£11. Tube: Russell Square.

Ristorante Olivelli Paradiso ★★ ITALIAN   Back in the day, this trattoria was so well-known that the Marx Brothers dined here on their only trip to Blighty. Today, it's an unpretentious place for good Italian food that, unlike most of the chains in town, actually has a pedigree. The homemade pastas are a notch more creative than other kitchens' at this level: saffron gnocchi topped with burrata mozzarella and caramelized onions, and ravioli asparagi stuffed with gorgonzola and walnut, both satisfyingly rich. This place is the 1934 original, but there's a second location near Waterloo at the Old Vic (61 The Cut, SE1. ✆ 020/7261-1221) and a third near Selfridge's (9 St Christopher's Place, W1. ✆ 020/7486-3196).

35 Store St., WC1. ✆ **020/7255-2554**. www.pizzaparadiso.co.uk. Pizzas £8, mains £9–£15. Tube: Goodge Street.

Inexpensive

Camera Café ★ INTERNATIONAL   Most of the joints around the British Museum hawk British stereotypes to tourists, but this locals' secret is tacked onto the back of Aperture Photographic, a small shop specializing in lenses and SLR cameras; the walls are decorated with shots taken by local artists. Food takes its sweet time in coming (at least there are lots of coffee-table books on art and Britain to borrow, plus a vintage Scrabble set) but arrives in a big way; the huge chow mein noodle bowls could serve two. The free Wi-Fi, plus the brewed coffees and teas, mean boho patrons tend to relax for hours.

44 Museum St., WC1. ✆ **07887/930826**. www.cameracafe.co.uk. Mon–Fri 11am–7pm, Sat noon–7pm. Mains £3.50–£7 Tube: Tottenham Court Road or Holborn.

Indian Veg Bhelpoori House ★ INDIAN   It ought to be protected by the National Trust. Not only is it meat-free, but it's also a top meal value in London. You pay just £5.50 for a giant all-you-can-eat-buffet—that's enough to make this off-the-beaten-track, multilevel restaurant ink worthy. You'll get a mix of spicy choices, conventional choices (onion bhajis, which go fast but get replenished), and weird choices (like curried Brussels sprouts). Its chatty decor—the walls are coated with propagandist slogans and dubious bar graphs extolling the virtues of vegetarianism—make it even more of a must. Many a broke student has survived thanks to the long-running deals. It even serves booze. There are other cheap no-limit buffets in town (a few are lined on Marchmont St. northeast of the British Museum), but no others come close in quality, range, or weird atmosphere.

92-93 Chapel Market, N1. ✆ **020/7833-1167**. Daily noon–11:30pm. Buffet £5.50, cash only. Tube: Angel.

SOHO & LEICESTER SQUARE

Visitors spend much of their time around here, the dining and entertainment hub of London. Naturally, a miasma of dining also-rans has sprung up, from junky steam-table buffets to the usual fast-food culprits to overpriced bistros that cook up a glitzy image better than anything they serve. Soho's southern fringe hosts a meager Chinatown in the neon-tinted two-block section between Leicester Square and Shaftesbury

Avenue. The district survives mostly as a tourist attraction, and I don't think many of its restaurants are distinguished enough to single out. Many of them use MSG, too, despite public health currents.

Expensive

10 Greek Street ★★★ CONTEMPORARY EUROPEAN Sometimes, restaurants get it so right—from friendly and knowledgeable staff to unfussy surroundings (chalkboard, mirrors) to pure, clean, well-made food—that you wonder why they can't all be this way. The menu, all a top value for the money, changes but the impeccable standards don't: frequent standouts include whole lemon sole with samphire (an edible coastal plant) and artichokes, zucchini flower stuffed with mushroom, elderflower sorbet, a continuous trickle of fresh-baked breads, and a wine list chosen with as much care as the fresh fish cuts. If there's a downside, it's that it will only take reservations for lunch, which means you risk missing out on dinner if you don't come early. Or just sit at the bar, where the people-watching is prime.

10 Greek St., W1. ⓒ **020/7734-4677**. www.10greekstreet.com. Mon–Sat noon–11:30pm. Mains £12–19. Tube: Tottenham Court Road.

Arbutus ★★★ CONTEMPORARY EUROPEAN A pair of celebrated city chefs, Anthony Demetre and Will Smith, opened an exquisite restaurant with the intention of serving magnificent modern food at reasonable prices, and they have triumphed, winning a Michelin star for their efforts (and you can buy Demetre's cookbook on bistro food). The menu changes according to what ingredients are in season and top-quality, but the slow-cooked dishes might include saddle of rabbit, English pea soup, Scottish organic salmon, or braised pig's head. Some of these may sound dauntingly adventurous, but deliciousness is assured. Service is also impeccable, and as another budget bonus, wines are available in carafes equal to a third of a bottle.

63-64 Frith St., W1. ⓒ **020/7734-4545**. www.arbutusrestaurant.co.uk. Mon–Thurs noon–2:30pm and 5–11pm, Fri–Sat noon–2:30pm and 5–11:30pm, Sun noon–3pm and 5–10:30pm. Mains £16–£21, £19 two-course/£21 three-course pre-theatre set menu 5–6:30pm. Reservations recommended; Tube: Tottenham Court Road.

Hix ★★ INTERNATIONAL Mark Hix is one of London's most of-the-moment serial restaurateurs, a scene-maker famed as much for his well-prepared British proteins as he is for his love-it-or-hate-it décor. The art, though by the latest contemporary names, is atrocious—avert your eyes from the miserable-looking stuffed flamingo mobile, ensnared in two hoops of neon. The food, though, compels. Fish, be it sea trout or Bideford Bay sole, is beautifully cooked and ample, the steak tartare gloriously citrusy, the Pimms jelly a thoroughly British dessert idea whose idea is long overdue. If you can't snag a table, the upstairs bar serves the same menu. The cellar cocktailerie, Mark's, is often even busier than the restaurant upstairs, and its leather chesterfields and tin ceiling attract young media types who want crave a Manhattan vibe, and the cocktails, which are delivered with a historic back-story, have an attitude to match: The Stiff Upper Lip, to take one, is made with Beefeater gin infused with green peas. If you're not eating upstairs, there's a £1.50 cover. To see Hix's antics taken to an extreme, visit Tramshed (p. 73).

66-70 Brewer St., W1. ⓒ **020/7292-3518**. www.hixsoho.co.uk. Mon–Sat noon–11:30pm, Sun noon–10:30pm, Mark's Bar until 1am. Mains £17.25–36.50. Reservations suggested. Tube: Piccadilly Circus.

The Ivy ★ TRADITIONAL BRITISH   A West End long-termer, it's where British celebrities (Look! Hugh Grant! Ooh! Simon Cowell!) have come to be seen while dining in its wood paneled, mullion-windowed halls, which have been serving for nearly a century. "The Ivy is like a safari park in which the rare and exotic creatures are nurtured," wrote *The Guardian*. Celeb sightings are rarer these days, but the food is reliable, and being chef here has launched many a career. The seasonal menu is British and somewhere between classic and conservatively contemporary: pea and Devon garlic soup, roasted Devonshire chicken with foie gras stuffing, double pork sausages with mash and gravy, and crumble with gooseberry and elderflower.

1 West St., WC1. ℰ **020/7836-4751**. www.the-ivy.co.uk. Mon–Sat noon–3pm and 5:30–midnight, Sun noon–3:30pm and 5:30–11pm. Mains £15–£20, set menu until 6:15pm on non-matinee days, two courses £22, three courses £26. Tube: Leicester Square or Covent Garden.

One Leicester Street ★★ MODERN BRITISH   A very rare English gourmet restaurant right off tourist-tilted Leicester Square, this easily overlooked one-room tablecloth restaurant with a narrow open kitchen maintains a sharing-plate menu that changes with the week even as it sticks to tradition. Expect locally infused dishes such as cockles with Jersey royal potatoes, pig's cheek that's cured for a week, and the ever-popular cod's roe with devilled pig's skin, which an American Southerner would call pork rinds with fish eggs. This little place, run by a Michelin-starred chef, punches harder than its weight, and the salted caramel with apple and crushed hazelnut is the knockout round. Also rare: Its value is sensible when you do the set "working lunch" meal: £16 for two courses and £19 for three. (Upstairs, the same owners also run a simple 15-room hotel done in a minimalist style, £165–225, although overnight noise in Leicester Square can be a bit much.)

1 Leicester St., W1. ℰ **020/3301-8020**. www.oneleicesterstreet.com. Sharing plates £7–16. Mon–Fri noon–3pm, 5:30–11pm, Sat 1–3:30pm and 5:30–11pm, Sun 1–4pm, 6–11pm. Tube: Leicester Square.

Moderate

Ceviche ★★★ PERUVIAN   This 2012 newcomer is already our firm favorite in Soho. Owner Martin Morales quit his job at Disney's European music division to pursue his true passion: food. Now he has a cookbook and runs this buzzing, no-attitude Peruvian hangout that re-creates the look of one of his favorite hangouts in Lima and pours the best pisco sour in town. Morales is like the Johnny Appleseed of Peruvian cuisine, and he's singlehandedly creating channels to import South American ingredients that London has never yet tasted. Favorite dishes include the lightly frothy, super-tangy wasabi ceviche of fresh sea bass, the don ceviche made with Amarillo chili tiger's milk, and the succulent corazón mío of beef skewers marinated in panca chili anticuchera. Once your tongue tastes its first citrusy zip, you'll want to come back, and I know tourists who have made this their hangout.

17 Frith Street, W1. ℰ **020/7292-2040**. www.cevicheuk.com. Mon–Sat noon–midnight, Sun noon–10:30pm. Small plates £7–12. Tube: Piccadilly Circus or Tottenham Court Road.

Ducksoup ★★ INTERNATIONAL   The sort of invisible hidey-hole you have to be told about, Ducksoup is barely marked, and indeed, when you first open its old door, the first thing you see is a stack of LPs and a record player, the sole sound system, that might be playing Grace Jones' "Nightclubbing" or Toots & the Maytals' "Funky Kingston." Today's menu hangs above the turntable on an office clip. The metal grille

> ## Changing Standards: From Arthur Frommer's *Europe on $5 a Day* (1957)
>
> "For your more exotic meals, go to **Soho**, a thickly-packed area of international restaurants, dives, and bars, located a short way from London's theatre section. Soho can be described as a combination of New York's Greenwich Village and San Francisco's Fisherman's Wharf. Main thoroughfare is Frith Street, exactly four blocks long, on which you'll find a score of real finds in restaurants. At 47 Frith Street [now Ronnie Scott's, p. 175], stands **Chez Auguste**, the self-styled "International Rendezvous of Gourmets." This restaurant serves nine different national dishes, sticks a flag on each plate to indicate its country of origin. The English dish is mixed grill ($1.10); American is fried chicken, corn fritters and fried bananas ($1.18); French is entrecote steak ($1.18); Polish is fried eggs on minced lamb (90¢); Turkish is shish kebab with pilaf ($1.04); Indian Madras curry of beef with rice (90¢); Hungarian, goulash; Italian medallions de veau Marsala ($1.18); and Greek, vine leaves stuffed with minced shoulder of lamb garnished with parsley and rice, for a paltry 90¢. Don't miss it."

on the windows and life-beaten walls make it look like a greasy caff that would sling a fry-up at you, but instead, there's a funky wine list and solid, whole-food selections such as steak tartare, grilled artichoke with lemon and capers, grilled leg of lamb, and chargrilled bream. It's non-scene, thoroughly neighborhoody, and at least in terms of the style and scars of the room it's in, feels like a London that went out with Thatcher—even if it's modern enough to notify friends of today's menu on Tumblr.

41 Dean St., W1. (℘ **020/7287-4599**. www.ducksoupsoho.co.uk. Mon–Sat noon–10:30pm, Sun 1–5pm. Mains £9–18. Tube: Tottenham Court Road.

Inamo ★ JAPANESE   A vibrantly patterned animated menu is projected from hexagonal ceiling pods onto your table, and using a circular trackpad embedded beside your plate, you can do things like preview dishes and order them, spy with the kitchen cam, request your bill, and order a taxi. The dining rooms, slotted with screens and lined with sheet fountains, recall a bamboo garden and attract birthday parties and group outings. A lesser restaurant could rely on the gimmick and slack on the food, but fortunately, flavors abound, be it in the Berkshire pork neck with spicy chocolate sauce, the many maki rolls, or the house cocktail of mandarin purée and muddled spring onion shaken with vodka and chili syrup. The prices are a touch high for what you eat (so restrain yourself from clicking away), but the interactive experience is memorably *Minority Report*.

4–12 Regent Street, SW1. (℘ **020/7484-0500**. www.inamo-stjames.com. Small dishes £4.25–£7.50, large dishes £10.50–£17.25. Mon–Thurs noon–3pm and 5–11pm, Fri–Sat noon–11pm, Sun noon–10pm. Tube: Piccadilly Circus.

Imli Street ★★ INDIAN/ASIAN   An affordable, thoroughly modern spin-off of Mayfair's exclusive Tamarind, it breaks its small-dish menu into four sections themed on Indian street food: seafood bites you might buy on the beach, kebabs and fried items you could buy from street carts, biryani and spicy chicken wings as served in the aisles of Indian Railways, and ideas that borrow from neighboring countries, such as ground lamb in lettuce cups and chili cheese toast. This isn't the India of dowdy curries; it's the India of peppy spice, smoky overtones, cashew nuts, and coconut, and the tapas imitation is suited to the rich cuisine.

167 Wardour St., W1. ✆ **020/7287-4243**. www.imlistreet.co.uk. Daily 8am–11pm. Sharing dishes £6–9. Tube: Piccadilly Circus or Tottenham Court Road.

Koya ★★ JAPANESE   A queue for a quick and cheap bowl of noodle soup? Well, ordinary soup wouldn't merit it. But this stuff is no mere soup. The dining room, which turns out customers quickly, is plain, bearing nothing more special than wood stick chairs, cheap chopsticks in cups, and rows of metal coat hooks. Even the menu of udon and more udon would appear to have no tricks. But then the finished product arrives in several parts, ferried by impish waitresses, for you to mix yourself, and the fog lifts. The pork udon is made of spring onion, salty roast pork crumble, a mystically umami broth base, and six ounces of pure Colombian cocaine. I'm not actually sure about that last ingredient, but it would explain a lot. You will drink the dregs from the bowl.

49 Frith St., W1. ✆ **020/7434-4463**. www.koya.co.uk. Daily noon–3pm, Mon–Sat 5:30–10:30pm, Sun 5:30–10pm. Mains £6.90–13.90. Tube: Tottenham Court Road.

Le Troisième ★ FRENCH   Somehow, a quiet, family-run French café has found sunlight among the choking jungle of chain restaurants around Leicester Square. Rather than slinging pizza or deep-fried filler, it offers a civilized space with street-facing windows to sip a glass of carefully chosen French wine and enjoy soothing Gallic comfort food such as Roquefort salad, beef bourguignon, duck breast with orange sauce, and minute steak. It serves as a pleasant reminder that Paris is only 2 hours away, after all.

3 Panton Street, SW1. ✆ **020/7930-2777**. Mon–Sat noon–3pm, 5–11pm. Mains £13 for two courses, £15 for three. Tube: Leicester Square.

Mildreds ★ VEGETARIAN   Usually packed, it's where vegetarians with palates go for a splashy date night. The menu is ever-changing but always assembled with more care than the usual bean and tofu: Sri Lankan sweet potato and cashew nut curry, chickpea and cauliflower tagine, and mixed mushroom and ale pie are three samples from its internationally derived menu. Big bowls and plates, appetizing presentation, and a vibe like a contemporary home have secured Mildreds a following even among carnivores. Save room for the peanut butter chocolate brownie—you won't believe it's gluten free.

45 Lexington St., W1. ✆ **020/7494-1634**. www.mildreds.co.uk. No reservations. Main courses £7.95–£10.50. Mon–Fri 9am–11pm, Sat noon–11pm. Tube: Tottenham Court Rd.

Inexpensive

Bar Italia ★★ COFFEE/ITALIAN   Italians settled Soho in the 1940s, and before they decamped for the suburbs, they installed a set of mod, gleaming coffee bars and caffs. This straggler from 1949 is a haunt of slumming celebrities and artists, yet modest enough for the rest of us. While this institution is busy all day—making simple sandwiches, delivering pastries—it swells with revelers after midnight. Even Rome doesn't have bars that steam, press, and shuffle cups of strong coffee across such defiantly worn '50s linoleum with such gusto. "Like everything in this city that Londoners really enjoy, it reminds us of being abroad," quipped the *Guardian*. Whatever; it practically leaks hipness.

22 Frith St., W1. ℂ **020/7437-4520**. www.baritaliasoho.co.uk. Mon–Sat 6:30am–4:30am, Sun 6:30am–2am. Coffee £3–4, pizza £10–11, panini £7. Tube: Leicester Square.

Café in the Crypt ★ INTERNATIONAL   The most delicious graveyard in town, and a perennial savior of budget travelers. Under the sanctuary of the historic St. Martin-in-the-Fields church at Trafalgar Square, atop the gravestones of eighteenth-century Londoners, one of the West End's sharpest bargains is served. The menu at this dependable cafeteria changes daily, but the satisfying options always include a few hot meat mains, a vegetarian choice, soups, salads topped with meats, and a traditional English dessert such as plum fruit cobbler or burnt cream chocolate mousse, all home-made—even the strawberries are topped with rich, fresh whipped cream. The soup-and-pudding deal is £6.10. If you're creeped out about dining near the bones, don't be—the vibe is modern, the crowds consistent, and the kitchen has a top rating from the food hygiene inspector.

Trafalgar Square, WC2. ℂ **020/7766-1158**. www.stmartin-in-the-fields.org. Mon–Tues 8am–8pm, Wed 8am–10:30pm with jazz after 6:30pm, Thurs–Sat 8am–9pm, Sun noon–6:30pm. Mains £6–8. Tube: Charing Cross.

Gordon's Wine Bar ★ INTERNATIONAL   In winter, the victuals are barely more than steam-table chow, but the atmosphere is matchless at London's most vaunted and vaulted wine bar. It was established in 1890 (when Rudyard Kipling lived upstairs) and, thank goodness, hasn't been refurbished since—look in the front display window and you'll see some untouched champagne bottles that have intentionally grown furry with dust. These crusty old cellars are wallpapered with important news-paper front pages from the 20th century—Thatcher's resignation, the death of King George VI—while ceiling fans threaten to come loose from their screws. Everything is suffused in a scorched-looking, mustardy ochre from more than 42,000 past eve-nings of indoor tobacco smoke (no longer legal). It's so resistant to change that tables are still candlelit, and music is not played—not that you could hear it over the din of conversation. Dozens of wines and sherries by the glass are around £5, you can select from a marble display of English and French cheeses, and in good weather, the event expands outside along Embankment Gardens with casual al fresco meals such as stuffed peppers and marinated pork loin. The scene is unmissable. Come down well before offices let out to secure seating in the tight, craggy cellars, which tunnel inti-mately in vaults beneath pedestrianized Villiers Street.

47 Villiers St., WC2. ℂ **020/7930-1408**. www.gordonswinebar.com. Mon–Fri 11am–11pm, Sun 11am–10am. Meals £7–10. Tube: Charing Cross or Embankment.

Mr. Kong ★★ ASIAN   One of the Chinatown rabble worth pausing for, Mr. Kong works from a lengthy Cantonese menu, and has worked it well since 1984. It's not much to look at (there's a lot more space downstairs), and its steely waiters treat patrons as little more than business transactions, but it's one of the few establishments in honky-tonk Chinatown to supplement Western-style Chinese dishes with daring ones (starring eel, soft-shell crab with chilies, and the like). In addition to laying claim to a following of Asian-born devotees, who order razor clams, crispy duck, and scal-lops by the bowlful, it's kid- and vegan-friendly and serves until the wee hours. The menu's daunting, so consider the £10.80 set that decides for you.

21 Lisle St., WC2. ℂ **020/7437-7341**. Mon–Sat noon–2:45am, Sun noon–1:45am. Mains £7.80–12. Tube: Leicester Square.

The Stockpot ★ INTERNATIONAL   High on function and low on glitz, it has been indispensable to scrimping visitors and families for years. It got me through many a lean day of backpacking. No dish, be it spaghetti Bolognese, pork steak, or coq au vin, will set you back more than £7, though everything's good and all portions over-flow their plates, and even dessert is £2.10—and that's the essence of its appeal. Staff waits around with dishrags at the ready on their shoulders, and the wall is hung with old drawings of gentlemen, just to class things up. On one memorable visit, a brief power outage interrupted dinner. "Just like the food," my neighbor inveighed, "it has a certain Eastern Bloc flavor." For those who can barely afford to visit London, the Stockpot is salvation. Forget the ravens at the Tower. When the Stockpot goes, London is over.

18 Old Compton St., W1. ℰ **020/7287-1066**. Mon–Tues 11:30am–11:30pm, Wed–Sat 11:30am–midnight, Sun noon–11:30pm. Mains £6–7, two-course set menu £7.50. Tube: Leicester Square.

Woodlands ★★ INDIAN   A 45-strong international vegetarian chain, mostly in India, it should be seen for what it is: a casual place for reliable South Indian food that's favored by South Asians. It's decorated as if someone raided a Crate and Barrel, although the recorded Asian music brings some authenticity back. Woodlands does a range of dishes, including snack-worthy *chaat* (crispy pastry rounds you stuff with chutneys), but its signature is the dosa, an enormous crepe made from soaked lentils and rice, formed into a cone, and stuffed with one of eight fillings. The onion *rava masala dosa,* our favorite, has a crepe flecked with sautéed green chilies and a filling of potatoes, onions, and peas. Of course, when a dosa arrives, your table suddenly looks like an old gramophone. Order Kingfisher, an Indian beer (slogan: "most thrilling chilled"). It's also at 77 Marylebone Lane (Tube: Bond Street).

37 Panton St., SW1. ℰ **020/7839-7258**. www.woodlandsrestaurant.co.uk. Daily noon–11pm. Mains £4.95–7.50. Tube: Leicester Square.

COVENT GARDEN

The area was once more interesting in general, but CAPCO, which governs the leases, has adopted a policy of squeezing out oddballs in favor of luxury brands such as Shake Shack, Chanel, Apple, and Balthazar.

Expensive

The Delaunay ★★ INTERNATIONAL   In 2012 Jeremy King and Chris Corbin, who did the acclaimed Wolseley (p. 67), opened another pitch-perfect evocation of a Continental café from a lost age. This one, just south of Covent Garden, is fitted with Deco brass fittings and lots of dark wood, and its menu, which does all three meals, is decidedly Teutonic, what with its schnitzels, seared mackerel, beef Stroganoff, and wieners. Next door, its much more affordable casual café, the Counter, is retro Vien-nese, and it's tempting to wile away an afternoon sipping espresso, eating sachertorte (£4.50) and fresh-made croissants (£1.80), and reading one of the provided newspapers at one of the benches with the crane-necked jeweler's lamps. There, it does an £12.95 tea after 3pm and sandwiches (salt beef, croque monsieur, and so forth).

55 Aldwych, WC2. ℰ **020/7499-8558**. www.thedelaunay.com. Mains £14.75–27, Counter cakes from £2, sandwiches £4.50–7. Mon–Sat 11:30am–midnight, Sun 11:30am–11pm;, Counter Mon–Wed 7am–7:30pm, Thurs–Fri 7am–9pm, Sat 10:30am–9pm, Sun 10:30am–5:30pm. Tube: Temple.

KEEPING THE BILL low

If you're watching your money, bear in mind these cultural differences:

Avoid Coke: It costs more than £2, and often for a puny glassful, no refills.

Avoid over tipping: Credit card slips often have a blank line for a tip—even if it was built in. Only tip (10–20%) if the menu says "service not included."

Avoid rice dishes: It's customary to pay £2 to £3 for a side dish of plain rice, even if you think it should come with what you ordered.

Avoid eating in: Some counter-service establishments charge as much as 20%

more if you decide to eat your purchases there.

Avoid water: Well, avoid it bottled. If you just order "water," waiters may bring expensive sparkling water, so if you want it for free, specify "tap water."

Avoid starters: Even where mains are £7, starters can be £4 to £6.

Avoid cocktails: Mixed drinks can cost a dizzying £8 to £11, and they're all the same middling strength because of measure standardization. If you do drink, stick to beer (£3–£4 a pint) or wine (around £5 a glass).

J. Sheekey ★★ SEAFOOD   Smartly turned out waiters prep you with so many strange fish-eating implements that your place setting starts to look like a workstation at Santa's workshop. Such presentational flourishes are appropriate to theatreland, where this has been a bistro-style classic for years, and although prices aren't generous, portions and quality are. The least expensive main dish option, fish pie, is fortunately its trademark, but there are plenty of other choices, from shrimp-and-scallop burgers to a delectable lemon sole, plus a changing slate of game and meats for the fish-averse. For all the folderol, children are welcomed. The adjoining horseshoe-shaped Oyster Bar (same hours without a mid-afternoon break) does a limited menu that includes a velvety rich crab bisque with cognac (£7.75).

28–32 St. Martin's Court, WC2. ℂ **020/7240-2565.** www.j-sheekey.co.uk. Main courses £15.75–£42. Weekend set lunch menu 3 courses £6.50. Mon–Sat noon–3pm and 5:30pm–midnight; Sun noon–3:30pm and 6–11pm. Reservations recommended. Tube: Leicester Sq.

Rules ★★ TRADITIONAL BRITISH   For a high-end kitchen that takes British cuisine seriously, make an iconic choice. In fact, it's London's oldest restaurant, having been cooking since 1798, and its patrons have included Graham Greene, Charles Dickens, Evelyn Waugh, and the Edward VII, who regularly dined here with his paramour Lillie Langtry. (The management is less than discreet about it; the nook they used is named for him.) Being a major stop on the tourist trail has gone slightly to its head, and its view of a dining experience is steeped in its own hype; beer comes in a "silver tankard," for example, and the landmarked dining rooms are an overdressed mélange of yellowing etchings, antlers, and rich red fabrics. But what's on the table is indisputably high-class London: English-reared meat like roast loin of roe deer, whole roast squab or grouse (it serves 18,000 game birds annually), and cocktails like that famous one made of tonic, juniper, and quinine.

35 Maiden Lane, WC1. ℂ **020/7836-5314.** www.rules.co.uk. Mon–Sat noon–11:45pm, Sun noon–10:45. Mains £18–29. Tube: Covent Garden.

Sarastro ★ MEDITERRANEAN   What if Mozart went insane? He'd open this flamboyant paean to the opulence of opera. In a design that must give the fire marshal sleepless nights, Sarastro's every cranny has been gilded, sheathed in shimmering fabric, or filled with erotic statuary (you can't miss the self-pleasuring Diablo, and let's not go into the art in the washrooms). Along the walls, ten intimate opera boxes, reached up precarious stairs, survey the silliness, which is often embellished by musicians. The menu—like it matters amid such eye candy—is Turkish, though not as fun as the setting, with lots of meats (beef bourguignon, "Guinea fowl supreme") and no shyness about the sauces. On Sundays and on Monday evenings, opera singers serenade diners. It's not dead cheap (two-course menus start at £15.50, three courses at £19.25), but it's an event. It isn't only tourists who come—locals celebrate events here.

126 Drury Lane, WC2. (C) **020/7836-0101**. www.sarastro-restaurant.com. Daily 12:30–midnight. Mains £12. Mains £15–23. Tube: Covent Garden.

Moderate

Bill's ★★ INTERNATIONAL   Handy for many uses—breakfast, lunch, dinner, tea, feeding kids, or downing cheap cocktails—this casual and affordable small group of restaurants, an import from success on the English shore, started as a green grocer a little over a decade ago and is still rigorous about quality ingredients. In few other London establishments will you find mac and cheese, burgers, pecan pie, and Caesar's salads together on the same menu, and fewer still have the cheek to charge a mere £3.95 for a Bloody Mary. It's a lifesaver when you're indecisive or in need of some decent, fuss-free grub served briskly, which is why you'll be glad to hear there are also locations near Piccadilly Circus (36–44 Brewer St., W1), off the Long Acre shopping street (St Martin's Courtyard, WC2; Tube: Covent Garden), and southeast of the British Museum (41 Kingsway, WC2; Tube: Holborn).

21 Wellington St., WC2. (C) **020/7836-8368**. www.bills-website.co.uk. Mon–Sat 8am–11pm, Sun 9am–10:30pm. Mains £8.50–13. Tube: Covent Garden or Temple.

Browns ★ TRADITIONAL BRITISH   In London, there's a Browns for fashion, and a Brown's Hotel, but Browns the spacious brasserie is the Browns you can afford. Installed in the former Westminster County Courts, this high-quality, Brighton-based English chain serves updated English food and imported beer. The globe lanterns, enormous mirrors, and staff buttoned into crisp white oxford shirts impart the sense of a Gilded Age chophouse. Expect lots of indulgently hearty dishes such as fish pie in cream and white wine sauce; steak, mushroom and Guinness pie; a house salad with beets, quinoa, pumpkin seeds, artichoke hearts and more; or a nice fat wild boar and chorizo burger. British tradition—starchy but welcoming to casual tourists—is the main product here: It also does a full afternoon tea for £10, cheaper than most places, or come for the Sunday roast served with meat, Yorkshire pudding, cauliflower cheese, and vegetables. There's another Browns at 47 Maddox St. in Mayfair (Tube: Oxford Circus), a riverside one southeast of Tower Bridge (Butlers Wharf; Tube: London Bridge or Tower Hill), and one at 2 Cardinal Walk (Tube: Victoria).

82-84 St. Martins Lane, WC2. (C) **020/7497-5050**. www.browns-restaurants.com. Mon–Thurs 8am–10:30, Fri 8am–11pm, Sat 10am–11pm, Sun 10am–10:30pm. Mains £8.50–15. Sunday roast £11–15. Tube: Leicester Square.

Great Queen Street ★★★ TRADITIONAL BRITISH   Here, the people behind the seminal Eagle (p. 73) present the essence of gastropub cuisine in the more convenient environs of Covent Garden. There's a pub feel—scuffed wood floors, burgundy walls, sconces capped with fringed mini-shades—but here, waiters come to you. And how: on one visit, I had no fewer than five servers attend to me, and one of them voluntarily gave me a free Negroni cocktail out of sheer conviviality. The slow-cooked dishes are clean and reassuringly ingredient-proud. Samples (they change) include Old Spot (a breed of pig) pork chops with sticky shallots, griddled quail with celery salt, and lamb's shoulder cooked for 7 hours and accompanied by gratin dauphinoise—that one feeds four, which hints at the sociable energy chefs foster here. The downstairs bar, often jammed after work, serves the cold dishes from the same menu.

32 Green Queen Street, WC2. ℗ **020/7242-0622**. Lunch Mon–Sat noon–2:30pm and Sun noon–3pm, dinner Mon–Sat 6–10:30pm. Mains £12–25. Tube: Covent Garden or Holborn.

Jamie's Italian ★ ITALIAN The current jewel in TV chef Jamie Oliver's food empire is this burgeoning chain where ingredients are thoughtfully sourced, appetizers are served on long wooden paddles called "antipasti planks," and pasta is made fresh on the premises. The menu is enormous and rangy enough to please the whole family (pastas, burgers, mains), and while the upstairs dining area is frenetic and loud, the booths downstairs impart a more soothing, vaulted feel. Considering the size of the menu and the volume of customers swarming through, it does a respectable job of forging delicious, honest food. Naturally, there's a gift shop for Oliver-branded swag—including those awkward planks. It starts rocking in here before showtime, so if you have tickets to something, try to arrive by 5:30pm.

11 St Martin's Lane, WC2. ℗ **020/3326-6390**. www.jamiesitalian.co.uk. Pasta £7–£13, mains £11.50–£18. Tube: Leicester Square.

Inexpensive

Dinner Jackets ★ TAKE-AWAY Often overlooked because it's just a mobile kitchen kiosk (and the endless line at the nearby Shake Shack is so distracting), this energy-packing standby bakes carb-rich baked potatoes ("jacket potatoes") with fillings including chicken curry, veggie chili, tuna mayo, and the like. No need belaboring this one; you come for carbs and value, and you get both. Park on the stone steps surrounding Covent Garden, watch the street performers, and you've got yourself a cheap meal that won't interrupt touring time.

Outside London Transport Museum, Covent Garden, W1. ℗ **020/7240-2677**. Daily 11am–6pm. Potatoes from £2.50. Tube: Covent Garden.

Food for Thought ★ VEGETARIAN This long-running vegetarian whole foods kitchen feels like a commune, what with the mismatched plates, and a changing slate of three or four dinner items (casseroles, salads, stir-fries, bakes, couscous, and the like). The basement dining room is elbow-to-elbow—just eight tables. The offerings (spooned out in huge portions) can be heavy on the beans, and you might make liberal use of the salt and pepper since the food is so "clean," but there's an earthy, doing-right-by-your-body sensation that comes after wiping your plate here. The fruity, sugary "scrunch" at dessert reverses some of the virtuous feelings. There's no doubt the price is right, especially for the area. It does vegan and gluten-free, too.

31 Neal St., WC2. ℗ **020/7836-0239**. www.foodforthought-london.co.uk. Mon–Sat noon–10:30pm, Sun noon–5:30pm. Mains around £5, cash only. Tube: Covent Garden.

Punjab Restaurant ★★★ INDIAN Ignore that it looks like every other hack kitchen sponging off the Covent Garden tourist trade—this place predates the recent curry trend, which is why it survived the crest of the popularity wave. Punjab has been cooking since 1947, when it was opened by Gurbachan Singh Maan, a wrestler, and his family still owns it. It proclaims itself the oldest North Indian restaurant in the U.K. Cooking is light on the oil and *ghee* (clarified butter), and many of its staff, some in turbans, have worked here, beneath the gold silk wallpaper, for decades. Meats and tandoori (the oven was installed in 1962) have been well marinated, and so they arrive tender. Ask for something not on the menu: *anari gosht*, or pomegranate-flavored lamb. ("That's only for the regulars," the waiter tells me. "No problem.") The flavors dovetail gorgeously with every bite, winding up with a slight spicy twang. The menu is cheeky, too: "If you have any erotic activities planned for after you leave us, perhaps you should resist this sensational garlic naan." Reserve ahead on weekends or face the queue.

80 Neal St., WC2. ✆ **020/7836-9787**. www.punjab.co.uk. Mon–Sat noon–11:30pm Sun noon–10:30pm. Mains £8–10. Tube: Covent Garden.

MAYFAIR, MARYLEBONE, KENSINGTON & KNIGHTSBRIDGE

Expensive

Coya ★★ PERUVIAN   Many Mayfair restaurants are too expensive or trendy to even bother turning a nose up at you, but this Peruvian-inspired newcomer—by Arjun Waney, an old hat at creating trendy hangouts—is a welcoming starting point where visitors and upscale young scenesters alike may meet over bold flavors and low light. It's not carefully Peruvian the way Ceviche (p. 59) is, although there is some excellent ceviche, of course. Instead the dishes corral influences from as far afield as Spain and India, and the meats (try the beef heart and the ribs) have the rich spiced undertones and fall-apart texture one would expect of the kitchen's high-end Josper grilling oven and the dining room's high-end clientele. The carefully distressed townhouse surroundings might be described as *calculated ennui*, but it's not totally democratic; upstairs, there's a members' lounge where you may not sip pisco sours unless you've paid the annual fee.

118 Piccadilly, W1. ✆ **020/7042-7118**. www.coyarestaurant.com. Lunch Mon–Sat noon–2:45pm, dinner Mon–Wed 6–10:45pm, Thurs–Sat 6–11pm, Sun 6–10:15pm. Small plays £7.50–11, two-course set lunch £19. Tube: Green Park.

The Wolseley ★★★ CONTEMPORARY EUROPEAN   "No Flash or Intrusive Photography please," chastises a footnote on the menu. That's because this opulent bistro in the Grand European style, posing with every polished surface to appear like something Renoir would want to paint, is home base for celebrities and power lunchers. Built as a luxury car dealership for a doomed manufacturer, then used as a bank, a decade ago it became the caviar-scooping, oyster-shucking, tea-pouring hotspot that fools nearly everyone who sips its pea-and-lettuce soup that it's always been this way. Waiters are attractive and look down their noses as they gingerly place salad Niçoise and Swiss souffle, enacting the calculated Continental crispness we crave.

160 Piccadilly, W1. ✆ **020/7499-6996**. www.thewolseley.com. Mon–Fri 7am–midnight, Sat 8am–midnight, Sun 8am–11pm. Sandwiches £11, mains £15–20. Tube: Green Park.

Moderate

The Hard Rock Café AMERICAN   You'll find one in every town from Key West to Kuwait. Its burgers (though excellent and sizable) hit an outrageous £15.50, much of the so-called memorabilia consists of instruments that big names played maybe once and tossed, and waiting up to 90 minutes for a table chews up time that could be used for more authentic touring. But this Hard Rock was the world's first, having opened in 1971, so there is at least one reason to visit. But it's also true that no rock star would be caught dead in here today. No stars, not for this review or among its clientele, but it's listed here because tourists demand to see it—and drop £18 on shirts.

150 Old Park Lane, W1. © **020/7514-1700**. www.hardrock.com. Mon–Sat 9:30am–11:30am, Sun 9:30am–11pm. Mains £11-16. Tube: Hyde Park Corner.

Ping Pong ★ DIM SUM   A chic fusion of Chinese dim sum and cocktail lounge, it boasts such a cutting-edge, glass-and-steel design (tip: check out the space-age toilets) that it appears at first to be one of the West End's many overpriced clubhouses for young, upper-class toffs. Yet it's affordable and well-adapted to the tourist's need for flexibility, with a service staff willing to walk newbies through the process. Baskets of piping hot dumplings arrive almost as quickly as they're ordered, and they're stacked in towers on your table as a trophy of your progress. If you can't decide, go for the "Selection" (£11), which buys 10 various pieces. The brand operates eight London locations including 10 Paddington St. (Tube: Baker Street), 29a James St. (Tube: Bond Street), the Southbank Centre (Tube: Waterloo); 48 Eastcastle St. in Fitzrovia (Tube: Oxford Circus).

45 Great Marlborough St., W1. © **020/7851-6969**. www.pingpongdimsum.com. Mon–Sat noon–midnight, Sun noon–10:30pm. Dim sum £2.95–£4.45. Tube: Oxford Circus.

Inexpensive

Busaba Eathai ★★ ASIAN   Founded by Alan Yau, the renegade who changed mainstream London tastes with his revolutionary Wagamama chain (p. 70) and London's celebrated (but pricey) Hakkasan restaurant, it duplicates its forebear's formula: a high-design dining area, convivial tables shared with strangers, and a Thai-inspired menu that abandons curry-and-rice banality. I've yet to sample a dish that I couldn't say something nice about, be it the wok-prepared ginger beef with spring onion, the spicy *sen chan phad Thai* (noodles with prawn, peanut, green mango, and crab meat), or the peppercorn scallops with asparagus and lime leaf. This high-minded yet populist-priced supper has enchanted the masses, so there are eight locations in central London, including in Soho (106–110 Wardour St., W1; Tube: Piccadilly Circus), Bloomsbury (22 Store St., WC1; Tube: Goodge Street), and Leicester Square (35 Panton St., W1) with similar hours.

8–13 Bird St., W1. Busaba.com. © **020/7518-8080**. Mon–Thurs noon–11pm, Fri–Sat noon–11:30pm, Sun noon–10pm. Mains £7.80–9.90. Tube: Piccadilly Circus.

Carluccio's ★★ ITALIAN   Another one of London's recommendable solid-value chains, each location fashions itself after an Italian grocery from Manhattan's Little Italy; you enter through a little shop selling pastas and sauces and then beg for attention from the harried staff (just like the real thing). Pastas, which reach beyond spaghetti into a lighter zone of fresh tomatoes, saffron, and ravioli, are well made and taste fresh but there are also salads, plates of prosciutto, meat entrees, and an extensive kids menu. There are so many branches around town (including a handy one by the South Kensington museums at 1–3 Old Brompton Rd.), check under your hotel room bed first.

St. Christopher's Place, W1. © **020/7935-5927**. www.carluccios.com. Daily 7:30am–11:30pm. Mains £9–16 Tube: Bond Street.

Leon ★★★ INTERNATIONAL The meat-and-all options are fashioned from a free-trade/organic shopping list and avoid refined sugar, which recently turned Leon into one of the city's fastest-growing counter-service names. At lunch, its block wood tables and chairs are crammed with office workers grabbing a healthy, casual meal. If it's full, pack your meal in one of the cute brown folding boxes and eat al fresco on Carnaby Street. The menu gets a tad heartier at dinner, but the best recurring options include "hot boxes" of Moroccan meatballs in plenty of red sauce with brown rice and slaw; a juicy grilled *halloumi* wrap, a "superfood" salad combining energizing ingredients such as kale and peanuts, and picnic boxes with potted mackerel and smoked salmon. There are plenty more locations around town now, including west of St. Paul's Cathedral (weekdays only; 12 Ludgate Circus); in King's Cross station, and behind the Tate Modern (7 Canvey St.).

35-36 Great Marlborough St., W1. © **020/7437-5280**. www.leonrestaurants.co.uk. Tube: Oxford Circus.

Muriel's Kitchen ★★ AMERICAN/INTERNATIONAL The front window is a fantasia of icing-blobbed, fruit-topped, sugar-dusted pastry temptation, but step inside this busy, rustic-style casual restaurant for locally grown, organic comfort foods such as beef lasagna; five-spice marinated pulled pork; chili con carne; and pork and pistachio balls with coriander lemongrass, and ginger. The high, wooden tables feel like something from an American farmhouse even as they look out on the neighborhood's French residents and the families on their way to the big Kensington museums around the corner. It's one of the few non-chain choices in South Ken, but that's about to change; at press time, a second location was staffing up in Old Compton Street in Soho.

1–3 Pelham St., SW7. © **020/7589-3511**. www.murielskitchen.co.uk. Mon–Sat 8am–11pm, Sun 9am–10pm. Mains £8–10. Tube: South Kensington.

Regency Café ★★★ TRADITIONAL BRITISH The midcentury "caff" diner, once a staple of London life, is rapidly being swept into Formica heaven by trendy bistros, coffee bars, and triangle sandwich sellers. As Edwin Heathcote puts it in his elegiac 2004 book *London Caffs*, "the increasingly sparse network of surviving refuges represents the dying, but still steaming, breath of a particular moment in the city's history." Among the few holdouts in central London is the 1940s Regency, an elegy to another age in black and white tiles. This isn't a gastronomic treasure (the fryer is in heavy use making fat English chips); it's an anthropological one, and so adored it played a recurring role in the 2004 Daniel Craig film *Layer Cake*. Big-value food is prepared with lightning speed, and when it's ready, your order is loudly announced by a throaty man so that you can come fetch it. Have a cuppa while it's still steaming. For another marvelous caff, see E. Pellicci (p. 76).

17-19 Regency St., SW1. © **020/7821-6596**. Mon–Fri 7am–2pm and 4:30–7pm, Sat 7am–noon. Mains £4–8. Tube: Pimlico or Westminster.

Wagamama ★★★ ASIAN   In the 1990s, this sociable noodle hall was one of the first to popularize Southeast Asian food on a wide scale in London, and now it's found all over town—happily so, because it suits parents with children and teens. This one is tucked behind Selfridges at Duke Street, perfect for Oxford Street shoppers. Diners are seated at long, communal wooden tables, so you'll have ample opportunity to meet your neighbor, and orders are transmitted by handheld tablets straight to the kitchen. Part of the appeal is the varied menu that includes noodles, teppan, ramen, chili men, and summer rolls, served in deep white bowls, no skimping on the ingredients or the spice (the Firecracker dish is more like an M-80), although the most intense stuff is marked. Some of the most convenient branches are in Bloomsbury (4 Streatham St.; Tube: Tottenham Court Road); 1 Tavistock St., south of Covent Garden (Tube: Covent Garden); 10a Lexington St. (Tube: Piccadilly Circus); Tower Place, next to the Tower of London (Tube: Tower Hill); at Harvey Nichols, 109–125 Knightsbridge (Tube: Knightsbridge); and Royal Festival Hall (Tube: Waterloo).

101a Wigmore St., W1. ☎ **020/7409-0111**. www.wagamama.com. Mon–Sat 11:30am–11pm, Sun 11:30am–10pm. Mains £7.80–11. Tube: Bond Street.

THE SOUTH BANK, SOUTHWARK & BOROUGH

Expensive

Oxo Tower Restaurant, Brasserie & Bar ★★ INTERNATIONAL   A top choice for an event dinner with a view, the Oxo commands a gratitude-inducing panorama of St Paul's and the City from Southbank, and its adjoining cocktail terrace is an ever-popular meeting spot for the city's smart young set. Chef Jeremy Bloor isn't one for faddish cooking techniques, although he does keep a waffle machine on hand for dishes such as sweet potato waffles with goat's cheese, beets, rosemary, and truffle honey dressing. Satisfyingly nuanced dinners are built around luxe proteins such as John Dory, Mallard, and South Devon beef, with a few sumptuous garnishes (lobster mash, oxtail spring roll) just to keep the fireworks going. The Brasserie section, which has live music in the evening, does less ostentatious food such as seared tuna and spring chicken for about £4 less per main. If you don't have reservations, try early during the seating period.

22 Barge House St., SE1. ☎ **020/7803-3888**. www.harveynichols.com/restaurants. Main courses £21.50–£35; 3 lunch courses £36.50. Mon–Fri noon–2:30pm and 6–11pm; Sat noon–2:30pm and 5:30–11pm; Sun noon–3pm and 6:30–10pm. Reservations recommended. Tube: Blackfriars or Waterloo.

Story ★★★ MODERN BRITISH   The moment you sit, your server lights a white taper and you slide your menu from the leafs of *Sketches by Boz* by Dickens, who started his life penniless nearby. By the time a fusillade of about six *amuse bouche* "snacks" hits you (paper-thin cod skin studded with emulsified cod roe, a sweet black eel mousse "Storeo"), your candle has quickly melted, you're told that the wax was actually edible beef fat, and you're handed a leather pouch of fresh-baked bread to sop up the rich drippings. And there are 10 more frivolously surprising small-plate courses to go. The dramatic and whimsical delights are by hot young talent Tom Sellers, and his prix fixe menu, which never stops amusing and dazzling with flavor duets, speaks of London cooking both old and new: scallop carpaccio with cucumber balls rolled in dill ash; Jensen's gin (Sellers loves gin) and apple consommé topped with garlic blossoms; and "Three Bears" porridge—one sweet, one salty, one just right. It's not just food you'll be talking about. It's food that makes you want to hang out with the chef over beers. Or gin.

201 Tooley Street, SE1. ℂ **020/7183-2117.** www.restaurantstory.co.uk. Tues–Sat noon–2pm, 6:30pm–9pm. Six courses £45, 10 courses £65. Reservations essential. Tube: London Bridge or Bermondsey.

Moderate

Wahaca ★★ MEXICAN   Mexican culture is relatively new to Londoners so it's sensible to name a Oaxaca tribute restaurant phonetically. Fashioned out of eight recycled shipping containers now sliced open and stacked in two levels to afford river views, it specializes in affordable bites it calls "street food"—soft corn-tortilla tacos, tostadas, quesadillas, fresh guacamole with warm chips, burritos, and that Spanish stalwart, *churros y chocolate*. Prices are kept low by cooking less with oil and more with hot ovens, as well as by sourcing ingredients locally—Lancashire sends cotija-style cheese, chili peppers are grown in plastic greenhouses in Bedfordshire, cows are grass-fed, and pigs reared outdoors. The adaptation works, and Wahaca has expanded to eight locations around town (this location trials recipes for them), including between Covent Garden at Trafalgar Square (66 Chandos Place, W1; Tube: Leicester Square).

Queen Elizabeth Hall, Southbank Centre, SE1. ℂ **020/7928-1876.** www.wahaca.co.uk. Mon–Sat noon–11pm, Sun noon–10:30pm. Mains £7–£10 Tube: Waterloo.

Inexpensive

Borough Market ★★★ INTERNATIONAL/TAKE-AWAY   Go when you're hungry and once you're back home, you will dream about it for months. A chronicle of overstimulation, it combines Victorian commercial hubbub with glorious, farm-fresh flavors, rendered as finger food for visitors. About a dozen greenmarket vendors sell their countryside meats, cheeses, and vegetables all week long, but the market blooms beneath its metal-and-glass canopy Thursdays through Saturdays, when more than 100 additional vendors unpack and the awe-inspiring, touristy scene hits full swing. The best time to arrive is ahead of the lunch crowds; Saturdays are plain nuts.

If there's any country that has farming down, it's England, and this market is its showplace. Follow the crowd to the west end of the fence by the cathedral to **Kappacasein** dairy from Bermondsey (www.kappacasein.com), which places great wheels of cheese under burners and sloughs bubbling swaths of it onto plates of boiled new potatoes (it's called *raclette*, £6, and the only thing to rival it for decadence is the same booth's goopy grilled cheese, £5, which you'll taste all day after eating). **Le Marché du Quartier** (www.marketquarter.com) does duck confit sandwiches (£5); the **Brindisa** booth (www.brindisa.com) facing Stone Street, feeds a steady line of punters its grilled chorizo sandwich with oil-drizzled pequillo peppers from Spain (£3.75); and **Shellseekers**, the fishmonger in the center, is famous for its fresh hand-dived Devon scallop, served in its own shell and topped with a bacon and sprout stir-fry (£5). **Roast** (www.roast-restaurant.com), which runs an expensive restaurant upstairs, has a stall for rich meats such as roast pork belly with crackling and Bramley apple sauce and

THE world COMES TO LONDON

Those who have been fortunate enough to travel broadly can attest to how sadly unusual it is to find places where people of wildly different colors, religions, and nationalities can live together without killing each other. London, though, like New York City, Toronto, or Sydney, is certifiably multi-ethnic—some 300 languages and 45 distinct ethnic communities—and the patchwork supplies the rare chance to sample cultures beyond the borders of our own. Take a few hours to explore the inexpensive restaurants, pubs, and specialized shopping that cater to newcomers who came to England to get a leg up—from pubs serving Kenyan mashed maize to Islamic shops selling prayer clocks and *jalabiya* robes, you'll find neighborhoods of all stripes everywhere, but here's the Tube or rail stop for some of the major concentrations so you can begin your own world travels:

Bangladesh: Bethnal Green, Whitechapel
Caribbean: Brixton, Willesden Junction
Egypt: Shepherd's Bush
Ghana, Nigeria, Congo, West Africa: Seven Sisters, Hackney Central or Hackney Downs (National Rail)
India, especially northern: Southall (National Rail)
Ireland: Kilburn
Kenya: Barking
Kurdistan: Manor House
Lebanon: Shepherd's Bush
Nigeria: Peckham Rye (National Rail)
Persia: Edgware Road
Poland: Hammersmith, Ealing Broadway
Somalia: Streatham (National Rail)
Sri Lanka and South India: Tooting (National Rail)
Syria: Shepherd's Bush
Turkey: Dalston Kingsland and Stoke Newington (National Rail)
Vietnam: Hackney Central or Hackney Downs (National Rail), Old Street

beef with horseradish cream (both £6.50). At **Maria's Market Café,** the moon-faced, second-generation proprietor slaves over a stove making fresh bubble (kind of a mushy version of home fries) that brings office workers from far and wide (it's £1 on a roll). Outside on Stone Street, opposite the well-stocked **Market Porter** pub, three more great finds in a row: **Monmouth Coffee** (www.monmmouthcoffee.com), which sends emissaries to check its single-farm beans in the field, is one of London's most revered roasters; **Gelateria 3bis** has an ultra-creamy *fior di latte* flavor made from rich English milk plus a warm chocolate fountain for pre-filling cones; and **Neal's Yard Dairy** (www.nealsyarddairy.co.uk), with its tables stacked high and clerks waiting in caps and aprons, is the gold standard for English cheese. Like almost everything at Borough, it's food you can only enjoy in London—and there are dozens more delicacies like it if you'll only explore with an empty stomach.

8 Southwark St., SE1. ℰ **020/7407-1002**. www.boroughmarket.org.uk. Mon–Wed 10am–3pm, Thurs 11am–5pm, Fri noon–6pm, Sat 8am–5pm. Tube: London Bridge.

M. Manze ★★ TRADITIONAL BRITISH   If you're truly fearless or your palate is truly twisted, brave the classic East End dishes of jellied or stewed eels. But if not, there's still a reason to visit: a jewel box of a shop with green glazed Victorian tile and wooden benches that is in such rare condition it's protected by the government. Manze, which was been serving since 1891, also does meat or vegetarian pastry pies—which to be fair, most customers prefer, as they have done since the days when this street was home to dockworkers and laborers. The parsley-made "liquor" sauce doesn't really taste like much, but the gravy and mash taste like nostalgia itself.

87 Tower Bridge Rd., SE1. ℂ **020/7407-2985**. http://manze.co.uk. Mon 11am–2pm, Tues–Thurs 10:30am–2pm, Fri 10am–2:30pm, Sat 10am–2:45pm.

THE CITY

Things tend to shut down around here after the bankers go home from work.

Expensive

Fifteen ★★ MODERN BRITISH   Jamie Oliver, the not-really-naked cookbook author and TV celebuchef, opened Fifteen in 2002 as a manifestation of his trademark idealism. The not-for-profit kitchen would be a place for disadvantaged youth to learn a trade as gourmet chefs. The experiment more than proved itself, and in 2013, it shifted its theme from Italian to British cuisine. Ingredients are assiduously sourced from around Britain and Europe and butchered on the premises, and menu selections are as bright and of-the-place as the concept: violet artichokes with girolles and Ticklemore cheese, cockles with pork belly, and Dorset crab with rye flatbread and fennel. You're tasting Britain while improving it.

15 Westland Place, N1. ℂ **0871/330-1515.** www.fifteen.net. Mains £13–27. Daily noon–3pm and 6–10pm. Reservations suggested. Tube: Old Street.

Tramshed ★ TRADITIONAL BRITISH   It essentially only does two things, chicken and steak, and the flavors are conventional, but what earns attention is its theatrics: Towering over the dining room, once an electrical plant for an Edwardian tram system, is a dangerous-looking tank of formaldehyde containing an entire cow carcass, plus a cockerel perched on her shoulder like a corsage. When the chemicals need replacing, the restaurant is shut down for safety. The work is by controversy hound Damien Hirst and the chef is local chef celeb Mark Hix, whose fixation on meat clearly exceeds your own. Is it appetizing to dine under a pickled Bessie? Can you stomach a seeing a whole chicken, trussed feet-to-the-sky like a torture victim, placed before you, awaiting your fork? Tramshed, which is nonetheless popular, represents London's trendy dining scene in all its self-important contradiction—nose-thumbing decor not quite a match for the earthy food—and its cock-and-bull shtick is something you'll argue about later.

32 Rivington Street, EC2. ℂ **020/7749-0478.** www.chickenandsteak.co.uk. Daily noon–10:30pm. Mains £20–£30. Tube: Old Street.

Moderate

The Eagle ★★★ TRADITIONAL BRITISH   By now, the gastropub trend is so widespread the term is virtually meaningless, but foodies note: It began here in 1991 (or so most agree) and shows no sign of fading (definitely). Behind the bar of a bare-to-the-wood former saloon, casual chefs prepare a changing selection of about a dozen flavorful and thoughtful dishes a day, from the likes of pork loin salad to pan roasted sole to the house specialty, the insidiously spicy Bife Ana steak sandwich dripping with marinated garlic and onion. Tables are shared, furniture reassuringly shabby and mismatched, and foodie crowds reliably in force—come early to ensure your share.

Order at the bar and get a beer while you're up there, because here, the food's the thing, and they'll bring your meal to you in their own sweet time. The point is to sit back and enjoy.

159 Farringdon Road, EC1. ✆ **020/7837-1353**. Mon–Fri noon–3pm, 6:30pm–10:30pm, Sat noon–3:30pm, 6:30pm–10:30pm, Sun 12:30pm–4pm. Mains £8–15. Tube: Farringdon.

Inexpensive

The Fryer's Delight ★★ TRADITIONAL BRITISH/TAKE-AWAY   In this age, no one would dare name their joint something as hydrogenated as The Fryer's Delight. Fortunately, this joint is not of this age. It's a true old-world chippy, where the fry fat is from beef drippings, chips come in paper wrappings, the wooden booths and chequered floor date to the lean postwar years, and the men behind the counter gruffly demand to have your order. Prices are anachronistic, too: Nothing's more expensive than £6. Seamy? Not at all—it's just one of the last hangers-on from the dying fish-and-chips tradition, so get a taste while you still can. Make sure to order yours with mushy peas, It's a 10-minute walk east of the British Museum; look for the logo of a codfish tipping his bowler hat (seriously).

19 Theobald's Rd., WC1. ✆ **020/7405-4114**. Mon–Sat noon–10pm. Tube: Holborn or Chancery Lane.

Little Bay ★★ INTERNATIONAL   Rarely has paying so little afforded such extravagance: The menu changes, but on one visit, I received an astounding 22 mussels in my mussels marinier (shallots, garlic, and white wine) for my piddly £3.45—and yes, they were fresh and well sauced. Mains are just as generous. Possibilities may include honey glazed pork belly, confit leg of duck, or sweet smoked spare ribs—yes, for only £7.25. The decor is beyond loopy, like the a penny arcade version of the

Vatican—a Romanesque fun house of plaster murals and gnarled chandeliers overseen by a massive mask of Zeus. Sunday is roast day: £8 including potatoes and Yorkshire pudding, and on Thursdays and Saturdays after 8pm, just to slam home the iconoclasticism, there's live opera. Little Bay is a find.

171 Farringdon Rd., WC1. ℰ **020/7278-1234**. www.littlebayfarringdon.co.uk. Mon–Sat noon–midnight, Sun noon–11pm. Mains £7.25. Tube: Farringdon.

SPITALFIELDS & DOCKLANDS

Expensive

The Narrow ★ TRADITIONAL BRITISH   It's too bad that Gordon Ramsay, the blustery celebrity chef, has cultivated an international aversion to his surly attitude, because it means people sometimes avoid the pleasant boathouse-style dining experience tucked in a pretty inlet on the north bank of the Thames east of the City. Here, in a skylit restaurant area with floor-to-ceiling conservatory window views, his must-be-henpecked minions deliver delicious, uncluttered British dishes and elevated pub fare (seasonal veg, fish, steaks, Cumberland sausage, sticky toffee pudding) with the near-religious emphasis on high-quality ingredients Ramsay has berated many over. The cozy bar area (no reservations, open fire in winter) also serves small snacks. Because of its culinary care, a location worth seeing, and the chance to taste food overseen by an international talent, this is a top value.

44 Narrow St., E14. ℰ **020/7592-7950**. www.gordonramsay.com/thenarrow. Mon–Sat noon–10:30pm, Sun noon–10pm. Reservations recommended. Mains £13–29., set meal £19 for two courses, £24 for three. Tube: Limehouse DLR.

St. John Bread & Wine ★★ TRADITIONAL BRITISH   Hand-in-hand with the gastropub trend is "nose-to-tail" eating. That's when your chef doesn't waste a single part of the animal, resulting in tastes that were commonplace to his agrarian English forefathers (heart, cockscomb, marrow, whole pigeon) but are new to most North American tongues. Most places charge, um, an arm and leg for it, but you can sample it at this lower-priced offshoot of the influential St. John restaurant, which in the 1990s brought back British cooking in a big way. Walls are simple white, chairs are plain wood, and the kitchen staff is serious about good food, no matter its form. Experience dishes like cold lamb with chicory and anchovy, smoked sprat (sardines) with horseradish, and laver bread (made with seaweed) with oats and bacon. A meal here can be an adventure (ever eaten dandelion?). St. John also makes terrific homemade bread served in the hippest restaurants in town. Don't skimp on dessert: brown bread ice cream is one such staple.

94–96 Commercial St., E1. ℰ **020/7251-0848**. www.stjohnbreadandwine.com. Mon–Fri 9am–11pm, Sat 9am–11pm, Sun 9am–9pm. Reservations recommended. Mains £6.50–9 before 6pm, around £15 after 6pm. Tube: Aldgate East or Shoreditch High Street.

Moderate

Giraffe ★★ INTERNATIONAL   Giraffe, a top choice for families and omnivores, quickly spread around town based on a rangy menu that includes big salads, burgers, Southeast Asian stir fries and noodle bowls, cocktails, and seven much-ordered brunch options available until 4pm daily. Normally, restaurants that try too many genres don't do well, but here, the food is generally satisfying, non-greasy, thoughtfully sourced, and successful (the chipotle BBQ chicken quesadilla is addictive). The staff is supernaturally friendly in a theatrical way that Europeans rarely are (maybe they're lifted by the cheerful Rod Stewart-era music). Children are especially well-treated: Look around the airy dining room during the day, and you'll see a forest of helium balloons swinging from each kid's high chair back. Weekdays from 5pm to 7pm, a meal of a starter and a main is £10. There are additional locations at Southbank Centre (Tube: Waterloo), the Brunswick Centre near the British Museum (Tube: Russell Square), 6 Blandford St. in Marylebone (Tube: Bond Street), 7 Kensington High St. (Tube: High Street Kensington), and 29–31 Essex Rd. (Tube: Angel).

Crispin Place, Spitalfields Market, E1. ✆ **020/3116-2000**. www.giraffe.net. Mon–Fri 8am–11pm, Sat 9am–11pm, Sun 9am–10:30pm. Mains £8–11. Tube: Liverpool Street.

Poppies ★★ SEAFOOD Big crispy portions flopping on big oval plates eaten with a big knife and fork to big 1950s sock-hop music: The franchise-ready Poppies does for British fish and chips what peppy jukebox diners have done for midcentury American food. For all its plastic theatricality, it hews to authenticity: The chief dish, cooked to order, is sustainably caught and sourced from third-generation fishmonger T. Bush at Billingsgate Market, and even the uniforms worn by the "Poppettes" waitresses—a red sailor frock with a jaunty, bellhoppy cap—come from Collectif in Camden's Stables Market. For those whose palates swerve differently, there's also chicken, the chance to try jellied eels, and lusher green salads than most London establishments serve. There's a second location near the markets of Camden Town (30 Hawley St., NW1; ✆ 020/7267-0440).

6–8 Hanbury St., E1. ✆ **020/7247-0892**. www.poppiesfishandchips.co.uk. Mon–Thurs 11am–11pm, Fri–Sat 11am–11:30pm, Sun 11am–10:30pm. Mains £10–12. Tube: Shoreditch High Street.

Inexpensive

Beigel Bake ★★ BAKERY The city's most famous bakery, Jewish or otherwise, never closes but there's often a line. The queue moves quickly here even if time doesn't—signs still post an area code that hasn't been active since 2000. The patronage is a microcosm of London, ranging from bikers to hipsters to arrogant yuppies to the homeless. Its beigels ("BI-gulls") are not as puffy or as salty as the New York "bagel" variety, and they even come filled for under £1.50—the same price, astonishingly, as a half-dozen plain ones. Its pastries are gorgeous, too: The chocolate fudge brownie, less than £1, could be nursed for hours. Watching the clerks slice juicy chunks of pink salt beef in the window, then slather it onto a beigel with nostril-clearing mustard from a crusty jar, is an attraction unto itself. Londoners complain it's gotten touristy, but what tourist trap serves 60p coffee?

159 Brick Lane, E1. ✆ **020/7729-0616**. Daily 24 hr. Tube: Shoreditch High Street.

E. Pellicci ★★ TRADITIONAL BRITISH London's tradition of midcentury diners, or "caffs," is quickly being gentrified into nostalgia, but this fry-up has been run by the affable Nevio family for generations, some of them were born upstairs, the matriarch of which has been in the kitchen for half a century. The Deco interior, a greasy spoon fantasia of sunburst icons and laminates, was designed just after World War II and is now protected by law. Besides serving as a hangout for artists (and once, for gangsters), many of whom have signed photos for the wall, meals are a steal. Italian dishes are done, but you'd most want to come for its English breakfast, when heaping

SAVE BREAD WITH sandwiches

Most of London's attractions are only open from about 10am to 5pm. That doesn't give you a lot of time to see what you came to see, so a marathon lunch will cost you precious hours. To dine like a true Londoner, have a big breakfast (your hotel probably serves it for free), and at midday, grab a carb-laden bite (a sandwich, a jacket potato) and get on with your day. Dinner is the time for table service.

You'll go all day without crossing paths with a bobby or a true Cockney, but you can barely walk a block without passing a sandwich shop The cheapest ones are what I call the **triangle sandwiches,** which are ready-made, sliced diagonally, and sealed into triangular containers. They are made fresh every day by the million. Triangle sandwiches range from £1.50 (for an egg salad/ "mayo" or other vegetarian selection) to about £4.25 (for triple-packs containing three sandwich halves with a variety of fillings).

More tips on decoding London sandwiches:

o *Pickle* is a tangy vegetable spread that tastes a bit like steak sauce.
o *Cress* is watercress.
o *Mayo* is like saying salad (like "tuna mayo"), but "salad" listed as an ingredient usually denotes just a cursory flap of lettuce.
o A *bap* is a round bread roll.

A few ubiquitous chains catering to the triangle sandwich trade are:

o **Eat** (www.eat.co.uk): Its quality is ahead of Pret, with a good selection of organics and whole grains.
o **Pret A Manger** (www.pret.com): Right behind Eat in clever flavors, with gourmet fixings in snazzy combinations.
o **Gregg's** (www.greggs.co.uk): Its sandwiches are average in every way, but it also does pies and hot meat rolls.
o **Marks & Spencer** (www.marks andspencer.com): Lots of cheap stuff, well done, and around dinnertime, it marks down its sandwiches by as much as 50 percent.

plates of beans, eggs, and chunky chips are flung about to assuage clubbers' hangovers. To call meals hearty would be more than accurate, although the heart is what suffers the most from their regular consumption. Help yourself to the range of on-table condiments (the HP sauce, in the brown bottle, is the best choice for potatoes). There's no more iconic caff in town.

332 Bethnal Green Rd., E2. © **020/7739-4873**. Mon–Sat 7am–4pm. Mains £6.40–8.20. Tube: Shoreditch High Street or Bethnal Green.

LONDON PUBS YOU'LL LOVE

Pubs are the beating heart of British life, and they have been for centuries. Hundreds are scattered throughout the city, and your neighborhood hangout is called your "local," but you might be shocked to learn that many of the oldest premises have been so well-loved (or so well-bombed) that most of their original features are gone, and most of them are company-owned and depressingly standardized and modern-looking, which may disappoint those looking for an evocative atmosphere. It's often easier to find a pint of Australian Foster's beer than a local brew. **The Campaign for Real Ale** (www.camra.org.uk) is devoted to advocating for the non-corporate community pub culture.

Beer in England usually has higher alcohol content than many varieties you may drink at home, and the percentage is clearly noted on taps. Ale and stout is often not chilled—it's not warm, just not ice cold—as intensely as it is where you live. Mixed drinks are also served, but don't expect a generous pour because measures are rigidly standardized across the country and since bartenders don't work for tips, they don't make them stronger as a favor. As for those hooks under the tables or the bar, they're for your coat.

The following pubs, all centrally located, should do you right. Be they truly ancient, stunningly beautiful, happily situated, or simply charming, they're all unlikely to let you down. All of them serve food of some kind (burgers, meat pies, and the like) for at least part of the day; you usually order at the bar, where you receive a numbered tag for your table so that servers can find you. Pubs commonly charge under £4 for a pint, the favored serving size of about 20 American ounces. Pints are usually cheaper than bottled beer.

The Anchor Pub ★★ Few pubs meld abundant history with an enviable location as perfectly. This Thameside patio in sight of St. Paul's dome is perhaps the most agreeable (and popular) spot in London at which to sit a spell with a fresh-pulled pint. There's been a tavern here at least since the 1500s, when Londoners ferried to Southwark by the hundreds to experience bear baiting, gardens, brothels, and Shakespeare (the playwright surely would have known the place). Diarist and royal confidant Samuel Pepys is said to have watched London burn to the ground from the safety of this shore in 1666. The industrial Anchor brewery that subsumed it for 200 years was cleared away in the 1980s, and the spacious (but always crowded) riverside terrace was added. Beer snobs kvetch that it has become a tourist draw, but that's all right with me; it's historic, and pubs have always been hangouts for the common man.

34 Park St., SE1. ✆ **020/7407-1577**. www.taylor-walker.co.uk. Mon–Wed 11am–11pm, Thurs–Sat 11am–midnight, Sun noon–10:30pm. Tube: London Bridge.

The Argyll Arms ★★ Having a beer in here can feel like drinking in a bejeweled, red velvet box. That's thanks to the many acid-etched glass screens that subdivide the busy bar into dignified drinking areas. Originally installed in 1895 to prevent brawls between the working and middle classes at a time when even subway rides were segregated, the screens somehow survived the 20th century. It's one of the prettiest pubs in London, and its location southeast of Oxford Circus (by several of the Tube's exits), makes it an easy stop.

18 Argyll St., W1. ✆ **020/7734-6117**. www.nicholsonspubs.co.uk. Mon–Thurs 10am–11:30pm, Fri–Sat 10am–midnight, Sun 10am–11pm. Tube: Oxford Circus.

The Chandos ★ A laid-back, spacious, wood-lined, and easy-to-find pub situated east across the road from the entrance to the National Portrait Gallery, the Chandos has an upper-floor Opera Room furnished with sofas. Big and relaxed, with lots of people who come for a drink before dashing out again, it looks older than it is (it was renovated in early 2006), but it's zero-attitude and makes a solid pre- or post-show choice. This is what an everyday pub is like.

29 St. Martin's Lane, WC2. ✆ **020/7836-1401**. Mon–Fri 11am–11pm, Sat–Sun 11am–midnight. Tube: Leicester Square or Charing Cross.

The Coach and Horses ★   The simple corner beerhouse in the thick of Soho's tourist crowd at Romilly Street dates to the mid-1800s, and although several pubs in London bear its name, few others share its history as a hangout for inebriated journalists. Stay downstairs for better prices, hang outside for air.

29 Greek St., W1. ⓒ **020/7437-5920**. www.coachandhorsessoho.co.uk. Mon–Thurs 8am–11:30pm, Fri–Sat 8am–midnight, Sun noon–10:30pm. Tube: Leicester Square.

The Coal Hole ★   A onetime haunt of actor Edmund Kean, who drank himself to an early curtain, was rebuilt in 1904 in the Arts and Crafts style and is still a hangout for performers at the adjoining Savoy Theatre. Use the entrance in back, by the stage door, to access the clubbier lower level. The antique street lamp on the Strand is a vestige of an experimental gaslight piping system that burned off sewage gases before the stink could overcome citizens. Bottoms up!

91 Strand, WC2. ⓒ **020/7379-9883**. www.nicholsonspubs.co.uk/thecoalholestrandlondon. Mon–Wed 10am–11:30pm, Thurs 10am–midnight, Fri–Sat 10am–12:30am, Sun 10am–10:30pm. Tube: Charing Cross or Embankment.

The Dove ★★   The 17th-century charmer houses many legends: that Charles II would cheat on his queen by sneaking off with Nell Gwynne here (probably false); that the composer of "Rule Britannia" lived, and died prematurely, upstairs (true); that dissolute artists Graham Greene, Ernest Hemingway, and Richard Burton all got wasted here (so very true, along with many other imbibers commemorated on the walls). It's a prototypical English pub with character, down to the low ceiling crossed by dark oak beams, brick facade, and open fire. But it's the terraced Thameside location that makes it endure. Sitting outside and watching the river, you'll understand why Hammersmith was a favored retreat from the city for so many centuries. Arrive early on weekends to snare a seat.

19 Upper Mall, W6. ⓒ **020/8748-9474**. www.dovehammersmith.co.uk. Mon–Sat 11am–11pm, Sun noon–10:30pm. AE, MC, V; Tube: Ravenscourt Park.

The George Inn ★★★   Unquestionably one of the most important ancient pubs still standing, the George traces its lineage to at least 1542, when a map of Southwark first depicted it; the Tabard Inn, from where Chaucer's pilgrims left in *Canterbury Tales,* was then a few doors south (it's gone now). The oldest part of the current structure, a galleried wood-and-brick longhouse, dates to 1677, after a horrific fire swept the district. It later functioned as an 18th-century transit hub, and its courtyard was encircled on three sides with a tavern, a hotel, stables, wagon repair bays, and warehouses. Shakespeare knew it, and Dickens memorialized it in *Little Dorrit,* but the rise of a railway nearly saw it destroyed, and only one side of the former complex survives. The National Trust now protects it, and in 2012, Pete Brown traced some of its *dramatis personae* in the book *Shakespeare's Local.* Sip ale in the low-ceilinged timber-and-plaster chambers, or sit in the cobbled courtyard and soak up the echoes of history.

77 Borough High St., SE1. ⓒ **020/7407-2056**. www.nationaltrust.org.uk/george-inn. Mon–Sat 11am–11pm, Sun noon–10:30pm. Tube: London Bridge.

The Grenadier ★★★   They say this was the Duke of Wellington's local bar and the unofficial clubhouse for his regiment, hence the battlefield artifacts on display, and they also say someone was beaten to death here for cheating at cards, hence the routine ghost sightings. This tiny plank-floored pub/restaurant, pretty as a picture in a cobbled mews, comes off like a boozer in some tiny upcountry village, with only 15 places at its island bar, part of which is still faced with its original pewter top. The clientele these days skews toward an international mix of students and businessmen. The pub is also unjustly known for its freshly mixed Bloody Marys (overrated). Find this secret place by heading down Grosvenor Crescent from Hyde Park Corner station, hanging a hard right upon arriving at Belgrave Square onto Wilton Crescent, and taking your first right on Wilton Row.

18 Wilton Row, SW1. ℂ **020/7235-3074**. www.taylor-walker.co.uk. Daily noon–11pm. Tube: Hyde Park Corner.

The Lamb and Flag ★★
Too tiny and thronged after work to supply much respite, it is nonetheless the epitome of a city pub, tucked as it is down an atmospheric brick alley and blessed with an original fireplace. It has been known throughout its 380 years as both the Coopers Arms and The Bucket of Blood, and its building is said to be Tudor in origin. No one can prove it, since it was heavily rebuilt in the 1890s. You'll find it on a lane just east of the intersection of Floral and Garrick streets. But you probably won't find a place to sit unless you start drinking after lunch, which the regular drinkers on its memorial wall surely did.

33 Rose St., WC2. ℂ **020/7497-9504**. www.lambandflagcoventgarden.co.uk. Mon–Sat 11am–11:30pm, Sun noon 11pm, Sun noon–10:30pm. Tube: Covent Garden or Leicester Square.

McGlynn's Public House ★
McGlynn's isn't hundreds of years old, or even important, but it fulfills the image of a "local" where the neighborhood folks hang out in peace and the landlord welcomes new faces. Its coal-blackened brick corner building, painted in old-fashioned green and red trim, is hard to find (it's southwest of Argyle Square in King's Cross), which accounts for some of its appeal. Its street is so quiet that, unlike at most London pubs, you'd actually consider loitering at one of its outdoor picnic tables in summer. It's the sort of place with a few "pokie" gambling machines jangling in the corner, and a rugby or football game on the TV every afternoon.

1-5 Whidborne St, WC1. ℂ **020/7916-9816**. www.mcglynnsfreehouse.com. Mon–Sat 11am–11pm, Sun noon–10:30pm. Tube: Russell Square or King's Cross St. Pancras.

The Narrow Boat ★★
Emblematic of a modern pub for hanging out, it's simply a smashing, contemporary place to pass a few hours on a pretty day. Picture windows overlook an attractive basin of the Regent's Canal, where you can watch barges, ducks, and wealthy folks in their waterfront loft conversions. Combine a visit with a stroll along the canal's footpath, and you've got one of the most romantic afternoons London has to offer. If there were pubs like this in your neighborhoods, you might never go home again. (Don't confuse this one with The Narrow, a pricey but delicious gastropub on the Thames in Limehouse.)

119 St. Peters St., N1. ℂ **020/7288-0572**. www.thenarrowboatpub.com. Daily 11am–midnight. Tube: Angel.

The Salisbury ★
The Covent Garden/Leicester Square location is unbeatable, and the ornate exterior and interior is unmistakably Victorian—ostentatious, just-how-drunk-was-the-designer Victorian, to be precise. Thrill to the Grecian urns in the brilliant-cut glass, the pressed-copper tables, and the nymphs entwined in the bronze lamps. Long a haunt of the city's theatrical community, it's now a suitable pit stop for any West End exploration. If you want food, try the "pie and a pint" including mashed

potatoes, seasonal veggies, gravy, and beer, for £9.50—although it does burgers and fish and chips, too.

90 St. Martin's Lane, WC2. ℰ **020/7836-5863**. www.taylor-walker.co.uk. Mon–Wed 11am–11pm, Thurs 11am–11:30pm, Fri 11am–midnight, Sat noon–midnight, Sun noon–10:30pm. Tube: Leicester Square.

The Ship & Shovell ★★   One of the most endearing configurations for any pub you'll ever see, it's cleft in two by a narrow alley trod by commuters on their way to Charing Cross station. On the north, there's a traditional Victorian-style space, and on the south, a cozier room with a charismatically sloping floor and private snugs. A cellar links the two halves. The bewigged tubby chap on the swinging sign is Admiral Cloudesley Shovell who, in 1707, wrecked his ship and instantly drowned 800 sailors, which certainly gives the interior's nautical theme an ignoble context. It's special for another reason, too, being one of the few pubs in town to pour Dorset ales from Hall and Woodhouse brewers, a family brewer dating to 1777.

1-2 Craven Passage, WC2. ℰ **020/8391-1311**. www.shipandshovell.co.uk. Mon–Sat 11am–11pm, Sun noon–10:30pm. Tube: Charing Cross or Embankment.

The Ten Bells ★   It's said that Annie Chapman, one of Jack the Ripper's victims, downed her last beer at this Spitalfields boozer while another, Mary Kelly, picked up her clients outside, and for an icky period in the '70s, the pub capitalized on infamy by being renamed for their slayer. All that unsavoriness is past, and the hipsters are here. The pub's Victorian tilework has been faithfully restored, and a new mural was added to celebrate the modern artistic vitality of the neighborhood. Today the clientele is young and friendly, the furniture casually mismatched, and the pub (which hosts a gourmet British restaurant upstairs) is a cheerful specimen of a well-aled "local" that parties more intensely as the evening advances. Nicholas Hawksmoor's Christ Church, which towers next door, silently observes the latest mortals at play.

84 Commercial Street, E1. www.tenbells.com. ℰ **020/7366-1721**. Mon–Wed, Sun noon–midnight, Thurs–Sat noon—1am. Tube: Liverpool Street.

Ye Olde Cheshire Cheese ★★★   Just the sort of rambling, low-ceilinged tavern you imagine London is full of (and was, once), it was built behind Fleet Street in the wake of the Great Fire in 1666, and because of steady log fires and regularly strewn sawdust, it still smells like history hasn't finished passing it by. In later generations, it played regular host to Dr. Samuel Johnson (who lived behind on Gough Square), Charles Dickens (who referred to it in *A Tale of Two Cities*), Yeats, Wilde, and Thackeray. You can get pretty well thackered yourself today: There are six drinking rooms, but the cozy front bar—of pallid light, candles in the fireplace, and antique paintings of dead fish—is the most magical. Observe the stuffed carcass of Polly the Parrot, enshrined above the bar since 1926 and "whose adept use of profanity would have put any golfer to shame," according to the *New York American*. Don't confuse this place with the Victorian-era Cheshire Cheese pub at nearby Temple.

Wine Office Court, off 145 Fleet St. ℰ **020/7353-6170**. Mon–Sat 11am–11pm. Tube: Blackfriars, Temple, or Chancery Lane.

Ye Olde Mitre ★★★   Suspended in a hidden courtyard and seemingly between centuries, this enchanter—no screens, no music—was once part of a great palace mentioned by Shakespeare in *Richard II* and *Richard III*. The medieval St.

Etheldreda's Chapel, the palace's surviving place of worship, stands just outside. This extremely tiny pub (established in 1546 but built in its present form in 1772) has two entrances that feed either side of the bar. The one on the left grants you access to "the Closet," a fine example of a semiprivate sitting area called a "snug." The entrance on the right brings you face-to-face with a case containing a blackened stump said to be part of a cherry-tree maypole that Elizabeth I danced around. (Yeah, right, drink another one.) Suck down one of the house specialties: pickled eggs, for less than 80p. To locate this hidden idyll, seek a little alley among the jewelry stores on eastern Hatton Garden between Holborn Circus and Greville Street. Leaving will be even more difficult.

1 Ely Court, off Ely Place, EC1. ℂ **020/7405-4751**. www.yeoldemitreholborn.co.uk. Mon–Fri 11am–11pm, closed weekends; Tube: Farringdon or Chancery Lane.

EXPLORING LONDON

Engand has been a top dog for 500 years, and London is where it keeps its bark. Many of the world's finest treasures came here and never left. Most cities store their best goodies in one or two brand-name museums. In London, riches hide everywhere. The major attractions could by themselves occupy months of contemplation. But the sheer abundance of history and wealth—layer upon layer of it—means that London boasts dozens of exciting smaller sights, too. You could spend a lifetime seeing it all, so you'd better get started.

Sightseeing discounts, such as 2-for-1s, are sometimes offered at **Last-Minute.com** under Experiences. The heavily publicized **London Pass** (www.londonpass.com), which gets you into a bevy of attractions for a fixed price (such as £45 a day or £61 for 2 days), is unlikely to pay off in the small amount of time you're given. Only the version that lasts 6 days (£97 adult, £67 child) would potentially pay off.

Historic Royal Palaces operates The Banqueting House (p. 103), Hampton Court (p. 132), Kensington Palace (p 105), Kew Palace (p. 134), and the Tower of London (p. 122). An annual membership pass will possibly save you money if you plan to see several of them; do the math (www.hrp.org.uk; ✆ 0844/482-7788; £45 one adult, £67 two adults, £57 for one adult and up to six children, £86 two adults and up to six children).

5

LONDON'S ICONIC SIGHTS

London-Wide Attractions

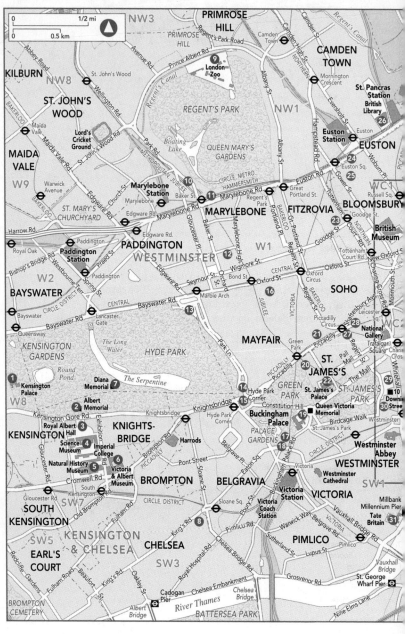

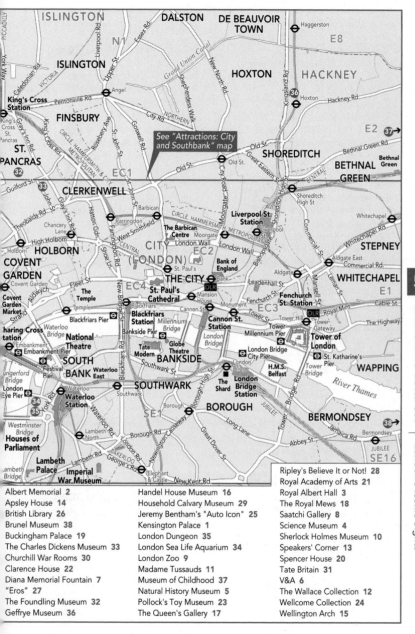

See "Attractions: City and Southbank" map

5

MUSEUMS

HISTORIC SITES

LANDMARKS

OTHER ATTRACTIONS

BLOOMSBURY, FITZROVIA & KING'S CROSS

The British Museum ★★★ MUSEUM Founded in 1753 and first opened in 1759 in a converted mansion, the British Museum is as much a monument to great craftsmanship as it is to the piracy carried out by 18th- and 19th-century Englishmen, who, on their trips abroad, plundered whatever goodies they could find and then told the bereft that the thievery was for their own good. Yet the exquisite taste of these English patriarchs is unquestionable, and now the British Museum may be the museum to beat all the rest. In fact, it's the top attraction in the country—5 and half million people visited in 2012. Put on your walking shoes because it's huge.

Holdings are grouped in numbered rooms by geography, with an emphasis on the Greek and Roman Empires, Europe, and Britain. Dominating the center of the glass-roofed **Great Court** like a drum in a box, the cream-and-gold, round **Reading Room,** completed in 1857 but closed to the general public until 2000, was once part of the British Library. Famous patrons, who had to apply for tickets, included Lenin and Karl Marx, who developed their political theories here; other habitués included Bram Stoker, Sir Arthur Conan Doyle, and Virginia Woolf, who wrote upon entering "one stood under the vast dome, as if one were a thought in the huge bald forehead which is so splendidly encircled by a band of famous names." On the southern wall (through which you enter), you can read panels on the museum's history. The Reading Room, which still houses some 25,000 books, often hosts exhibitions, although with the 2014 addition of a giant new space on the museum's northwest flank, its future purpose is being decided.

It's impossible to choose the *most* priceless item in a welter of pricelessness, but if you have only a few hours to see the most famous and instructive selections, first orient

---

Prices & Opening Hours

Children's prices generally apply to those 15 and under. To qualify for a **senior discount,** you must usually be 60 or older. Students require ID for discounts. Some places offer **Family Tickets** for up to three kids who enter with adults. Museums may post prices that include a voluntary donation, but you may ask to have it removed. In addition to closing on public holidays and on December 25 and 26 (Boxing Day), some heritage properties only open in the summer.

yourself in the Great Court. Hit the Info Desk for details on tours, including some 15 daily EyeOpeners, focused on particular rooms, and Hands On, which allow you to touch some things. Consider renting a hand-held audio/video tablet (£5) that spotlights 200 of the best objects. The website also has free themed tour plans—useful because maps cost money. But don't miss:

o The museum's most famous, and most controversial, possessions are the so-called **Elgin Marbles**, which the museum gingerly refers to as **The Sculptures of the Parthenon** (rooms 18 and 19) to disguise their imperialist provenance. These slab sculptures (called friezes and Metopes), plus some life-size weathered statuary, once lined the pediment of the famous Parthenon atop Athens' Acropolis but were defaced (literally—the faces were hacked off) by invading vandals (not literally—they were Persian) in the 500s. They suffered further indignities in a 1687 gunpowder explosion before being sawed off and carted away by Lord Elgin. They're laid out in the gallery in the approximate position in which they appeared on the Parthenon, only facing inward so you can admire them. The government of Greece has lobbied for years for their return, but the British have argued that they're better cared for in London. If you've ever seen the smog-burnt portions left behind in Athens, it's easy to see their point, which makes a muddy political issue murkier.

o Fragments of **sculptures from The Mausoleum at Halikarnassos,** one of the lost Seven Wonders of the Ancient World, loom in room 21. So colossal are these chunks—a woman, once one of 36 such figures, carved from a single block of stone; a bulging horse's head that measures 2.1m long (7 ft.)—that they call into question everything we think about ancient peoples' limited technology and culture.

o The pivotal **Rosetta Stone** (196 B.C.), in room 4, is what helped linguists crack hieroglyphics, and its importance to anthropology can't be exaggerated. Napoleon's soldiers found it in Egypt in 1799, but it was nabbed in 1801 by the British. Consider it his first Waterloo.

o The grisly array of **Egyptian Mummies** in rooms 62, 63, and 64 have petrified children for years, and on your visit, they'll probably be thronged with school groups as usual. In addition to the wizened, raisinlike corpses, there are painted coffins; the hair and lung of the scribe Sutimose, dating to 1100 B.C.; and scarabs galore. In room 64, check out the body from 3400 B.C., found in a fetal position without a coffin, which was preserved by dry sand. Beside it is another body, 400 years younger that rotted to bones and soil because it was laid to rest in a basket.

o Kids also love leather-faced **Lindow Man** in room 50; he was discovered, throat slit, in a Cheshire bog nearly 2,000 years after his brutal demise. Preserved down to his hair and fingernails, he looks like he could spring to life and pound the glass of his case. Nearby (room 49) is the **Mildenhall Treasure,** a hoard of silver Roman tableware unearthed by Gordon Butcher, a Suffolk farmer, as he plowed his fields in 1942; the saga of how Butcher was cheated of his fortune was chronicled by writer Roald Dahl. (Yes, pillage is something of a hidden theme in this place.)

Room 70, on the upper floor, holds three remarkable holdings: **The Portland Vase,** a black, cameo-glass jug that's very difficult to make even today; the bronze **head of Roman Emperor Augustus,** found in the Sudan and lifelike to an unsettling degree (it still has its painted eyeballs, as most statues of the time did); and **The Warren Cup,** a First Century silver chalice graphically depicting homosexual sex in relief. The Warren Cup's acquisition in 1999 for £1.8 million caused some juvenile titters; the jibes are made more amusing by the fact visitors have to bend over to inspect its indecorous decorations.

There's a **restaurant** above the Reading Room that serves a full afternoon tea for just £19.50—a bargain (℗ 020/7323-8990).

Great Russell Street, WC1. ℗ **020/7323-8299**. www.thebritishmuseum.org. Free. Sat–Thurs 10am–5:30pm and Fri 10am–8:30pm, closed New Year's Day, Good Friday, and Dec 24–26. Tube: Tottenham Court Road or Holborn or Russell Square.

The British Library ★★★ MUSEUM One of the planet's most precious collections of books, maps, and manuscripts, the **Treasures of the British Library** exhibition, is displayed in a cool, climate-controlled suite of black cases and rich purple carpeting. It ought to be mobbed, but isn't. The library holds approximately 150 million items and adds 3 million each year, so when it puts the cream (about 200 items) on display, you will be floored. A portion of the trove (100 of which are highlighted in a $6 app) includes:

- Two of the four known copies of the Magna Carta, 800 years old in 2015
- The Beatles' first lyric doodles: "A Hard Day's Night" on Julian Lennon's first birthday card (there's a choo-choo on it) and "Strawberry Fields Forever," sketched far from suburban Liverpool on Lufthansa airline notepaper
- The Diamond Sutra, the oldest known printed book, which was found in a Chinese cave in 1907 and was probably made by woodblock nearly 600 years before Europeans developed similar technology
- The *Codex Sinaiticus,* one of the two oldest Christian Bibles (the Pope has the other) and illuminated manuscripts from Buddhism, Jainism, and Islam
- Jane Austen's diary and writing desk
- Michelangelo's letter to his dad telling him he had finished the Sistine Chapel and pages from Leonardo da Vinci's notebook, in mirror writing
- Music in the hand of Mozart, Handel, Beethoven, and Mendelssohn (*The Wedding March*)—you can listen to the final works on headphones
- Lady Jane Grey's prayer book, handed to a lieutenant at the Tower seconds before her beheading, and the Earl of Essex's death warrant
- An 11th-century copy of *Beowulf* on vellum, in Old English; it's the only surviving manuscript, written when Ethelred the Unready was king.

The King's Library, some 85,000 tomes owned by King George III, floats in a glassed-in central tower and forms the core of the collection, like Thomas Jefferson's library does for Washington's Library of Congress—which means the King who lost America and a principal engineer of the loss provided the seed for their respective

Free Entry, A La Carte Touring

Many of London's biggest museums are free to enter, but there's a catch: To make up the cash they miss out on, they find lots of other revenue streams. Most institutions charge £1 for a map and about £10 to see major temporary exhibitions. Fortunately, this funding model also give museums an incentive to operate superlative shops, publish a variety of keepsake guidebooks, and run gorgeous cafés that even attract customers off the street.

JEREMY BENTHAM'S "auto icon"

England's own Ben Franklin, Jeremy Bentham (1748–1832) was a renaissance man, a philosopher, a progressive, and a subversive. Prison reformer, supporter of suffrage and the decriminalization of homosexuality, educator, and pen pal of U.S. president James Madison, Bentham worked to enable equal access to courts and schools, and he coined the words *international*, *maximize*, and *codification*.

He was so ahead of his time, he refused to stay in the past: His will stipulated eternal access to his corpse—the gift that keeps on giving, really. Starting years before his death, he purportedly carried around a pair of glass eyes that were intended for his future "Auto Icon" (auto = self, icon = image), which would represent him forever. After he expired, his body was dissected for students. In 1850, a colleague dressed his remains and Bentham's severed head was placed between his own feet. There his remains remain, in a lobby at University College London. His skeleton is under his original clothing and gloves. Unfortunately, his noggin was preserved artlessly, and kids kept swiping it (in 1975, some hooligans held it for a £10 ransom), so today, it's stashed in the vaults, staring blankly with its long-pocketed blue eyeballs. You can see it on an electronic display. "Some visitors find it disturbing to look at," confesses the caption after you're already looking at the leathery, white-haired thing. His new head has a lifelike, doughy face that sagely observes the current scholarly crop at UCL from beneath a straw hat. You'll find this freak show on the east side of Gower Street between University Street and Grafton Way, opposite the red-brick Cruciform Building. Go in the gates, veer right, and enter the door marked South Cloisters. Then hang a right and head for the stone lions (Tube: Euston Square).

nations' libraries. The hall contains the **Philatelic Exhibition,** 500 vertical drawers containing thousands of rare stamps.

You can't handle books unless you're an accredited scholar, but the Library encourages anyone to hang out in its public spaces. In addition to the Treasures, rotating exhibitions are on display. Head to the info desk; the librarians schedule frequent talks (many are podcasted online) and chances to inspect items from the stacks—including, oddly, non-bibliophilic objects such as locks of Napoleon's hair and the ashes of the poet Shelley. Twice a day, you can book an £8 tour of the facilities and its conservation standards.

96 Euston Rd. ⓒ **087/0444-1500**. www.bl.uk. NW1. Free. Mon and Wed–Fri 9:30am–6pm, Tues 9:30am–8pm, Sat 9:30am–5pm, Sun 11am–5pm. Tube: King's Cross St Pancras.

Other Area Attractions

Pollock's Toy Museum ★ MUSEUM   A few mildewed old apartments were barely altered before being fitted with cases of whacked-out bygone toys for those with a specialized interest. The collection is exhausting, if not exhaustive: Mechanical cast-iron banks, 1950s rocket toys, puppets, Gollywogs, wax dolls, the 1921 forerunner to G.I. Joe (Swiss Action Man), doll's houses, and a board game based on the Falkland Islands invasion that was banned for being in poor taste. The vintage kitsch factor is through the roof, and its ground-floor shop, free to enter, has some terrific, hard-to-find toys that don't cost much, including reproduction tins, lots of handmade items, and cardboard theaters—the museum takes its name from the last great printer of toy theaters.

1 Scala St., W1. ℂ **020/7636-3452**. www.pollockstoymuseum.com. £6 adults, £5 seniors/students, £3 children. Mon–Sat 10am–5pm, last admission 4:30pm. Tube: Goodge Street.

Wellcome Collection ★★ MUSEUM   Once upon a time, there was a very strange Midwestern pharmacist named Henry Wellcome. Henry got very rich and developed a taste for hoarding medical oddities, such as Napoleon's toothbrush, hair from George III, oil paintings of childbirth, and Japanese sex toys. When he died, he bequeathed a museum for them, which is now slick and modern and makes for a highly amusing hour's visit. Get goose bumps with some of his rarities in the first section (there's a free audio tour) before seeing the second half, which takes a contemporary art approach to the all the ways we deal with our bodies. This unexpected theme is augmented by a couple of changing exhibitions (such as an assortment of skeletons found under London building sites, or a moving exhibition of before-and-after portraits of people who were willingly photographed both before and after their deaths). It's one of the most compelling, most offbeat exhibitions in town, and it courts families, Addams or otherwise, with activity packs for kids and an appealing lobby café.

83 Euston Road, NW1. ℂ **020/7611-2222**. www.wellcomecollection.org. Free. Mon, Tues, Fri, Sat 10am–6pm, Weds 10am–10pm, Sun 11am–6pm. Tube: Euston Square or Warren Street.

SOHO, COVENT GARDEN & WEST END

The Courtauld Institute of Art Gallery ★★★ MUSEUM   The masses don't visit it, but art historians consider the Courtauld one of the most prestigious collections on earth. Its small two-level selection is supreme, with several masterpieces you will instantly recognize. Among the winners are Manet's scandalous *Le Déjeuner sur l'herbe,* depicting a naked woman picnicking with two clothed men and the artist's *A Bar at the Folies-Bergère,* showing a melancholy barmaid standing in front of her disproportionate reflection. There are multiple Cézannes, Toulouse-Lautrecs, and Tahitian Gauguins. Degas' *Two Dancers on a Stage* is popular, as is Van Gogh's *Self-Portrait with Bandaged Ear.* Especially rare is a completed Seurat, *Young Woman Powdering Herself,* which depicts his mistress in the act of dressing and initially included his own face in the frame on the wall—he painted over it with a vase of flowers to avoid ridicule. **Somerset House**, its home, was once a naval center and later was where Londoners came to settle taxes and research family history. The central courtyard, beneath which lie the foundations of a Tudor palace, has a grove of 55 ground-level fountains that delight small children, and it's the scene of both popular summer concerts and a winter ice rink, plus a café by the popular charcuterie-bakery Fernandez & Wells. Check out the changing free exhibitions at the **East Wing Galleries** and see if anything interesting is showing at the **Embankment Galleries**, which charges £10 adults, £8 seniors/students depending on what's on display. The terrace overlooking the Thames (from across the street) can be enjoyed for free.

Somerset House, Strand, WC2. ℂ **020/7848-2526**. www.courtauld.ac.uk. Daily 10am–6pm, until 9pm one Thurs a month. £6 adults, £5 children/seniors/students, £3 Mondays. Tube: Temple.

The Hardy Tree

In 1866, as laborers dug their way through his churchyard to create the new St Pancras Station just to the south, the Vicar of St Pancras noticed with horror that they were tossing aside thigh-bones and skulls. His cemetery contained the remains of Mary Wollstonecraft, J.C. Bach, Sir John Soane, and Ben Franklin's son, the last colonial governor of New Jersey, so the Vicar assigned Thomas, a young architecture student, with the unenviable task of overseeing the relocation of some 8,000 bodies. As he worked, Thomas carefully arranged their discarded headstones around a tree. The tree survives today, having become one with the grave markers. It is called the Hardy Tree—because young Thomas, who created this eerie living monument, eventually became the famous novelist Thomas Hardy. *(St Pancras Old Church, Pancras Road, NW1; ℰ 020/7424-0724; www. posp.co.uk. Tube: King's Cross St Pancras).*

The Foundling Museum ★★ MUSEUM   Small but devastating, it tracks the history of the Foundling Hospital, which took in thousands of orphans between 1739 and 1953. This was a period in which kids were treated like rubbish: For example, in 1802 a law was passed limiting the time children could work in mills—to 12 hours a day. By that measure, it's clear that the benefactors, who seem needlessly harsh today, were actually helping kids by locking them in this borderline prison. Don't miss the heartbreaking cases of tokens that mothers left at the doorstep with their babies. These tiny objects, into which a lifetime of hopes was imbued, never made it to their children's hands lest they compromise a mother's anonymity. Also take the time to listen to the oral histories by some of the last kids to be raised by the Hospital; at the time of recording, they were elderly but still obviously quite shaken. Upstairs is the Hospital's modest but solid collection of 18th-century English works (Hogarth, Reynolds, Gainsborough), which believe it or not was one of the first permanent art exhibitions in the world. The composer Handel loved the Hospital so much that he bequeathed many of his papers to it, including a score to his *Messiah* that was written as a benefit for the facility in 1754; it's on public display. The exercise grounds are now a called Coram's Fields. Fittingly, it is the domain of the child; adults are not permitted to enter without one.

40 Brunswick Square, WC1. ℰ 020/7841-3600. www.foundlingmuseum.org.uk. £7.50 adults, free for children under 16, £5 seniors/students; Tues–Sat 10am–5pm, Sun 11am–5pm. Tube: Russell Square.

London Transport Museum ★★ MUSEUM   It's hard to imagine London without its wheeled icons: the red double-decker bus, the black taxi, and the Tube are the best of their kind in the world and a draw for visitors. In this soaring Victorian-era hall, which takes about 2 hours to tour, their development and evolution are traced with impeccable technology (lots of video screens and illuminated boards) and detail (there are even fake horse apples beneath the antique carriages). Besides some pedigreed vehicles, such as Number 23, a steam locomotive that powered the Underground in its earliest and most unpleasant days, there's also plenty of the system's famous Edwardian and Art Deco posters, many of which are so stunning they could qualify for an art gallery—because of them, the gift shop, which doesn't require a ticket, could satisfy an hour by itself. Illustrators and designers will appreciate the background on Johnston, the distinctive and oft-imitated typeface created by Frank Pick in 1916 for the Underground that could now be considered London's unofficial font. Along the way, you'll learn a great deal about the shifts in everyday London life, and you'll likely feel a twinge of embarrassment about the state of your own town's public transportation. Be warned that kids run wild here, so adults who come to learn history must learn patience first.

Covent Garden, WC2. ℰ **020/7565-7298**. www.ltmuseum.co.uk. £15 adults, £11.50 seniors/students, free for kids under 16. Sat–Thurs 10am–6pm, Fri 11am–6pm, last admission 45 min. before closing. Tube: Covent Garden.

National Gallery ★★★ MUSEUM   When the bells of St. Martin-in-the-Fields peal each morning at 10am, the doors promptly open on this artistic fireworks show—each famous picture follows an equally famous picture, many of which you'll instantly recognize. Few museums can compete with the strongest, widest collection of paintings in the world—one of every important style is on display, and it's almost always the best in that genre. If a painter isn't here, though, he isn't worth knowing. There are 2,300 Western European works—mostly royal-owned, originally—which is plenty to divert you for as long as you can manage, and 5 million visitors are drawn here every year.

The building replaced a stables in 1835; Trafalgar Square was selected because it was central, and therefore accessible to the poor. Even today, crowds swell around lunchtime as working people pop in for a free art infusion. As you enter via the main Portico Entrance, galleries imperceptibly surge through time in a clockwise arrangement. The rooms jumble together, so grab a £1 map—but drop a coin in the slot or a sentry will bark. The best course is to start in the Sainsbury Wing (through room 9 or from Pall Mall East) and backtrack, which will order viewings more or less chronologically.

Among the museum's many noteworthy holdings:

Sainsbury Wing
- Piero della Francesca, one of the most sought-after Renaissance painters, is represented by *The Baptism of Christ* (1450s, room 66) with its then-advanced use of light and foreshortening. The faces of its subjects verge on bemusement, and the dove, representing the Holy Spirit, seems to fly into viewers' faces.
- Sandro Botticelli fell under the spell of the hardline reformer Savonarola. He burned many of his finest paintings in the Bonfire of the Vanities and changed to an inferior style, so his best works are rare; *Venus and Mars* (1485, room 58), depicting the lovers reclining, is one of them, and it's in a room full of others.

The Main Building
- Michelangelo's *The Entombment* (around 1500, room 8) is unfinished but powerful. The feminine figure in the red gown is now thought to be St. John, but it's hard to know for sure, since the artist favored strong masculine traits.
- Kids love Holbein's *The Ambassadors* (1533, room 4), full of symbolic riddles that refer to the guy on the left, and famous for a stretched image of a skull that can only be viewed in proper perspective from the side. Get close; the fine brushwork extends even to the feathers on the shoes.

- Kids also love the grotesque, porcine old lady in *A Old Woman* ("*The Ugly Duchess*"; 1513, room 5), thought to be a satire on ladies who try to look younger than they are, but possibly a woman suffering from a disease.
- Rembrandt has two self-portraits. One at age 34 (room 24) is pridefully detailed to declare ego and prosperity; by age 63 (room 23), he's in simple clothes and broadly dolloping paint with a palette knife. The pair makes for a universal story of preening youth giving way to confident old age.
- The Gallery is rich in Peter Paul Rubens, with some 25 works attributed to him. His *Samson and Delilah* (1609–10, room 29) is known for Samson's muscular back and Delilah's crimson robe.
- Edouard Manet's *The Execution of Maximilian* (1867–68, room 43) was sliced into five sections after the artist's death, but Edgar Degas reassembled what he could; the missing patches lend the firing-squad scene further tension.

My list of recommendations could continue: George Seurat's almost pointillist *Bathers at Asnieres* (1884, room 44), Van Gogh's *Sunflowers* (room 45), Leonardo da Vinci's *The Virgin of the Rocks* (room 2), Jan van Eyck's *The Arnolfini Portrait* (Sainsbury Wing, room 56), a mysterious but fabulously skillful depiction of light that dates to 1434, years ahead of its time. **Brueghels. Cézannes. Uccellos.** There's so much art here that you may want to go twice during your visit, and the Gallery is so centrally located that you can.

Touring can sometimes be heavy mental work. Posted signs are awfully straight-laced. Audio tours covering 1,200 of the 2,000-odd works are £3.50 and come in themed varieties, a $2 app catalogs more than 1,500 paintings, and a free version supplies 183 highlights. Your visit would be best illuminated by some expert input. Check the info desk for events, such as the "Ten Minute Talks" about a single work; 30-minute, 1pm "Lunchtime Talks" about a specific work or artist; storytelling for kids; or the few hour-long tours (often at 11:30am and 2:30pm, plus another weekends at 4pm). The permanent displays are usually supplemented by temporary exhibitions, one free and one paid (around £8). The Gallery schedules most family activities for Sundays. The two restaurants are top-quality but overpriced, and the view from the restaurant at the National Portrait Gallery (see below) is better, but don't miss the superlative gift shops, which will print you a color-matched custom copy of any of 1,200 of the works to take home.

Trafalgar Square, WC2. ☎ **020/7747-2885.** www.nationalgallery.org.uk. Free. Sat–Thurs 10am–6pm and Fri 10am–9pm. Tube: Charing Cross or Leicester Square.

The National Portrait Gallery ★★★ MUSEUM   On paper, the concept of a portrait gallery sounds like Field Trip Hell. But actually, you'll be surprised how the best works capture the sparkle of life behind history's most charismatic shapers. Here, the names from your high school textbook flower into flesh-and-blood people, and the accompanying biographies are so sublimely evocative (Samuel Johnson is described as "massive, ungainly, plagued with nervous tics.") that subjects come alive.

The ancient kings and queens have the most heft, partly because it's hard to wrap your brain around the fact that in many cases, the actual people posed in the same room as these very canvases. One of the most instantly recognizable paintings is the **Ditchley portrait of Elizabeth I** (room 2), in which the queen's jeweled gown spreads like wings and Her Majesty firmly glares at the viewer under stormy skies. Right away, it becomes clear that many artists are slyly commenting on the disposition of their sitters.

The troublesome **Henry VIII** is shown in several likenesses. One is a delicate 1537 paper cartoon by Hans Holbein the Younger (for a mural at Whitehall—a rare survivor from that palace), in which the king suspiciously peers with flinty grey eyes—hinting at a shiftiness that His Majesty probably couldn't recognize in his own likeness, but that all who knew him feared (room 1). One painting of **King Edward VI,** painted when he was 9, is executed in a distorted perspective (called anamorphosis) that requires it to be viewed from a hole on the right side of its case (room 1). You'll also find **George Washington** (he was born an Englishman, after all), and one of the only authoritative images of **Captain James Cook** (room 14), who was so pivotal in colonial expansion. In room 15, look for the newly acquired **Chevalier D'Eon**, a male diplomat and fencing champion who lived as a woman in the late 1700, and in room 18, for the sketch of **Jane Austen** by her sister—friends admitted, kindly, that it stank. The three **Brontë Sisters** appear together in an 1834 portrait found folded atop a cupboard in 1914; their brother Patrick, the artist, was painted out but his ghostly image is eerily re-appearing (room 24).

Fortunately, the portraits don't stop when cameras were invented. The image of **Margaret Thatcher**, soft and demure in a chair, makes the Iron Lady look sweet as your granny (room 32). The bust of artist **Marc Quinn** is formed by eight pints of his frozen blood (room 38). In contrast, a 1950 sitting-room portrait of **Queen Elizabeth II** with her parents, **King George VI** and the **Queen Mum,** mines Rockwell-esque, just-us-folks imagery (Mum's about to pour tea, Dad's smoking) to make the Royal Family seem as normal and as middle-class as The Cleavers (room 31). Modern portraits tend to change often because there's simply not enough room to show everything. Just about everything can be printed as a poster in the gift shop.

To start, take the escalator to the top floor and work your way down over about 2 hours. The oldest works (Tudors, Jacobeans, Elizabethans) will come first, and you'll progress forward in time—adding photography when canvas fatigue sets in. Frankly, it helps to have a little historical knowledge so that these pictures ring some bells, so consider visiting near the end of your trip, when many of these names will be fresh in your mind from your tours. The £3 audio guide can be dull at the start, but by the end, it uses archival recordings of the famous people you're looking at, which is cool, and there's a $2 smartphone app of the highlights. Bring along kids; the desk has free discovery trails for those 3 and up.

IT'S free!

All of the following attractions charge no admission fees for their permanent collections. Not a shabby lineup!

Free all the time:
The Bank of England Museum; The British Library; The British Museum; The Hunterian Museum; Museum of Childhood; Museum of London; Museum of London Docklands; The National Gallery; The National Maritime Museum; The National Portrait Gallery; The Natural History Museum; The Old Naval College, Greenwich; The Queen's House, Greenwich; The Royal Observatory (partly); Saatchi Gallery; The Science Museum; Sir John Soane's Museum; The Tate Britain; The Tate Modern; The V&A; The Wallace Collection; The Wellcome Collection.

Also consider it for its pre-theatre menu (£17.50 for two courses, £20.50 for three) served from 5:30 to 6:30pm in the rooftop Portrait Restaurant, which has a breathtaking view taking in Nelson's Column and Big Ben's tower (📞 020/7312-2490; www.searcys.co.uk).

St. Martin's Place, WC2. 📞 020/7312-2463. www.npg.org.uk. Free. Sat–Wed 10am–6pm, Thurs–Fri 10am–9pm, last admission 45 min. before closing. Tube: Leicester Square.

Sir John Soane's Museum ★★ MUSEUM   A doorman will politely ask you to check your bags. With good reason: These two town houses on the north side of Lincoln's Inn Fields are so overloaded with furniture, paintings, architectural decoration, and sculpture, that navigation is a challenge. The Georgian architect, noted for his bombastic neoclassical buildings (the Bank of England) as much as for his aesthetic materialism, bequeathed his home and its contents as a museum for "amateurs and students," and so it has been, looking much like this since 1837. It's as if the well-connected eccentric has just popped out to purloin another Greek pilaster, leaving you to roam his creaking wood floors, sussing out the *objets d'art* from the certifiable treasures. His oddball abode, which his will decreed must be left precisely as it was on the he day he died, is a melee of art history in which precious paintings and sculpture jostle for space like baubles in a junk shop. Ask to join a tour of the **Picture Room,** built in an 1823 expansion, so you can watch its hidden recesses be opened, revealing layer upon buried layer of works (such as William Hogarth's 8-painting *The Rake's Progress*, a documentary of dissolution), filed inside false walls. Look sharp for Canalettos (which often fetch £9 million at auction) and a J. M. W. Turner (ditto). Curation appears convoluted and haphazard: The guides swear that although sunshine appears to pour onto the masterpieces through skylights, there are UV filters—yet architectural fragments from Whitehall Palace are plainly betrayed to the elements in the courtyard ("It was never covered because that's the way he wanted it," a guide says.) You have to wonder how Soane could legally acquire antiquities such as the sarcophagus of Seti I, carved from translucent limestone, and you won't know because nearly nothing is marked. (Just how the elitist Hogarth hoarder wanted it.) Download one of three free MP3 tours to make sense of the untidiness. Or take a tour: Tues and Fri at 11:30am, Weds and Thurs at 3:30pm. Mostly, a visit reminds you of the unseemly way in which privileged Englishmen used to stuff their homes with classical art as a way of stocking up on a sense of righteousness, but that doesn't mean it's not wondrous.

12 Lincoln's Inn Fields, WC2. 📞 020/7405-2107. www.soane.org. Free. Tues–Sat 10am–5pm, candle-lit nights the first Tues of the month 6pm–9pm; Tube: Holborn.

Other Area Attractions

The Benjamin Franklin House ★ LANDMARK   The only residence of the portly politico left standing in the world operates as a sort of architectural preserve. Astonishingly, Franklin lived here in this boarding house by the Thames without his wife for nearly 16 years, much longer than many Americans realize—during the Boston Tea Party, the enactment of the Stamp Act, and his invention of the armonica—and it was only the Revolution that forced him to leave his adopted home and move back to the Colonies. For much of his life Franklin was a fervent loyalist who, even as late as 1775, felt that the differences between Britain and the Colonies could be settled in "half an hour." Tours are conducted by a young actress playing the landlady's daughter,

Polly Hewson, who became such a dear friend to Franklin she later moved to Philadelphia and was with him when he died. Polly tells wistful tales as recordings chime in with other voices from her memory. The rewards of a tour are mixed. On the one hand, the spiel crowds out questions, exhibits are sparse (one exception is the ghoulish deposit of human bones in the backyard, likely left over from dissections by Franklin's doctor neighbor), and there are few kids' activities. But on the other hand, it's rare for a famous home of this age to have survived into our lifetimes. It's also humbling to see how this giant man made do with such small quarters; his study is no larger than the smallest London hotel rooms. The worn wooden staircase, on which the he got his exercise when French trollopes weren't available, is so well preserved it feels ghostly.

36 Craven St., WC2. *C* **020/7839-2006.** www.benjaminfranklinhouse.org. Tours (required) £7 adults, £5 seniors/students, free for children under 16; 5 timed tours daily, Wed–Sun noon–4:15pm; Tube: Embankment or Charing Cross.

"Eros" ★★ LANDMARK   Some say the fleet-footed, winged lad atop the Shaftesbury Monument in Piccadilly Circus is Eros, the Greek god of sex, erected in 1893 by Alfred Gilbert and one of the first to be cast in aluminum. They are wrong. It's actually based on Anteros, Eros' brother, the god of selfless love. In fact, the work, dedicated to a Victorian philanthropist, is officially called *The Angel of Christian Charity*. But Anteros, gallant deity that he is, lets Eros cop the glory. Until World War II, his arrow pointed up Shaftesbury Avenue; now he aims down Lower Regent Street and is a primary snapshot target and perch for loiterers.

Piccadilly Circus. Tube: Piccadilly Circus.

Hunterian Museum ★ MUSEUM   This ghoulish exhibition at the Royal College of Surgeons, now 2 centuries old, chronicles the life's work of John Hunter (1728–93), who elevated surgery from something your barber dabbled in to something a saw-wielding, germ-spreading "scientist" would, ahem, undertake. It's a macabre scene, crowded with thousands of specimens, including extinct animals, all tastefully presented in a modern, gleaming, two-level hall. See Napoleon III's bladder stone and Winston Churchill's gold dentures, designed to fix his childhood lisp. Most of your time will be spent squeamishly perusing some 3,000 black-lidded jars of human and animal pathology and anatomy (many originally obtained by grave-robbers, a common practice then), plus a bone-grinding collection of crude surgical instruments that could rattle even the steeliest physician. Check out the cross-section of a chicken's head that Hunter grafted with a human tooth. Such Frankenstein projects funded his school of anatomy. Upstairs, as part of a history of surgery, you'll find an ill-conceived amputation buzz saw. In its first use, it became slick with blood, slipped, and lopped off a nurse's hand; both patient and nurse were killed by subsequent infection. Ask the good-humored staff questions, or else catch the weekly free guided tour, Wednesdays at 1pm (book ahead if possible). A treat—but don't eat first.

35-43 Lincoln's Inn Fields, WC2. *C* **020/7869-6560**. www.rcseng.ac.uk/museums. Free. Tues–Sat 10am–5pm. Tube: Holborn.

The Charles Dickens Museum ★ MUSEUM   Although Dickens moved around a lot, his last remaining London home, which he rented for £80 a year when he was 30, is now his testament. A museum since 1925, and restored to a period look in 2012 (when the attic and kitchen were opened for the first time), these four floors don't exude many vibes from the old guy; after all, he departed in 1839 after staying less than 2 years. It could be anyone's humble home. Still, his celebrity got a kick-start while he lived here: *Oliver Twist* and *Nicholas Nickleby,* arguably his biggest hits, were written while he was in residence, a short stroll from the Foundling Hospital for orphans. As you inspect his desk, his razor, bars from a prison where his spendthrift dad was locked up, an unpleasant realization sets in: Charles Dickens was a compelling character but also a jerk. Tough on his kids and unfaithfully cruel to his wife, his greatest possession seems to have been his ego. Ironically, his audience still feeds it, nearly 150 years after his death.

48 Doughty St., WC1. © **020/7405-2127**. www.dickensmuseum.com. £8 adults, £4 kids 6–16, £6 seniors/students. Daily 10am–5pm. Tube: Chancery Lane or Russell Square.

Cleopatra's Needle ★ LANDMARK   Cleopatra's Needles—which Cleopatra had nothing to do with—were originally erected in Heliopolis, Egypt, around 1450 B.C., and their inscriptions were added 200 years later. The Romans moved the granite spires to Alexandria, where they were toppled and buried in the sand, preserving them until the early 1800s. New York's Cleopatra's Needle was installed in Central Park in 1881, and after much peril during its delivery, London's was erected 3 years earlier. Two sphinx were installed to guard it (some say backwards, since they face the sculpture, not away from it). Just 130 years in London wrecked what 20 African centuries didn't: In 1917, German bombs scarred the southern sphinx, and pollution has rendered the hieroglyphs illegible. There's a third needle in Paris.

Victoria Embankment. Tube: Embankment or Temple.

WESTMINSTER & ST JAMES'S

For information on the Changing the Guard ceremony, please see p. 139.

Buckingham Palace ★★ HISTORIC SITE   Let's be honest. If you were to fall asleep tonight and wake up inside one of the **State Rooms,** you'd never guess where you were. Is it opulent? No question. But if ever gilding, teardrop chandeliers, 18th-century portraits, and ceremonial halls could be considered standard-issue, Buckingham Palace is your basic palace. Queen Elizabeth's mild taste in decor—call it "respectable decadence" of yellows and creams and pleasant floral arrangements, thank you very much—is partly the reason. Remember, too, that much of this palace was built or remodeled in the 1800s—not so long ago in the scheme of things—and that the Queen considers Windsor to be her real home.

All tickets are timed and include an audio tour that rushes you around too quickly. The route threads through the public and ceremonial rooms (nowhere the Royal Family spends personal time, and besides, the Palace is open only 2 months a year, when they're in Scotland) at the back of the palace. (If you want to see highlights of the formal gardens, that's another £8.75.) Highlights include the 50m-long (164-ft.) **Picture Gallery** filled mostly with works amassed by George IV, an obsessive collector; the 14m-tall (46-ft.) **Ballroom,** where the Queen confers knighthoods; the parquet-floored **Music Room,** unaltered since John Nash decorated it in 1831, where the Queen's three eldest children were baptized in water brought from the River Jordan; and a stroll through the thick **Garden** in the back yard. It's definitely worth seeing—how often can you toodle around the spare rooms in a Queen's house, inspecting artwork given as gifts by some of history's most prominent names? But it's no Versailles. If you're in London any time other than August or September and spot her standard of red, gold, and blue flying above, you'll at least know the Queen is home. (If it's the Union Jack, she's gone.) So near, yet so far.

Buckingham Palace Rd., SW1. ℓ 020/7766-7300. www.royalcollection.org.uk. £19 adults, £10.85 children 5–16, £17.50 seniors/students; late July to late Aug daily 9:30–7pm, Sept. 9:30am–6pm, last admission 2 hr. 15 min. before closing. Tube: Victoria or Green Park.

Churchill War Rooms ★★★ MUSEUM/HISTORIC SITE

One of London's most fascinating museums is the secret command center used by Winston Churchill and his staff during the most harrowing moments of Word War II, when it looked like England would become German. We regard the period with nostalgia now, but the abject terror of life then cannot be exaggerated; a staggering 30,000 civilians were killed by some 18,000 tons of bombs in London alone and more than 65,000 innocent people were killed in Britain as a whole. Here, in the cellar of the Treasury building, practically next door to 10 Downing Street, the core of the British government hunkered down in secret, but one ill-placed bomb could have buried the lot of them.

When the War ended, the bunker was abandoned, but everything was left just as it was in August 1945, and when it was time to make it a museum, everything was intact—from pushpins tracing convoy movements on yellowed world maps to rationed sugar cubes hidden in the back of a clerk's desk drawer. Although the hideout functioned like a small town for 526 people, with sleeping quarters kitchens, radio rooms, and other facilities that would enable leaders to live undetected for months on end, it feels a lot more like your old elementary school, with its painted brick, linoleum walls, and round clocks.

Midway through your tour, you disappear into the **Churchill Museum,** surely the most cutting-edge biographical museum open at this moment. Exhaustively displaying every conceivable facet of his life (his bowtie, his bowler hat, and even the original front door to 10 Downing Street), it covers the exalted statesman's life from entitled birth through his antics as a journalist in South Africa (where he escaped a kidnapping and became a national hero), to, of course, his years as prime minister. You even learn his favorite cigar (Romeo y Julieta) and brandy (Hine). Although the entire museum is atwitter with multimedia displays, movies, and archival sounds, the centerpiece will blow you away: a 15m-long (50-ft.) Lifeline Interactive table, illuminated by projections, that looks like a long file cabinet and covers every month of Churchill's life. Touch a date, and the file "opens" with 4,600 pages of rare documents, photos, or, for critical dates in history, animated Easter eggs that temporarily consume the entire table (select the original Armistice Day or the *Titanic* sinking to see what I mean). You could play for hours, dipping into his life day by day.

Clive Steps, King Charles St., SW1. ℓ 020/7930-6961. www.iwm.org.uk. £15.45 adults, free for children under 16, £12.35 seniors/students, posted prices are higher and include a "voluntary donation." Daily 9:30am–6pm, last admission 5pm. Tube: Westminster.

The Houses of Parliament ★ LANDMARK

Did you know that the building most people call Big Ben is actually named Elizabeth Tower? Big Ben is the bell within. These are the things you learn in this modern-day castle dedicated to government. Throughout the Middle Ages, this was considered one of the monarch's main homes, only to burn down in 1512 and again in 1834, when it was rebuilt into the Gothic citadel now used for the day-to-day running of the Empire. Your Blue Badge guide will refer to it as a "palace" because technically, the Crown still owns it. It's roughly divided into three areas: those for the House of Lords (whose members inherit seats, done in rose); the House of Commons (by far the most powerful, elected by the people, seats of blue-green, with a chamber dating only to 1950); and a few Royal sitting rooms and the "Robing Room" (golds, browns, burgundies), which the Queen flits through when she shows up once a year to kick off sessions. The walls of Westminster Hall, essentially England's highest all-purpose events space, were built in 1097, and both William Wallace (remember *Braveheart?*) and the Gunpowder Plot conspirators were tried in it. The Hall, the only part of the original Westminster Palace to survive an 1834 fire except for the Jewel Tower (see below), is cherished for its oak hammer-beam ceiling, Europe's largest, dating to 1399; during World War II, it was saved at the expense of the House of Commons itself. Considering all the ornate mosaic flooring, peaked windows, and statues stacked in niches, you would be forgiven for mistaking the complex for a church. It's certainly the high altar of secular Britain.

Frustratingly, The Elizabeth Tower (1859) above the Houses—it contains the 13.5-ton bell known as Big Ben plus four smaller bells—is only open to U.K. residents. At least there's a virtual tour of it on the website. But visiting the rest of the complex is a possibility. Visitors may tour only on some Saturdays and in summer (around Aug 1–Sept 30), when the government is not in session. Booking ahead is advisable, but you can try your luck for last-minute openings at the ticket office, which opens from mid-July next to the Jewel Tower, across the street from Parliament. Sometimes temporary explicate the otherwise impenetrable nuances of the British system.

Bridge St. and Parliament Square, SW1. © **0844/847-1672**. www.parliament.uk/visiting. August: 9:15am–5:30pm except Mondays, 1:15pm–5:30pm, Sept.–early Oct: 9:15am–4:30pm, most Saturdays throughout the year. 75 min. tour £16.50 adults, one child 5–15 free with paying adult or £7, children under 5 free, £14 seniors/students. Reservations recommended. Tube: Westminster.

Spencer House ★★ MUSEUM   A home so lush that its current owners are the Rothschilds, who host diplomatic and corporate events here that make the world go round, is the only surviving London mansion with an intact 18th-century interior. Tours of the ground floor and a portion of the first floor are conducted by very proper guides employed by the Rothschild banking group, who are prone to peering down their noses at weekend sightseers. The home was begun in 1756 as a love nest by Diana Spencer's ancestors (and, by extension, the future king's), and the lavish gilt and carved decor repeatedly invoke the symbols of fidelity and virility. War damage spooked the Spencer clan, who moved out in the 1920s, and since then, they've gradually transferred the most precious elements to their estate at Althorp, 193km (120 miles) north of the city, and replaced them with equally fantastic facsimiles—the fireplace library, for instance, took 4,000 hours to carve. Expect your jaw to drop: three Benjamin West paintings are on loan from the Queen, a chair in the Palm Room has a companion in the Museum of Fine Arts in Boston, and the original Painted Room suite was once at the V&A. Groups are limited to 20, so arrive early to secure a spot.

27 St. James's Place, SW1. © **020/7499-8620**. www.spencerhouse.co.uk. £12 adults, £10 children under 16/students/seniors. Sun 10:30am–5:45pm, closed Jan and Aug. Tube: Green Park.

Tate Britain ★ MUSEUM   Tourists often wonder what the difference is between the Tate Modern and this, its sister upstream on the Thames. Well, the Modern is for contemporary art of any origin, and the Britain is exclusive to British-made art made after 1500. Not to diminish the quality of the grade-A work on display here, but you won't spot many recognizable masterpieces. Britain has a historic knack for collecting international art, not so much for creating it, so a lot of the work on display is rich with relevance but highly imitative of classical or Renaissance styles. The main collection has corporate sponsorship by BP, which has not done as good of a job handling oil as the artists represented on the walls. Although the oldest portion of the collection, full of documentary or moralist works by William Hogarth, William Blake, and Joshua Reynolds, skillfully illustrates British life from centuries ago, it's hard to shake the feeling that, artistically speaking, Britain was playing catch-up with the rest of Europe. That changes when the galleries progress chronologically into the modern era, and works by visionaries such as Francis Bacon and James Abbott McNeill Whistler (granted, not English, but an American who lived in England) reveal the ebullient colors that were latent in the national mind.

Descriptions are often didactic (works are described, emptily, to be "questioning" or "explorations") and many paintings are placed at such altitude that glare makes them inscrutable. It's all very good stuff, but a bit too textbook. One-hour tours go at 11am, noon, 2pm and 3pm.

Shifting objectives consistently rotate beloved paintings into storage, a frustrating habit with Tate, but some masterpieces can be relied upon. J. M. W. Turner's trenchant *The Field of Waterloo* (room 1810) was painted in 1818, 3 years after the battle; its gloomy piles of corpses, and of bereaved family members searching them, makes the now-unknown battle suddenly vivid and touching. The oil-on-canvas *Carnation, Lily, Lily, Rose* (room 1840) depicts children holding paper lanterns so luminous that visitors often halt in their tracks as they pass it. John Singer Sargent (another American who settled in London) is the genius responsible. Check out the sculpture, too, including forms by **Henry Moore**, who gets two rooms, and Barbara Hepworth. But the crowning attraction here is the **Turner Galleries,** with their expansive collection of J. M. W. Turners. Turner (1775–1851), the son of a Covent Garden barber, was a master of landscapes lit by misty, perpetual sunrise, and the dozens of paintings and sketchbooks testify to both his undying popularity and his doggedly British tendency to convey information purely by implication. Turner's work is lovely, if sleepy, and there's a mania for him (in 2010, one of his works fetched £29.7 million at auction). Just don't sully his name in these halls; even his crusty paint box and his fishing rod are dotingly preserved.

Millbank, SW1. ℂ **020/7887-8888**. www.tate.org.uk/britain. Free. Daily 10am–6pm. Tube: Pimlico.

Westminster Abbey ★★★ HISTORIC SITE If you have to pick just one church to see in London—nay, one church in the entire *world*—this is the one. The

---

The Tate-to-Tate Boat

The best way to get between the Tates is not via Tube (a circuitous route) but via the **Tate Boat** (ℂ **020/7887-8888.** www.tate.org.uk/visit/tate-boat. £6.50 adults, £3.25 children under 16, Oyster rare £5.85, Travelcard rate £4.30 adults, £2.15 children), a 220-seat catamaran that zips along the Thames every 40 minutes from 10am to around 5pm between the docks in front of the Tate Britain and the Tate Modern. Along the way, it stops by the London Eye and also supplies the only view of the Houses of Parliament that isn't spoiled by angular fences and gun-fondling guards. Tate's entertainment!

echoes of history are mind-blowing: The current building dates from the 1200s, but it was part of a monastery dating to at least 960. Every English monarch since 1066 has been crowned here (with three minor exceptions: Edward V, Edward VIII, and possibly Mary I). Seventeen monarchs are interred here (their deaths date from 1066–1760), as are dozens of great writers and artists. Even if England's tumultuous history and the thought of bodies lying underfoot don't stir your imagination, the interior—in places, as intricate as lace—will earn your appreciation. A visit should take about 3 hours and should begin early, since entry lines are excruciating.

Unlike St. Paul's Cathedral, which has an airy, stately beauty, the much smaller Westminster is more like time's attic, packed with artifacts, memorials, tombs, and virtuosic shrines. It's easy to feel overloaded after just a few minutes; by the time you've pocketed the (paltry) change from your admission ticket, you're already treading on the final resting place of poor William Bradford (died 1728 at age 32). It only gets busier from there. Take your time and don't get swept along in the current of visitors. Let them pass. There are stories to be told in every square meter of this place.

Inside the sanctuary, tourists are corralled clockwise from the North Transept. The royal tombs are clustered in the first half of the route, in the region of the High Altar, where coronations and funerals are conducted. The most famous rulers of all time are truly *here*—not in story, but in body, a few inches away behind marble slabs. Some are stashed in cozy side chapels (which once held medieval shrines before Cromwellians bashed them to pieces during the Reformation; some vandalism is still visible), but the oldest are on the sanctuary side of the ambulatory (aisle). The executed **Mary Queen of Scots** was belatedly given a crypt of equal stature to her rival, **Elizabeth I,** by Mary's son **James I,** who gave himself only a marker for his own tomb beneath **Henry VII**'s elaborate resting place. James I's infant daughter Sophia, who died aged 3 days, was given a creepy bassinet sarcophagus in the Lady Chapel.

If you have questions, approach anyone in a red robe; they're "vergers," or officers who attend to the church. They lead 90-minute tours (usually at 10am, but up to five times daily, for £3) and if you stump them, you may win an invitation to the atmospheric Library, a creaking loft that smells of medieval vellum and dust, where an archivist can answer you.

The South Transept is **Poet's Corner,** where Britain's great writers are honored. You'll see many plaques, but most (Shakespeare, Austen, Carroll, Wilde, the Brontës) are merely memorials. The biggest names who truly lie underfoot are Robert Browning, Geoffrey Chaucer (he was placed here first, starting the trend), Charles Dickens, Thomas Hardy (buried without his heart), John Gay, Rudyard Kipling, Dr. Samuel Johnson, Laurence Olivier, Edmund Spenser, and Alfred Lord Tennyson. Ben Jonson is commemorated here but is actually buried in the Nave near Isaac Newton and Charles Darwin.

Now for a few Abbey secrets:

o That oak seat between the Sanctuary and the Confessors' Chapel, near the tomb of Henry V, is the **Coronation Chair.** Unbelievably, every English monarch since 1308 has been crowned on this excruciating-looking throne. The slot under the seat is for the 152kg (336-lb.) Stone of Scone, said to be used as a pillow by the Bible's Jacob, and a central part of Irish, Scottish, and English coronations since at least 700 B.C. After spending 7 centuries in the Abbey (except for when Scottish nationalists stole it for 4 months in late 1950), the Stone was returned to Scotland in 1996, where it's on view at Edinburgh Castle. It will return for every future coronation.

- **Oliver Cromwell,** who overthrew the monarchy and ran England as a republic, was buried with honors behind the High Altar in 1658. Three years later, after the monarchy was restored, his corpse was dug up, dragged to Tyburn (by the Marble Arch), hanged, decapitated, the body tossed into a common grave, and its head put on display outside the Abbey. (Didn't they realize he was already dead?) Today his much-abused cranium is at Sidney Sussex College in Cambridge. Cromwell's daughter, who died young, was mercifully allowed to remain buried in the Abbey.
- The **Quire** is where the choir sings; it comprises about 12 men and 30 or so boys who are educated at the adjoining Westminster Choir School, the last of its type in the world. The wooden stalls, in the Gothic style, are Victorian, but are so delicate they're dusted using vacuum cleaners.

The Abbey's oft-overlooked **Museum,** beside the Pyx Chamber, contains some astounding treasures, including **Edward III's death mask** (thought to be the oldest of its kind in Europe; it's made of walnut and doesn't ignore his facial droop, which resulted from a stroke), **ancient jewelry** "found in graves" (we know what that means—pried from skeletons), the **fake Crown Jewels** used for coronation rehearsals, 14th-century leather shoes and Roman tiles unearthed on the grounds, and the fateful **Essex Ring,** which Elizabeth I gave to her brilliant confidant Robert Devereux, telling him to send it if he needed her. He tried to, but his enemies intercepted it, and he was beheaded at the Tower of London in 1601. Oops.

Time seems suspended in the **Cloister,** or courtyard. But better gardens are hidden away. At the Museum, head for the corridor to the left and you'll find the fragrant and fountained **Little Cloister Garden,** blackened by 19th-century coal dust, and beyond that to the right, the wide **College Garden,** a tempting courtyard with daffodil beds, green lawns, and five plane trees dating to 1850. The garden has been continuously planted for 900 years, when it grew herbs for an adjacent hospital. Westminster School, started by the abbey's monks in the 1300s, stands nearby. (Incidentally, there haven't been monks in this complex for 550 years, yet Londoners persist in calling it an "Abbey.")

Get a real sense of the majesty of the space at a service. Evening prayer with choirs from around the world are at 5pm weekdays and Sung Eucharist Sundays at 11:15am, plus a Sunday organ recital at 5:45pm and evening service with simple hymns at 6:30pm (but check ahead, since services are sometimes shuffled to smaller, but equally historic, chapels). Holy Communion is daily at 12:30pm in the Nave. It's not all history and tradition: You can subscribe to its sermons on iTunes.

Next door, pop into **St. Margaret's Chapel** (free), which the monks built so they'd be left alone in peace. The Germans didn't comply: Some southern windows were destroyed by a bomb and were replaced by plain glass, and in addition to damage to the north wall, Pew 3 remains charred.

Broad Sanctuary, SW1. ✆ **020/7222-5152**. www.westminster-abbey.org. £18 adults, £8 children 11–15, £15 seniors/students. Mon–Tues and Thurs–Fri 9:30am–4:30pm, Wed 9:30am–7pm, Sat 9:30am–2:30pm, last admission 1 hr. before closing, closed Sun. for worship. Tube: Westminster.

Other Area Attractions

The Banqueting House ★ HISTORIC SITE   The glorious palace of Whitehall was home to some of England's flashiest characters, including Henry VIII. In a wrenching loss for art and architecture—to say nothing of bowling heritage, since

Henry had an alley installed—it burned down in 1698. But if you had to pick just one room to survive, it would have been the one that did, designed with Italianate Renaissance assurance by Inigo Jones and completed in 1622, which means Henry never set foot in it, but another fateful king set his *last* foot in it: In 1649, Charles I walked onto the scaffold from a window that stood in the present-day staircase, and met his doom under an axe wielded by Cromwell's republicans. The reason to come here is to gape at the nine grandiose ceiling murals by Peter Paul Rubens in which the king is portrayed as a god. They give you a bold clue as to why the rabble would want to see His Highness brought low. Thoughtfully, mirrored tables help you inspect the ceiling without craning your head to behold why Charles lost his.

Whitehall at Horseguards Ave., SW1. © **084/4482-7777**. www.hrp.org.uk. £5 adults, children under 16 free, £4 seniors/students, including audio tour; daily 10am–5pm. Tube: Charing Cross or Westminster.

Clarence House ★ HISTORIC SITE   The Queen dictates who in her family lives at which palace, and she herself lived at this four-story mansion, a part of St. James's Palace, just before she took the throne. Her mother dwelled here for nearly half a century until her 2002 death at age 101, and now it's chez Charles and Camilla. Prince Charles, having a keener sense of public relations than perhaps any royal before him, decided to open the house, where royals have lived since 1827, to tourists during the summer months when the family is away. You won't get to poke around the Prince's medicine cabinet on your hour tour since you can only see the ground floor, which still feel like an old lady's house despite being recently renovated. It feels much more like a grand town house than a mansion fit for a future king and reflects the Windsors' homey, cluttered decorating style, heavy on paintings of horses and light on the gilding and glitter.

Stableyard Rd., SW1. © **020/7766-7303**. www.royalcollection.org.uk. £9 adults/seniors/students, £5 children 5–16. Daily, early Aug to early Oct 10am–5:30pm, last admission 4:30pm. Tube: Green Park.

Jewel Tower ★ HISTORIC SITE   Built around 1365, it's one of only two remnants left from the 1834 fire that ravaged the Royal Palace of Westminster. This stone three-level tower, once a moatside storehouse for Edward III's treasures, has walls so thick it was later considered an ideal setting for taking accurate measurements. So you'll see some explanation of weights-and-measures standards and some relics dug up from the moat (a 1,200-year-old sword, a bulbous bottle from The Sun, a 17th-century tavern where Samuel Pepys drank). It's quiet and easily overlooked.

Abingdon St., SW1. © **020/7222-2219**. www.english-heritage.org.uk. £3.90 adults, £2.30 children 5–15, £3.50 seniors/students; Apr–Oct daily 10am–5pm, Nov–Mar daily 10am–4pm. Tube: Westminster.

KENSINGTON & KNIGHTSBRIDGE

Apsley House ★★ MUSEUM   This is how you'd be rewarded if you became a national war hero: You got Hyde Park as a backyard. In 1815, Arthur Wellesley defeated Napoleon and became the Duke of Wellington and later, prime minister. The mansion, still in the family (they maintain private rooms), was filled with splendid thank-you gifts showered upon him by grateful nations, including a thousand-piece silver set from the Portuguese court, but he never seemed to get his nemesis off his mind. Under the grand staircase stands a colossal nude statue of Napoleon that the little emperor despised; the Duke cherished it as a token of victory. Aspley's supreme art stash, which was largely looted by the French from the Spanish royal family and never went home, includes a few Jan Bruegel the Elders, Diego Velazques' virtuosic *The Waterseller of Seville* (you can understand why it was the artist's favorite work, since just looking at it makes you thirsty); and Correggio's *The Agony in the Garden,* in a case fitted with a keyhole so the Duke could open it and polish it with a silk hanky. The Duke and his best friend lived here together after their wives died, and the whiff of faded masculine glory pervades the place like cigar smoke. In other circumstances, the Duke and Napoleon, who both liked fancy finery and fancier egos, would have been buddies. If you're also visiting Wellington Arch (see below), a joint ticket will save £2.50.

149 Piccadilly. ℰ **0870/333-1181**. www.english-heritage.org.uk. £6.70 adults, £4 children, £6 seniors/students, including an audio tour. Open Weds–Sun, closed until April 2014 for refurbishment. Tube: Hyde Park Corner.

Diana, Princess of Wales Memorial Fountain ★ LANDMARK

In July 2004, the Queen came to Hyde Park to open a beautiful fountain designed to conjure the memory of the mother of her grandchildren and a longtime thorn in her side, Princess Diana. As designed by American architect Kathryn Gustafson, this graceful o-shaped fountain undulates down a gentle slope, sending two flumes of water rushing and bubbling into a calm collecting pool. At three points, bridges carry you to the center. One day after the opening, trouble began. It clogged with leaves. Then visitors started falling—the planners hadn't considered algae growth. So for 5 months in 2005, it closed while an asphaltlike path was laid around it, spoiling lawsuits and the effect alike. After it re-opened, hairline cracks were found in its 545 blocks of Cornish granite. The bill for that? £5.2 million. Londoners decided they don't miss Di *that* much. Rather than putting me in a state of remembrance, it may put you into a state of wanting to ride it on an inner tube. For all that, the Fountain, which is gated and switches off exactly on time, makes expensive gurgly sounds. Reach it from the Alexandra Gate at Kensington Gore, Knightsbridge, up Exhibition Road.

Between West Carriage Dr., Rotten Row, and The Serpentine, Hyde Park. ℰ **030/0061-2350**. www.royalparks.org.uk. Free. Nov–Feb daily 10am–4pm, Mar and Oct daily 10am–6pm, Apr–Aug daily 10am–8pm, Sept daily 10am–7pm. Tube: South Kensington. Check website for maintenance closures.

Kensington Palace ★ HISTORIC SITE

[ST]Most people know it as the place where Lady Diana raised Princes William and Harry with Prince Charles from 1984 to 1996, but now it's where Prince William, Kate, and George live. (Sorry. You won't run into them in the bathroom.) It has been a royal domicile since 1689, when William and Mary took control of an existing home (then in the country, far from town, which inflamed William's asthma) and made it theirs. Handsome and haughty, with none of the symmetry that defined later English tastes, the red-brick palace is not as ostentatious as you might expect.

At least from the outside. A 2013 refit ruined the experience within. Some design firm must have done some fancy talking to convince Historic Royal Palaces to reinterpret priceless spaces with junky art installations based on scandals that happened here (voices whispering from gramophones, graffiti-like quotations scrawled across carpets and walls) that strip the venerable palace of a sense of import and give it the aspect of a spook house. Cheap paper background cards hang ignored from hooks, and visitors wander listlessly with an unquenched thirst to learn something. Thankfully, the walk-through still includes the magnificent King's Staircase, lined with delicate canvas panels whose perimeters are rigged with tissue paper slivers designed to tear as a warning of shifting or swelling. The staircase is considered so precious that it was only opened to the public in 2004, 105 years after the rest of the palace first accepted sight-seers. Also, in the Gallery there's a working Anemoscope, which has told the outside wind direction since 1694, and has a map of the world as known in that year. But you'll only know both those things because I told you.

Queen Victoria has her own section, but she's given the trashy treatment, too, and rather than teaching visitors about what enabled her to successfully control the most powerful empire in the world, she is shown, misogynistically, in terms of gender roles: as a good girl, a loving wife, and a grieving widow. You do see cases of her toys (including her favorite doll, named after her favorite ballerina, Taglioni), some clothes, and the bedroom where she learned of her ascension, at age 18, in 1837. The room draped in black leads you to believe Prince Albert died in it, but no, he died at Windsor. You'll also get a chance to see gowns worn by HM the Queen, Diana, and Princess Margaret, who also lived here. Overall, through, if you're short on time, the Palace is no longer a must-see.

5 Kensington Gardens, W8. ℰ **084/4482-7777**. www.hrp.org.uk. Admission £16.50 adults, children under 16 free, £13.75 seniors/students including audio tour, online reservations £1 less, posted prices are higher and include "voluntary donation". Mar–Oct daily 10am–6pm, Nov–Feb daily 10am–5pm, last admission 1 hr. before closing. Tube: High Street Kensington or Queensway.

The Natural History Museum ★★ MUSEUM   Some cities have an equivalent, but few have an equal. You know: a hall of dinosaur bones, cases of colorful rocks, a taxidermist's menagerie, and sobering reminders of just how many animals are on their way to being snuffed out for eternity. The commodious NHM, good for several hours' wander, has all that and more. Organization is a cut above. Even the dinosaurs (in the Blue Zone) are supplemented by scary robotic estimations of how they sounded and moved. On weekends, the queue for that can be an hour long (after all, 5 million people a year come here), so go early, and enter through Exhibition Road for lighter crowds. A Martian meteorite that fell to Morocco in July 2011 (the **Green Zone**) is a visitor favorite, as is the **Red Zone** (the Earth Galleries), a just-rehabbed multimedia display about how the planet works. The **Darwin Centre's** Cocoon looks like a seven-story egg laid in the back atrium; hidden inside are some 20 million bottled specimens (including those that came back on the *Beagle*) on 27km/17 miles of shelves. Most of the discussion here, and throughout the museum, is aimed at a child's mind, with signs answering insipid questions such as why scientists name things and why we study stuff, but now and then, you'll see an expert through a window into the stacks of Centre who can use a microphone to answer more serious questions.

Even if you don't give a hooey about remedial ecology, the 1880 Victorian building is a landmark worth seeing. It crawls with carved monkeys whimsically clinging to the terra-cotta and plants creeping across ceiling panels. Daily Nature Live talks are given at 12:30pm on a huge range of topics, they're streamed online, too. The Museum's brainiacs even cultivate a garden and pond (the Orange Zone; open Apr–Oct) that attracts a range of English creatures and flowers. Families are well catered for: Kids under 7 can borrow free Explorer backpacks with pith helmets, binoculars, and activities themed to Monsters, Birds, Oceans, or Mammals (they tend to run out early on weekends); and those 7 to 14 should look for the free Investigate hands-on lab in the basement (afternoons are less crowded). All that—and the requisite blue ceiling whale.

Cromwell Rd., SW7. © **020/7942-5000**. www.nhm.ac.uk. Free. Daily 10am–5:50pm. Tube: South Kensington.

Royal Albert Hall ★★ LANDMARK   In addition to being a great concert venue, the Royal Albert is also one of London's great landmarks, and you don't need a seat to enjoy it. Conceived by Queen Victoria's husband Albert and opened in 1871, a decade after his death from typhoid (Vicky was so distraught that she didn't speak at the opening ceremonies). You can take a 1-hour tour. The hall contains such oddities as Britain's longest single-weave carpet (in the corridors), the Queen's Box (still leased to the monarchy), and a spectacular glass dome (41m/135 ft. high and supported only at its rim). Be warned: You don't go backstage (that's for groups only). Some 320 performances a year are presented, many with less than 24 hours' set-up time, and a flow of sightseers would be in the way.

Kensington Gore, SW7. © **0845/401-5045**. www.royalalberthall.com. Admission to lobby free, tours £11.50 adults, £9.50 seniors/students. Tours available most days, times vary; generally 9:30am–4:30pm. Tube: South Kensington.

Saatchi Gallery ★★★ MUSEUM   In Chelsea, the most celebrated (or, depending on your viewpoint, reviled) collection of Britart, ranging from shockingly revealing self-sculpture to immovable hyper-realistic depictions of homeless people, belongs to adman Charles Saatchi, a gossip column denizen with a knack for selecting trenchant pieces that make you think. The impressive collection is the resident in the three-story, 6,500-sq.-m (70,000-sq.-ft.) former Royal Military Asylum building (1801) in Chelsea, complete with a cafe, bookshop, and massive exhibition halls. The socially risky, eye-bending experiments—pieces made entirely of paper, China's most daring protest artists—make the Tate Modern look as oblique and conservative as it is. No fan of contemporary art should miss it.

Duke of York Square, SW3. © **020/7811-3070**. www.saatchi-gallery.co.uk. Free. Daily 10am–5pm. Tube: Sloane Square.

Science Museum ★★ MUSEUM   Around the corner from the Natural History Museum and across the street from the V&A, it's really two museums, one classic and one far-out, that have been grafted together, but both are about the triumph of man over his environment and not so much about the tenets of electricity or chemistry. So many interesting exhibitions are on display here that you'll probably run out of time. The old-school section, which began collecting in 1857 and is split over six levels, is an embarrassment of riches from the history of science and technology. Exhibits are similar to what lots of science museums have, but in almost every case, they display the most original or most rare specimen available: 1969's *Apollo 10* command module; "Puffing Billy," the world's oldest surviving steam engine; and a 1950 computer pioneered by Alan Turing. The rarely updated upper floors are full of subjects like model ships and early computers (second floor), a history of veterinary medicine (fifth floor), and in the hangarlike third floor, aviation. Highlights: a complete De Havilland Comet, which was the first jetliner (1952), and a modified Vickers Vimy bomber, the first plane to cross the Atlantic without stopping. It was flown by Arthur Whitten Brown, who promptly became the first person to report something you may be feeling now: jet lag. He called it something less catchy: the "difficulty of adjustment to the sudden change in time."

The high-concept wing buried in the back of the ground floor is easy to miss, but seek it out. A cobalt-blue, humming, multileveled cavern dedicated to interactive games and displays, it bears little relation to the mothballed museum you just crossed through. The Antenna exhibition (ground floor) is exceptionally cutting-edge, and updated regularly with the latest breakthroughs; past topics have included biodegradable cell phones implanted with seeds and people missing the DNA to enable them to feel pain. The interactive exhibits of Launchpad (third floor; heat-seeking cameras, dry ice, and the like) enchant kids. But not everything in the museum is enchanting. The gift shop (mostly mall-style toys) and guidebook disappoint. And when you've got the actual Model T and Enigma code breaker, why charge £10 for a gimmicky IMAX 3-D cinema or £6 on motion simulator rides? Among fans of actual learning, hopes are high for the debut of Information Age, a massive new wing examining the progression of communication that will open in September 2014.

Exhibition Rd., SW7. © **087/0870-4868**. www.sciencemuseum.org.uk. Free. Daily 10am–6pm. Tube: South Kensington.

V&A ★★★ MUSEUM   As a decorative arts repository, the Victoria & Albert is about eye candy. This means that although the museum occupies a haughty High Victorian edifice more suited to a courthouse or a capitol, it subjectively celebrates beauty and style. If it's good-looking, fabulous, or well designed, it'll be here.

The ground floor, a jumbled grid of rooms, has lots of good stuff, but lots more bric-a-brac (Korean pots, 1,000-year-old Egyptian jugs of rock crystal) that you'll probably walk past with polite but hasty appreciation. The second, third, and fourth levels have less space and therefore are more manageable.

The V&A, which, tellingly, was endowed by the proceeds from the first world's fair (the Great Exhibition of 1851), is very much about fine objects from everyday life, so letting things catch your eye is the point. Rooms are arranged by country of origin or by medium (ironwork, tapestries, and the like) but you'll want to see the **20th Century** (rooms 74, 76; level 3), which surprises by including objects you may have once kept in your home (a Dyson vacuum cleaner, mobile phones); the U.K.'s only permanent **Architecture** gallery (rooms 127–128a, level 4), for a nautilus-like preconstruction model of the Sydney Opera House; and endless slices of **medieval stained glass** (rooms 83–84, level 3) Wherever you go, if you see a drawer beneath a display case, open it, because many treasures are stored out of the light. More not to miss:

○ The seven **Raphael Cartoons** (room 48a), dating from 1515, are probably the most priceless items in the house. These giant paper paintings—yes, paper—were created by the hand of Raphael as templates for the weavers of his ten tapestries for the Sistine Chapel. Before Queen Victoria moved them here, they hung for around 175 years in the purpose-built Cartoon Gallery at Hampton Court Palace. The colors are fugitive, meaning they're fading: Christ's red robe, painted with plant-based madder lake, has turned white—his reflection in the water, painted with a different pigment, is still red.

The Spiritualist Association of Great Britain, which has catered to clairvoyants and mediums since 1872, owns a humdrum Victorian town house in tony Knightsbridge, where it holds workshops on the psychic arts. You can attend one of the hour-long "demonstrations," in which a medium stands at the front of the room and reports on the ghosts and psychic vibrations swirling around the few dozen members of the audience. You won't get quivering tables or milky crystal balls; in truth, the plain meeting area is about as spooky as the function room of a Midwestern Presbyterian church, and some guests will be relieved to know that most leaders acknowledge God during their sessions. I've had mediums pick me out of the crowd and tell me things no other person could know, but I've also been singled out to be told my father was an RAF pilot from the Midlands, which was patently ludicrous. Still, on almost every occasion, I have seen evenings here suddenly take an eerily heart-wrenching turn when some visitor became emotional about what the mediums plucked out of the ether—or *appeared* to. Demonstrations take place Mon–Sat at 3:30pm and Sunday at 5pm. Even if you're a skeptic, it's one of the most electrifying cheap nights out in town. The house is on the southeast side of the square; combine a visit with a drink at The Grenadier pub (p. 79) off the square's opposite side—an appropriate choice, since the pub is said to be haunted. *33 Belgrave Square, SW1.* ☏ **020/7931-6488.** *www.spiritualist association.org.uk. Demonstrations £4. Tube: Hyde Park Corner.*

○ None of the sculptures in the sky-lit **Cast Court** (rooms 46 and 46a) are original. They're casts of the greatest hits in Renaissance art, and they crowd the room like a yard sale. They were put here in 1873 for the poor, who could never hope to travel and see the real articles for themselves. Find Ghiberti's doors to the baptistery at Florence's San Giovanni, whose design kicked off the artistic frenzy of the Renaissance. Michelangelo's *David,* floppy puppy feet and all, looks down from his pedestal; he was fitted with a fig leaf for royal visits. Depressingly, many of these replicas are now in better shape than the originals.

○ Tipu Sultan of India hated imperialist Europeans. So in the 1790s he commissioned an automaton of a tiger devouring one. A crank on **Tippoo's Tiger** (room 41) activates a clockwork that makes the Englishman's hand flail and an organ makes his gaping mouth moan. In the end, Tipu was killed by Europeans and the English got his Tiger after all. It has been a crowd favorite since 1808, when it was part of the East India Company's trophy museum.

○ **The Great Bed of Ware** (room 57), a ten-by-11-foot four-poster of carved oak that dates to about 1590, was apparently once a tourist attraction at a country inn, renowned enough for Shakespeare to mention it in *Twelfth Night:* "big enough for the bed of Ware." As you admire it, consider that in those days, bed canopies were installed to protect sleepers from insects that might tumble out of their thatched roofs and into their mouths. Canopied beds, a mark of luxury today, were a sign of a humbler home. Nearby is James II's embroidered wedding suit (1673, room 56).

○ The **Ardabil carpet,** the world's oldest dated carpet (copies have appeared on the floors of 10 Downing Street and Hitler's Berlin office alike), is part of the Islamic

5

EXPLORING LONDON | Kensington & Knightsbridge

arts gallery. To preserve its dyes, the carpet is lit for just ten minutes at a time on every half-hour.

○ The **Hereford Screen** (1862, Ironworks balcony) is a liturgical riot by Gilbert Scott, the architect of the Renaissance St Pancras (p. 23). It took 38 conservators 13 months to restore the 8-ton choir screen to its full golden, brassy, painted, Gothic glory.

○ The **Gilbert Collection** (rooms 70–73) of impossibly fine decorative arts (jewel boxes, cameos, silver, fine mosaics) amassed by a rich enthusiast is so impressive it once had its own museum at Somerset House.

Planning ahead will pay off: Download a map and you'll save £1, and download its free app to anticipate what paid exhibitions you'll need to buy tickets for. The big one in 2013 was on David Bowie, and it sold out weeks in advance. Free 1-hour introductory tours are given at 10:30am, 12:30pm, 1:30pm, and 3:30pm, with one for the Medieval and Renaissance galleries at 11:30am and another for the British galleries at 2:30pm. Kids can borrow delightful "Back-Packs," which contain activity sets that engage them in some of the museum's most eye-catching holdings. More goodies for kids are list at www.vam.ac.uk/families and exhibited at the Museum of Childhood (p. 126). Make a side visit to the V&A's western exterior. Scarred during The Blitz, the stonework was left alone as a memorial. If the damage was this bad in Kensington, just imagine the scene in the Germans' main target, East London.

Cromwell Road, SW7. ✆ **020/7942-2000**. www.vam.ac.uk. Free. Daily 10am–5:45pm, Fri until 10pm. Tube: South Kensington.

Other Area Attractions

Albert Memorial ★ LANDMARK   Albert, Queen Victoria's German-born husband (and, um, first cousin), was a passionate supporter of the arts who piloted Britain from one dazzling creative triumph to another. But when he died suddenly of typhoid (some say Crohn's disease) in 1861 at age 42, the devastated Queen abruptly withdrew from the gaiety and remained in mourning until her death in 1901, shaping the Victorian mentality. She arranged for this astounding spire—part bombast, part elegy—to be erected in 1872 opposite the concert hall he spearheaded. Some of its nearly 200 figures represent the continents and the sciences, and some, higher up, represent angels and virtues. It's Victorian high-mindedness in stone. At the center, as if on an altar, is Albert himself, gleaming in gold. Tours of the interior go at 2 and 3pm on the first Sunday of each month, June to December (no reservations required; £6).

Kensington Gardens. Tube: South Kensington.

Wellington Arch ★ LANDMARK   When it was finished in 1830, it was intended as a triumphal entry to Buckingham Palace. Minor anecdotes of its relocation and the switch from Wellington's original statue on top to a smaller statue (*Peace descending upon War,* the largest bronze sculpture in Europe) are all this handsome landmark can muster in its little museum, which also discusses the period when the Arch served as a police station. If you buy a joint ticket with the Apsley House, across Piccadilly (see above), you'll save about £2.50; you can take an elevator up with the admission price.

Hyde Park Corner, Apsley Way, W1. ✆ **020/7930-2726**. www.english-heritage.org.uk. £4 adults, £2.4 children 5–15, £3.60 seniors/students; late Mar to early Nov Wed–Sun 10am–5pm, Nov–Mar Wed–Sun 10am–4pm. Tube: Hyde Park Corner.

MARYLEBONE & MAYFAIR

The Wallace Collection ★★★ MUSEUM   A little bit V&A (decorative arts and furniture), a little bit National Gallery (paintings and portraits), but with a boutique French flair, the Wallace celebrates fine living in an extravagant 19th-century city mansion, the former Hertford House. Rooms drip with chandeliers, clocks, suits of armor, and furniture, usually of royal provenance, and there's not a clunker among the paintings. While other museums were stocking up on Renaissance works, the Wallaces, visionaries of sorts, were buying 17th-century and 18th-century artists for cheap, and now its collection shines. You might recognize Jean-Honoré Fragonard's *The Swing* (Oval Drawing Room), showing a maiden kicking her slipper to her suitor below. Peter Paul Rubens' *The Rainbow Landscape* is also here (East Drawing Room), as is the world's most complete room of furniture belonging to Marie-Antoinette (Study; look for her initials hidden around a keyhole on one cabinet). Thomas Gainsborough's *Mrs. Robinson 'Perdita'* (West Room) depicts the sloe-eyed actress in mid-affair with the Prince of Wales; she holds a token of his love, a miniature portrait, in her right hand. If she exudes a suspicious mood, it's for good reason—the Prince dumped her before the paint was dry. Be in the Ground Floor State Rooms at the top of the hour, when a chorus of golden musical clocks announce midday direct from the 1700s. Kids should grab a free trail map, which leads them to the most attention-holding works. The Wallace Restaurant, in the covered courtyard, has an exemplary atmosphere but stupidly high prices, although its French-styled afternoon tea is a reasonable £15.

Hertford House, Manchester Square, W1. ℂ **020/7563-9500**. www.wallacecollection.org. Admission free. Daily 10am–5pm. Tube: Bond Street.

Royal Academy of Arts ★★ MUSEUM   Britain's first art school was founded in 1768 and relocated here to Burlington House, a Palladian-style mansion, in Victorian times. Only a few of its lushly restored 18th-century state rooms, the six John Madejski Fine Rooms, can be seen on tours, but what's displayed there is worth a half-hour: John Singer Sargents, Thomas Gainsboroughs, Stanley Spencers, and even Winston Churchills (the old bulldog was good at everything). The paintings change regularly, but they're always strong. Charles Darwin's *Origin of the Species* papers were delivered for the first time in the Reynolds Room on July 1, 1858; the space now displays 20th-century paintings. Beyond those, you'll pay £7 to £11 for whatever crowd-pleasing exhibition is on—about David Hockney, Australian art, always impeccably selected. The museum's biggest event is the annual **Summer Exhibition,** which since the late 1700s has displayed the best works, submitted anonymously; careers have been made by it. Its podcast series zeroes in on specific works at www.royalacademy.org.uk/podcasts.

Burlington House, Piccadilly, W1. ℂ **020/7300-8000**. www.royalacademy.org.uk. Free. Sat–Thurs 10am–6pm, Fri 10am–10pm, last admission 30 min. before closing. John Madejski Fine rooms by free tour only: Tues–Fri 1pm, Weds–Fri also at 3pm, Sat 11:30am. Tube: Piccadilly Circus or Green Park.

The Handel House Museum ★ MUSEUM/HISTORIC SITE   Here's a pleasant *Messiah* complex. This Mayfair building, the German-born composer's home from 1723 (he was its first tenant) to his death in 1759, has lived many lives—before the museum's 2001 opening, conservators chipped 28 layers of paint off the interior walls to uncover the original grey color. You'll see a 15-minute video on Handel's life, and then move on, often attended by old dears serving as volunteers, to see the few humble rooms. They're furnished with period furniture that wasn't his, but not many artifacts. There's a small alcove where kids can try on period costumes and grown-ups can listen to Handel's greatest works. You're best off coming during one of the house's many concerts, held every week or so in a plain recital room (£7–£10 depending on performance). Handel fans should also investigate the composer's collection at the Foundling Museum (p. 92), where he was a crucial patron.

25 Brook St., W1. ℂ **020/7495-1685**. www.handelhouse.org. £6 adults, £2 kids aged 5–16 except Sat–Sun (free), £5 seniors/students; Tues–Wed and Fri–Sat 10am–6pm, Thurs 10am–8pm, Sun noon–6pm; Tube: Bond Street.

Speakers' Corner ★ LANDMARK   Near the northeast corner of Hyde Park, where Edgware Road meets Bayswater Road, Londoners of yore congregated for public executions. By the early 1800s, the gathered crowds were jeering at hangings instead of cheering them, and the locale's reputation for public outcry became entrenched. An Act of Parliament in 1872 finally legitimized it as a place of free speech, and its tradition of well-intentioned protest has evolved into a quirky weekend attraction. Laborers and suffragettes fomented social change here, but these days, you're more likely to encounter a rogues' gallery of kooks and idealists. Anyone can show up, always on Sunday mornings after 7am, with a soapbox (or, these days, a stepladder), plus an axe to grind, and orate about anything from Muslim relations to the superiority of 1970s disco—but if they don't have the wit to appease the crowd, they stand a good chance of being jibed, or at the very least vigorously challenged. In true British style, most speakers refrain from profanity. Even the heckling is usually polite. ("Communists, violent racists, vegetarians," reported Arthur Frommer in 1957. "They undergo the finest heckling in the world, a vicious repartee…") While audience participation at this scholarly circus can be heated, it's usually based on facts rather than emotion—the American talk radio hosts are not models for success. The blather continues until late afternoon.

Tube: Marble Arch, exits 4, 5, 8, or 9.

THE SOUTH BANK, SOUTHWARK & BOROUGH

Imperial War Museum London ★★★ MUSEUM   One of London's unexpectedly great museums has plenty to do, and not just for military buffs. This is no gunfondling storehouse. Instead of merely showcasing implements of death, the IWM, the latest tenant of the commodious former mental hospital known as Bedlam, takes great care to help visitors understand the sensations, feelings, and moods of soldiers and civilians caught in past conflicts. In addition to giving visitors an easy-to-grasp background on major wars, the museum, intelligently balances tanks and planes with displays that connect you to the human experience. Highlights include The Trench Experience, a walk-through mock-up of a muddy fortification in Somme, 1916 (it was just renovated along with the World War I galleries); The Blitz Experience, a rousing recreation of an air raid shelter under aural assault; a comic kids' exhibition about spies themed to the popular *Horrible Histories* books; and an exceptionally thoughtful

Holocaust exhibition. It would be difficult to emerge from here without having learned or felt something. Beware: The facilities are undergoing a messy renovation that will cause considerable closures until summer 2014.

Lambeth Rd., SE1. ℭ **020/7416-5000**. www.iwm.org.uk. Free. Daily 10am–6pm; Tube: Lambeth North or Elephant & Castle.

London Eye ★★★ OBSERVATIONAL WHEEL   The Eye, once sponsored by British Airways but now stickered by EDF Energy, was erected in 1999 as the Millennium Wheel, and like many temporary vantage points, it became such a sensation—and a money-minter—that it was made permanent. It rises above everything in this part of the city—at 135m/443 ft. high, it's 1½ times taller than the Statue of Liberty. The 30-minute ride above the Thames affords an unmatched and unobstructed perspective on the prime tourist territory. On a clear day, you can see to Windsor, but even on an average day, the entire West End bows down before you. That's why you should either go as soon as you arrive in the city, to orient yourself, or (my choice), on your last day in town, when you can appreciate what you've seen. The whirl is adulterated by a lame "4D Experience" movie (the camera moves through London while a fan blows in your face—Orlandofied twaddle) but it's included in the price.

Each of the 32 enclosed capsules, which accommodate up to 28 people at once, is climate-controlled and rotates so gradually that it's easy to forget you're moving—which means it will upset only the desperately height-averse. By the time you reach the top, you'll have true 360-degree views unobstructed by the support frame. The ticket queue often looks positively wicked, but in fact, it moves quickly, chewing through 15,000 riders a day, 800 per revolution. The Shard (p. 116) is much higher (and £10 more), which is why you have a much better chance of appreciating what you're seeing aboard the Eye. *Tip:* Booking on the Web saves waiting in the ticketing queues, and it gives other advantages: You can pick your time ahead and you'll save 10 percent off the price listed above. There's a host of ticket options—basically, you can pay more to go anytime you want rather than stick to a reservation, but a standard ticket satisfies your needs.

Riverside Building, County Hall, SE1. ℭ **0871/781-3000**. www.londoneye.com. £19.20 adults, £12.30 children 4–15, free under 5, £15.30 seniors, Family of two adults and two kids £63, save 10% online; Jan–March and Sept–Dec. 10am–8:30pm, April–June 10am–9pm, July–August 10am–9:30pm; Tube: Waterloo or Westminster.

The Old Operating Theatre Museum & Herb Garret ★★ MUSEUM   In the mid-1800s, before general anesthesia, St. Thomas' Hospital used the attic of a neighboring church for a space in which surgeries, mostly amputations and other quick-hit procedures, could be conducted where students could watch but other patients couldn't hear the agonized screams. When the hospital moved in 1862, it was abandoned, sealed away, and forgotten. It was considered lost until 1956, when an enterprising historian thought to look in the attic, and he found the secret surgical stadium behind a wall. Creep up the wooden spiral staircase once used by the bell-ringer and you'll find the theatre, now the centerpiece of a ghoulish, but carefully educational, museum delving into medical methods of the early 1800s, from herbal remedies to leeches. On a recent visit, a 7-year-old boy in a visiting school group nearly passed out during a mock bloodletting show-and-tell; the staff, accustomed to fainters, casually produced a pillow and a glass of water and without halting the demonstration, proving that in the old days, medicine was less about science and more about soldiering on.

9a St. Thomas St., SE1. ℭ **020/7188-2679**. www.thegarret.org.uk. £6.20 adults, £3.50 children under 16, £5 seniors/students. Daily 10:30am–5pm, closed Dec 15–Jan 5. Tube: London Bridge.

Shakespeare's Globe ★ MUSEUM/LANDMARK   A painstaking recreation of an outdoor Elizabethan theater, it tends to bewitch fans of history and theater, but it can put all others to sleep. Arrive early in the day, since the timed 40-minute tours fill up. Get a bad time, and you'll be stuck waiting for far too long in the UnderGlobe, the well-crafted but exhaustible exhibition about Elizabethan theater. Also avoid matinee days, since tours don't run during performances. The open-air theater was made using only Elizabethan technology such as saws, oak framing, pegs, and plaster panels mixed with goat's hair (the original recipe called for cow's hair, but the breed they needed is now extinct). The first Globe burned down, aged just 14, when a cannon fired during a performance caused its thatched roof to catch fire. It took a special act of Parliament, plus plenty of hidden sprinkler systems, to permit the construction of this, the first thatched roof in London since the Great Fire. The original theater was the same size (and stood 180m/591 ft. to the southeast), but it crammed 3,000 luckless souls. Today, just 1,600 are admitted for performances. If you'd like to see location of the Rose Theatre, a true Shakespeare original, go around the corner to 56 Park Street, where its foundations, discovered in 1989 and now squatted over by a modern office building, are open for visitors on Saturdays from 10am to 5pm. There's a video on how it was discovered and it also hosts regular performances. (ℭ020/7261-9565. www.rose theatre.org.uk, free.)

21 New Globe Walk, SE1. ℭ **020/7401-9919**. www.shakespearesglobe.com. £13.50 adults, £8 children 5–15, £12 seniors, £11 students. Daily early Oct to Apr 9:30am–5pm, late April to early Oct 9am–5pm. Tube: London Bridge.

Southwark Cathedral ★ HISTORIC SITE   Pick up an antique panoramic map of London and look next to old London Bridge on the southern bank. See that church with the square Early English tower? The one flying a pinnacle, and tending to the destitute river men? It still stands. Called St. Saviour's until its elevation to an Anglican cathedral in 1905, the retro-choir, choir, and choir-aisles, dating to the 1200s, constitute the earliest surviving Gothic building in London, but the roof and nave were rebuilt in the mid-1800s. Its Refectory is a cheap place for lunch, and there's even an excavated swath of an old Roman road you can view. It's included in the walking tour on p. 193.

London Bridge, SE1. ℭ **020/7367-6700**. http://cathedral.southwark.anglican.org. Free but £4 donation suggested. Mon–Fri 8am–6pm, Sat–Sun 9am–6pm. Tube: London Bridge.

Tate Modern ★★★ MUSEUM   In 2000, Bankside's chief eyesore, a goliath power station—steely and cavernous, a cathedral to soulless industry—was ingeniously converted into the national contemporary art collection and is now as integral to London as the Quire of Westminster Abbey or the Dome of St. Paul's, with 5.3 million annual visitors, making it Britain's number-two attraction. The mammoth Turbine Hall, cleared of machinery to form a meadowlike expanse of concrete, hosts works created by major-league artists (its Unilever Series app chronicles them in high-resolution glory), and people of every background frolic there as if it were a park. This building is a star.

The flow through the galleries, stacked from floors two to six on the river side of the building, is natural. Holdings focus on art made since 1900 and are divided into four loose areas of thought: On Level 2, there's Poetry and Dream (about surrealism) plus a changing exhibition (usually £10); on Level 3, you'll see Transformed Visions (post-war works) and another paid exhibition; on Level 4, Structure and Clarity (abstract art) and Energy and Process (arte povera, a radical movement). The top floor is the café.

The formidable collection, one of the world's best for breadth, is always shifting, not just because the museum owns more than it can display (even in this hangar), but also because works shuffle around on short-term loans. You could visit once a year and see new stuff each time. Some heavy hitters never leave. My favorite: In room 6 of Transformed Visions, the monotonal series created by Mark Rothko for New York City's Four Seasons restaurant never fails to put visitors in a meditative mood. The Tate website is updated with what's on display either here or in the Tate Britain down the river, which is helpful considering the facilities will be in continuous upheaval until 2016, when a 10-story southern expansion is completed.

Some may argue that the selection suffers from over-representation of establishment works and a dearth of truly challenging stuff, but the conservative selection is approachable for most people. True, the descriptions too often dwell on the incestuous art world culture, something the Tate tries to ameliorate with its "Modern Art Terms" glossary smartphone app, but fortunately, the daring of the pieces speak louder than the curators' self-satisfied descriptions.

The Tate's exceptional array of touring aids can make sense of oddity. For £4, rent a tremendous multimedia tour of the highlights on a smartphonelike video device that embellishes on the works' meaning and context. There are four free daily guided tours, usually at 11am, noon, 2pm, and 3pm; ask at the ground floor information desk to find out where they meet. At the family desk open on weekends and busy days, kids can pick up free art-related activities, such as a drawing kit or a tour based on sounds. The gift shop, on the bottom floor by the West entrance, is tops anywhere.

The sit-down Tate Modern Restaurant on Level 6 can be inhospitable due to crowds (make a reservation: ℭ 020/7401-5014)—but its panorama of St. Paul's and the Thames is indelible. Afternoon tea is just £15, and the fish and chips platter with mushy peas has my approval for flavor if not price (£16). You can get the same dish for £4 less in the cafe on the second floor, but without that stirring view. At lunch, kids under 12 eat free if a grown-up buys a main course.

Bankside, SE1. ℭ **020/7887-8888**. www.tate.org.uk/modern. Free admission; Sun–Thurs 10am–6pm, Fri–Sat 10am–10pm. Tube: Southwark.

View from the Shard ★ OBSERVATION DECK   In 2013, the newly opened Shard, the tallest building in Europe (but not even in the top 50 worldwide), added an extremely expensive observation deck with timed tickets. The jagged 306m/1,016 ft.-tall tower doesn't exactly fit in with its neighbors, and it doesn't want to; signs works hard to incessantly remind you how big it is. Even the souvenirs it sells depict the Shard as an enormous spire amongst teeny versions of London landmarks, starting with its primary competition, the Eye. Everyone agrees it's the biggest new erection in town, so why the Napoleon complex? Even its prices have to be tackier: souvenir photos cost £22. After two ear-popping fast lift rides, you emerge 244m/800 ft. up to some weird angel-like synth music and vertiginous floor-to-ceiling windows far, far over the city—so far that after the initial impression, the casual visitor isn't likely to pick out most of what they're seeing. A few levels up (you have to hoist yourself up stairs for the last three floors), there's a second, half-outdoor level, shielded at body-level from the elements. There is no seating (although staff will fetch a folding chair if you need one), no restaurant, and no washrooms, but if you can brave the aerial deprivation, you can spend as much time as you want. There is one novel addition: Point a "digital telescope" in the distance, and attached screen reveals the same view at different times of day. Of course, the screens also go out of their way to diss rival buildings, pointing out that St George's wharf to the west "has twice won the accolade of 'Worst Building in the World.'" The unblinking truth is that the Eye is more connected to its surroundings and a more original observational experience.

Joiner St., SE1. ℭ **0844/499-7111**. www.theviewfromtheshard.com. Adults £30, kids 4–15 £19, £5 discount booked 24 hr. ahead. Sun–Weds 10am–7pm, Thurs–Sat 10am–10pm. Tube: London Bridge.

Other Area Attractions

Brunel Museum ★ MUSEUM/HISTORIC SITE   Although the engineering contributions of Marc Brunel and his son Isambard Kingdom Brunel are largely taken for granted, here they're given their due. With the help of a shield system they invented, these pioneers executed the first tunnel to be built under a navigable river, but London's soft earth didn't make it easy. It took from 1825 to 1843, and this red-brick building marked by a chimney, was where steam engines pumped the seeping water out as diggers toiled. The tunnel, lined with arches and Doric capitals, was a commercial flop that deteriorated into a subterranean red-light district. But it later found new purpose as a part of the Overground Line and new respect through this museum, which often creates special events to bring guests into the tunnel. One regular opportunity London Walks' £9 "Bermondsey to Brunel Museum" tour Tuesdays at 6:15pm, which ends at the museum; it stays open until 9:30pm that night for the walkers.

Railway Ave., SE16. ✆ **020/7231-3840**. www.brunel-museum.org.uk. £3 adults, £1.50 children/seniors/students. Daily 10am–5pm. Tube: Rotherhithe.

The Design Museum ★ MUSEUM   Just east of the Tower Bridge on the southern bank of the Thames, you'll find strictly contemporary top-drawer talent—the cool kids of current style. To me, that makes it more of a gallery than a museum. The steep fee also means it's best for devotees of high design, not for average sightseers. Shows are puffed-up explorations of random topics (race cars, the creation of everyday objects, fashion celeb Paul Smith), but if they're sometimes ostentatious, at least they're thought-provoking. Each spring, the museum hosts its prestigious Designs of the Year competition, and mounts mini-shows by each nominee. The gift shop stocks some strange oddities such as artist-conceived housewares, dolls, and office supplies. A free iPad app previews 59 of the best objects. In 2015, superstar architect Zaha Hadid, one of those design cool kids, takes over this building and the museum will relocate to Kensington.

Shad Thames, SE1. ✆ **020/7940-8783**. www.designmuseum.org. £10.85 adults, free for children under 12, £9.70 seniors, £6.50 students. Daily 10am–5:45pm, until 6:45pm in July and Aug, last admission 5:15pm. Tube: London Bridge or Tower Hill.

The Golden Hinde ★ MUSEUM   Tucked into one of the few remaining slips that enabled ships to unload in Southwark (another is Hay's Galleria, downstream by the HMS *Belfast,* now converted to a boutique shopping area), is a 1:1 replica of Sir Francis Drake's square rigged Tudor galleon, which circumnavigated the world from 1577 to 80. This 1973 version, which is so tiny you will forever feel pity for those old explorers, made its own circumnavigation in 1980. Self-guided and guided tours are available daily, but it also hosts broadly comic Pirate Fun Days and Tudor Fun Days (£7 adults, £5 children) for kids as well as sleepovers (£43, March to October) during which the little ones can dress in period clothes, hear tales from costumed actors, and help with shipboard tasks on an imaginary voyage.

Pickfords Wharf, Clink St., SE1. ✆ **020/7403-0123**. www.goldenhinde.com. £6 adults, £4.50 children/seniors/students. Daily 10am–5pm. Tube: London Bridge.

HMS Belfast ★ MUSEUM   You'll feel as if the powerful 1938 warship, upon being retired from service in 1965, was simply motored to the dock and instantly opened as an attraction. Nearly everything, down to the grey-and-red checked flooring and decaying cables, is exactly as it was (although those mannequins with the bad toupees might have been added), making the boat a fascinating snapshot of mid-century maritime technology. The authenticity also makes it a devil to navigate, especially if you have any bags with you—sorry, no cloakrooms, sailor. Getting around her various decks, engine rooms, and hatches requires dexterity and a well-calibrated inner compass. You can roam as you wish, visiting every cubby of the ship from kitchen to bridge, all the while being thankful that it wasn't you who was chasing German cruisers (the *Belfast* sank the *Scharnhorst*) and backing up the D-Day invasion in this tough tin can. The price is too high for those with a lukewarm interest, but the new Upper Deck bar, atop the visitor center (a wine bar over a warship—appropriate?), has stellar views of the Tower of London and Tower Bridge—and an afternoon Prosecco cream tea that costs just £9. Thanks, World War Two!

Morgan's Lane, Tooley St., SE1. © **020/7940-6300**. www.iwm.org.uk. £13.15 adults, free for children under 16, £10.55 seniors/students, posted prices are higher and include a "voluntary donation"; Mar–Oct daily 10am–6pm, Nov–Feb daily 10am–5pm, last admission 1 hr. before closing. Tube: London Bridge.

The Hayward Gallery ★ MUSEUM The principal exhibition space of the Southbank Centre, a non-profit arts center, hosts some terrific blockbuster shows, usually about £10, which have included Ansel Adams, Roy Lichtenstein, 1920s Surrealism, and a 60-artist panorama of modern African art. Some smaller exhibitions (too bad you missed the coral reef rendered in crochet) are free, and so are frequent music events at its cafe/bar, the Concrete. There are major plans to overhaul the space—but no one can agree into just what. For now, don't miss the Undercroft, a neglected concrete space under the building along the Thames, which, for years, skateboarders have turned into a landmark in their sport. Naturally, the Southbank Centre's artistic director, Jude Kelly, wants to evict them so she can charge someone rent.

South Bank Centre, Belvedere Rd., SE1. © **087/1663-2501**. www.southbankcentre.org.uk. Daily 10am–6pm, until 8pm Thurs & Fri. Tube: Waterloo.

THE CITY

Museum of London ★★★ MUSEUM The tale of London is the tale of the Western world, so this repository's miraculous cache of rarities from everyday life wouldn't be out of place in the greatest national museums of any land. But here, they're cataloged in a place that most tourists, judging by the name, might assume will be lame. Well, it's not. This huge storehouse, smartly presented, contains so many forehead-smackingly rare items that by the time you're two-thirds through it, you'll start to lose track of all the goodies you've seen. When it comes to the history of this patch we call London, no stone has been left unturned—literally—because exhibits start with local archaeological finds (including elephant vertebrae and a lion skull) before continuing to 3,500-year-old spearheads and swords found in the muck of the Thames. Voices from the past come alive again in chronological order: There's a 1st-century oak ladder that was discovered preserved in a well, Norman chain mail, loaded gambling dice made of bone in the 1400s, a leather bucket used in vain to fight the Great Fire of 1666, a walk-in wooden prison cell from 1750, Selfridge's original bronze Art Deco lifts, and far, far more. The biggest drawback is that you need to budget a few hours, otherwise you'll end up in a mad rush through the entire lower floor covering the Great Fire to now—and it'd be such a shame to miss Tom Daley's tiny Stella McCartney swim trunks from the Olympics. You also don't want to miss the Victorian Walk, a kid-friendly re-creation of city streets, shops and all, from the 1800s (grab a card at its entrance to know what you're seeing). You also can't miss the Lord Mayor's state coach, carved in 1757, which garages here all year awaiting its annual airing at the Lord Mayor's Show in November. The museum, which overlooks a Roman wall fragment outside, is easy to combine with a visit to St. Paul's, and sells one of the best selections of books on city history. It also runs an excellent second

City & Southbank Attractions

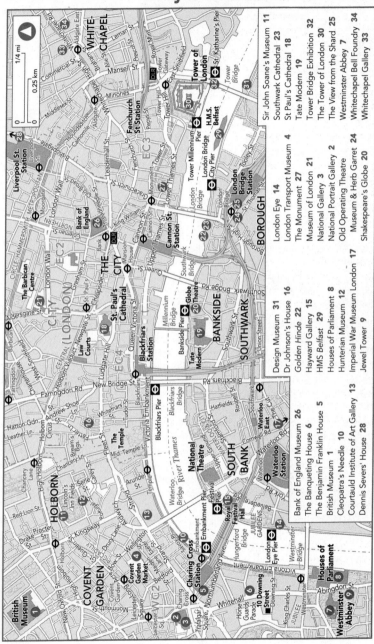

Bank of England Museum 26
The Banqueting House 6
The Benjamin Franklin House 5
British Museum 1
Cleopatra's Needle 10
Courtauld Institute of Art Gallery 13
Dennis Severs' House 28

Design Museum 31
Dr Johnson's House 22
Golden Hinde 22
Hayward Gallery 15
HMS Belfast 29
Houses of Parliament 8
Hunterian Museum 12
Imperial War Museum London 17
Jewel Tower 9

London Eye 14
London Transport Museum 4
The Monument 27
Museum of London 21
National Gallery 3
National Portrait Gallery 2
Old Operating Theatre
Museum & Herb Garret 24
Shakespeare's Globe 20

Sir John Soane's Museum 11
Southwark Cathedral 23
St Paul's Cathedral 18
Tate Modern 19
Tower Bridge Exhibition 32
The Tower of London 30
The View from the Shard 25
Westminster Abbey 7
Whitechapel Bell Foundry 34
Whitechapel Gallery 33

A Poignant Pocket Park

Little-known **Postman's Park** is beloved by those lucky enough to have stumbled across it. Hemmed in between buildings, its central feature is the moving **Watts Memorial,** a collection of plaques dedicated to ordinary people who died in acts of "heroic self sacrifice." Have a seat on a bench and ponder John Clinton, 10, "who was drowned near London Bridge in trying to save a companion younger than himself" in July 1894. In 1893, William Freer Lucas tantalizingly "risked poison for himself rather than lessen any chance of saving a child's life and died." The commemorations ceased in Edwardian times, making these forgotten faces seem forgotten once again. Playwright Patrick Marber gave new life to at least one of the fallen; a character in his film *Closer* took her name from Alice Ayres, who in 1885 saved three children from a burning house "at the cost of her own young life." On the silver screen, Alice got to sleep with Jude Law. *West side of St. Martin's-Le-Grand between St. Paul's Cathedral and the Barbican Centre; open 8am–dusk; Tube: St. Paul's or Barbican.*

museum in East London about Docklands (p. 127). Download its superlative (and free) Streetmuseum app, which serves you archival images and historic facts based on wherever you're standing in London.

150 London Wall, EC2. © **020/7001-9844**. www.museumoflondon.org.uk. Free. Daily 10am–6pm. Tube: Barbican or St. Paul's.

St. Paul's Cathedral ★★★ HISTORIC SITE   The old St. Paul's, with its magnificent spire, stood on this site for 600 years before it was claimed by 1666's Great Fire. It was so beloved that when Sir Christopher Wren was commissioned to rebuild London's greatest house of worship, he tried to outdo the original, devoting 40 years to the project and going one further by crowning it with a mighty dome—highly unusual for the time. My, how people talked.

St. Paul's cost £750,000 to build, an astronomical sum in 1697 when the first section opened for worship, and now, it costs £3 million a year to run. Wren overspent so badly that decoration was curtailed; the mosaics weren't added until Queen Victoria thought the place needed spiffing up. Stained glass is still missing, which allows the sweep and arch of Wren's design to shine cleanly through. Many foreigners were introduced to the sanctuary during the wedding of Prince Charles and Lady Diana Spencer in 1981, but the cathedral also saw a sermon by Martin Luther King in 1964 and Churchill's funeral the following year.

The **High Altar** has a canopy supported by single tree trunks that were hollowed out and carved, and its 15th-century crucifix and candlesticks require two men to lift. (They're nailed down, anyway. As one docent, a half-century veteran of Cathedral tours, lamented, "You'd be surprised what people try to steal.") Behind it is the **American Memorial Chapel** to the 28,000 American soldiers who died while based in England in Word War II. In a glass case, one leaf of a 500-page book containing their names is turned each day. The **organ**, with 7,000 pipes, was regularly played by Mendelssohn and Handel, and the lectern is original. The **Great West Doors,** largely unused, are 27m high (90 ft.) and on their original hinges; they're so well-hung that even a weakling can swing them open. In 2005, the Cathedral completed a £10.8-million cleaning program; a stone panel beside the doors was left filthy to show just how bad things were.

Eight central pillars here support the entire weight of the wood-frame Dome; Wren filled them with loose rubble. In 1925, engineers broke them open to find the debris had settled to the bottom, and they filled them again with liquid concrete. If you're fit, you can mount the 259 steps (each an awkward 13cm/5 in. tall, with benches on many landings) to the **Whispering Gallery,** 30m/98 ft. above the floor. Famously, its acoustics are so fine you can turn your head and mutter something that can be understood on the opposite side. That's in theory; so many tourists are usually blabbing to each other that you won't hear a thing, although it is a transcendent place to listen to choir rehearsal on a mid-afternoon. Climb higher (you've gone 378 steps now) to the **Stone Gallery,** an outdoor terrace just beneath the Dome, and catch your breath, if you choose, for the final 152-step push to the **Golden Gallery,** which requires you to scale the inner skin of the Dome, past ancient oriel windows and along tight metal stairs. It's safe, but it's not for those with vertigo or claustrophobia. The spectacular 360-degree city view from the top (85m/279 ft. up), at the base of the Ball and Lantern (you can't go up farther), is so beautiful that it defies full appreciation. For more than 250 years, this was the tallest structure in London, and therefore the top of the world.

If you miss the **Crypt,** you'll have missed a lot. In addition to memorials to the famous dead (such as Florence Nightingale and plenty of obscure war heroes), you'll find the tombs of two of Britain's greatest military demigods: **Admiral Horatio Nelson** (whose body was preserved for the trip from the battlefield by soaking in brandy and wine; the 72,000-ton weight of the Dome is borne by the walls of this small chamber), and **Arthur Duke of Wellington** (flanked by flags captured on the field of battle; they will hang there until they disintegrate). To the right of the OBE Chapel, in **Artists Corner,** there's a monument to poet **John Donne** that still bears the scorch marks it suffered in Old St. Paul's during the Great Fire (they're on its urn, and it was the only thing that survived the conflagration), and you'll find the graves of the artists **J. M. W. Turner** and **Henry Moore,** plus **Christopher Wren** himself, who rests beneath his masterpiece. "I build for eternity," he once said, and so far, so good: In 2010, the cathedral celebrated 300 years since its completion. If you're hungry, scope out the cafe, since it's one of the cheaper options in this neighborhood.

Keep a Church but Lose the City

Most people are familiar with the famous 1940 photograph of the **Dome,** lit purely by firelight during the Blitz, which has come to symbolize London's fortitude during Word War II. What most people don't know is that St. Paul's was hit, many times—a bomb blasted the floor of the North Transept (photos of the devastation are in the Crypt), and another obliterated the east end. So many people were assigned to stamp out incendiary bombs before they could melt through the Cathedral's lead-lined roof that huge areas of The City were left unmanned—much of London was lost so that St. Paul's could be saved, a bittersweet fact.

Tours by volunteers, called "supers," leave at 10 and 11am, 1 and 2pm. Listen closely, because they are the elder statesmen; many have been here for decades. Lest you forgot it's actually a cathedral, you can also worship here outside of sightseeing hours—for free.

St. Paul's Churchyard, EC4. ✆ **020/7246-8357**. www.stpauls.co.uk. £16 adults, £7 children 7–16, free children under 6, £14 seniors/students, including guide and audio tour, up to £1,50 cheaper online. Mon–Sat 8:30am–4:30pm, open for worship only on Sun, Whispering Gallery and Dome cleared and last admission at 4pm. Tube: St. Paul's.

Tower Bridge Exhibition ★★ LANDMARK   In the late 1800s, there was no bolder display of a country's technological prowess than a spectacular bridge. Consider The Brooklyn Bridge or the Firth of Forth Bridge. This celebrates one such triumph. The museum is like two attractions in one. The first satisfies sightseers who have dreamed of going up in the famous neo-Gothic towers and crossing the high-level observation walkways. For them, it's a close encounter with a world icon. The second aspect delves into the steam-driven machinery that so impressed the world in 1894, and that will hook the mechanically inclined. The original bascule-raising equipment, representing the largest use of hydraulic power at the time, remains in fine condition despite being retired in favor of electricity in 1976. The raising of the spans is now controlled by joystick from a cabin across the road from the entrance (check "Bridge Lift Times" on the website to find out when). How could such a proud monument survive the Blitz when everything around it got flattened? The Luftwaffe needed it as a visual landmark. It discounts tickets with entry to the Monument (for both: £9 adults, £4 kids 5-15, £6.20 seniors/students). Its app is just a silly photo puzzle, but it does provide a £2-off voucher for its gift shop.

Tower Bridge, on the side closest to the Tower of London, SE1. ✆ **020/7403-3761**. www.tower bridge.org.uk. £8 adults, £3.50 children 5–15, £5.60 seniors/students. Apr–Sept daily 10am–6pm, Oct–Mar daily 9:30am–5:30pm, last admission 30 min. before closing. Tube: Tower Hill or Tower Gateway DLR.

The Tower of London ★★★ MUSEUM/HISTORIC SITE   Every morning at 9am a military guard escorts the keys to the Tower and the its huge wooden doors yawn open again for outsiders. It's the most famous castle in the world, a UNESCO World Heritage Site, and a symbol of not just London, but also of a millennium of English history. Less a tower than a fortified minitown of stone and timber, its history could fill this book. Suffice it to say that its oldest building, the four-cornered White Tower, went up in 1078 and the compound that grew around it has served as a palace, prison, treasury, mint, armory, zoo, and now, a lovingly maintained tourist attraction that no visitor should neglect. It's at the very heart of English history, and exploring its sprawl should take between 3 and 5 hours.

Tickets are sold outside the battlements. Hit the Welcome Centre, just past the Ticket Office, and grab a copy of the free "Daily Programme," which runs down the times and places of all the free talks, temporary exhibitions, and miniperformances. Plenty are offered—the Tower at times feels more like a theme park than a living museum with 1,000 years of history behind it. The prime excursion is the **Yeoman Warder's Tour,** led with theatrical aplomb by one of the Beefeaters who live in the Tower (there are about 100 residents, including families, but only one Beefeater, Moira Cameron, is female) and preserve it. Those leave every 30 minutes from just inside the portcullis in the Middle Tower. They're engaging, but juvenile—expect bellowing and histrionics, each recites an identical script with a gleeful fetish for yarns about beheadings and torture. (In truth, you can count the people executed inside the Tower on your fingers and toes; it was considered an honor to be killed here, since it was private.) For reasons I'm about to explain, I suggest you double back and join the tour later in the day. If you'd like your history delivered without vaudevillian shenanigans, head to the gift shop on the right after Middle Tower and grab an audio tour (£3.50, but do it early; headsets run out). The official guidebooks (£5) here are pretty good, and they certainly help with orientation.

The key to touring the Tower is to arrive close to opening. At 9am, there's a short ceremony (see p. 139) during which guards unlock the gates for the day. Make a beeline for the two star attractions since intimidating queues form by lunch: the Crown Jewels, in the Waterloo Block at the north wall (farthest from the Thames) and the White Tower, in the center.

As you enter the **Crown Jewels** exhibition, you'll see archival film of the last time most of the jewels were officially used, at the coronation of Queen Elizabeth in 1952. After passing into a vault, visitors glide via people-movers past cases of glittering, downlit crowns, scepters, and orbs worn (awkwardly—they're 2.3kg/5 lb. each) by generations of British monarchs. Check out the legendary 105-carat Koh-I-Noor diamond, once the largest in the world, which is fixed to the temple of the **Queen Mother's Crown** (1937), along with 2,000 other diamonds; the Indian government has been begging to get the stone back. The 530-carat Cullinan I, the world's largest cut diamond, tops the Sovereign's **Sceptre with the Cross** (1661). The **Imperial State Crown,** ringed with emeralds, sapphires, and diamonds aplenty, is the one used in the annual State Opening of Parliament. After those come candlesticks that could support the roof of your house, trumpets, swords, and the inevitable traffic jam around the **Grand Punch Bowl** (1829), an elaborate riot of lions, cherubs, and unicorns that shows what it would look like if punch bowls could go insane. Because Oliver Cromwell liquidated every royal artifact he could get his hands on, everything dates to after the Restoration (the 1660s or later). Clearly, the monarchy has more than made up for the loss.

Touring the four levels of the cavernous **White Tower** requires much stair-climbing but takes in a wide span of history, including a fine stone chapel, Norman-era fireplaces and toilets, the gleaming **Line of Kings** collection of the Royal Armoury (even small children can't help but notice the exaggerated codpiece of King Henry VIII's intricately etched suit from 1540), and some models depicting the Tower's evolution

The Ravens, Forevermore

Ravens probably first visited the Tower in the 1200s to feast on the dripping corpses of the executed, who were taken from Tower Hill (the public execution ground, near the present-day Tube stop) and hung outside the battlements as a warning. You've probably heard the modern legend that if the ravens ever leave the Tower, England will fall—so seven of the carnivorous birds are kept in cages north of Wakefield Tower, where they are fed raw meat, blood-soaked cookies, and the occasional finger from a tourist dumb enough to stick their hands between the bars.

(it's been much altered, but the six smallest arched windows on the White Tower's south side are original to the 11th century). After you're finished in here, you'll have an excellent overview of how the whole complex worked.

Once you've got those two areas under your belt, take your time exploring the rest. I suggest a stop in the brick **Beauchamp Tower** (pronounced "BEECH-um," 1280), where important political prisoners were held and where you can still glimpse graffiti testifying to their suffering. In front of it on Tower Green is the circular glass memorial designating the **Scaffold Site,** where the unlucky few (including sitting queens Anne Boleyn and Lady Jane Grey) are said to have lost their heads. In reality, we don't know exactly where they were killed, but Queen Victoria wanted a commemorative site set, and because of the obvious dangers of displeasing the queen, this spot was chosen.

The **St. Thomas's Tower,** from the 13th century, is closest to the Thames and re-creates King Edward's bedchamber with authentic materials. Beneath it, **Traitor's Gate,** once called Water Gate, originally was used to ferry prisoners in secret from the Thames. Torture was never a part of English law, but it happened here anyway, and the **Bloody Tower** was where some of the worst stuff went down. Don't forget to climb the ramparts for that classic photo of the Tower Bridge. But save the extra quid and skip the Royal Fusiliers Regimental Museum, a dreary hodgepodge of military memorabilia.

Daily at 2:50pm, the guards parade outside the Waterloo Block to the Byward Tower. On Sundays, your admission ticket allows you to attend services at the **Chapel Royal of St. Peter ad Vincula,** the Tower's church, at 9:15 or 11am; otherwise, the only way to get in, and to see the marble slab beneath which Boleyn and Grey's decapitated bodies were entombed, is with a Yeoman Warder's Tour.

Tower Hill, EC3. ✆ **084/4482-7777**. www.hrp.org.uk. £19.50 adults, £9.75 children 5–15, £16.50 students/seniors, £52 family of up to 5, posted prices are higher and include a "voluntary donation". Nov–Feb Tues–Sat 9am–4:30pm and Sun–Mon 10am–4:30pm, Mar–Oct Tues–Sat 9am–5:30pm and Sun–Mon 10am–5:30pm, last admission 1 hr. before closing. Tube: Tower Hill or Tower Gateway DLR.

Other Area Attractions

Bank of England Museum ★ MUSEUM   The intermittently compelling tale of the B of E is recounted in appealingly patronizing but generous detail, accompanied by plenty of antiques from the vaults. That's fine if you understand finance, but most people lose the plot pretty quickly. Along the way are some fun oddities, including a million-pound note, printed in the early 19th century for internal accounting, and reimbursement claims from families of *Titanic* victims. There's lots of expensive swag, such as a primitive safe from 1700, heaps of silver treasures, and a gold bar so pure (1 part in 10,000 impure) that it was given to Queen Elizabeth as a coronation gift. Guess she didn't need it. It's also fun to watch Her Majesty age on the money over the years. The most popular exhibit is probably a 28-lb. standard gold bar encased in a clear plastic box, that you're challenged to lift. The rest of the Bank isn't open, but you can peek inside with the free Bank of England Virtual Tour app.

Threadneedle St., EC2. ✆ **020/7601-5545**. www.bankofengland.co.uk/museum; free. Mon–Fri 10am–5pm. Tube: Bank.

Dr. Johnson's House ★ MUSEUM/HISTORIC SITE   A rare surviving middle-class home from the 18th century (built in 1700), this slouching and brick-faced abode happens to be that of the famous lexicographer Samuel. He lived here from 1748 to

1759. If you're hoping to learn a lot about him, you'll have to spring for a book in the gift shop. Little substance is provided in the house itself, which fortunately merits some mild interest on its own terms (the corkscrew latch on the front door, which prevented lock-picking from above, is an example). The rooftop garret in which Johnson and his six helpers toiled to publish the first comprehensive English dictionary was burned out in the Blitz, ironically, by a barrel of burning ink which flew out of a bombed warehouse; you can still see some scorch marks on the ceiling timbers. Ink defined the house and nearly destroyed it, but it also saved it, because the printers who used it in the intervening years boarded up the walls, preserving them. While you're here, pop round the corner to the wonderful Ye Olde Cheshire Cheese pub (p. 81). Dr. Johnson sure liked to.

17 Gough Square, EC4. (C) **020/7353-3745**. www.drjohnsonshouse.org. £4.50 adults, £1.50 children, £3.50 seniors/students. May–Sept Mon–Sat 11am–5:30pm, Oct–Apr Mon–Sat 11am–5pm. Tube: Blackfriars.

The Monument ★ LANDMARK   Back in 1677, it was the tallest thing (61m/200 ft.) in town and it made people gasp. Today, it's easy to miss. The Monument was erected to commemorate the destruction of the city by the Great Fire in 1666. Its 61m (202 ft.) height is also the distance from its base to the site of Thomas Farynor's bakery in Pudding Lane to the east, where the conflagration began. There's only one thing to do in this fluted column of Portland stone: Climb it. The spiral staircase of 15cm (6-in.) steps, which has no landings, gradually narrows as it ascends to the outdoor observation platform—a popular suicide spot until 1842, when a cage was installed. They'll tell you it's 311 steps to the top, but they're lying. It's 313 if you count the two before the box office. (Sissies can watch live pictures of the view from the base.) Go on a pleasant day unless you'd like a good wind whipping. Check out the metal band snaking down the north side; it's a lightning rod, and it crosses along an inscription, in Latin, that blamed Catholics for starting the fire (the insult was chiseled off in 1831). It discounts tickets in package deals with the Tower Bridge Exhibition (for both: £9 adults, £4 kids 5-15, £6.20 seniors/students).

Monument St. at Fish St. Hill, WC4. (C) **020/3627-2552**. www.themonument.info. £3 adults, £1.50 children. Daily 9:30am–5:30pm. Tube: Monument or Bank.

EAST LONDON & DOCKLANDS

The part of London east of the City encompasses many square miles and dozens of separate neighborhoods, but most visitors will only hear it referred to broadly as "East London." Docklands, the rehabbed area bordering the river, is rich in upscale condos and corporate offices. Greenwich is a gorgeous townlike neighborhood on the southern bank of the Thames. And in Stratford, the biggest population center of East London, the Queen Elizabeth Olympic Park is undergoing an intense overhaul. Some of its arenas and buildings are being retooled for use by schools and sporting teams, and others have been put online as concert venues, but in general, the district won't be ready for tourist visits until the middle of 2014. When it is, the sculptural ArcelorMittal Orbit observation tower will become a draw.

Dennis Severs' House ★★★ MUSEUM   This 1724 town house was dragged down by a declining neighborhood until the late 1970s, when an eccentric Californian named Dennis Severs purchased it for a pittance, dressed it with antiques, and delighted London's intelligentsia with this amusingly pretentious imagination odyssey—he called it "Still Life Drama" and a "game." Other museums are unrealistically neat and cordoned off, but his house looks lived-in to make the past feel as real as it truly was. As Severs, who died in 1999, put it, "In this house it is not what you *see*, but what you have only just *missed* and are being asked to imagine."

This unforgettable home tour has a complicated opening schedule, but here's the bottom line: Go on Monday after dark for "Silent Night." When you do, as you approach, the shutters are closed and a gas lamp burns. You're admitted by a manservant who speaks very little. He only motions you to explore the premises, room by room, silently and at your own pace. Suddenly, you're in the parlor of a reasonably prosperous merchant in the 1700s, and the owners seem to have just left the room after a mysterious memorable incident. Candles burn, a fire pops in the hearth, the smell of food wafts in the air, and a black cat dozes in the corner. Out on the street, you hear footsteps and hooves. Room by dusky room, without rules or guards, you silently explore corners overflowing with the implements of everyday life of past ages. Wherever you go, it's as if the residents were just in the room, leaving toys on the stairs, beds rumpled, tobacco in bowls, mulled wine freshly spilled, buttered toast and tea growing cold, and cosmetics half-applied from their oyster shells. The effect gives you a powerful sense of the period. By the time you reach the last of ten rooms, the attic, you'll have accompanied the house and its occupants through its decay into a collapsing slum. "Silent Night" one of London's most invigorating diversions.

18 Folgate St., E1. ℅ **020/7247-4013**. www.dennissevershouse.co.uk. Day visits: Sun noon–4pm, selected Mondays noon–2pm, Silent Night: Mon 6–9pm, also Weds 6–9pm from October through May, Reservations required only for evenings. Monday day visits £7, Sunday visits £10, Silent Night visits £14. Tube: Liverpool Street.

Geffrye Museum ★★ MUSEUM   Founded in 1914 as a resource for the furniture industry, the Geffrye is beloved by local families and design students. The complex, a U-shaped line of dignified brick houses built in 1714 for ironworkers, feels removed from the rush of the East End. Inside is a walk through the history of the home: re-creations of typical middle-class London abodes from the 1600s to the late 20th century, artfully arranged to appear lived-in, and complete with explanations of each item on display, including illuminating information about which pieces were necessary and which were merely trendy. To some, they're rooms full of furniture. To others, the Geffrye is a chance to understand how people of the past lived. You know which person you are. One building here is a restored almshouse for the poor; book timed tours to see how charity cases lived back in the day (some Saturdays and Wednesdays; £2.50 adults, free for children under 16). On weekends, curators plan discussions, lectures, and kid-oriented crafts workshops, which gives the place much more energy than you'd expect from a design-based attraction. Especially on fine days from April to October, the grounds are an exceptional place to relax. The walled herb garden encourages touch, to release scents, and its period plots are historically accurate, cultivated with plants used in several eras, including Elizabethan and Victorian times.

136 Kingsland Rd., Shoreditch, E2. ℅ **020/7739-9893**. www.geffrye-museum.org.uk. Free, including audio tour, Tues–Sun 10am–5pm. Tube: Hoxton.

Museum of Childhood ★★ MUSEUM   The awesome V&A Museum chronicles kiddom through the ages here, pulling from its considerable collection of toys,

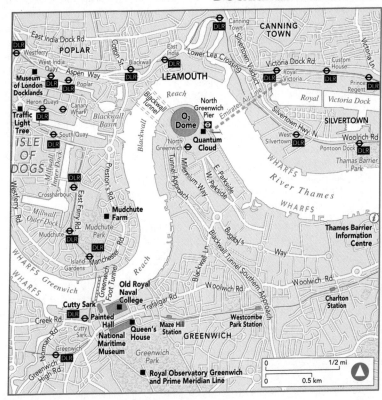

clothing, dollhouses, books, teddy bears, and games. Objects are placed at kids' eye level with simplified descriptions. Some young ones don't grasp the concept—toddlers burst into tears when they see a crib behind glass that they can't climb into. Just as often, though, the outbursts are from parents, who feel the sensation of withering youth when they see an old slot racer car set sealed inside a museum exhibit. Child-rearing history is also addressed; look for the "Princess Bottle" of 1871, which had a reservoired shape that allowed for quick milk dispensing but also incubated bacteria, a fact that wasn't realized until countless babies died. The MoC's glass-and-steel building is itself an artifact; it began its life in South Kensington as the home of the nascent V&A collection but was re-erected here in the 1860s—the fish-scale mosaic floor was made by female prisoners, many of whom were separated from their own kids.

Cambridge Heath Rd., E2. ⓒ **020/8983-5200**. www.museumofchildhood.org.uk. Free. Daily 10am–5:45pm. Tube: Bethnal Green.

Museum of London Docklands ★★★ MUSEUM
If you dig the head-spinning Museum of London (p. 118), here's a similarly lush, ultimately redeeming treatment to life in London's East End. Many of the city's other museums would have you

believe that London was always a genteel bastion of graceful gentlemen. This place tells the real story of the working men who sweat to put the teacups into more privileged, manicured hands, and the labor that circulated profits from the slave trade into City banks. Housed in a brick rum-and-coffee warehouse from 1804, the three-floor museum, strong on plain-speaking explanations, traces the history of working on the Thames starting, starting with Anglo-Saxon times and ending now. You can inspect an intricate model of the medieval London Bridge, which like the Florentine Ponte Vecchio was stacked with homes and businesses but clogged the river's flow so drastically that it was a threat to life. You'll also roam "Sailortown," a creepy warren of quayside alleys, all shanties and low doorways, meant to evoke the area's early 19th-century underworld. Finally, the spotlight shifts to the harrowing Blitz, when the whole area was obliterated by fire from the sky and forced to reinvent itself as a corporate citadel. The whole circuit takes several hours. There's also an interactive, river-themed play area for kids, Mudlarks.

No. 1 Warehouse, West India Quay, Canary Wharf, E14. ☎ **020/7001-9844**. www.museumin docklands.org.uk. Free. Daily 10am–6pm. Tube: West India Quay DLR or Canary Wharf.

Whitechapel Bell Foundry ★ MUSEUM/HISTORIC SITE   America's Liberty Bell. Montreal Cathedral's Great Bell. Big Ben himself. Name an important chimer from Western history, and chances are Whitechapel Bell Foundry cast it. Sure, the Liberty Bell cracked, by which time it was too late to exchange it, but the foundry's craftsmanship is not in question—Guinness verified it as Britain's oldest manufacturing company, established in 1570, with lineage traceable to 1420. Back then, fulsome industries such as metalworking were found in the East End, where the prevailing winds would carry the grime out of town. This foundry, still operating in a brick-front building from the late 1600s, conducts tours of its cramped, messy workshops on some Saturdays—always when workers are off duty, because flying sparks and molten metal sting a little. A visit isn't plastic in any way; tours (full weeks or months ahead) dodge piles of metal dust, sand, shavings, and aged workbenches to collect around heavyweight bells cooling in their molds. Every aspect of the craft, from casting to buffing, is given its due. You'll even learn that the foundry uses a siren to tell workers when it's time for a break. Why? "Well," says Hughes, "When you work in a bell factory . . . ." There's also a small museum and shop (teeny bells, musical scores for handbells), open weekdays, which don't require tickets.

32-34 Whitechapel Rd., E1. ☎ **020/7247-2599**. www.whitechapelbellfoundry.co.uk. Shop open Mon–Fri 9am–4:15pm, tours 2 Saturdays monthly at 10am, 1:30 and 4pm, £12, no one under 14 admitted. Tube: Aldgate East.

Whitechapel Gallery ★★ GALLERY   When it opened in 1901, contemporary art was viewed as a degenerate indulgence. Since then, the Whitechapel has reliably led the development of new artistic movements. There's no permanent exhibition, freeing it to import whatever will grip audiences, so every new visit is a fresh experience. In 1939, it brought Britain Picasso's newly painted *Guernica* as part of an exhibition protesting the then-current Spanish Civil War. Later it introduced Jackson Pollock's abstracts (now they're staples in the Tate museums), and now it gives berth to titillating British sculptors such as Sarah Lucas and Rachel Whiteread. It's also something of a community center, and there's always a talk or screening going on.

77–82 Whitechapel Rd., E1. ☎ **020/7522-7888**. www.whitechapelgallery.org. Free admission. Tues–Sun 11am–6pm, Thurs to 9pm. Tube: Aldgate East.

GREENWICH

As soon as you step off the ferry 30 minutes east of Central London, you're in a UNESCO World Heritage Site. If you don't have time to go into the countryside, Greenwich will give you that English small-town English feel.

Cutty Sark ★★ HISTORIC SITE   This handsome wooden ship, launched in 1869 when it was expected to last only 30 years, is today the only tea clipper left in the world and a symbol of English economic muscle. Against the odds, she still has nearly all of her fabric and riggings—a 2007 fire didn't consume them because they were in storage for a restoration that was already underway. The restoration provided an opportunity for a lavish presentation (and to nearly triple admission fees). Now she floats over a dry dock that's skirted by a glass canopy so visitors can go inside, topside under tarps, and peeping beneath her shining brassed keel. It's a slight cheat, because she originally had a hull coated with Muntz metal, bitumen, and felt, but hey, she looks incredible. She'll never be speedy again, but she'll always look hot.

King William Walk, SE10. ✆ **020/8312-6608**. www.rmg.co.uk/cuttysark. £12 adults, £6.50 kids 5–15, £9.50 seniors/students. Mid-Sept–July 10am–5pm, late July–mid-Sept, 10am–6pm, last admission 1 hr. before closing. Tube: Cutty Sark DLR, Greenwich river ferry, or Greenwich National Rail.

Maritime Greenwich ★★★ HISTORIC SITE/LANDMARK   Situated on a picturesque slope of the south bank of the Thames, Greenwich once was home to Greenwich Palace, where both Henry VIII and Elizabeth I were born. The last part of the palace to be constructed, **The Queen's House** (1616, Inigo Jones, p. 130), still stands, but most of the grounds were rebuilt in the late Georgian period as the equally palatial Royal Hospital, a convalescence haven for disabled and veteran sailors now known as the **Old Royal Naval College** (p.130). High on the hill, in Greenwich Park, is the **Royal Observatory** (p. 130), and between them stands the **National Maritime Museum** (see below). So many of these treasures are owned by the state that many entrance fees are waived; you can play the whole day without paying more than a few pounds. Stop by the visitor center, alongside the *Cutty Sark*, for background information.

Old Royal Naval College, SE10. ✆ **020/8269-4747**. www.ornc.org. Free admission. Grounds open 8am–6pm. Tube: Cutty Sark DLR or Greenwich National Rail.

The National Maritime Museum ★★ MUSEUM   Don't be put off by the topic. The world's largest maritime museum is extraordinarily kid-friendly, brimming with buzzy set-piece toys such as steering simulators and a giant playground that looks like a world map. So it's not as, ahem, dry as most would expect. Since so much of Britain's history from the 17th to 20th centuries was transacted via the high seas, this place isn't just about boats and knots. The facility has an endless supply of Smithsonian-worthy artifacts that would do any museum proud. Highlights include a musical stuffed pig clutched in a lifeboat by a *Titanic* passenger; and, most ghoulishly, the bloodstained breeches and bullet-punctured topcoat that Admiral Lord Nelson wore on the day he took his fatal shot (in a new gallery devoted to the man). Get the creeps from relics from Sir John Franklin's ill-fated 1848 Arctic expedition, including lead-lined food tins that likely caused the explorers to go mad and probably eat each other. Also excellent is the Atlantic Worlds display, which plumbs the British role in the slave trade, something few London museums touch upon. The museum is also not too flashy to present the viewpoint that through the East India Company, England looted India—in fact, the English word *looted* has Hindi origins. It's not all so gloomy, though; there are big set pieces such as figureheads, models, antique instruments, and entire wooden vessels. Weekends are full of free kids' events (storytelling, treasure hunts) that bring suburban London families pouring into the gates, and the fun Greenwich Market is running nearby then, too.

Romney Rd., Greenwich, SE10. ⓒ **020/8858-4422**. www.nmm.ac.uk. Free. Daily 10am–5pm. Tube: Cutty Sark DLR, Greenwich river ferry, or Greenwich National Rail.

Old Royal Naval College ★ HISTORIC SITE/LANDMARK   This 1696 neo-classical complex, primarily the work of Wren, is mostly used by a university but offers two main sights: the Painted Hall and the Chapel. The **Painted Hall** has incredible paintings by Sir James Thornhill that took nearly 2 decades to complete. It was the setting for the funeral of Admiral Nelson, but it may never have looked more glorious than today, because a 2013 restoration removed years of candle grime and even crusty food splatters from rowdy pensioners' banquets. **The Chapel**, in the Greek Revival style, is the work of James Stuart. Tours by accredited guides run daily at 11:30am and 2pm. If the ORNC's stately symmetry rings a bell, that's because it was used as a stand-in for Paris in the movie musical *Les Misérables*. It's also where you'll find **Meantime Brewing Company** (www.meantimebrewing.com), one of the city's hottest microbrewers and a supplier of restaurants across the city. It has plenty of garden space where you can kick back with very stiff pints.

Greenwich, SE10. ⓒ **020/8269-4747**. www.ornc.org. Free. Grounds daily 8am–6pm, buildings daily 10am–5pm, Royal Chapel opens Sun at 11am for worship. Tour reservations ⓒ 020/8269-4799, 90 min., £5 adults, free admission for children under 16. Tube: Cutty Sark DLR, Greenwich river ferry, or Greenwich National Rail.

The Queen's House ★ MUSEUM/HISTORIC SITE   Viewed from the river and framed by the newer Old Royal Naval College, the Queen's House enjoys as elegant a setting as a building could wish for. Inigo Jones took 22 years to come up with a then-revolutionary, Palladian-style summer retreat for Charles I's wife, Henrietta Maria, but it was completed only in 1638, just before the Civil Wars cut both Charles and his building schemes off at the head. Henrietta scurried off to France. The house today has a few ho-hum galleries and displays (lots of paintings of ships and battles) and is connected to the National Maritime Museum by a colonnade. Its nautilus-shaped Tulip staircase, plus other rooms, are considered to be haunted by an unknown specter, so have a camera ready.

Romney Rd., SE10. ⓒ **020/8312-6565**. www.rmg.co.uk. Free admission. Daily 10am–5pm; Tube: Cutty Sark DLR, Greenwich river ferry, or Greenwich National Rail.

The Royal Observatory ★★ HISTORIC SITE/MUSEUM   Commanding a terrific view from the hill in Greenwich Park, with the towers of Canary Wharf spread out in its lap, the Observatory is yet another creation of Christopher Wren (from 1675), and the place from which time zones emanate. Historically the Empire's most important house for celestial observation, it houses significant relics of star-peeping, but since it began charging in 2011, the paid areas became a tourist trap. Most of the good stuff—marked on the map in red—is free, including a small Astronomy Centre and an exhibition on time. The only things admission get you is an unremarkable ceiling-projection planetarium and the bulk of the Flamsteed House by Wren, which includes a collection of clocks that cracked the mystery of measuring longitude, ushering the English Empire to worldwide dominance. Most people plunk down admission not because they care about those but to get access to The Meridian Courtyard. The Prime Meridian, located at precisely 0° longitude (the equator is 0° latitude), crosses through the grounds and interminable queues of coach tourists pay at least £7 to wait an hour the for a silly Instagram moment of straddling the line with a foot in two hemispheres at once—but the dirty secret is they don't have to. The line continues on the walkway north of the courtyard, where it's free and there's never a wait. In the old days, the red Time Ball fell precisely at 1pm daily so that the city could synchronize their clocks; it still rises at 12:55pm and drops 5 minutes later. You could set your watch by it, but technically, you already do.

Greenwich Park, SE10. ℂ **020/8312-6565**. www.rmg.co.uk. Free admission for most of grounds. Flamsteed House and Meridian Courtyard £7 adults, £5 seniors/students, £2 kids under 16; planetarium £6.50 adults, £4.50 seniors/students/kids; combination ticket £11.50 adults, £5.50 kids under 16, £8 seniors/students. Daily 10am–6pm, last admission 5:30pm. Tube: Cutty Sark DLR, Greenwich river ferry, or Greenwich National Rail.

Up at the 02 ★★ TOUR   Climbers, about 10 at a time, hook into a safety rigging system and follow a guide over a tensile fabric catwalk laid a few feet over the Dome's (see box) roof, from south to north, to an observation platform at the zenith of the structure. There they pause for 15 minutes of photos of East London (the City is mostly hidden behind Canary Wharf's towers). Beneath them, humming like a ship at sea, is a Dome conquered. The excursion isn't for the height-averse—at your highest, you're 171 feet (52m) above the ground, and it's not for big eaters or children, either (the weight cutoff is 286 lbs. (130kg) and you have to be at least 10 years old), but it's also not scary since you're tethered, the shoes they lend you grip well, and if the weather's bad, you get matching jumpsuits like Ooompa-Loompas. The climb, which is more like a stroll up a steep hill, takes 45 minutes, and the rest of a 90-minute experience consists of getting harnessed and psyched up.

Peninsula Square, SE10. ℂ **020/8463-2000**. www.the02.co.uk/upatthe02. Climbs from £25. Climbs begin at 10am and end at 6pm to 10pm, depending on the season. Tube: North Greenwich or North Greenwich ferry.

OUTER LONDON

Dulwich Picture Gallery ★★ MUSEUM   A 15-minute train from Victoria and a 15-minute walk from the station lands you in a pretty villagelike enclave of South London. The Gallery, which keeps one of the world's most vital collections of Old Master paintings of the 1600s and 1700s, is so ideal it was once a household name. Magnanimous collectors made it England's first public gallery (opened 1817), designed with a surplus of space and light by Sir John Soane (who left us his own cramped museum; p. 96). A visit is almost indescribably serene. Soane's skylight system was so novel that it more or less invented the private-gallery genre—you'll see shades of it in the Getty Museum in Malibu, California—and the collection was so well-assembled that after it opened, Britain wasted little time in creating its own National Gallery.

Gallery Rd., Dulwich Village, SE21. ℂ **020/8693-5254**. www.dulwichpicturegallery.org.uk. £6 adults, free for children under 18, £5 seniors/students. Tues–Fri 10am–5pm, Sat–Sun 11am–5pm. National Rail: West Dulwich Station.

Dome Ask, Dome Tell

The Millennium Dome was built on a toxic peninsula wasteland in the Thames in the '90s. Conceived as a showplace for what turned out to be a poorly attended turn-of-the-century exposition, it had some elements that were clever in theory: The world's largest domed structure, it was (and is) supported by a dozen 100m-tall yellow towers, one for each hour on the clock in honor of nearby Greenwich Mean Time. But that preening and meaningless symbolism cost a shocking £789 million, and then it stood empty for a half a decade while locals cursed the eyesore and argued about how to use it. In 2007, it was finally reborn as the city's finest performance arena, with 20,000 seats, scads of women's restrooms, and seemingly limitless corporate branding potential. There are still plenty of Londoners who would love to stomp on it, and with the debut of Up at the O2, now they can.

The Freud Museum ★ MUSEUM   In a hilly Hampstead neighborhood of spacious brick-faced homes, Sigmund Freud, having just fled the Nazis, spent the last year of his life. His daughter Anna, herself a noted figure in psychoanalysis, lived on in the same house until her own death in 1982. The eight rooms and their contents, though original and passionately preserved by Anna (Elektra complex, indeed), are not well explained, so don't expect to learn much about the Freuds' pioneering methods. Sigmund's study and library, which came from the doctors' famed offices at Berggasse 19, Vienna, were left precisely as they were on the day he died—which he did on a couch, of course.

20 Maresfield Gardens, NW3. ⓒ **020/7435-2002**. www.freud.org.uk. £5 adults, free for children under 12, £3 seniors/students. Wed–Sun noon–5pm. Tube: Hampstead.

Hampton Court Palace ★★★ MUSEUM/HISTORIC SITE   If you have to pick just one palace to visit in London, select this one because there's so much more to do than look at golden furniture. A 35-minute commuter train ride from the center of town, Hampton Court looks like the ideal palace because it defined the ideal: The red-brick mansion was a center for royal life from 1525 to 1737, and its forest of chimneys stands regally in 24 hectares (59 acres) of achingly pretty riverside gardens, painstakingly restored to their 1702 appearance. Visitors come looking for vibrations left by Henry VIII during the 811 days he spent here (yes, that's all; he had more than 60 houses), and the Crown still stocks many of the 70 public rooms, which start out Tudor and end up Queen Anne, with rare art.

Guides pander to Tudor scandals to make history more interesting, and days are full of events, which may include re-enactments of gossipy events by costumed actors, Tudor-style cook-offs in the old kitchens, Shakespeare plays in the hammer-beamed Great Hall, or ghost tours. Whatever you do, don't neglect the 24-hectare (59-acre) **gardens** and make time to lose yourself in the Northern Gardens' shrubbery **Maze**, installed by William III and; kids giggle their way through to the middle of this leafy labyrinth. The well-mannered **South Garden** has the Great Vine, the oldest vine in the world, planted in 1768; its grapes are sold in the gift shop in August.

East Molesey, Surrey. ⓒ **084/4482-7777**. www.hrp.org.uk. £16 adults, £8 children 5–15, £13.40 seniors/students. March to late Oct daily 10am–6pm and late Oct to Mar daily 10am–4:30pm, last admission 1 hr. before closing. National Rail: Hampton Court.

Royal Botanic Gardens, Kew ★★★ PARK/GARDEN/MUSEUM The 121-hectare (300-acre) gardens earned a spot on the UNESCO list of World Heritage Sites in 2003. As you'd expect, the gardens and glasshouses are world-class—there are 2,000 varieties of plants, many descended from specimens collected in the earliest days of international sea trade. Of the seven conservatories, the domed **Palm House**, built from 1844 to 1848 and jungle-warm, is probably the world's most recognizable greenhouse, while the **Temperate House** is the world's largest glasshouse containing the world's largest indoor plant (the 17.7/58-ft.-tall Chilean wine-palm, planted in 1843—not a typo). It's undergoing a £34 million restoration until 2018 but they've relocated most of its plants (except the *Encephalartos woodii* cycad, extinct in the wild and too fragile to move). Other attractions include a bamboo garden, a water lily pond, **Treehouse Towers** (a tree-themed play area for children aged 3–11), and, providing a chilly contrast to the hot houses, an Alpine glasshouse. The gardeners are champs; in 1986, they coaxed a bloom from a portea that hadn't flowered in 160 years. Kew's contributions to botanical science are ongoing since 1759, but not mired in the past; it also provides a free app that lets you scan labels to learn more and find blooms. But it's expensive, and at 10km/6⅓ miles from the city, visiting eats up a lot of a day. Also be aware that many of the goodies clamp down in winter (including Kew Palace, included in the price, p. 134), so this is best in the summer.

Royal Botanic Gardens, Kew, Richmond, Surrey. ✆ **020/8332-5655**. www.kew.org. Daily 9:30am–4:15pm in winter, until 5:30pm in spring, 6pm in fall, and 6:30pm in summer. £16 adults, £14 seniors/students. free for children under 17. Tube: Kew Gardens.

Warner Bros. Studio Tour London—The Making of Harry Potter ★★★ MUSEUM London's most popular new family outing is like a DVD extra feature that comes to life, and it's as gripping as the fine museums can be. On the very lot where the eight movies of history's most successful film franchise were shot, it seems that every set, prop, prosthetic, wig, and wand—and I mean every last thing—was lovingly saved for this polished, informative, and exhaustive walk-though feast. You could spend hours grazing the bounty, from the students' Great Hall to Dumbledore's roost to Dolores Umbridge's den to the actual Diagon Alley. There's little filler, so book your entry time for early in the day so you'll have time to wander. Even if you care nothing about the movies, you will be blown away that items that got barely two

TAKING THE thames TO HAMPTON COURT OR KEW

From April to September daily, you can take **London River Services** (www.wpsa.co.uk. ✆ 020/7930-2062. £15 adults, £10 seniors, £7.50 kids) all the way from Westminster in central London, the way Henry VIII did on his barges, but it can be a commitment of 4 hours and tides sometimes play such havoc with schedules that you may arrive too late to see much. You will have to take the train the other way. Trains go twice an hour from Waterloo, take 35 minutes, and let you off across the river from the Palace: much easier. Kew is simpler: The ferry's return fare is £18 adults, £12 seniors, and £9 kids. It goes four times a day and takes 90 minutes.

seconds of long-lens screen time could possess such intricate craftsmanship. The finale, an astounding 1:24 scale model of Hogwarts Castle embedded with 2,500 fiber optic lights, is 50 feet across and takes up an arena-size room lit to simulate day and night. Midway through the tour, in an outdoor area containing 4 Privet Drive and the actual Knight Bus, you'll find the only place outside of Orlando where you can taste Butterbeer (£3). And you won't *believe* the gift shop. Easy 15-minute trains go three times an hour from Euston Station—but not, fans sigh, from Platform 9¾ at King's Cross. (Although there, an enterprising Potter souvenir stall affixed a sign and takes pictures for £9).

Warner Bros. Studios Leavesden, Aerodrome Way, Leavesden, Hertfordshire. *C* **08450/840-900**. www.wbstudiotour.co.uk. £29 adults, £21.50 kids, £85 family of four, return train ticket £9.80. Reservations required. First tours 9am–10am and last tours 4pm–6:30pm, closes 3 hrs. after last tour time. National Rail: Watford Junction, then a £2 shuttle bus that meets trains.

Other Area Attractions

Horniman Museum ★ MUSEUM The legacy of a dilettante tea trader that opened in 1901 is a hike into South London. But this international-minded repository of some 350,000 items has something for everyone, including a cherished collection of 7,000 musical instruments plus a huge range of stuff regarding anthropology (masks, puppets, folk art) and natural history (stuffed creatures galore), and a modest aquarium. The grounds are fantastic, too.

100 London Rd., Forest Hill. *C* **020/8699-1872**. www.horniman.ac.uk. Free. Daily 10:30am–5:30pm. Tube: Forest Hill Overground.

Kew Palace and Queen Charlotte's Cottage ★ MUSEUM/HISTORIC SITE Remember George III? He's the ruler who, during his reign from 1760 to 1820, lost his American colonies and went crazy from suspected porphyria: see the movie *The Madness of King George* for the tragic tale. Kew Palace was where he lived, 10km (6⅓ miles) southwest of London, while his dream home, the Castellated Palace, was being built just to the east. His son hated that never-finished building so much (critics

Pearly Kings & Queens

One of the most iconic symbols of London life is that of the Pearly King and Queen. You've seen pictures: grinning folks in suits outrageously embroidered with white buttons and baubles. The tradition began in the Victorian markets, when traders trumpeted their status by decorating their seams with smoke pearl buttons. A poor street sweeper named Henry Croft evolved this esoteric nomenclature into fully embellished outfits, weighing up to 14kg (30 lb.) and worn to attract charitable donations. Soon the idea spread to a whole league of approved wearers, each with their own suit representing a different borough of London. The tradition is dying out, and costumes are increasingly more likely to be found hanging in a museum than on the backs of people. Some of those appearances are announced on the official site of the loosely organized **London Pearly Kings and Queens Society** (*C* **020/8778-8670**; www.pearly society.co.uk), but you can usually find them in the third Saturday of every month at Covent Garden, from 10:30am to 2:30pm.

said it looked like a French prison; fightin' words) he blew it up with gunpowder as soon as he could. Anyway, his secondary crash pad near the Thames, recently restored with scientific exactitude, is only the size of a standard manor house. The little Queen Charlotte's Cottage, an imitation of a humble village home, was probably built for a zookeeper of a long-gone menagerie.

Royal Botanic Gardens, Kew, Richmond. © **020/8332-5655**. www.hrp.org.uk. Admission to Kew Gardens is required: £16 adults, £14 seniors/students. free for children under 17. Kew Palace: Mar–Sept 9:30am–5:30pm, closed Oct to late Mar. Cottage: Mar–Sept Sat–Sun 10am–4pm. Tube: Kew Gardens.

Mandir ★ LANDMARK   Among London Hindus, the Swaminarayan movement claims the most adherents; the breathtakingly gorgeous, many-pinnacled Mandir in northwest London is the largest Hindu temple outside of India. This fabulous temple was only completed in 1995. Some 5,500 tons of Italian Carrara marble and Bulgarian limestone were carved in India and shipped here, where they were assembled by volunteers—its dome was built without using steel or lead. The Mandir's interior is delicately carved, as complicated and as white as a doily, and is apt to amaze even people generally unimpressed by such virtuosity. The adjoining Haveli, equally astonishing, is an intensely carved wooden structure that includes a massive 50m-wide (164-ft.) prayer hall made without pillars and suitable for simultaneous use by 4,000 souls. The work, done entirely by hand, is eye-popping. Tourists are welcomed—there's even an "Understanding Hinduism" exhibition. If you're entering, shorts or skirts must not fall higher than the knee (although ankle-length is preferable and sarongs are available to borrow); visitors must also remove their shoes.

105-119 Brentfield Rd., NW10. © **020/8965-2651**. www.mandir.org. Free. Daily 9am–6pm. Tube: Neasden, then 112 or 232 bus.

Thames Barrier Visitor Centre ★ LANDMARK/MUSEUM   People forget that London floods. Parliament has been under water, and in 1953, surges killed 307 people in the U.K. The reason it took so long to settle Southwark is that it's a natural marsh. At least, London *used* to flood. One of the capital's great pieces of modern engineering, the Thames Barrier is the city's primary defense against it and comprises ten 20m (66-ft.) steel-and-concrete gates. These can be raised to block the 520m (1706-ft.) span of the river in just 10 minutes. Most of the time you can't see the gates themselves, which rest on the riverbed, but the piers that raise and lower them are always visible, strung across the river like a row of mini Sydney Opera Houses. At the visitor center you plumb the Barrier's construction and, if you're lucky, see a test raise. On the north bank of the Thames, opposite the visitor center, next to the barrier, is the 8.8-hectare (22-acre) **Thames Barrier Park.** Established in 2000, it's a pretty place to be, scattered with angular hedges and dancing fountains. It's open from sunrise to sunset, and is a 5-minute walk from Pontoon Dock DLR station. Pick one side or the other, because it's arduous getting between them.

Unity Way, Woolwich, SE18. © **020/8305-4188**. www.environment-agency.gov.uk. Admission £3.50 adults, £3 seniors and students, £2 children 5–15, free for children 4 and under. Thurs–Sun and bank holiday Mon 10.30am–5pm. Rail: Woolwich Dockyard.

Wimbledon Lawn Tennis Museum ★ MUSEUM   Most of us can't get to the tournament. For us, there's still something to see the rest of the year. It's sort of like a Hall of Fame with an emphasis, of course, on Wimbledon, with artifacts going back to

It's easy watching the Wimbledon Championships on TV for 2 weeks in late June and early July, but seeing it in person is a trickier matter. Because tickets for the final matches go to VIPs, you're more likely to catch famous players during the early rounds, when the club's 19 grass courts are all in use. Roaming access to all but three of those (surcharges of £37–£101 are levied for Centre, No. 1, and No. 2 courts, and tickets are distributed by lottery the previous summer) can be had for the price of a "ground pass" (which cost, at most, £20). Around 6,000 ground passes are distributed each morning starting at 9:30am, so arrive before that (the local council gets angry if it's before 8am), and if you snag one, you'll probably be inside by noon, when matches begin. Another clever way to get in is to bum tickets off people as they get tired and leave for the day (just don't offer money—the organizers hate that because they sell unused tickets, too, for charity). A few more ground passes are resold after 3pm for £5 to benefit charity. On weekdays and rainy days, your chances of getting unfilled seats for the best courts are better, since people are working or huddling indoors. And after 5pm, ground-pass rates dip to, at most, £14, which isn't such a bad deal since matches continue until 9pm. It's all ridiculously complicated, so check ahead to make sure the rules are the same.

5

1555, although the British have never been prouder than they are now that Scotsman Andy Murray brought home the trophy after 77 years. There is no other museum in the world where a ghostly video apparition of John McEnroe appears in a locker room to vent about opponents. He comes in peace. No need to duck.

Church Rd., SW19. ⓒ **020/8946-6131**. www.wimbledon.com/museum. 10am–5pm; £8.50 adults, £4.75 children, £7.50 seniors/students; Tube: Southfields or Tooting Broadway, then bus 493, or National Rail to Wimbledon Station, then bus 493.

OVERRATED ATTRACTIONS

In every city, you will invariably find attractions that are heavily publicized but, once seen, revealed to be time poorly spent. In every city, you will also find a subset of visitors who have no idea why they came. Unfortunately, London provides a variety of overpriced pursuits catering to people with an unaccountable aversion to its true treasures. Parents of bored children might also discover these inauthentic sights are just the tonic to jolt them back into a compliant mood.

Emirates Air Line OBSERVATION GONDOLA   Opened in time for the Olympics as a Thames crossing between the ExCeL convention center and the O2 dome, it's simply an enclosed, 10-person gondola that shuttles between two places most tourists never go, and it's too far from the City to be of much panoramic use, although you will see the ArcelorMittal Orbit Olympic tower (which will reopen to tourists in the spring of 2014). Transport for London considers it part of its network, so Oyster cards work on it.

ⓒ **0843/222-1234**. www.emiratesairline.co.uk. Mon–Fri 7am–9pm, Sat 8am–9pm, Sun 9am–9pm. 5 to 10 min. journeys £4.30 adult, £2.20 child (without Oyster) or £3.20 adult, £1.60 child (with Oyster). Tube: North Greenwich or Royal Victoria DLR.

The Household Cavalry Museum MUSEUM   Along Whitehall, where guards try mightily to ignore buffoonish tourists who try to get them to crack a smile, this tiny museum pays soporific tribute to the martial ceremonies of the Queen's Life Guard. You might see troopers groom horses through a glass partition or regard cases of uniforms and regalia with glazed eyes, but nothing against these dedicated men, you won't get much back on your investment. On the hour, mounted dutymen change, and at 11am, the Life Guard changes, but you can see those outside for free.

Horse Guards, Whitehall, SW1. ℂ **020/7930-3070**. www.householdcalvalrymuseum.co.uk. April-Oct. 10am–6pm, Nov-March 10am–5pm. £6 adults, £4 kids and seniors.

The London Dungeon HAUNTED HOUSE   Avoid it like the plague. It's a sophomoric gross-out with locations in 8 cities that sops up overflow from the London Eye. Costumed actors bray at you as you're led through darkness from set to set, each representing a period of English history as a 13-year-old boy might define them. Plague-ridden rubber corpses "sneeze" on passersby, a whore exposes one of Jack the Ripper's mutilated victims, and Sweeney Todd commands you to sit in his chair. The climax is a pair of indoor carnival rides. If you dread being picked on by bad stand-up comics, you're going to hate this place. Booking ahead may not save you having to queue.

County Hall, Westminster Bridge Road, SE1. ℂ **0871/243-2240**. www.thedungeons.com. £24.60 adults, £19.20 kids 5–15, £22.50 students, £7–8 cheaper booked online. Times shift constantly but are roughly daily 10am–6pm. Tube: Westminster or Waterloo.

London Sea Life Aquarium AQUARIUM   Sure, it's fun to see sharks under your feet and penguins on a faux floe. But sorry Charlie, the truth is there is nothing here you can't see at other fish zoos, there are 43 other Sea Life locations, and this tank farm feels as cramped as a 16th-century galleon.

County Hall, Westminster Bridge Rd., SE1. ℂ **0871/663-1678**. www.sealifelondon.co.uk. Mon-Thurs. 10am–6pm, Fri-Sun 10am–7pm, last admission 1 hr. before closing. £20.70 adults, £15 kids 3–15, kids under 3 free, 10% discount online. Tube: Waterloo or Westminster,

The London Zoo ZOO   It's not about the pedigree. No, it has an esteemed history going back to 1828 as a menagerie for members of the Zoological Society of London. It's just that it's ultimately just a zoo, and a smallish one at that, with few large animals. A pair of Sumatran tigers arrived in 2013, but they're not enough to justify the high-ticket price, especially for a first-time London visitor who could be learning about the city instead.

Outer Circle Rd., Regent's Park, NW1. ℂ **020/7722-333**. www.zsl.org. £23 adults, £17 children 3–15, £20.45 seniors/students, save 10% online. Daily 10am-5:30pm. Tube: Camden Town, then 274 bus.

Madame Tussauds TOURIST MUSEUM   Have you ever heard of Shah Rukh Khan? Cheryl Cole? Jonny Wilkinson? If your answer is no, you're not going to get much joy out of this wax trap. The execution of its doppelgangers, which you can usually touch (Harry is behind ropes, girls), is generally superb. That's not the issue. But the focus of this world-famous waxworks is on British celebrities, so you're not going to be consistently engaged for the ferocious price. A 5-minute, Disney-esque ride, "The Spirit of London," invokes every conceivable London stereotype, from the Artful Dodger to plague victims. As you glide through, you'll suddenly wonder if you're the real dummy here.

Marylebone Road, W1. ℂ **0871/894-3000**. www.madame-tussauds.com/london. Pricing is complicated based on time of year and time of day, but it peaks at £30 adults, £26 children, £19 seniors, up to 25% discount online or via its app, £15 for entries after 5pm; daily 9:30am–5:30pm, slightly longer on weekends and holidays, tours continue at least 45 minutes past posted closing time. Tube: Baker Street.

The Queen's Gallery MUSEUM   The Queen inherited the mother of all art collections—7,000 paintings, 30,000 watercolors, and half a million prints, to say nothing of sculpture, furniture, and jewelry—but she shows only a tiny fraction. The few works (budget 1 hr.) are undoubtedly exceptional (one of the world's few Vermeers, a Rubens' self-portrait given to Charles I, glittering ephemera by Fabergé), but they're not the cream of what she owns. There's more exciting stuff to be had for free at the National Gallery. The Gallery and the Royal Mews can be seen on a joint ticket (£16.25 adults, £9.10 children 5–16, £14.90 seniors/students).

Buckingham Palace Rd., SW1. ℂ **020/7766-7301**. www.royalcollection.org.uk. £9.50 adults, £4.80 children 5–16, £8.75 seniors/students. Daily 10am–5:30pm, last admission 4:30pm. Tube: Victoria.

Ripley's Believe It or Not! TOURIST MUSEUM   Like foot fungus, the worthless rip has spread wherever people maintain low standards. Now it's in London. Its halls of oddities (sample: a portrait of Diana made from lint) are useless and not worthwhile even for the kitsch value. This is the definition of a tourist trap. And it costs more than Westminster Abbey!

1 Piccadilly Circus, W1. ℂ **020/3238-0022**. www.ripleyslondon.com. Daily 10am–midnight. £27 adults, £25 seniors, students, £22 kids. Save £4 online. Tube: Piccadilly Circus.

The Royal Mews MUSEUM   Most visitors pop in to what amounts to the Queen's garage in about 15 minutes. You'll see stables fit for a you-know-who (they barely smell at all) and Her Majesty's Rolls-Royces (many of which, at Prince Charles' behest, run on green fuels). You'll also overdose on learning about regulations for when this set of harnesses may be used and when that leather must be polished. The Queen's Gallery and the Mews can be seen on a joint ticket (£16.25 adults, £9.10 children 5–16, £14.90 seniors/students).

Buckingham Palace Rd., SW1. ℂ **020/7766-7302**. www.royalcollection.org.uk. April to Oct 11am–5pm, November to March 10am–4pm.,last admission 45 min. before closing. £8.50 adults, £5.30 children 5–17, £7.75 seniors/students. Tube: Victoria.

The Sherlock Holmes Museum TOURIST MUSEUM   Set up a house as if it were really the home of a fictional character, prop up some shabby mannequins, and then charge people to see it. That's the scheme and it has worked for years, so much so there's often a line. Tourists are not the most intuitive detectives: Do I really have to tell them that Sherlock Holmes didn't actually exist and all of this is nonsense?

221b Baker St., NW1. ℂ **020/7224-3688**. www.sherlock-holmes.co.uk. £8 adults, £5 children under 16; daily 9:30am–6pm. Tube: Baker Street.

OUTDOOR LONDON

Epping Forest ★★★ PARK/GARDEN   Mostly because its soil is unsuitable for farming, for a millennium it remained a semi-virgin woodland, so it's the best place to get a feel for what Britain felt like before humans denuded its land. It's the largest open space in London, 6,000 acres, 12 miles long by 2½ miles wide, and

RITUAL abuse

I'm only telling you this because I love you: **Changing the Guard** (Buckingham Palace; www.royal.gov.uk; Free; 11:30am daily in May–July, and every other day in other months, cancelled in heavy rain; Tube: St. James's Park, Victoria, or Green Park), sometimes called Guard Mounting, is an underwhelming use of 40 minutes of your time. Arrive at Buckingham Palace at least 45 minutes ahead if you don't want to face the backs of other tourists—Buckingham Palace sells a 69p smartphone app that will help decode the ritual. A marching band advances from Birdcage Walk (often, playing themes from *Star Wars*, *West Side Story*, or ABBA—so much for traditional English customs), then members of the Queen's Life Guard—two if the Queen's away, three or four if she's in—do a change around their sentry boxes. And that's it, give or take additional prancing.

Guards patrol all day, without crowds, at both Buckingham Palace and at Horse Guards Arch on Whitehall (which does its own, uncrowded change at 11am, 10am Sun). Or park yourself at **Wellington Barracks,** just east of the Palace along Birdcage Walk, by 11am, and catch the Inspection of the Guard that happens before the same guards march over to the Palace for the main event. Then use the day's golden hours for something less touristy.

Ceremony of the Keys (Tower of London; ✆ **020/3166-6278;** www.hrp.org.uk; free admission; 9:53pm nightly; Tube: Tower Hill or Tower Gateway DLR), held every night as the Yeomen lock up the Tower of London, has been a routine for more than 700 years—not even German bombs cancelled it. But it's an awful lot of work for not much payoff: You must enter the Tower at 9:30 (several hours after closing time, so you can't combine it with a day's visit) and won't leave until around 10:05pm, even though the whole show takes less than 7 minutes—plus, photos aren't allowed. As for the event, the Chief Yeoman Warder approaches the heavy wooden gate with keys and a lantern, is asked "Halt, who comes there?," passes muster, and locks up the gates to a bugle call. The end. If you want to see that, apply for tickets by mail only with two International Reply Coupons (the equivalent of an SASE, available at your post office) to Ceremony of the Keys Office, Tower of London, London, EC3N 4AB, Great Britain; include the names of all attendees with a maximum of six April through October (max. 15 November through March), plus two possible dates that are at least 2 months in advance (three for summer).

containing a universe of diversion—650 plant species, 80 ponds where waterfowl splash, and even some 1,500 species of fungi. Getting lost in the wood is feasible, but not likely, since it stretches in a single direction. Henry VII built a timber-framed hunting lodge in 1542 that was inherited by his daughter Elizabeth and, astoundingly, still stands: **Queen Elizabeth's Hunting Lodge** (reach that via the Chingford rail station).

Rangers Road, Chingford, E4. ✆ **020/8529-6681**. www.cityoflondon.gov.uk. Free admission. Daily 6am–dusk, Lodge: Daily 10am–5pm. Tube: Snaresbrook or Wood Street, National rail: Chingford.

Hampstead Heath ★★★ PARK/GARDEN Some 7 million visitors a year come to the 320-hectare (791-acre) Heath, in northwest London, to walk on the grass, get enveloped by thick woods, and take in the view from the magnificent Pergola, a beguiling, overgrown Edwardian garden, and a true London secret. The Heath is a perennial locale for aimless strolls and (it must be confessed, George Michael) furtive trysts. The Heath has several sublime places to rest, including the just-restored **Kenwood House** (Hampstead Lane, NW3; ✆ 020/7973-1286; www.english-heritage.org. uk; Tube: Hampstead or Highgate), a sumptuous neoclassical home from 1640 adorned with miles of gold leaf and important paintings by Reynolds, Turner, and Vermeer (The Guitar Player); and **Spaniards Inn** (Spaniards Rd. at Spaniards End, NW3; www.thespaniardshampstead.co.uk; ✆ 020/8731-8406; Tube: Hampstead), a garden pub dating to 1585 that has a pistol ball, said to be fired by the legendary outlaw Dick Turpin, framed above the bar. The Heath's hilltop is another favored lookout point. The Heath isn't considered a park by locals, but a green space. The difference, if there is one, is irrelevant. It's transporting.

✆ **020/7606-3030.** www.cityoflondon.gov.uk/hampsteadheath. 7:30am–dusk. Tube: Hampstead or Hampstead Heath Overground.

Hyde Park and Kensington Gardens ★★★ PARK/GARDEN Bordered by Mayfair, Bayswater, and Kensington, is the largest park (138 hectares/340 acres) in the middle of the city. It's the tourist favorite, mostly because of its handy location. It's home to the famous **Speakers' Corner** (Tube: Marble Arch, p. 112), a meandering lake called the Serpentine, and the Diana, Princess of Wales Memorial Fountain (Tube: South Kensington, p. 105). The most famous promenade is Rotten Row, probably a corruption of "Route de Roi," or King's Way, which was laid out by William III as his private road to town; it runs along the southern edge of the park from Hyde Park Corner. Hyde Park is where many historic open-air concerts, such as Live 8, were held, and it's where screens are erected for overflow crowds during critical national events. Kensington Gardens, which flows seamlessly from Hyde Park, only opened to plebes like us in 1851, and it hasn't yet shed its country-manor quality. Calming but a bit too busy for perfect peace, it's where you'll see George Frampton's famous statue of Peter Pan playing the pipes (Tube: Lancaster Gate). You'll also find the **Serpentine Gallery** (west of West Carriage Drive and north of Alexandra Gate. ✆ **020/7402-6075.** www. serpentinegallery.org. Daily 10am–6pm. Free. Tube: South Kensington), a popular venue for modern art exhibitions. Each summer, a leading architect creates a fanciful pavilion there. Volunteers sometimes run guided tours of the park's quirks; check the bulletin boards at each park entrance to see if one's upcoming.

Hyde Park, W2. ✆ **030/0061-2100.** www.royalparks.org.uk. Free admission. Hyde Park open daily 5am–midnight, Kensington Gardens open daily 6am–dusk. Tube: Hyde Park Corner, Marble Arch, or Lancaster Gate.

The Green Park ★ PARK/GARDEN The area south of Mayfair between Hyde Park and St. James's Park, was once a burial ground for lepers, but now is a simple expanse of meadows and light copses of trees. It doesn't have much to offer except pastoral views, and most visitors find themselves crossing it instead of dawdling in it, although its springtime flower beds (which bloom brightest in Mar and Apr) are marvelous.

Piccadilly, SW1. ✆ **030/0061-2350.** www.royalparks.org.uk. Free admission. Open 24 hours. Tube: Green Park.

Greenwich Park ★★ PARK/GARDEN   Decently sized (183 acres), it was once a deer preserve maintained for royal amusement; a herd of them still have 13 acres at their disposal. It's been a Royal Park since the 15th century, although the boundary wasn't formally defined until James I erected a brick wall around it in the early 1600s, much of which still survives. On top of its clean-swept main hill are found marvelous views of the Canary Wharf district, and the world-famous **Royal Greenwich Observatory** (p. 130), commissioned in 1675 by Charles II, serves as the intersection point for the Prime Meridian as well as the center of Greenwich Mean Time. Most people combine a visit with the many other museums of Greenwich.

Greenwich Park, SE10. ℭ **030/0061-2380.** www.royalparks.gov.uk. Free. Daily 6am–dusk. National Rail: Greenwich or Maze Hill, or Cutty Sark. DLR or Greenwich ferry.

St. James's Park ★★ PARK/GARDEN   The easternmost segment of the contiguous quartet of parks that runs east from Kensington Gardens, is bounded by Whitehall to the east and Piccadilly to the north. Its little pond, St. James's Park Lake, hosts ducks and other waterfowl. The Russian ambassador made a gift of pelicans to the park in 1664, and the Brits can't give up tradition, so six (three of them a 2013 gift from the city of Prague) still call it home; they're fed their 13kg (28 lb.) of whiting daily at 2:30pm at the Duck Island Cottage. The park has a fine view of Buckingham Palace's front facade, where royal couples smooch on balconies. The real draw is people-watching, since a cross-section of all London passes through here. Not a place for picnics or ball throwing, there's little in the way of amenities or activities, unless you count voyeurism, and why wouldn't you?

The Mall, SW1. ℭ **030/0061-2350.** www.royalparks.org.uk. Free. Open 24 hours. Tube: St. James's Park.

Regent's Park ★★★ PARK/GARDEN   It's the people's park (195 hectares/487 acres), best for sunning, strolling long expanses—it can take a half-hour to cross it—and darting into the bohemian neighborhoods that fringe it. Once a hunting ground, it was very nearly turned into a development for the buddies of Prince Regent (later King George IV), but only a few of the private terrace homes were built; Winfield House, on 5 hectares (12 acres) near the western border of the park, has the largest garden in London, after the Queen. The American ambassador lives there—surprised? The most breathtaking entrance is from the south through John Nash's elegant Park Crescent development, by the Regent's Park and Great Portland Street Tube stations. North of the park, just over the Regent's Canal and Prince Albert Road, **Primrose Hill Park** (Tube: Chalk Farm or Camden Town) affords a panorama of the city from 62m (203-ft.) high.

Regent's Park, NW1. ℭ **030/0061-2300.** www.royalparks.gov.uk. Free. Daily 5am–dusk. Tube: Baker St., Great Portland St., or Regent's Park.

Victoria Park ★ PARK/GARDEN   The largest and finest open space in East London, this was, when it opened in 1845, the capital's first public park. Bordered by canals and divided in two by Grove Road, it covers an area of just under 87 hectares (220 acres) and contains two lakes, formal gardens, sports facilities, and a bandstand. Other notable features include a Grade II-listed 1862 drinking fountain and two arches from the pre-1831 London Bridge—now turned into benches. In summer, big music events such as Lovebox come here. The park also forms the central section of the

THE hidden park

Sure, everybody knows about London's famous green spaces, but there's one recreation area, which stretches from London's northwest to its east through gentrified lanes and industrial wasteland alike, that few tourists are told about. It's the **Regent's Canal**, which threads from Paddington through Camden, Islington, and East London before joining with the Thames (86 feet lower) just before Canary Wharf. It was completed in 1820 to link with canals all the way to Birmingham and feed the city's massive seagoing trade. In those days, barges were animal-drawn and the districts along the waterway were rat-infested and perilous, but today, it's one of the frontiers for development; many of the horse tracks are leafy promenades and shadowy warehouses have become affluent loft condos. A new development north of King's Cross station is revealing even more glories. Along the shore, you'll pass docks where houseboat barges tie up; their owners can be found topside, making conversation with passersby. The most popular segment is probably the crescent just north Regent's Park. The **London Canal Museum** (12-13 New Wharf Rd., N1. ☎ **020/7713-0836.** www. canalmuseum.org.uk. Tues–Sun 10am–4:30pm. Tube: Kings Cross St Pancras; £4), in a former icehouse, is devoted to the waterway, and it operates regular tours of its towpath and, in summer, a 1-hr Sunday boat tour (£8.50) of the Islington Tunnel, which stretches for three quarters of a mile under the streets.

5

Jubilee Greenway Walk, a route marked out in 2009 with glass paving slabs in honor of the Queen's Diamond Jubilee, and stretching for exactly 60km (37 miles)—one km for each year of her reign—from Buckingham Palace to the Olympic Park. She doesn't use it.

Grove Rd., E3. ☎ **020/7364-2494.** www.towerhamlets.gov.uk/victoriapark. Free. Daily 6am–dusk. Tube: Mile End/Overground: Hackney Wick or Homerton.

Walking Tours

There are so many guides to choose from—the best ones are government-accredited "Blue Badge" professionals—that you could fill a week with walking tours alone. Plenty of qualified operators cater to custom business, but also check the "Around Town" section of *Time Out* magazine, where museums and organizations announce one-off tours.

City of London Guided Walks ★★
The government gives written and performance-based exams to the experts who lead its excellent weekly tours. The experience is less theatrical and denser with facts than what London Walks generally provides, and group sizes tend to be smaller, too. Christopher Wren is the topic Wednesday at 1pm, Fleet Street's messy history (newspapers, Sweeney Todd) comes Thursdays at 11am, and Smithfield is Fridays at 2pm.

City Information Centre, St. Paul's Churchyard, EC4. www.cityoflondonguides.com. £7 adult, free for children under 12, £6 seniors/students; 90 min. to 2 hr.; Tube: St. Paul's.

City of Westminster Guides ★★
Westminster, the area of London west of the City that includes Whitehall, also contracts officially tested guides to lead

tours including "Tarts and Tiaras" (the high life of Mayfair), "The Streets to the Stars" (Theatreland), and "Exclusive Clubs and Posh Shops" of St James's. Advance booking isn't required.

www.westminsterguides.org.uk. £8 adults, £6 seniors/students, kids under 12 free. 90 min. to 2 hr. Locations vary.

Greenwich Guided Walks ★   Like London, Greenwich operates its own official tours with carefully vetted guides. There are usually two basic 90-minute tours daily from the Greenwich Tourist Information Centre taking in the main sights plus the Royal Observatory and the Meridian Line.

© **020/8858-6169**. www.greenwichtours.co.uk. £8, £7 seniors/students, children under 14 free.

London Beatles Walks ★   Richard Porter, an extensive writer on the Fab Four, has led tours for 2 decades; the most regular are the Magical Mystery Tour (landmarks in the development of the band; Sun, Wed, and Thurs) and In My Life (landmarks in their lives; Tues and Sat). You don't have to book ahead.

© **020/7624-3978**. www.beatlesinlondon.com. Tours £9.

London Walks ★★★   Undoubtedly one of the city's best tourist services, its tour list is inspiring. On weekdays, there are often more than a dozen choices, and on weekends, nearly 25, which means that if you ever find yourself with a few hours to kill, you can always find instant occupation. Every tour (most are £9) departs from a Tube stop, which makes arrangements easy. The marquee tour is probably "Jack the Ripper Haunts," which heads out to the streets of Whitechapel around sunset and, in the pursuit of ghoulish entertainment, employs considerably more grotesquerie than uncontested facts. Many of the group's other walks are more informative, including "The Blitz," "Old Westminster," "Rock 'n' Roll London," and "Behind Closed Doors," which includes a visit to the Royal Courts of Justice, guided by a barrister. Other topics that can supply authoritative tours on lesser-visited themes such as Hampstead village, the "Little Venice" near Regent's Canal, places few other touring companies touch. The group also provides guidance for sightseeing staples such as the British Museum and Westminster Abbey, as well as "Great Escapes!" of Bath, Brighton, Cambridge, Oxford, and other day-trip favorites (entry fees and train transit are included in the price, which is usually in the mid-£20s; they may go weekly or seasonally). If there's any fault with London Walks, it's that some groups swell to untenable sizes, and many of the guides, although proven knowledgeable when pressed, rely too commonly on canned performance shtick (in fact, many are actors, but then again, histrionics are preferable to a narcotic delivery). The best way to remedy both problems is to pick a tour with narrower appeal; you'll have a better chance to ask questions.

© **020/7624-3978**. www.walks.com. Most tours £9. Locations vary.

Unseen Tours ★★★   London is more than kings and art. See it from a raw angle, and plumb its modern issues, on a walk guided by homeless and former homeless residents. Walks run Friday through Sunday on four different routes—around Shoreditch, Covent Garden, London Bridge, and Brick Lane.

© **0751/426-6775**. www.sockmobevents.org.uk. Tours £10.

Escorted Tours

There are many reasons to lean against those hop-on, hop-off bus tours. First, they're expensive. Also, after 10 minutes of rolling down the streets in these tourist-processing machines, everything you've seen will blend into a miasma of antiquity. Third, these tours are like playing Russian roulette, because your experience depends on the skill and brains of your guide and/or the quality of the amplification system, over which you have no control.

Narrated bus tours often make you wait 20 to 30 minutes to catch your next leg, which can add up to hours wasted, and although your ticket will be good for 24 hours, don't expect to catch anything between 6pm or so until after 9am the next morning. Day tickets may come with one free walking tour (Changing the Guard, Jack the Ripper) and a hop-on, hop-off pass for the river shuttle boat (although some reports say paying customers may crowd out passholders like you). Unfortunately, both of those perks must often be used during the same 24 hours as the bus ticket's validity, demolishing their usefulness.

In sum, London is a walker's city, and you're better off getting an overview on foot or, if you really want a ride, from a window seat on a real double-decker bus, which is £4.40 for the whole day if you use Oyster pay-as-you-go (see p. 182 for the best routes for sightseeing), or £19.60 for the whole week. But if you insist on perceived convenience, you can buy tickets at any marked bus stop.

HOP-ON, HOP-OFF

The Big Bus Company Like its competition, it offers three circuitous routes, although two of them (Red and Blue) cover much of the same ground with and narration is frequently prerecorded with out-of-date information. It doesn't matter at which of the 50-odd stops you get on, but drivers often change at Green Park on Piccadilly, so you'll avoid that wait by starting there. You can catch this one at any stop, but most people get on at Marble Arch, Regent Street south of Piccadilly Circus, Charing Cross Road north of Trafalgar Square, or under the South Bank Lion at Westminster Bridge. Prices can be a few pounds higher if you don't book ahead.

48 Buckingham Palace Road, SW1. © **020/7233-9533.** www.bigbustours.com. £30 adults, £12 children 5–15, including free City Cruise tour and free walking tour, save £6 booking online, 48-hour tickets an additional £6/£3. Departures daily 8:30am–6pm.

Golden Tours Open Top Bus Tours The discount option. Golden Tours is one of the big machines in town, offering every permutation of bus tour and day-trip excursion you can imagine. None are particularly special, but they get the job done, and they do it with a flesh-and-blood narrator at low-ish prices, which means crowds. Its main product is a system of routes granting 24-hr. access to a network of 44 stops, generally from 8am to 5pm, plus one free walking tour and one free river boat ride. It also offers a 3-hr. guided tour (£16 adults/£8 kids 5-15) that doesn't allow you to get off and on. Its Blue Line covers most of the core city including South Kensington, and the Red Line forgoes South Ken for the Docklands area. Commensurate with the lower prices, buses are in poorer repair.

11a Charing Cross Road, WC2, 156 Cromwell Road, SW7, and 4 Fountain Square, 123-151 Buckingham Palace Road, SW1. © **020/7630-2028** (U.K.) and **800/509-2507** (North America). www.hoponhopoffplus.com. £20 adults, £10 kids 5-15, £55 for family of two adults and two children, including one free river cruise and one free walking tour. Add £4 adults/£2 kids for a second 24-hr. period. 9am–4:30pm.

The Original Tour London Sightseeing Tours, conducted on open-top coaches, are covered for 24 hours with a ticket, so you can go around five times if your feet hurt. You can catch the bus (three interconnecting circuits that supply solid coverage of the main sights) at any of the 80-odd stops on the routes, but most people begin at Piccadilly Circus, Trafalgar Square, Embankment Station, near Victoria Station, or outside Madame Tussauds. Live narrators only appear on the Yellow Line, which covers the broadest swath of town, while the other lines are more likely to have recorded spiels, sometimes too quiet.

17-19 Cockspur St., SW1. ℂ **020/8877-1722**. www.theoriginaltour.com. £28 adults, £14 children 5–15, £3/£2.50 discount online, including a river cruise. Daily 8:30am–6pm.

OTHER TOURS

Brit Movie Tours Increasingly, people feel more connection with movies and TV than with the history that actually wrought them, and for them, it hosts an array of excursions ranging from walking tours to full-day coach, including an 8-hour *Downton Abbey* visit (£55 adults, £40 kids) and tours for James Bond, Doctor Who, and Harry Potter locations (£20/£15).

ℂ **0844/2471-007**. www.britmovietours.com.

City Cruises When you take a standard trip on its generously glass-sided and -topped boats, live narrators point out details of interest. The "Red Rover" ticket allows you to hop on and off all day. Boats go every 30 min., generally between 9am and 9pm, at four piers: Westminster, London Eye, the Tower, and Greenwich. Note that two of those stops are across the river from each other, leaving the stretch between the London Eye and the Tower of London (the meatiest section) without a stop. Using it to add Greenwich can save money off buying several one-way tickets on standard ferries, but simple return tickets are cheaper on Thames Clippers. The lunch tours (£27) and afternoon tea excursions (£22) are less of a value since you can't get off to explore.

ℂ **020/774-0400**. www.citycruises.com. 24-hr. passes £17 adult, £8.50 kids, £11.90 senior/student, £34 for two adults and up to three kids, 10% online discount. 48-hr. passes £24.50 adults, £12.25 kids, £17.15 senior/student.

London Ducktours Tacky? Totally. But fun. Like their forebears that have plied the Wisconsin Dells for decades, these 75-minute tours are conducted in clumsy, American-made DUKW amphibious vehicles, which roll down streets like buses and then plow into the Thames and motor along briefly as boats. Roofed and mostly splashless, these vehicles were developed as Word War II transports. You can't hop off and you only see Whitehall, Westminster and Vauxhall, but if you have kids to educate, it's a spoonful-of-sugar option.

55 York Rd., SE1. ℂ **020/7928-3132**. www.londonducktours.co.uk. Daily 10am to late afternoon. 75 min. rides £23 adults, £15 children 12 and under, £18 seniors/students 13–17. Reservations recommended. Tube: Waterloo.

Muggle Tours Although it's based on a mass-appeal trend, it's worthy. This well-assembled 2-hr. tour dispenses reams of Harry Potter trivia, from the books, the movies, and locations from the movies. Groups of 20 start at London Bridge, near Borough Market (p. 71), and wind up in Leicester Square, and because so much London history is folded in, there's enough for non-Potterheads. Book online.

ℂ **07917/411-374**. www.muggletours.co.uk. £12 adults, £10 children 11 and under.

Thames Rib Experience   Touristy to the core, this outfit loads you in semi-inflatable RIB speedboats with twin 245-horsepower engines and flits you downriver to Canary Wharf or Greenwich from Embankment. Make a lasting memory of St. Paul's flying past, blurry from cold estuary spray in your face.

Victoria Embankment, WC2. © **020/3432-6856**. www.thamesribexperience.com. 50 to 75 min. rides £36-50 adults, £22-31 kids. Tube: Embankment or Charing Cross.

LONDON SHOPPING

B lame Elizabeth I. Sure, the old girl loved her baubles and gold-embroidered bodices, but her biggest contribution to English consumerism was defeating the Spanish Armada. You see, that established England as the dominant player on the high seas, which opened up channels of international trade and soon, the Thames was more jammed with bounty than the parking lot at the mall on Christmas Eve. Ever since then, London has had a hankering for the finer things. Gird your pocketbook!

Stores across the city generally open at 9 or 10am daily and close at 7 or 8pm, although boutiques may close at 6pm and the department stores and Oxford Street shops are often open as late as 9pm. On Sundays, relatively new terrain for British shopping, 11am or noon to 6pm is common (although arcane laws mean some stores won't make a sale until noon); very few places will stay open past then. Expect crowds on weekends, when people pour into town from the countryside.

THE GREAT SHOPPING STREETS

Appropriately for a city obsessed with class, London's prime shopping streets aren't usually defined so much by what they sell as by how much you'll spend to bring home their booty.

THE ARCADES OF PICCADILLY & OLD BOND STREET

Tube: Green Park: There are several iron-framed, skylighted "arcades" (closed Sun), built by 19th-century blue bloods for shopping in any weather along these streets. The best include the longest one, Burlington Arcade, a block long parallel to Old Bond Street at Piccadilly (silverware, cashmere, handbags, Ladurée macaroons); the Royal Arcade, south of Burlington Gardens (antiques, shoes, watches); and Piccadilly Arcade, across from Burlington Arcade (men's tailoring; it leads to Jermyn St., once the heart of haberdashery).

CARNABY STREET

Tube: Oxford Circus or Piccadilly Circus: This used to be for the mod crowd, but today its legendary hyperalternative looks are mostly found on Memory Lane. Instead, expect mainstream sporty choices such as North Face and Vans. Better for browsing is Kingly Court, a former timber warehouse converted into a mini-mall for 30-odd upcoming designers. (carnaby.co.uk)

CECIL COURT

Tube: Leicester Square: Distinguished by glazed-tile buildings, matching green-and-white shop signs, and a refreshing lack of cars, this block is a holdout of the antiquarian book trade that once dominated Charing Cross Road, its western anchor. Foyles (p. 153) started trading here. A favorite is Marchpane, at 16, a trove of vintage children's literature. (www.cecilcourt.co.uk)

FLORAL STREET

Tube: Covent Garden: Every lane around Covent Garden (Long Acre, Henrietta St.) is an obvious shopping drag, full of the usual brands but increasingly some one-off names. This side street gives respite from the same old tourist tat. Duck in when you want to browse some originals. (www.coventgardenlondonuk.com)

KENSINGTON HIGH STREET

Tube: High Street Kensington: London's coolest department store street in the '60s, the big ones have decamped for the malls, and it's now a hodgepodge of upmarket brand names, young trendy stuff on the east end, plus some boutiques on Kensington Church Street.

KING'S ROAD

Tube: Sloane Square or South Kensington: The Chelsea avenue where affluent "Sloaneys" spend is where you go to dream—increasingly, about what King's Road used to be. Most of the truly unique stores have recently been elbowed aside by the same old names, but amid the familiar (Ted Baker, Rag & Bone, Anthropologie), you'll find a few independent boutiques, high-end mommy wear, and some designer furnishings That doesn't mean the French cafes on Sloane Square aren't prime real estate for watching those happy rich kids pass bay.

NEW BOND STREET

Tube: Bond Street or Green Park: The ultimate high-end purchasing pantheon runs from Oxford Street to Piccadilly, partly as Old Bond Street. Every account-draining trinket maker has a presence, including Sotheby's, Van Cleef & Arpels, Graff, Alexander McQueen, Harry Winston, Tiffany & Co., Chopard, and Boucheron. Asprey's, at 165-169, sells adornments few can afford, but its Victorian facade is a visual treat for all incomes. Nearby, South Molton Street continues the luxury, but at half-step down in expense, with Brown's Ted Baker, Karen Millen, and other fashion houses.

REDCHURCH STREET

Tube: Shoreditch High Street: This down-at-heel Shoreditch alley, once rammed with cabinetmakers, is at the forefront for stylists. The 150-year-old menswear brand Sunspel opened its first retail shop, Labour & Wait vends desirable kitchen toys, Maison Troi Garçons does slick interiors, and Terence Conran's super-chic hotel/restaurant/café complex Boundary seals the deal for scenesters. Around the corner, Boxpark, a hipster mall comprised of five dozen rehabbed shipping containers, hosts pop-up boutiques and slumming corporate brands alike.

OXFORD STREET

Tube: Marble Arch, Bond Street, or Oxford Circus: The king of London shopping streets supports the biggest names, including Topshop, H&M, the ever-mobbed

Primark, and a few lollapalooza department stores like Selfridges, John Lewis, and Marks & Spencer. Boy, are weekends crowded! (www.oxfordstreet.co.uk)

SLOANE STREET

Tube: Knightsbridge: Offshore millionaires come here to feast at the top of the consumerist food chain: Bulgari, Valentino, Miu Miu, Prada, Armani, and everything else haute and showy. And no farther than you can throw a chocolate truffle, Harvey Nichols and Harrods. (www.sloane-street.co.uk)

TOTTENHAM COURT ROAD

Tube: Tottenham Court Road or Goodge Street: Locals sniff, but the street's lower half, between Oxford and Store streets, is their only drag for cut-rate electronics (including voltage converters). North to Torrington Place, pickings shift to brilliantly designed housewares and furnishings at Habitat (p. 159) and London's grande dame of smart styling, Heal's (p. 159).

UPPER STREET

Tube: Angel: Islington's chief avenue is emerging as a low-key location for boutiques, vintage outfits, and kitchen-sink junk shops, all pleasantly spelled by unpretentious pubs and cafes. While you're south of the Green, explore the sidewalks of Camden Passage, known for antiques and bric-a-brac.

THE SHOPPING PALACES

Fortnum & Mason ★★★   So venerable is this department store, which began life in 1707 as the candlemaker to Queen Anne, that in 1922 archaeologist Howard Carter used empty F&M boxes to tote home the treasures of King Tut's tomb. The veddy British department store, which has a special focus on gourmet foods, is renowned for its glamorous hampers, which were first distributed in the days before World War I, when soldiers' families were responsible for feeding their men on the field. Such picnic sets now come with bone china and can cost £300, and the tables of its ground floor food hall are immoderately piled with a cornucopia of such tongue-teasing triumphs as jarred black truffles and fresh Blue Stilton cheese in ceramic pots. In addition to a huge selection of tea packaged in distinctive canisters, F&M makes its own "parlour ice" (ice creams) and something called Rubies in the Rubble (chutney made from fruits obtained in London's markets). There's something to be said for a store that maintains its own beehives for honey. Don't scan too quickly or you'll miss the dark chocolate scorpions and reindeer pâté. Content yourself, as most do, with a wander through the hushed upper-floor departments, which are lit by chandelier, accented by wooden cases, and illuminated by a lotuslike atrium skylight. The fragrance department smells like a rose garden. High tea can be taken in the top-floor St. James's tearooms, among the city's most sumptuous (reservations: ℂ 0845/602-5694), while lunching ladies can be found in the banquettes of the Fountain Restaurant. When the clock strikes the hour over the store's Piccadilly entrance, two mechanical representations of Mr. Fortnum and Mr. Mason emerge, bow to each other approvingly, and return to business inside.

181 Piccadilly, W1. ℂ **020/7734-8040**. www.fortnumandmason.co.uk. Tube: Green Park or Piccadilly Circus.

Harrods ★   Now owned by the Qatari royal family's financiers, a miraculous hold-over from the golden age of shopping has been retooled into a vertical mall appealing to free-spending, not-too-discerning visitors. Still, based on its prior reputation (or maybe because it's become such a bombastic parody of itself), many visitors prioritize a visit right behind Westminster Abbey or the Tower. Its thronged Food Hall rooms are still a glut of exorbitantly priced meats and cheeses, its ornate seven-floor facade is still emblazoned like a Christmas tree after dark, its endless floors are still spiked with jewelry and staff ready to ply the husbands of spoiled wives with champagne until they give in. But much floor space, where too-loud rock beats blare non-stop, is devoted to brands you'd find for a third of the price at your local mall. The artificial environment, from clerks wearing straw hats to the souvenir "emporium" on the 2nd floor (£17 for sandwich-sized gusset bags; £15 mugs; teddy bears aplenty), would be more authentic at Disneyland than anywhere in the London of old, so don't think you're participating in something traditional. Of the many escalator banks, the most interesting is the uproarious Egyptian-themed one at the store's center. At its base is a tacky brass fountain memorial to Dodi Al-Fayed and Princess Diana, who died together in Paris in 1997—his father owned Harrods at the time and campaigned to prove Prince Philip ordered the murder of Diana lest she marry a Muslim. A wine glass from the couple's final tryst is preserved along with a ring with which al-Fayed claims his son intended to propose to Diana. Tacky! If you crave a real British department store experience, visit Fortnum & Mason or Selfridges; if you want to be flabbergasted by the pompous excesses of the jet-set, Harrods is the overly shellacked circus for you.

87-135 Brompton Rd., SW1. ✆ **020/7730-1234**. www.harrods.com. Tube: Knightsbridge.

Harvey Nichols ★   *Absolutely Fabulous'* shallow anti-heroines Patsy and Edina spoke of it with the same breathless reverence most people reserve for deities. You'll need the income of a god to afford a single thread of Harvey Nick's women's and men's fashion, and although the British-owned store isn't as popular as it used to be—it's been here since the 1880s—a stroll through this eight-floor spendthrift's heaven is entertaining. In addition to the lunching ladies on display in the Fifth Floor Restaurant—think of it as a zoo for old money.

109-125 Knightsbridge, SW1. ✆ **020/7235-5000**. www.harveynichols.com. Tube: Knightsbridge.

John Lewis ★★   Every Englishman knows that if you want a sound deal, you go here, where there's a price guarantee; it employs an army of people to scout for the lowest prices in the area, which it matches. That may sound like the gimmick of a low-rent wannabe, but John Lewis, established in 1864, is in fact a respected cooperative owned by its employees, and their interest in its success shows in their attentive service and seemingly limitless product line. It also has some exceptional buyers; you'll find things here no other store carries (the bedding department is renowned). Art fans shouldn't miss the building's eastern face, upon which is mounted an abstract cast-aluminum sculpture, *The Winged Figure* (1960), by one of the most important artists of the twentieth century, Dame Barbara Hepworth. She's also in the Tate Britain (p. 100)

Oxford St. at Holles St. ✆ **0844/693-1765**. www.johnlewis.com/oxfordstreet. Tube: Oxford Circus.

Liberty ★★   Founded in 1875, it made its name (and earned some mockery) as an importer of Asian art and as a major proponent of Art Nouveau style. Now its focus is distinctly British. The timber-and-plaster wing looks Tudor, but is actually a 1924 revival constructed from the salvaged timbers of two ships, HMS *Impregnable* and HMS *Hindustan;* the length of the latter ship equals the building's length along Great Marlborough Street. The store's stationery and scarf selections are celebrated, as are its fabrics (many of which are designed in-house), and the beauty hall is one of the best. The soft wooden spaces are creaky and seductive, which the staff service is so obsequious it evokes a bygone era.

210-220 Regent St., W1. ℰ **020/7734-1234**. www.liberty.co.uk. Tube: Oxford Circus.

Marks & Spencer ★★★ Fresh off a reinvention, the beloved M&S is back on top as the country's favorite mid-level department store for good-looking clothing staples. Its own-brand clothing, once shoddy and ill-fitting, has been re-envisioned as affordable riffs on well-tailored fashions, and customers are drifting back to enjoy the good buys. M&S is particularly beloved for its underwear, but its crowning achievement is its giant **food halls ★★★** (usually tucked underneath the store but sometimes a stand-alone shop called **Simply Food**), which sell an astonishing array of prepared meals, soups and sandwiches, and well-selected yet inexpensive wines. M&S is a national treasure, with nothing like it in other countries, and it's about time the English remembered that.

Flagship: 458 Oxford St., W1. ℰ **020/7935-7954**. www.marksandspencer.co.uk. Tube: Marble Arch.

Selfridges ★★★ Aside from Harrods' olive drab sacks, no shopping bag brags louder about your storied shopping preferences than a canary yellow screamer from Selfridges. It's unquestionably the better of the two stores, since it's not merely a sprawling sensory treat, but it also sells items you'd actually want. Since its 1909 opening by an American marketing executive from Marshall Field's in Chicago (it was designed by Daniel Burnham of Chicago and Manhattan's Flatiron Building fame), Selfridges has pioneered standard department store practices, including placing the perfumes near the front door, filling its 27 ground-floor windows with consumerist fantasias, and inventing the phrase "the customer is always right." Some one million products are for sale, and the beauty department is Europe's largest. The thicket of food counters on the ground floor is mobbed at lunchtime, and the rest of the store is just as popular at other times; some 17 million visits are recorded each year—in the basement, there's a Quiet Room so they can escape the crush and have a think. Selfridges has traded in history, too; the first public demonstration of television was held on the first floor in 1925, and 3 years later, the store sold the world's first set. During much of the Blitz, Churchill's transatlantic conversations with FDR were encoded via a scrambler stashed in the cellar. The store's popularity is enjoying a goose thanks to the 2013 series *Mr. Selfridge*, with Jeremy Piven barking his way through the title role, that gives the store's early years the soapy treatment.

400 Oxford St., W1. ℰ **0800/123-400** (U.K.) or 113/369-8040 (from overseas). www.selfridges.com. Tube: Bond Street or Marble Arch.

RECOMMENDED STORES

For a city world-famous for shopping, where people from around the world arrive with one fat wallet and leave with 10 stuffed suitcases, there's no way to give proper celebratory due to everything that is wonderful and for sale. Some stores, though, are so original and site-specific that they can sweeten the experience of being in London even if you don't buy a thing.

Antiques

After Noah ★   More like an upscale junk shop, it makes its name on vintage toys, crockery, bathroom fittings, cheerful celluloid jewelry, and wooden desks and bedsteads, sadly too large to get home. Its refurbished mid-20th-century telephones are particularly sought-after.

121 Upper St., N1. ✆ **020/7359-4281**. www.afternoah.com. Tube: Angel.

Bermondsey Market ★   The earlier you come, the more you'll find at this weekly event that yields some of the city's broadest inventory (a trove of Edwardian and Victorian ephemera), plus some stuff that probably fell off a lorry. It kicks off at 6am Fridays, and is history by 2pm.

Bermondsey St. at Long Lane, SE1. ✆ **020/7234-0805**. Tube: London Bridge.

Blue Mantle ★   For dream renovations back home, the largest antique fireplace showroom in the world salvages the good stuff with warm English touches when developers knock down classic buildings.

306-312 Old Kent Rd., SE1. ✆ **020/7703-7437**. www.bluemantle.co.uk. Tube: Borough.

Camden Passage ★★   Plenty of tourists swing through the booths, so bargains aren't always very easy to come by. Still, shimmering examples of china, silverware, cocktail shakers, military medals, coins, and countless other hand-me-downs overflow the cases. Despite the name, it's in Islington.

Off Upper Street, N1. www.camdenpassageislington.co.uk. Wed and Sat only. Tube: Angel.

Grays ★★   Not the place to go if you're looking for the lowest deal (it's in Mayfair), but it's definitely a source for variety. There are some 200 vendors, many experts registered in the official antiques societies, split among two buildings, and they sell everything from Victorian jewelry to toys to strange bric-a-brac and collectible silverware. Weekdays are best.

58 Davis St., W1. ✆ **020/7629-7034**. www.graysantiques.com. Closed Sun. Tube: Bond Street.

LASSCo ★★   From stained glass to paneling and faucets to wood flooring, you'll get an incredible selection of fittings and furniture rescued from museums, churches, pubs, and homes at LASSCo (The London Architectural Salvage and Supply Company).

41 Maltby St., SE1. ✆ **020/7394-8061**. www.lassco.co.uk. Tube: Bermondsey. Also at Brunswick House; 30 Wandsworth Rd., SW8. ✆ **020/7394-2100**. Closed Sun. Tube: Vauxhall.

Books

The territorial nature of publishing means that many books that are for same in London won't be in print back home. Take time to trawl the used book stores along **Charing Cross Road** and the adorable collectible bookstores lining **Cecil Court**, which runs from to St Martin's Lane. For scripts, acting guides, and performers' biographies, **French's Theatre Bookshop** (52 Fitzroy St., W1; ✆ 020/7255-4300; www.samuel french-london.co.uk; Tube: Warren Street), north of lovely Fitzroy Square, is the city's most reliable publisher and supplier. But you mustn't ignore the **National Theatre**

Bookshop (Royal National Theatre, Southbank, SE1; © 020/7452-3456; http://shop. nationaltheatre.org.uk; Tube: Waterloo). **Pleasures of Past Times** (11 Cecil Court, Charing Cross Road, WC2; © 020/7836-1142) is a collector's shop with a fine selection of old playbills, vaudeville cards, and out-of-print histories.

Daunt Books ★★   Lined with oak galleries and lit by a long, central skylight, it prides itself on its travel collection, which is located down a groaning wooden staircase. Everything is arranged by the country it's about—Third Reich histories under Germany, Tolstoy under Russia. It's no slouch in the general interest categories, either. Clerks seem to know what will interest the vaguest browser, and the cashier's desk is always piled with choice curiosities.

83 Marylebone High St., W1. © 020/7224-2295. www.dauntbooks.co.uk. Tube: Baker Street.

Foyles ★★   In business since 1903, this institution has thus far navigated the onslaught of high rents and low readership. After the 1999 death of its tyrannical owner, the store was once again passed to the next generation of the Foyle family, and it caught up with modernity just in time to avoid closure; among other tweaks, it installed a jazz club. Now its huge inventory of 200,000 titles (sold by computer, fully browsable) straddles both popular and specialty topics, and writers favor the store for signings. There are smaller outlets at St. Pancras, and the Southbank Centre, but this is the H.Q., and in early 2014 it moves to a newly constructed building at 107-109 on the same block.

113-119 Charing Cross Rd., WC2. © 020/7437-5660. www.foyles.co.uk. Tube: Tottenham Court Road.

Hatchards ★★   Although the Duke of Wellington and the Queen herself are counted among its customers, Hatchards, the oldest bookseller in the city (1797), is also noted for its famous shoplifters: An 18-year-old Noël Coward was apprehended as he stuffed a suitcase full of books. (Characteristically, he talked his way out of trouble.) It has been trading since 1801 at its current location, which means it was selling books before Hardy, Dickens, or the Brontës were writing them. You'll find it not far west of Waterstone's (listed below).

187 Piccadilly, W1. © 020/7439-9921. www.hatchards.co.uk. Tube: Piccadilly Circus.

Housmans Booksellers ★   London supports a vibrant protest community—don't forget this is where Karl Marx fashioned his views that changed the world. Since 1945, the city's pre-eminent store for radical books has been Housmans. It also boasts the United Kingdom's largest collection of magazines and newspapers, with some 200 titles on offer at any time, plus stationery and a cafe (free trade all the way). You're not going to find most of the stuff here published back home. Wednesdays at 7pm, an author speaks.

5 Caledonian Rd., N1. © 020/7837-4473. www.housmans.com. Closed Sun. Tube: King's Cross St. Pancras.

Stanfords ★★★   Since 1901, it has peddled globe-trotting goodness, from guides to narratives to fiction with a worldview. Should you accidentally leave your map in your hotel room, beeline to the basement; the floor there is covered with an oversized reproduction of the London A-Z map. There are also reams of maps for purchase, including for walking trails across Britain.

12-14 Long Acre. © 020/7836-1321. www.stanfords.co.uk. Tube: Covent Garden.

The Royal Warrant

When you're snooping around the stuffy shops of St. James's or Mayfair, keep an eye out for a royal crest near the store's sign. That insignia is a seal of approval—its presence means that the store counts a member of the royal family as a customer and has done so for at least 5 years. To earn Prince Charles' plumed crest, stores have to do even more, and prove they abide by a sustainable environmental policy. The Queen is represented by a lion and a unicorn, but William doesn't have any warrants registered yet. Once a business wins a warrant—about 800 have done it, even elevator repair services—it's extraordinarily rare to see it withdrawn, but to its humiliation, Harrods lost its seal in 2000. Which hotel does the Queen prefer? The Goring (p. 31), which earned its warrant in 2013. But don't ask what specific items businesses are delivering to the Palace; shopkeepers aren't permitted to tattle. To learn which companies supply the Windsors—say, where the Queen buys her corgis' dog food—search the current warrant holders at www.royalwarrant.org.

Waterstones ★★★   Built in 1936 as Simpson's clothiers, the Art Deco model for Grace Brothers in the saucy Britcom *Are You Being Served?,* this branch of the chain is Europe's largest bookshop. Even if Waterstones (in 2012, it dropped its apostrophe in its name to make Web references easier) is the McDonald's of bookselling, it handles the stewardship of that dubious title with dignity; there are six sweeping floors, an enormous London section, plenty of easy chairs for freeloaders, and a dedicated events space for visiting authors. The top floor's panoramic cafe, 5th View, hops after work and into the evening.

203 Piccadilly. ✆ **0843/290-8549**. www.waterstones.com. Tube: Piccadilly Circus.

Clothing

Albam ★★   Unusually, this men's boutique seeks out well-constructed, honest clothing (made in the U.K.) but doesn't mark it up by insane factors. Although its prices are similar to those of high-casual chain stores, the store has a following among guys because its clothing lasts longer.

23 Beak St., W1. ✆ **020/3157-7000**. www.albamclothing.com. Tube: Piccadilly Circus or Oxford Circus.

Beyond Retro ★★   A one-stop for classic items (jeans, jackets, boots, and other casuals), it's a haunt of the poor and stylish, who can put together an off-margin look without overdrawing. There's a branch in Soho (58-59 Great Marlborough St., W1; ✆ 020/7434-1406; Tube: Oxford Circus), but this is the location with the cat Tiny, who lives in the store and has become a local mascot.

110-112 Cheshire St., E2. ✆ **020/7613-3636**. www.beyondretro.com. Tube: Shoreditch High Street or Whitechapel.

Browns ★★   Some 100 designers, all of them for higher-end purchasers, fill the five connected shops at the top of Mayfair. For 40 years, it's been a marketplace for upscale women, but increasingly, it's pitching to a younger and more casual set.

23-27 South Molton St., W1. ✆ **020/7514-0000**. www.brownsfashion.com. Tube: Bond Street.

Dover Street Market ★   A high-minded multidesigner concept, heavy on pretentious industrial architecture, has launched couture (Comme des Garçons, Boudicca) by fusing it with multimedia art installations, all in a six-story department store–like space with a bakery on the top floor.

17-18 Dover St., W1. ⓒ **020/7518-0680**. www.doverstreetmarket.com. Tube: Green Park.

Diverse ★   One of the first boutiques to move into Upper Street, it keeps stock changing even as it spotlights white-hot labels, many of which go on to greatness. Clothes tend toward arty, which is to say interesting but not irresistible.

294 Upper St., N1. ⓒ **020/7359-8877**. www.diverseclothing.com. Tube: Angel.

Eleven Paris ★★   After 16 stores in France and 8 in Paris, in 2013 the French rocker brand hit London, bringing with it its smart-aleck tees and natty casual wear with a sophisticated urban edge. Next target: the U.S.A.

46 Carnaby St., W1. ⓒ **020/7434-1171**. www.elevenparis.com/en. Tube: Oxford Circus.

Gap ★   Don't laugh: For some reason, its inventory is different from the baggy junk clothing it offers in North America. It's still affordable and non-challenging, but it fits better. It's worth a look.

376-384 Oxford St., W1. ⓒ **020/7408-4500.** www.gap.co.uk. Tube: Oxford Circus.

H&M ★   The Swedish chain is an international byword for flashy and of-the-moment clothing bargains. It's where the fashion conscious can find astoundingly cheap outfits—they won't last more than a season or two, of course. This main store, on the corner of Oxford and Regent streets, has the widest selection, including men's; the location nearby at 234 Regent St. also has a wide range; the outpost a few blocks east at 174-176 Oxford Street also has stuff for the home; and the one at Covent Garden (27-29 Long Acre) is small but has a good inventory.

Oxford Circus, W1. ⓒ **0844/736-9000**. www.hm.com. Tube: Oxford Circus.

Jack Wills ★★   "Fabulously British," it brags, but this line comes off a bit like American Eagle Goes to Eton. It goes for a sporty prep school look with rugby shirts, polos in zippy colors, cute striped trunks, and brightly hued jumpers. It has expanded internationally, but here's the three-story flagship.

136 Long Acre., WC2. ⓒ **020/7240-8946**. www.jackwills.com. Tube: Marble Arch.

Jimmy Choo ★   The legendary Malaysian cobbler started his luxe line in 1996 with a fashion editor from the British edition of *Vogue*. Today, he designs a couture line that is sold by appointment only at 18 Connaught Street (ⓒ 020/7262-6888), a location so exclusive it's not posted on the corporate website. If you're not a celebrity or MP's wife, you'll have to content yourself with the flagship store.

27 New Bond St., W1. ⓒ **020/7493-5858**. www.jimmychoo.com. Tube: Bond Street.

The Laden Showroom ★★   Barry Laden takes chances on eager, young designers when no one else will. Since 1999, this lifelong Whitechapel resident has given counsel and space—a shelf here, a cubicle there—to newbie designers, about 40 at a time. Once you go in, it's tough to leave without something. Most items, but not all, are for women.

103 Brick Lane, E1. ⓒ **020/7247-2431**. www.laden.co.uk. Tube: Whitechapel.

New Look ★★   Another reliable High Street chain that does a huge amount of cute casual wear fashionably and cheaply. Its specialty is women's clothes, but it does a few men's.

500-502 Oxford St., W1. ℂ **020/7290-7860**. www.newlook.co.uk. Tube: Marble Arch.

Office ★★★   The H&M of footwear rips off designer styles cheaply but effectively, and you'll find it everywhere in town, but one of the most convenient locations is in the Seven Dials area of Covent Garden.

57 Neal St., WC2. ℂ **020/7379-1896**. www.office.co.uk. Tube: Covent Garden.

Old Hat ★★   I say, old chap, what happened to all the tweed coats and bowler hats the British men were famous for wearing? They're gathering dust here, where classic British fashion, if that's the term, can be found for cheap.

66 Fulham High St., SW6. ℂ **020/7610-6558**. www.davidsaxby.com. Closed Sun. Tube: Putney Bridge.

Opening Ceremony ★★   The first European outpost of the American marketplace that promotes the most promising local artists, the shop sells a variety of British designers, new and established, cult favorites and its own house label, in a mix that appeals to a fashion-obsessed crowd.

35 King St., WC2. ℂ **020/7836-4978**. www.openinceremony.us. Closed Sun. Tube: Putney Bridge.

Primark ★★★   The most intense, most crowded, most oppressive store on Oxford Street roils with young families stuffing baskets with cheap-as-chips fashionable outfits, shoes, luggage, and outrageously lowballed accessories. Unfortunately, we're also talking about a clientele that discards garments wherever they want, staff that cleans up the rubble with big push brooms, no washrooms, and products that won't last a year. But the bargains! Oh, the bargains—paying more than £10 is unusual, and £1 deals are common. You just can't help leaving with sacksful. "The devil wears Primark," mutter the snobs.

213 Oxford St., W1. ℂ **020/7495-0420**. www.primark.co.uk. Tube: Marble Arch and 14-18 Oxford St., W1. ℂ **020/7580-5510**. Tube: Tottenham Court Road.

River Island ★★   Another of the popular, affordable women's High Street fashion brands, it's headquartered in West London and designs most of its wares in-house. Dresses are affordable, shoes are cool, leather jackets well-cut, and there's a kid's line. In 2013, Rihanna tried her hand at formulating a collection for the brand. Police had to restrain the crowd.

470-482 Oxford St., W1. ℂ **0844/826-9835**. www.riverisland.com. Tube: Marble Arch; 207-213 Oxford St., W1. ℂ **0844/847-2666**. Tube: Oxford Circus; 309 Oxford St., W1. ℂ **0844/395-1011**. Tube: Oxford Circus.

Rokit ★★   Because it's been cool for longer than many of its competitors have been in business, it has a strong following. Probably the largest collection in the city, Rokit sells retro and vintage threads, shoes, and accessories that are funky and hipster-prone, from 1950s industrial uniforms to tracksuits.

42 Shelton St., WC2. ℂ **020/7836-6547**. www.rokit.co.uk. Tube: Covent Garden. Also in Whitechapel (101 and 107 Brick Lane, E1; ℂ **020/7375-3864**; Tube: Shoreditch High Street) and Camden (225 Camden High St., NW1; ℂ **020/7267-3046**; Tube: Camden Town).

WHAT CAN I bring home?

Although you should always claim edibles when you pass through Customs, very few things will be confiscated. Most stuff, including baked goods, honeys, vinegars, condiments, roasted coffee, teas, candy bars, crisps, pickles, and homemade dishes, are good to go. Always check your country's requirements, but these things are certain to make the inspector dog's nose twitch:

○ Meat and anything containing meat, be it dried, canned, or bouillon.

○ Fresh fruit and vegetables.

○ Runny cheeses, but not firm ones, which make up most cheeses (rule of thumb: if you have to keep it chilled, leave it behind).

○ Rice. As if you would import rice.

○ Plants, soil, wood, and seeds (non-edible). Ask the nursery whether you need paperwork, because many varieties are permitted. And be warned that officers in Australia respond to wood like it's kryptonite.

Topshop ★★★ At this 8,361-sq.-m (90,000-sq.-ft.) store, some 1,000 employees are on hand, many charged expressly with helping shoppers put together a smashing new outfit. The range of accessories is dizzying. It's not just women, either, because the incorporated **Topman** is crammed with deal seekers, too. Designs are at the vanguard of youth fashion, yet the prices are defiantly low, which makes this forward-thinking store a primary stop.

214 Oxford St., W1. ✆ **020/7636-7700**. www.topshop.com. Tube: Oxford Street.

Uniqlo ★★★ Savvy, huge, cheap, and of unexpected extraction like H&M and Zara, the Japan-based, rapidly multiplying megastore is another staple on any sensible Oxford Street shopping spree. It does jeans and tops well, but it's also known for cool socks, and its hallmark is poppy colors and sporty casuals.

311 Oxford St., W1. ✆ **020/7290-7701**. www.uniqlo.co.uk. Tube: Oxford Street.

World's End ★ For a few years in the 1970s, Vivienne Westwood's shop was the coolest place on the planet. The clock at this guerilla boutique still runs backwards, but London's punk heyday is long over, and Westwood went from rebel to royalty. Never mind the bargains—her Anglomania label is a living museum, but it's not cheap. Still, the fanciful couture inventions, flowing with fabric, are outlandish enough to enchant.

430 Kings Rd., SW10. ✆ **020/7352-6551**. www.viviennewestwood.com. Tube: Fulham Broadway.

Food

Also take a gander at the markets in the city, listed at the end of this chapter, and at the food halls of the shopping palaces, earlier in this chapter.

A Gold ★★ English food has been a punch line for so long that even the British were starting to believe the reputation. A. Gold looks longstanding because of its vintage fittings but is actually a newcomer. It peddles country comfort food that you can't even find at the English supermarkets anymore, such as Cornish salted sardine filets,

Romney's Kendal mint cakes, Moffat toffee, and Yorkshire brack—okay, those names don't help, do they?

42 Brushfield St., E1. ✆ **020/7247-2487**. www.agoldshop.com. Closes at 4pm. Tube: Liverpool Street.

Hope and Greenwood ★★ A contemporary evocation of an old-fashioned confectionery, with striped wallpaper, a back wall gleaming with glass jars filled with goodies, and wooden tables piled high with additive soft Terrific Toffees, Salt Caramel Popcorn, boiled sweets, and lavender-and-geranium truffles.

1 Russell St., WC2. ✆ **020/7240-3314**. www.hopeandgreenwood.co.uk. Tube: Covent Garden.

The SAvanna ★ Try some biltong or droëwors, two flavorful jerkies made of local beef, which are eaten like potato chips back in the former colony of South Africa. SAvanna will also sell you antipodean candy bars (Lunch Bar), groceries, and sodas—the Stoney ginger beer will curl your toes.

Unit 1, London Bridge Station, Railway Approach, SE1. ✆ **020/7357-931**. www.thesavanna.co.uk. Tube: London Bridge.

Health & Beauty

Boots ★ Do I dare suggest you patronize the ubiquitous High Street brand that has devoured all other drugstores? Yes, I certainly do. Something like 80% of fragrance sales in the U.K. are conducted over Boots' counters, and the chain's endless 3-for-2 promotions almost always include something worth taking home, be it soaps, razors, or other toiletries. Makeup costs a few pounds less than at most other stores. It's authentically British, too—its founder, John Campbell Boot, the 2nd Baron Trent, has his picture in the National Portrait Gallery.

Multiple locations. www.boots.co.uk.

Neal's Yard Remedies ★★★ At the forefront of Britain's powerful green movement, it supplies beauty aids, holistic treatments, massage oils, and even make-your-own-cosmetics ingredients, all cruelty-free, clear of toxins, and naturally formulated. Its products—London's answer to the New York beauty boutique Kiehl's—are respected for their quality and ethical standards, and the brand is expanding rapidly across the city. The primary store is squirreled away between Monmouth Street and Shorts Gardens, just northeast of Seven Dials.

15 Neal's Yard, WC2. ✆ **020/7379-7222**. www.nealsyardremedies.com. Tube: Covent Garden.

Penhaligon's ★★★ I don't want to picture Prince Charles lighting a Lily of the Valley candle and anointing his body with English Fern eau de toilette, but the fact is that Penhaligon's, established in 1870, is listed as an official supplier to the Prince of Wales, so it may be happening right now. It hand-squeezes and custom designs its own fragrances for both men and women—generally floral-based and gentle—and sidelines in luxury shaving and grooming products. A picturesque location is at 16-17 Burlington Arcade (Tube: Green Park).

41 Wellington St., WC2. ✆ **020/7836-2150**. www.penhaligons.co.uk. Tube: Covent Garden.

Housewares

Conran Shop ★★ Gorgeous, contemporary, smartly selected pieces made its name in housewares, and its flagship store is a master class in elegant urban furnishings and desirable home accessories. Its building is just as worthy: the 1911 Art Nouveau headquarters of the Michelin Tyre Company, coated with decorative tiles of era racing cars and Bibendum.

81 Fulham Rd., W1. ℂ **020/7589-4000**. www.conranshop.co.uk. Tube: South Kensington.

Habitat ★★★ Consider it not for furniture but for its cheerful linens, kitchen tools, and bath fabrics. In pursuit of the department store's mandate (set by founder Sir Terence Conran) to bring high design to the masses at affordable prices, A-list artists (Tracey Emin, Manolo Blahnik) have been recruited to contribute temporary items, and products are always peppy and practical. Although this store is Habitat's showpiece, a nice-size outpost is at 208 King's Rd. in Chelsea (Tube: Sloane Square or South Kensington).

196-199 Tottenham Court Rd., W1. ℂ **084/4499-1122**. www.habitat.co.uk. Tube: Goodge Street.

Heal's ★★ A stalwart since 1810, but not stuffy like one, Heal's (like Liberty, p. 150), was instrumental in forwarding the Arts and Crafts movement in England, and its furniture and housewares, which are usually defined by chic shapes, have proven so influential that in 1978 it donated its archive to the Victoria & Albert museum. The kitchen department is popular. There's another location on tony King's Road (234 King's Rd., SW3; ℂ 7349/8411).

196 Tottenham Court Rd., W1. ℂ **020/7636-1666**. www.heals.co.uk. Tube: Goodge Street.

Stationery

Paperchase ★★★ Paperchase does for stationery what Habitat does for chairs and tables: imbues them with infectious style, bold colors, and wit. Its journal selection is incomparable. Starting in summer, stock up on holiday cards, not only since they're much cheaper in the U.K. than abroad, but also because some proceeds go to charity. There are many so-so branches in this chain, but this three-floor flagship is a big paper cut above. There's even a busy café.

213-215 Tottenham Court Rd., W1. ℂ **020/7467-6200**. www.paperchase.co.uk. Tube: Goodge Street.

Ryman Stationery ★ If you're into office supplies (admit it—it's time to come out of the supply closet), the ubiquitous chain, which makes an appearance on almost

---

Cracking the DVD Code

In their drive to ensure they extract the maximum amount of cash from every economy, Hollywood studios release DVDs with "region codes." American and Canadian players will only play Region 1 discs, and Australia and South America are zoned Region 4, but the DVDs you buy in the U.K. will be coded Region 2. This is annoying, to put it politely for a family-friendly guidebook, because many DVDs for sale in Britain—TV shows, documentaries, and so forth—simply aren't available anywhere else. The only legal solutions for now: Buy DVDs marked "All Regions," (sometimes noted as Region 0) or, back home, pick up a "multizone" DVD player that accepts discs from any region. Those are often sold in neighborhoods where recent immigrants have settled.

every busy shopping street, is a good place to stock up on hard-to-find English-sized A4 paper, envelopes, and convenient "box files" (strangely absent from many countries' stationers), available in a spectrum of sprightly colors.

Multiple locations; www.ryman.co.uk.

Smythson of Bond Street ★★★　In addition to a line of leather journals, organizers, and handbags, it does stationery impeccably. The Queen, a one-woman thank-you note industry, buys her paper here. The cotton-fiber content is probably higher than in your bedsheets.

40 New Bond St., W1. ✆ **020/7629-8558**. www.smythson.com. Closed Sun. Tube: Bond Street.

Toys

Hamleys ★★★　Remote-control helicopters in your hair, magicians at your elbow, rugrats at your knees. This high-octane toy store is run by a gaggle of cheerful young floor staff, themselves kids at heart, who giddily demonstrate the latest toys. The experience will send you into sensory overload. The seven floors are stuffed with amusements—the fifth floor is nothing but sweets. Depending when you go, there may be free pirate face painting, a caricaturist, or even a beach party. It's one of the world's few department stores devoted just to children, and the only must-see toy store in London—even if you don't have kids with you.

188-196 Regent St., W1. ✆ **0871/704-1977**. www.hamleys.com. Tube: Oxford Circus.

LONDON'S GREATEST MARKETS

Unfortunately, with the inexorable spread of megastores like Tesco, Sainsbury's, and the Walmart-owned Asda, outdoor markets that have been feeding Central Londoners since the Dark Ages are finding themselves extinguished. The following markets soldier on. Not every market sells something you can take home, unless you count memories: For example, the **Columbia Road Flower Market** (Sundays at 8am; Tube: Old Street), is an Eden for English blooms, which get cheaper around 2pm, near closing time. **Borough Market**, which is fully described on p. 71, is all about prepared foods or things you can't get past Customs. Even if you aren't keen to buy anything, a stroll down one of the market lanes. It's like a front-row seat to the ongoing opera of everyday life. It's London as it was—and hopefully will continue to be.

> ### Market Hours
>
> Unless otherwise noted, markets are mostly outdoors and generally kick off at around 8 or 9am in the morning and start packing up at around 3pm.

BERWICK STREET MARKET ★

Berwick St. around Broadwick St.; www.berwickstreetlondon.co.uk; daily except Sun; Tube: Piccadilly Circus.

Good for: Fruit and vegetables and basic wares; it's small, but it's the last daily street market in the West End, dating to the crowded days of the 1840s.

Also check out: Interesting punk clothing and record shops along the route.

BRICK LANE MARKETS ★★★

Brick Lane at Buxton St.; www.bricklanemarket.com; Tube: Shoreditch High Street.

Good for: The Vintage Market (clothes), Backyard Market (crafts), Boiler House (food), and Tea Rooms (antiques), all open on weekends. On Sundays, UpMarket does trendy fashions and food.
Also check out: The Beigel Bake (p. 76) for London's version of a bagel.

BRIXTON MARKET ★

Electric Ave. at Pope's Rd.; daily except Sun; Tube: Brixton.

Good for: Exotic produce, spices, halal meats, sold to reggae and hip-hop.
Also check out: Brixton Village, stalls selling African and Caribbean clothes, foods, and housewares; Ritzy's Art Fayre, a designer market, every Saturday.

CAMDEN ★★

Camden High St. at Buck St.; daily (but weekends are best); Tube: Camden Town.

Good for: Tourists favor this rambling warren of 700 stalls for vintage fashions, sunglasses, leather, goth wear, and fast foods, partly in a dockside setting. Between the Lock Market, the Market Hall, the Horse Stables, and Camden Lock Village across the street, options seem never-ending, but the crowds can be tiring.
Also check out: Stables Market, on the other side of the railway off Chalk Farm Road, sells vintage clothes, antiques, and pop culture knick-knacks; Electric Market (on Camden High Street) is an indoor fair of cool T-shirts, fake furs, and goth wear, Saturday and Sunday.

CHAPEL MARKET ★★

Islington; daily except Mon; Tube: Angel.

Good for: Cheese, dumplings, meat pies, toiletries—it's a real catch-all working-class market that actually feeds workaday Londoners.
Also check out: The antithesis of a market, the gleaming N1 Islington mall, dominates the eastern end of the street; it's New London versus Old London.

GREENWICH MARKETS ★★

11A Greenwich Market; www.greenwichmarket.net; Wed–Sun, but best weekends; Tube: Cutty Sark DLR or Greenwich National Rail.

Good for: Antiques, crafts, honeys, breads, cakes under a historic market roof.
Also check out: The cafes lining the covered Craft Market.

LEATHER LANE MARKET ★

Leather Lane between Clerkenwell Rd. and Greville St.; weekdays from 10:30am–2:30pm; Tube: Farringdon.

Good for: Hot and ready-to-eat food, be it Jewish (latkes, salt beef), Mexican (burritos), or universal (salads); sweat suits and skirts, shoes, jeans.
Also check out: Ye Olde Mitre pub (p. 81), a street away.

MALTBY STREET MARKET ★★★

Maltby Street, SE1; www.maltby.st; ✆ **020/7237-9247;** Sat 9am–4pm, Sun 11am–4pm. Tube: London Bridge or Bermondsey.

Good for: Refugee vendors from overrun Borough Market decamped to here, south of the Tower Bridge, and they share railway vaults with an antiques salvage company.

HACK THE tax attack

First, the good news: when you see a price in England, that's the full price. Tax is always included. Now, the bad news: that tax is usually charged at a rate of 20%. It's called VAT (Value-Added Tax), and it goes to enviable programs such as national health care, so that any British citizen who needs emergency care doesn't have to go into debt to get it.

And more good news: tourists can often get a little of that back. As long as the store you're patronizing participates in the VAT Retail Export Scheme (many don't) and you get the paperwork from them while you're there (stores have varying minimum-purchase requirements), you can apply for a refund, minus a dismaying chunk for administrative fees. The only purchases it doesn't work for are vehicles, unmounted gemstones, and anything, except antiques, requiring an export license. The system mostly benefits those who spend hundreds or thousands of pounds.

To get money back:

- Be a non–European Community visitor to the U.K.
- Obtain stamped tax refund documents from each retailer. At big

stores, you may have to wait in line with I.D. and receipts for as long as half hour and the store may take a cut of several pounds as a processing fee.

- On the day you leave Britain, present that document to the VAT refund desk at the airport. The line may be extreme. You must also have the goods on hand, which means a) you must put them in your carry-on or b) you pack the goods in your baggage but first check in at your airline to pick up your travel documents, then bring your yet-to-be checked baggage for inspection, and then re-submit your baggage at the airline counter once that is finished. This process can take up to 2 hours, and even then you may only get £7 back for every £100 you spent, so decide if it's really worth the hassle and then plan ahead.

Britain maintains information via ℂ 029/2050-1261 or www.hmrc.gov.uk.

Shuffle along gathering gorgeous flavors such as pork with sweet chili jam, mugs of horseradished Bloody Marys, and "African volcano" hot sauce.

Also check out: Historic pie and mash vendor M. Manze (p. 72) is nearby.

PORTOBELLO ROAD MARKET ★
Fri and Sat; www.portobelloroad.co.uk; Tube: Notting Hill Gate or Westbourne Park.

Good for: Antiques, hot foods, jewelry, vintage clothes, tourist tat by the ton. Overcrowded and overrated, but thanks to the movies, it's not going anywhere.

Also check out: The packed pubs along the route; the galleries and antiques shops in the storefronts, where prices can be better than at the stalls.

QUEEN'S MARKET ★
Green St. at Queen's Rd.; Tues and Thurs–Sun; Tube: Upton Park.

Good for: 80 stalls and 60 local stores for ingredients from Asia, Africa, Russia, the Caribbean, and elsewhere; international clothes and rugs. Although it's not very posh, it is very Everyday London. Sunday is a quieter day.

Also check out: Its defenders' website, www.friendsofqueensmarket.org.uk, which has argued their market is half as expensive as Walmart.

RIVERSIDE WALK MARKET ★★

Southbank under the Waterloo Bridge; daily noon–7pm in good weather; Tube: Waterloo.

Good for: Tables of used books, maps, lithographs, and wood engravings.

Also check out: Lower Marsh Market on Lower Marsh between Westminster Bridge and Baylis roads (south of Waterloo station), for a classic produce market.

SPITALFIELDS MARKET ★★

Commercial St. between Brushfield St. and Lamb St.; www.visitspitalfields.com; daily except Sat; Tube: Liverpool Street.

Good for: Up-and-coming designers and artists, prepared world food, handmade housewares, jewelry, vintage cinema posters. It's the most gentrified market in town, and there are lots of one-of-a-kind clothing items for sale, not all of them affordable. The rollicking success of this market has been one of the major reasons that East London is now considered a hip hotspot.

Also check out: Visit the Style Market for fashions on Saturday afternoons.

WALTHAMSTOW MARKET ★

Walthamstow Market St.; www.walthamstowmarket.com; Tues–Sat.; Tube: Walthamstow.

Good for: 450 stalls selling everything, from knockoff clothes to food to Chinese-made batteries—it's the longest market street in Europe.

Also check out: You may not have the energy to see much else in this multicultural neighborhood, since the market is a kilometer long.

LONDON NIGHTLIFE

7

Let no one tell you that London tucks itself into bed early. Perhaps that was true in your grandfather's day, but nowadays, the U.K. rocks all night. The Tube may shut down after midnight, but the entertainment rollicks until dawn. London, simply put, is an entertainment dynamo. With hundreds of theaters, nightclubs, cinemas, and music halls, London has more to offer on a single night than many cities can muster in an entire year.

That said, London's nights aren't perfect. The city's prevailing liquor laws, to say nothing of a Tube system that often closes after midnight, force even top clubs to sometimes unceremoniously dump their clientele on the streets in mid-toast. Whereas in Spain, Greece, and New York, the night rarely begins before 1am, that's usually when the DJ packs up at many of London's top clubs. Recent changes to the law have only added an extra hour to a few clubs' operations. That can put a crimp in plans since it forces those who can't afford taxis to choose just one or two activities in a single night: dinner, theater, or club. The Night Bus system (p. 233) assuages some of the financial pain, but it's a buzzkill to end a festive night out with your legs crossed while you crane your next for the bus.

GETTING THE SCOOP   The best way to know what's going on is to do what the locals do: Hit the newsstand. Londoners turn to their newspapers and magazines for announcements of the latest to see, hear, and do. The most complete listings information for entertainment is published on Saturday in the daily papers. You can also start with these resources:

○ *Time Out* **magazine:** The original publication of what's now an international brand, Time Out's weekly pages constitute the most comprehensive listing of goings-on, and in 2012, it began publishing for free. (www.timeout.com/london)

○ **Visit London:** The "What's On" section of its website is assiduously updated and, even better, it's free. (www.visitlondon.com)

○ *Metro:* Free in racks at Tube stations, most copies are gone by mid-morning, but commuters leave copies behind on the trains; it's considered green to recycle a pre-read newspaper. (www.metro.co.uk)

○ The *Evening Standard:* Free near Tube stop entrances in the afternoon—some days, there's an accompanying lifestyle-centric magazine section; it's usually in a nearby stack. ES is also available online for free. (www.standard.co.uk)

THEATER

If you leave London without seeing at least one stage show, then you'll have missed one of this city's most glittering attractions. This is where Shakespeare defined great writing and Gilbert and Sullivan shaped modern musical theater. London's influence isn't just in antiquity; the great work continues to this day, and if you doubt it, look at the lists of Oscar, Emmy, and Tony winners from the past decade. With that kind of heritage, London theatres are intrinsically more daring than American ones, where an over-emphasis on profits and critics mar creativity.

Whenever you hear the phrase "West End" in relation to shows, think of the term as describing the 60-odd top-tier theatres in the middle of town. These are the shows that most tourists flock to see, but that doesn't mean they're always the best—the West End is increasingly clogged with mediocre dramas propped up by Hollywood names and by so-called "jukebox" musicals that are the intellectual equivalent of bubble gum.

A great many West End shows begin their lives at companies found elsewhere in town. For challenging work mounted by producers intent on taking artistic risks, look to them. Many of them have designed and built facilities expressly for pumping out fresh projects, and each of them has a devoted following of fans and donors that most tourists, because of the circles they travel in, don't hear about. What's more, you're just as likely to catch stars—all at prices that are half what you'd shell out for a West End megamusical that was created by committee.

Standard curtain times range from 7:30 to 8pm for evening shows, and matinees start anywhere between 2 and 4pm. Every theatre is different, so check your ticket. Nearly all shows are closed, or "dark," on Sundays.

It's easy to make a night of it. Every theatre has its own bar, and many sell ice cream and snacks at intermission ("interval"). Companies with their own buildings might even run their own mid- to high-end restaurants.

Theater Tickets for Less

If you are desperate to see a specific show, book tickets before you leave home to ensure you won't be left out. Check with **The Society of London Theatre** (www.officiallondontheatre.co.uk), the trade association for theater owners and producers (established in 1908), for a rundown of what's playing and soon to play, as well as discount offers. Keep in mind that many links, including Visit London's, will deliver you to ticket sellers who'll hit you for a premium of as much as 20 percent for your booking. Only use that method if you'd be heartbroken to miss a particular show.

Given a lead-time of a few weeks, the established **LastMinute.com** sells tickets for half price, as does **LoveTheatre.com** (click "Special Offers"). **BroadwayBox** (www.broadwaybox.com/london) posts the known discount codes for the West End shows. **London.Broadway.com** also sometimes advertises slight discounts, but make sure you see evidence of a price cut, because many of its ticketing offers are, in fact, at regular retail rates.

Once you get to London, grab a copy of The *Official London Theatre Guide,* dispensed for free in nearly every West End theater's lobby and at countless brochure racks; it tells you what's playing, where, for how much and how long, and the location of each theater. Unless you buy discounted seats directly from the box office of the theater, there's only one intelligent place to get same-day tickets: **TKTS** (South side of Leicester Square; www.tkts.co.uk; Mon–Sat 10am–7pm, Sun noon–3pm; Tube:

saving ON THE STAGE

Apart from using TKTS, how can you save on a show?

o **Matinees are often cheaper than evening shows.** Unfortunately, they also cut into your available daylight touring time.

o **Ask about standing room tickets and "day seats."** Not all theaters have them, but the Donmar, the National, and the Old Vic, to take three examples, may sell standing room for a tenner (£10) to £20. "Day seats" are a daily allotment of cheap seats that you'll have to queue for in the morning. The Book of Mormon holds a fun lottery for cheap seats 2½ hours before curtain.

o **Buy at the box office** to avoid paying booking fees.

o **In one of the older theaters, you can often settle for a restricted-view seat.** You may have to crane your neck to see around the edge of the balcony or a pillar, but you'll be in the room. They cost about a third what top-price seats do. Theatremonkey.com posts theatre-specific ratings of them.

o **If you're a student,** some box offices (but not TKTS) may offer you discounts of 20 to 40 percent. Make sure you have a recognized ID card.

Leicester Square), operated by the Society of London Theatre. It sells same-day seats at mostly half-price—the best stuff is sold in the first hour of opening. While the white-hot shows won't be represented here, about 80 percent of West End shows are—TKTS posts a list of its available shows on its website, which is handy for getting a handle on what may be on sale when you get there. Musicals are half off, around £30–£40, up to full price; and plays cost £20–£30, although the prices fluctuate per production with up to a £3 per ticket service charge. Come armed with a magazine or a newspaper that lists what the shows are about because TKTS offers no descriptions.

The West End is dotted with closet-size stalls hawking tickets to major shows and concerts. Don't deal with them. They are for audiences who simply must get tickets to their chosen show regardless of the fees as high as 25 percent over cost. Before you give your money to any of these outfits, check with the self-policing **Society of Ticket Agents and Retailers** (© 0844/879-4272; www.star.org.uk) to find out who is reputable. Scalpers, called **touts** here, often issue counterfeit tickets or abscond with your cash before forking over anything at all. Some sightseeing discount cards also brag about discounts, but their deals are mostly for the longest-running, touristy shows and they don't save you nearly as much as TKTS would—only around £20 off the top price.

London's Landmark Theaters

The Barbican Centre ★★ In the 1950s, earnest but misguided city fathers turned their attentions toward redeveloping a bombed-out crater. The end result was a haltingly forbidding, mixed-use residential/business concrete complex that took more than 20 years to finish. They optimistically planned for lively crowds by adding Europe's largest arts and conference center, too, with a concert hall, two theaters, three cinemas, and two galleries, and now they're the best thing about the place—and one of the best things about London arts in general. You can't always find something going on in all of its venues, and even when things are rocking full-tilt, the bunkered Barbican is so windswept it makes *Blade Runner* look like Candy Land, but what does play here is rarely dull. It's nearly impossible to classify the Barbican's fare, since it receives a wide range of the world's great orchestras, singers, and composers, plus a handful of banner festivals each year, particularly in the realm of contemporary music and experimental theater. Its cinemas often screen features fresh from major film festival triumphs, and the long-running Bite festival brings in work from new names and white-hot international producers.

Silk St., EC2. ℂ **020/7638-8891** www.barbican.org.uk. Tube: Barbican.

The Bush Theatre ★★★   The Bush, which for more than 40 years has created a formidable output from new writers, started as a pub theatre and in 2011, thanks to a lifesaving campaign that rallies support from the likes of Judi Dench and Daniel Radcliffe, got its own facility in a disused Victorian library. Besides attracting exciting writers, it brings in stars (like Kate Beckinsale and Alan Rickman) who want to connect with audiences.

7 Uxbridge Rd., W12. ℂ **020/8743-5050** www.bushtheatre.co.uk. Tube: Shepherds Bush.

Donmar Warehouse ★★★   You can't often snag a last-minute ticket to the 250-seat house without standing in line for returns. Its productions, mostly limited runs of vividly reconceived revivals, are edgy and buzzy. Past coups for this comfortably converted brewery warehouse include the *Cabaret* revival that introduced Alan Cumming to the world and appearances by world-class performers such as Ian McKellen and Nicole Kidman. The front row of full-price, same-day tickets are dished out each morning at 10am sharp Mondays for performances 2 weeks later, with a maximum of two tickets per person.

41 Earlham St., WC2. ℂ **0844/871-7624.** www.donmarwarehouse.com. Tube: Covent Garden.

Menier Chocolate Factory ★★   In an intimate setting among exposed beams and cast iron columns, converted you-know-what from the 1870s, is where some of the city's hottest musical revivals have been mounted. Its *Sunday in the Park with George* and *A Little Night Music* transferred to the West End and later to Broadway. This company, which also does plays, is one of the few to do Sunday shows; it's dark Mondays.

51-53 Southwark St., SE1. ℂ **020/7378-1713.** www.menierchocolatefactory.com.Tube: London Bridge.

Old Vic ★   American star Kevin Spacey moved to London to run the Old Vic, and the fruits of his stewardship have been largely successful. His choices (generally mountings of talky, meat-and-potatoes drama—stuff actors love to sink their teeth into) are reliable, and he often hires stars like Vanessa Redgrave, Kim Cattrall and, yes, himself. There's little doubt that the 200-year-old building is pulling bigger crowds than it did before, and The Pit Bar, downstairs, is a stylish pre- and post-show hangout.

The Cut at Waterloo Rd., SE1. ℂ **0844/871-7628.** www.oldvictheatre.com. Tube: Waterloo or Southwark.

Royal Court Theatre ★★   The pre-eminent writer's theatre, it has fought censorship and unveiled international brilliance for so long that it's now a pre-eminent actor's theatre as well. On the east side of jaunty Sloane Square, it devotes a hefty portion of its schedule to important premieres in two theatres to premieres by the likes of Bruce Norris and Caryl Churchill to performances from fierce actors such as Ben Whishaw and Fiona Shaw. Among the plays launched here include *Look Back in Anger, The Rocky Horror Picture Show* (in its upstairs studio theatre), George Bernard Shaw's *Major Barbara* and *Heartbreak House* and most recently, *Cock.*

Sloane Square, SW1. ℂ **020/7565-5000.** www.royalcourttheatre.com. Tube: Sloane Square.

Royal National Theatre ★★★   The government-subsidized powerhouse people simply call The National is perhaps the country's most noted showpiece for top-flight drama and classical acting, and its three houses are frequently the birthplaces of the city's hottest tickets, so when you're planning shows, check here first. Nicholas Hytner, its director until 2015—Laurence Olivier was its first one—is one of the theater world's luminaries, and he plans a diverse repertoire for its three spaces permanent that runs from envelope-pushing musicals (*Jerry Springer: The Opera*) to classic revivals (the *Oklahoma!* that made Hugh Jackman a star) to immersive spectacles with no seats (Punchdrunk's *The Drowned Man*) to a huge range of dramas (*War Horse* began here) to world premieres of well-made plays by famous writers cast with household names. Actors consider it a career highlight to tread the boards at this modern theatrical mulitplex, and the season runs year-round. As the people's theatre, pricing is populist. Some 95,000 tickets a year are discounted to £12 for the Travelex season (ℂ 020/7452-3000). It also runs 75-minute tours (£8.50) showing off the backstage areas, and the lobby bookstore is performing arts heaven.

South Bank, SE1. ℂ **020/7452-3000.** www.nationaltheatre.org.uk. Tube: Waterloo.

Sadler's Wells ★   Sadler's Wells has been a part of the fabric of London life for so long (since 1683) that its current two-house home, dating to 1998, is actually the sixth. You can turn to this Islington establishment to catch some of the world's greatest companies in movement- or rhythm-based performances that transcend language. Its specialties are ballet (Matthew Bourne is a frequent guest artist), contemporary dance, and opera (Rufus Wainwright's *Prima Donna* premiered here). It also programs the Peacock Theatre on Portugal Street near the Holborn Tube.

Rosebery Ave., EC1. ℂ **020/7863-8198.** www.sadlerswells.com. Tube: Angel.

Southbank Centre ★★★   Like the Barbican, it's a bleak canvas-colored slab architects don't know quite how to fix. It was conceived as a postwar pick-me-up, but age was not kind; despite a peerless riverside location, it's got a reputation as a forbidding architectural scowl that looks more like a pile of sidewalk curbs than an artistic capitol. It's perkier on the inside. Some 1,000 programs a year go down here at its three concert venues as well as in its huge central hall, which has a cafe and is open to everybody. Dance, classical and contemporary music, the London Jazz Festival, and films fill the bill, but by no means define it.

Belvedere Rd., SE1. ℂ **020/7863-8198.** www.southbankcentre.co.uk. Tube: Waterloo.

London's Great Smaller Theaters

Almeida Theatre ★★   The inviting Almeida, which has its own contemporary pub, sticks to its guns, mounting intelligent plays (some new, some unfairly forgotten, many new) without much regard for pushback—the winter of 2014 will see *American*

THE QUIRKS OF LONDON theatregoing

London theater can be a new experience for outsiders:

o Programs are not free; they cost from £3 (for plays) to £5 (for musicals). Big productions will also sell a glossy souvenir brochure for £7 to £10.

o Some seats are equipped with plastic opera glasses, which can be rented for the show with a 50p or £1 coin.

o What North American theaters call "orchestra" seats, London houses call the "stalls." And instead of a "mezzanine," they have a "Dress Circle," and above that, "Upper Circle" or "Royal Circle." If there happens to be a third, topmost level, that is the "balcony," or sometimes, the "gallery." And because many theaters were constructed in a class-obsessed era, there will likely be a separate street entrance for each area.

o The break between acts is called an "interval," not "intermission."

o The big snack? Ice cream, sold by ushers (or "attendants").

o Older theaters are required to deploy the "fire curtain," which seals the stage from the auditorium in the event of flames, once during every performance. It's usually done discreetly during the interval.

o Leave big bags at the hotel, because these old seats can be real knee-knockers. And ladies, cover your knees, because in the Circles, they will likely be at head-level of the person sitting in front of you.

Psycho—the musical. The resulting experience is often thought-provoking. Lucy Kirkwood's *Chimerica,* about the Tiananmen Square tank photograph, was a 2013 smash.
Almeida St. off Upper St., N1. ☎ **020/7359-4404.** www.almeida.co.uk. Tube: Angel.

Hackney Empire ★ One of London's greatest and most ornate old houses (1901) was where, once upon a time, you could catch Charlie Chaplin as a vaudeville act. The slate still presents the best of variety, but with an urban, multicultural twist: kids' shows, opera, comedy acts like British smarm-meister Jimmy Carr, hip-hop drama, and concerts.
291 Mare St., E8. ☎ **020/8985-2424.** www.hackneyempire.co.uk. Tube: Hackney Central Overground.

Lyric Hammersmith ★ It may look like a fusty Victorian jewel-box theater, but you'll find spectacular stuff—a mix of multimedia-based shows, avant garde experiments, and an annual Christmas show to write home about. Its kids' shows are its bread and butter.
Lyric Square, King St., S6. ☎ **020/8741-6850.** www.lyric.co.uk. Tube: Hammersmith.

Roundhouse ★★ Located in a rehabbed 1846 locomotive shed, picks up on the maverick spirit of neighboring Camden with a frisky lineup of innovative creations such as musical dramas and spectaculars, many of them given a crowd-pleasing, dance-inflected, shock-to-the-system twist. In the 1960s, it was one of London's most important stages, particularly for counterculture concerts: In more recent seasons, you're just as likely to see one-off comedy events or concerts (The B-52s, David Byrne).

Chalk Farm Rd., NW1. ✆ 084/4482-8008. www.roundhouse.org.uk. Tube: Chalk Farm.

Soho Theatre ★   The Soho functions like an one-building arts festival; it casts a wide net in looking for the latest voices in theater, comedy, and cabaret. On weekend days, come for kids' shows.

21 Dean St., W1. ✆ 020/7478-0100 www.sohotheatre.com. Tube: Tottenham Court Road.

The Unicorn Theatre ★   A children's theater that caters to kids without suffering from a debilitating case of preciousness, it runs at least two productions, one for each of its theater spaces, at a time. Some are script-based and some sensory-based for younger kids and kids with autism. Many are designed to expose kids to other cultures, places, and classic stories for the first time. If only every city had a kids' facility as lush.

147 Tooley St., SE1. ✆ 020/7645-0560. www.unicorntheatre.com. Tube: London Bridge.

Young Vic ★   Spry and in top form, it programs a mixed bag of sturdy plays, conversational touchstones, edgy musicals, and affordable opera, then stands back and hopes for frisson. It often achieves it, and if it fails, it doesn't dally long, since it has three theaters (seating 500, 160, and 80) to fill. There's nearly always something high-quality to plumb here.

66 The Cut, SE1. ✆ 020/7922-2922. www.youngvic.org. Tube: Waterloo or Southwark.

Pub Theatres

In the early 1970s, a new form of alternative theatre swept London: the pub theatre. Often just a tatty back room where you can bring your beer from the scruffy front bar, your typical theater pub is where some of the city's most affordable, idiosyncratic, let's-try-this-and-see-if-it-works theater is found—which is why so many megastar actors were launched to fame from them. Some of the most respected fringe venues in town are pub theaters, and they have just as much artistic power as many better-heeled West End palaces. Five fantastic ones are:

The Etcetera Theatre ★★   Odd, challenging fare (sometimes several different shows a night) in its very small black box. 265 Camden High St., NW1. ✆ 020/7482-4857. www.etceteratheatre.com. Tube: Camden Town.

Hen & Chickens ★   Frequent comedy bookings as well as strong writing presented by a resident company. 109 St. Paul's Rd., N1. ✆ 020/7354-8246. www.henand chickens.com. Tube: Highbury & Islington.

The King's Head ★★★   Alums include Kenneth Branagh, Clive Owen, Joanna Lumley, Ben Kingsley, Juliet Stevenson, Hugh Grant, and John Hurt in their younger, braver, poorer days. 115 Upper St., N1. ✆ 020/7478-0160. www.kingsheadtheatre.com. Tube: Angel.

Landor Theatre ★   Basically just a large room seating about 60, this space specializes in palatable musicals, cabaret, and comedy. 70 Landor Rd., SW9. ✆ 020/7737-7276. www.landortheatre.co.uk. Tube: Clapham North.

Old Red Lion ★   The very pubby ORL hires its 60-seat space to a variety of aspiring producers and hosts the occasional comedy night. 418 St. John St., EC1. ✆ 020/7837-7816. www.oldredliontheatre.co.uk. Tube: Angel.

OPERA

Opera can a budget-breaker. Frugal travelers should try the street singers who perform daily at the **Covent Garden Piazza** (Tube: Covent Garden). That's not a joke: Performers are auditioned before being awarded buskers' licenses, so the caliber here is high. Also check to see if there's a touring opera putting down stakes at Sadler's Wells (p. 168). Of course, nothing compares to these institutions:

English National Opera ★★   With the Royal Opera entrenched as the country's premium company, the ENO can be the progressive one. Gadaffi has been fodder for one opera, and in 2013, Philip Glass' bio-opera *The Perfect American,* was a *Citizen Kane* version of Walt Disney's life. The rest of its 9-show slate consists of classics *(Aida, Rigoletto).* In an ongoing "Secret Seats" promotion (only bookable online), buy an unallocated seat for £20 and be guaranteed a seat worth £25 or more somewhere in its gorgeous London Coliseum theatre.

St. Martin's Lane, WC2. ✆ **020/7845-9300.** www.eno.org. Tube: Leicester Square.

Royal Opera House ★★   Opera fans don't need to be reminded of the role the ROH plays on the world scene, but outsiders might be surprised at how inviting and attractive its terrace and café are. The main house, which is shared by the equally prestigious Royal Opera and Royal Ballet, is supplemented with two smaller spaces for chamber opera and studio dance. Happily, 40 percent of the tickets cost £40 or less—if you move quickly—and surtitles appear on little screens or monitors. There are three daytime tours available, too: backstage, or workshops, or its 2,256-seat, horseshoe-shaped auditorium (✆ 020/7304-4002; £7.50–12; Calendar online).

Bow St., Covent Garden, WC2. ✆ **020/7304-4000.** www.roh.org.uk. Tube: Covent Garden.

DANCE PERFORMANCE

London's dance scene has yet to achieve the vibrancy of New York's or Germany's, but hat's not to say there's nothing to see; it's just that some of the best terpsichorean productions are put on by visiting companies, not by Londoners. The first thing to do is check the schedules at The Barbican (p. 166), Roundhouse (p. 169), Sadler's Wells (p. 168), and Southbank Centre (p. 168), which present a cornucopia of performance genres. The country's premier company, **Royal Ballet ★★** shares space with the Royal Opera (Bow St., Covent Garden, WC2; ✆ 020/7304-4000; www.roh.org.uk; Tube: Covent Garden). The more adventurous **English National Ballet** tours Britain much of the time but when it's in London, its home is the London Coliseum and sometimes the Barbican (St. Martin's Lane, WC2; ✆ 020/7845-9300; www.ballet.org.uk; Tube: Leicester Square).

The Place ★★★ (17 Duke's Rd., WC1; ✆ **020/7121-1100;** www.theplace.org.uk; Tube: Euston) is known for contemporary dance—specifically, as the home of the Richard Alston Dance Company—and the host venue of some 100 companies a year from around the world. **Laban Theatre** (Creekside, Greenwich, SW8; ✆ **020/8691-8600;** www.laban.org; Tube: Cutty Sark DLR) The lucky tenant of a gleaming translucent building by the same team that designed the Tate Modern puts on a mixed bill of works from around the world and by up-and-comers from its dance school. To find out about one-off performances, check Time Out's "Dance" section. Also check out the listing for the Barbican (p. 166), the Southbank Centre (p. 168), and the city's lunchtime concerts (p. 172).

CLASSICAL MUSIC

Cadogan Hall ★   With 900 seats, the onetime Christian Scientist church is now the home of the Royal Philharmonic Orchestra and, in summer, the BBC Proms, which books it during the summer for its chamber music as a supplement to its concerts at Royal Albert Hall.

5 Sloane Terrace, SW1. ℰ **020/7730-4500.** www.cadoganhall.com. Tube: Sloane Square.

King's Place ★★   Since only 2008, this new development has become the city's most versatile, exciting music venue. Bright ideas include year-long series on a single composer (2013: Bach), 50 great chamber concerts determined by a vote, comedy, and literary festivals.

90 York Way, N1. ℰ **020/7520-1440.** www.kingsplace.co.uk. Tube: King's Cross St Pancras.

Royal Albert Hall ★★★   Imposing, ornate, and adored by music lovers worldwide, it's one of the few performance arenas on earth where, once they have performed there, artists can truly claim to have made it. During the summer, the storied BBC Promenade Concerts (the Proms) fill this historic, 5,200-seat circular hall with classical music, but the rest of the year, the space books a hodgepodge of tours, arena-style musicals, Cirque du Soleil, concerts (the house organ is 21m/69 ft. tall and has 10,000 pipes)—even tennis matches. See p. 107 to tour it.

Kensington Gore, SW7. ℰ **0845/401-5034.** www.royalalberthall.com. Tube: South Kensington.

St. Martin-in-the-Fields ★★★   Right in the thick of Trafalgar Square, this handsome church's evening candlelight concerts and lunchtime performances are London traditions. It's non-fussy with clean acoustics.

Trafalgar Square, WC2. ℰ **020/7766-1100.** www.stmartin-in-the-fields.org. Tube: Charing Cross.

Wigmore Hall ★★   Opened in 1901 as a recital hall for the Bechstein piano showroom that was once next door, it was seized (along with the company) as enemy property in World War I. A nasty start, but today, it's known for ideal acoustics and a roster of some 400 concerts a year.

36 Wigmore St., W1. ℰ **020/7935-2141.** www.wigmore-hall.org.uk. Tube: Bond Street.

THE MUSIC SCENE

Just as many of London's live music venues don't draw a heavy line between the genres they present, no rigid division exists between gig venues and dance venues; in fact, many spaces switch from live music to dance in a single evening. That's one of the things that make the city's nightlife so vibrant, but it's also why it's important to check programming in advance. Students can often get discounts on entry—as if you needed any more proof that education is valued in England.

Live Music, Including Jazz, Pop, Folk & Rock

Dozens of theaters and arenas in town book concerts by recognizable names, but it would be fruitless to list them since they're almost all rented by promoters and don't

PRINCE CHARLES CINEMA: THE WORLD'S silliest MOVIE THEATER?

The family-friendly "Sing-a-Long-a" *The Sound of Music*, a silly participatory screening of the 1965 classic, was born here in 1999 and swept the world. Participants—some of whom arrive dressed as Nazis and nuns, without regard to gender—receive a "magic moment" bag with edelweiss, curtain swatches, and a party popper to deploy at the moment of Maria and the Captain's kiss. And it hasn't stopped with "Do-Re-Mi." On Friday nights, other Netflix favorites are given the call-and-response treatment, *Grease, Moulin Rouge, Bugsy Malone, Willy Wonka*, and *Dirty Dancing* among them. On other nights, it's a "quote-along" to *Mean Girls, Anchorman*, or *Ghostbusters*. Or a *Labyrinth* Masquerade Ball. Or an all-night sleepover to John Hughes movies. Or an *Animal House* Frat Party (don't tell your hotel you're wearing its sheets). Is this the giddiest movie theatre in the world? 7 Leicester Place; ℂ 020/7494-3654; www.princecharlescinema.com; Tube: Leicester Square.

always have something going on. The better advice is to stay on top of who's playing by checking *Time Out* (www.timeout.com) or *New Musical Express* (NME; www.nme.com) magazines. Since big shows sell out months in advance, the best recourse is to book ahead via **See Tickets** (ℂ 087/1220-0260; www.seetickets.com); **Stargreen** (ℂ 020/7734-8932; www.stargreen.com), which has a small office at 20/21a Argyll St., outside the Oxford Circus Tube station; **Ticketweb** (www.ticketweb.co.uk) or its partner **Ticketmaster** (www.ticketmaster.co.uk; both are at ℂ 08444/999-999), all of which levy fees but let you buy from abroad.

The 100 Club ★   Many decades have passed since it was a prime hangout for U.S. servicemen homesick for the jazzy sounds of Glenn Miller and his colleagues. In 1976, after passing through an R&B and jazz period that had Louis Armstrong puckering up for audiences, it sponsored the world's first punk festival, and bands like the Sex Pistols—unsigned at the time—took the stage. This red-walled club still can't decide which era to honor, so it careens between punk, swing, R&B, and jazz.

100 Oxford St., W1. ℂ **020/7636-0933**. www.the100club.co.uk. Cover £7–£21, 25% discounts often available in advance. Tube: Tottenham Court Road.

12 Bar Club ★★★   The postage stamp–size club is a central place to find a range of music, indie pop to funk, booking four acts a night, it costs a found pounds to hear all of them until 3am.

22-23 Denmark Place, WC2. ℂ **020/7240-2120**. www.12barclub.com. Closed Sunday. Tube: Tottenham Court Road.

Barfly ★   Launch pad for a thousand indie bands, some that actually ended up soaring (Coldplay, Blur, and the like), Barfly is a dark, intimate bar/performance space with a good mix of students, musicians, and old-time locals. Beware the sometimes over-zealous moshers. When the bands wrap up, a house DJ spins for a few more hours while the audience chills.

49 Chalk Farm Rd. ℂ **084/4847-2424**. www.barflyclub.com. Tube: Chalk Farm.

The Betsey Trotwood ★★ An adorable, wood-floored Victorian pub on three levels that hosts a few singer-songwriters a month—Jason Mraz appeared here early in his career. Thursdays are for bluegrass.

56 Farringdon Rd., EC1. © **020/7253-4285.** www.thebetsey.com. Tube: Farringdon.

Borderline ★ A Soho institution since 1992, this modest (capacity 275) basement space, which was recently renovated to install much-needed AC, books country, folk, Britpop, and blues. Cheap beer, young crowd.

Orange Yard, Manette Street, W1. © **020/7734-5547.** www.mamacolive.com/theborderline. Tube: Tottenham Court Road.

Dingwalls ★ An ever-popular house of rock, folk, and acoustic guitar since 1973, this former industrial space by Camden Lock grants audiences the dignity of seating and tables for enjoying the music, which has included Mumford and Sons, Jello Biafra, and Foo Fighters.

Middle Yard, NW1. © **020/7428-5929.** www.dingwalls.com. Tube: Camden Town.

Dublin Castle ★ Any bar that proclaims itself the birthplace of the '70s ditty band Madness would not on the surface seem to be a place you'd want to enter without prior insobriety. But it has street cred. It was the first bar in London to win a late liquor license from the government, so it became an important nightspot. Really no more than a threadbare, greenish pub with a teeny backroom stage, it hosts bands struggling to make it—and a few (Blur, for one, and Madness for two) that actually have.

94 Parkway, NW1. © **020/7485-1773.** www.thedublincastle.com. Tube: Camden Town.

Electric Ballroom ★★ One of those dicey, utilitarian halls that never loses the lingering smell of old beer, it has hosted the likes of Sid Vicious, The Clash, and Garbage. Steel yourself for a weeklong roster of punk, goth, industrial, glam, hardcore, metal, and other genres whose aficionados are unlikely to do more architectural damage to the premises than what's already been done by the ravages of time and benign neglect.

184 Camden High St., NW1. © **020/7485-9006.** www.electricballroom.co.uk. Tube: Camden Town.

Green Note ★★ Much of London nightlife is mired in dance music and the illusion of luxury, this welcoming vegetarian café/bar books acoustic live gigs, from folk to jazz, roots to singer-songwriters. Softened by pillows and upholstered seating, it's a laid-back scene, and food prices are sensible (no meat, all organic), but you can swing in just for the shows.

106 Parkway, NW1. © **020/7485-9899.** www.greennote.co.uk. Tube: Camden Town.

Jazz Café ★★★ The prime venue for "names" keeps the music going from to 2am, usually in the form of acts (jazz, soul, bluesy vocalists) with followings. Converted from a bank, there's both cabaret tables and an upstairs gallery with food; show up early for a good position.

5 Parkway, NW1. © **0844/847-2514.** www.jazzcafe.co.uk. Tube: Camden Town.

Koko ★ Favored by visiting indie bands, in its first life as the Camden Palace this 1,500-place, multileveled space saw performances by Charlie Chaplin. In the '70s and '80s, it became an epicenter for pop—The Eurythmics, Boy George, and Wham!

played their earliest gigs here, it's where and Madonna made her UK debut. The name Koko brings respect.

1A Camden Rd., NW1. ✆ **087/0432-5527**. www.koko.uk.com. Tube: Mornington Crescent.

Pizza Express Live ★★ Unlikely as it is for a chain restaurant, it hosts host concerts in on-site jazz club by respected acts such as Jamie Cullum, Noah Jones, and Roy Haynes. Even Amy Winehouse played here.

10 Dean St., W1. ✆ **084/5602-7017**. www.pizzaexpresslive.com. Tube: Tottenham Court Road.

Ronnie Scott's Jazz Club ★ Since the 1960s, it has been the standard bearer in London for stylish, American-style jazz, and it honors a long tradition of pairing visiting U.S. greats with local acts. But the old dive got ritzy. After a £2.1-million renovation, the 255-seater began charging prices in the £45 range. But it's true that the club draws important names, including Patti Austin, Van Morrison, Tom Waits, and Cleo Laine.

47 Frith St., W1. ✆ **020/7439-0747**. www.ronniescotts.co.uk. Tube: Leicester Square.

Scala ★★ When it was a cinema, Stanley Kubrick shut it down for screening his A Clockwork Orange without permission. Good thing he did, or this 1920 theatre might not have been reborn as is a pleasing place to catch an acoustic or lyrical band. Its three levels give nearly everyone a good view of the stage, fostering a sense of intimacy appropriate to its capacity of around 1,000 people. A mazelike warren of rooms confuses the drunk ones and conceals the shy ones. Weekdays, it hosts gigs by indie bands, and weekends, it turns to club nights.

275 Pentonville Rd., N1. ✆ **020/7833-2022**. www.scala-london.co.uk. King's Cross St. Pancras.

The Water Rats ★★ If you're not a headbanger, its singer-songwriters may appeal more than Camden's squalling pubs. Bob Dylan made his U.K. debut in the back room in 1963, Oasis braved London audiences for the first time here in 1994, and Katy Perry played its cramped stage before arenas. It's little wonder why the record-label scouts brave the grime to listen to the new acts, be they alt-country, rock, or hip-hop.

328 Gray's Inn Rd., WC1. ✆ **020/7209-8747**. www.themonto.com. Tube: King's Cross St. Pancras.

Major Venues

If you want to get into the best shows, you have to book ahead, before you arrive. The most important venues post their schedules and link to ticket sellers on their websites. The grittier, midsize venues include **Bush Hall** (www.bushhallmusic.co.uk); the **O₂ Academy Brixton** (www.02academybrixton.co.uk); the **O₂ Academy Islington** (www.02academyislington.co.uk); the **Hammersmith Apollo** (www.hammersmithapollo.com); the **O₂ Shepherds Bush Empire** (www.02shepherdsbushempire.co.uk); plus the **Electric Ballroom** and **Koko** (see below). The most massive venues—where your favorite artist will look like a tiny, bouncing smudge on the far side of 10,000 sweaty fans—are the just-renewed **Queen Elizabeth Olympic Park** (www.queenelizabetholympicpark.co.uk); the cavernous **Earl's Court Exhibition Centre** (www.eco.co.uk), doomed to redevelopment in the as-yet-undetermined near future; and **Wembley Arena** (www.wembleyarena.co.uk). Sometimes you'll also see big gigs on the sports pitches at **Arsenal's Emirates Stadium** (www.arsenal.com/emiratesstadium) or **Twickenham Stadium** (www.rfu.com/microsites/twickenham), well outside of town.

The O₂   The £789-million boondoggle on the Thames in East London, is a dome the volume of ten St Paul's. It's where the gargantuan acts appear, packing in their own religious followings, in a 20,000-place arena (ladies, there are 550 toilets for you, too) fringed by a mall for food and clubs. Michael Jackson was in rehearsal for a concert series for the O₂ when he died, and during the 2012 Olympics, it housed gymnastics and basketball. For those not keen to squint at their favorite artist reduced to a tiny smudge on a distant arena stage, there's O₂ dome's "intimate" performance space, **IndigO₂** although with 2,350 places in an acoustically superior, contemporary room, it's still plenty big, has four bars, and attracts major talent (Prince, Leonard Cohen). Even if you aren't carrying a ticket for a show, it's worth exploring the massive open spaces inside. The bubbly-blue mega-chandelier hanging above the main entrance is enough to blow your mind, but if you need something more jolting, you can take a safe, 2-hour climb above it on its Up at the O2 roof-walking attraction (p. 131). One of the keys to O₂'s explosive success has been the fact the Jubilee Line's sleek North Greenwich station runs beneath it, making getting there fuss-free.

Peninsula Square, London, SE10. ℂ **020/8463-2000.** www.theo2.co.uk. Tube: North Greenwich.

Clubs

The city's dance scene, being embedded in the style scene, is various and shifting, and by the time you read this, the variety will have shifted again. The best source for tips on parties you stand a chance of getting into is Time Out (www.timeout.com/london/clubs). Although the clubs around Shoreditch, Old Street, and King's Cross were until recently the markers of cool, both gentrification and development has squeezed the most cutting-edge stuff northeast to Dalston, which makes getting home in the middle of the night expensive—freelance cabbies charge double.

The king of clubs remains **Fabric** (77a Charterhouse St., EC1; ℂ **020/7336-8898;** www.fabriclondon.com. Cover £8–£24; Tube: Farringdon or Barbican), a former butchery that for more than a decade has had lines around the block. Its all-weekend parties (from Sat at 10pm to the cock crows on Monday) are engineered to drill teeth-chattering bass frequencies into the souls of those who dare to submit, Friday is dub-step and drum-and-bass night, Saturdays is deep house. The City is not lost to the nerds yet; the heavy, 200-capacity dance pen at **Plastic People** (147-149 Curtain Road, EC2; ℂ **020/7739-6471;** www.plasticpeople.co.uk; Tube: Old Street) is still pumping out eardrums with funk and bass, and in September 2012, the pedigreed managers of **XOYO** (32-37 Cowper St., EC2; ℂ **020/7729-5959;** www.xoyo.co.uk; Tube: Old Street) turned a former printworks into a stripped-down sound tank, and succeeded. It sometimes throws approachable parties at the South Place Hotel (p. 39) before shifting all night to its home base. The **Ministry of Sound** (103 Gaunt St., SE1; ℂ **020/7740-8600;** www.ministryofsound.com; Tube: Elephant & Castle) set the beats for a generation with its top-notch sound system, upper-crust DJs, and extreme cover charge in the low £20s. Otherwise, wander Dalston for the leading edge and basement clubs. The **Dalston Superstore** (117 Kingland High St., E8; ℂ **020/7254-2273;** www.dalston-superstore.com; Tube: Dalston Kingsland Overground) is a pansexual party mix of DJs, disco, and ravey go-go boys. **Nest** (36-44 Stoke Newington Rd., N16; www.ilovethenest.com; ℂ **020/7354-9993;** Tube: Dalston Junction rail) is intimate, affordable, and at times sweaty, but has the quality line-up and sound system of a mini Fabric.

Comedy Clubs

London's comedy scene—counter-intuitively—is dominated by Edinburgh's. Each August in the Scottish capital, hoards of wannabe laughmakers head north for the city's famous festival season, where they vie for awards, audiences, and perversely, that shiniest of brass rings, a major London booking. The rest of the year, it seems that half the stages in town are either helping artists groom material for Edinburgh (June and July's schedules are packed with new shows) or cashing in on its past successes. The fevered competition has created a comedy scene that has less in common with the stand-and-discuss neuroses of New York clubs and more to do with the brittle high concepts of, say, Monty Python or Ricky Gervais. You may miss a few local references, but you're sure to appreciate the wit.

All comedy venues serve food and drink, and tickets are almost always under £10 unless it's big name or a very central location. Main shows are usually at 7:30 or 8pm and finish in time for you to catch the Tube home.

Amused Moose ★★★   Screen comics Ricky Gervais, Dave Gorman, and Mackenzie Crook have all performed here. Its banner show is its Saturday night showcase at the Soho pub Moonlighting—big-name comics like Eddie Izzard or Stephen Merchant sometimes appear here without a peep of advance word to test out new material—but it books nights at four other venues around town. The company decamps for Scotland in August.

Soho: Moonlighting Nightclub, 17 Greek St., W1. ℭ **020/7287-3727.** www.amusedmoose.com. Tube: Tottenham Court Road.

Canal Café Theatre ★   This cluttered, candle-lit room puts on more than a dozen shows a week, including some sketch and improv outings. The big draw is "NewsRevue" (www.newsrevue.com) a weekly send-up of current events running since 1979 that holds the Guinness record for the longest-running live comedy show; it plays Thursday through Sunday.

The Bridge House, Delamere Terrace, W2. ℭ **020/7289-6054.** Tube: Warwick Avenue.

The Comedy Store ★★   The 400-seat space was created in 1979 in imitation of clubs popular in New York but wound up pioneering the distinctly British alternative movement that elevated Jennifer Saunders, Eddie Izzard, and Ben Elton to fame. On Wednesdays and Sundays, improv comics (including Whose Line Is It Anyway?'s Josie Lawrence) entertain, while Thursday, Friday, and Saturday are for stand-up.

1a Oxendon St., SW1. ℭ **084/4871-7699.** www.thecomedystore.co.uk. Tube: Leicester Square or Piccadilly Circus.

Downstairs at the King's Head ★   It may appear to be an iffy hole in the wall, but in fact it's an admired (and affordable) haunt for well-known comedians who want to try out new stuff. The best value is "Comedy Try Out Night" Thursdays, when 16 new acts appear.

2 Crouch End Hill, N8. ℭ **020/8340-1028.** www.downstairsatthekingshead.com. Tube: Finsbury Park.

Jongleurs ★   There are nine locations around the U.K., and so while it brings in some names and tickets aren't hard to get, it also brings in a less discerning clientele (think bachelorette parties and crummy food).

Covent Garden location: 61-65 Great Queen St., WC2. ℭ **08700/111-960.** www.jongleurs.com. Tube: Holborn. Also at 80 Haymarket, SW1. Tube: Piccadilly Circus.

Pleasance Theatre Islington ★★   With two spaces squeezed into a former wood warehouse, it has stronger ties than most to Edinburgh; it operates the Scottish festival's chief comedy venue. It also presents theater, bringing its total to 180 new shows a year. Russell Brand's a regular.

Carpenters Mews, North Rd., N7. © **020/7609-1800.** www.pleasance.co.uk/islington. Tube: Caledonian Road.

Cinema

Major movie premieres attended by major movie stars are routinely held at one of Leicester Square's giant cinemas, including the **Odeon** (24-26 Leicester Square, WC2; © **087/1224-4007;** www.odeon.co.uk; Tube: Leicester Square), from 1937, the largest cinema in the country, with seating for about 1,700. But tickets for Leicester Square theaters cost an outlandish £14. For better prices—in even more historic houses—you'll have to look elsewhere. Because so many handsome old cinemas have survived, movie-going can still feel like an event. In most theaters, you even select your seats when you buy your ticket.

Coronet ★   One of the oldest houses showing movies in London was built as a small variety house in 1898. In 2004, it was sold to an area church. History buffs despaired of losing this fine institution, done up in rich reds and woods, until the church proudly revealed that it intended to spruce it up and continue operating it as a cinema. Just more proof that Britain is now a truly secular society. The cinema, which shows first-run movies, made an appearance in Notting Hill, when Hugh Grant's character wistfully attended a movie starring his estranged girlfriend (Julia Roberts).

103 Notting Hill Gate, W11. © **020/7727-6705.** www.coronet.org. Tube: Notting Hill Gate.

The Electric Cinema ★★★   One of the great screens in the world: The leather seats are softer and deeper than anything you have at home, and each one is equipped with a footstool, table, and a wine basket—it's a luxurious, romantic way to pass a few hours. The bar in the back of the house sells everything you need, from crudites to booze, and downstairs is a barrel-roofed French-American diner. Meanwhile, the films, which change daily, hop between first-run and well-received art house movies—nothing too obscure. Shockingly, this place stood derelict from 1993 to 2001, and only a fierce campaign saved it. Now it's run by the exclusive Soho House.

191 Portobello Rd., W11. © **020/7908-9696.** www.electriccinema.co.uk. Tube: Ladbroke Grove or Notting Hill Gate.

BFI Southbank ★★★   The programming of the British Film Institute (BFI), is mind-bogglingly broad and savvy, from classics to mainstream to historic—more than 1,000 titles a year. For example, on a day in a recent July, its three screens unspooled a retrospective of Indian director Satyajit Ray, Alfred Hitchcock's Dial M for Murder in 3-D, a mid-century series from the largely forgotten Boulting Brothers, and outdoor screenings of gothic monster schlock. As the country's preeminent archive and exhibitor, it also programs plenty of talks, special previews, and the occasional free screening. The on-premises **Mediatheque** is a arcade for quiet, on-demand viewing of tons of titles you'd never see abroad because of rights issues, and its shop stocks an uncompared list of rare DVDs, including many treasures the BFI has personally restored and re-released—Charlie Chaplin's 1914 Keystone films being a 2009 triumph.

Belvedere Rd., South Bank, SE1. © **020/7255-1444.** www.bfi.org.uk/whatson. Tube: Waterloo.

Phoenix Cinema ★   Thought to be the oldest purpose-built cinema in the U.K., it was constructed as the Premier Electric Theatre in 1910; by 1985, despite its handsome Edwardian barrel-vault ceiling, it was nose-to-nose with the wrecker's ball before fans (including director Mike Leigh) rallied. It screens an immense range of films from across eras and borders, plus frequent transmissions of live theatre. It also has a liquor license.

52 High Rd., East Finchley, N2. ℂ **020/8444-6789**. www.phoenixcinema.co.uk. Tube: East Finchley.

Gay & Lesbian

London has the most varied and vibrant gay and lesbian scene in the world. The city boasts more than 100 pubs, clubs, and club nights, and a dozen saunas—beat that, San Francisco or New York! The music seems to crank a few notches louder when the jolly and outrageous **Pride London** (www.londoncommunitypride.org) season rolls along, in late June or early July.

Daily gay-oriented pursuits have traditionally been centered around Soho, where the bars and clubs take on a festive, anyone-is-welcome flair, and after work, guys spill into the streets. But as a mark of a truly integrated city, now nearly every neighborhood has its own pubs and gay nights. Where you spend an evening depends on your proclivities and willingness to commute. At most places, there aren't usually cover charges unless an event or show is on, when they're about £5 at bars and £11 for clubs. Lesbians who want to go out at night must usually plan a little because most girls' events take the form of weekly scheduled nights in bars that might cater to other niches during the rest of the week. The Sapphically inclined should turn to Gingerbeer (www.gingerbeer.co.uk) for listings.

Grab one of two weekly magazines. **Boyz** (www.boyz.co.uk) and **QX Magazine** (www.qxmagazine.com) publish schedules that favor club events. *Time Out* also has a weekly "Gay and Lesbian" section that dwells more on clubbing than on well-rounded pursuits.

These standout venues in every flavor are welcoming to tourists and will provide a good overview of the culture.

Barcode Vauxhall ★★   Thanks to its cobalt-and-steel design it seems on the surface like a snooty setting, but in reality it attracts a varied crowd of friendly over-25s on their pre-club rounds, and it gets far cruisier than its style might suggest.

Arch 69, Albert Embankment, SE1. ℂ **020/7582-4180**. www.bar-code.co.uk. Closed Tues, Wed. Tube: Vauxhall.

The Black Cap ★★   Drag has mainstream acceptance in Britain, where the Dame role is a staple in children's shows. This pubby institution, which has a roof garden, has for a half-century cultivated a fierce following, and it's shoulder-to-shoulder during its weekend drag and cabaret performances.

171 Camden High St., NW1. ℂ **020/7485-0538**. www.theblackcap.com. Tube: Camden Town.

Candy Bar ★   One of London's best-known (and only 7-days-a-week) lesbian bars, and given that there aren't too many girl bars in town, it attracts a wide spectrum of types—even tagalong men.

4 Carlisle St., W1. ℂ **020/7287-5041**. www.candybarsoho.com. Tube: Tottenham Court Road.

Central Station ★ For those who like it sexually charged, no other large space in the city can compete. Three floors plus a roof terrace and a drag cabaret mean there can be events of various spiciness going on at once, so it's essential to check its schedule beforehand. Fetish nights aren't the only thing going down in cellar cruise spaces.

37 Wharfdale Rd., N1. ℂ **020/7278-3294.** www.centralstation.co.uk. Tube: King's Cross St. Pancras.

The Duke of Wellington ★★ Just a gimmick-free, down-to-earth pub with normal, friendly guys. In good weather its sidewalk scene is the best in Soho, and it's amid prime tourist stomping grounds.

77 Wardour St., W1. ℂ **020/7439-1313.** Tube: Piccadilly Circus.

The Edge ★★ Despite having four levels, it gets incredibly crowded with man-flesh. The coolest thing about it is its location right on Soho Square, and patrons often duck out to kick back in the park, giving this hotspot a less frenetic vibe than many other trendy places. In summer, sidewalk tables are laid out.

11 Soho Square, W1. ℂ **020/7439-1313.** www.edgesoho.co.uk. Tube: Tottenham Court Road.

G-A-Y ★★ Once renowned for their literary prowess and symbolic subterfuge in hinting at their sexuality, London's homosexuals have allowed their wit to become somewhat less nimble. The unimaginatively named G-A-Y is about partying, cruising, and dancing. The main event is the Saturday night club, No other dance club in Europe, gay or straight, comes close to attracting such a pantheon of legendary live performances: Kylie, the Spice Girls, Cyndi Lauper, Bjork, and of course, Madge, all performed here at the height of their fame, and some have been known to drop by unannounced to collect laurels from 2,000 chipper young things. Every night, G-A-Y also runs a bubblegum-light pre-show hangout, G-A-Y Bar where a young, twink crowd steeps in cheery Europop, and watches videos on the plasma screens. And you can imagine the vibe at its G-A-Y Late venue, which goes until 3am.

Club: Heaven, Under the Arches, Villiers Street, WC2. Tube: Charing Cross or Embankment. Bar: 30 Old Compton Street, W1. ℂ **020/7494-2756.** www.g-a-y.co.uk. Tube: Leicester Square. Late: 5 Goslett Yard, W1. ℂ **020/7734-9858.** Tube: Tottenham Court Road.

Ku Bar ★★ A manageably sized, young-skewing, three-level bar and lounge it's the place you go when you don't want a scene, but you also don't want a dusty cave populated with trolls stuck to their barstools. It stays open until 3am.

30 Lisle and 25 Frith sts., WC2. ℂ **020/7437-4303.** www.ku-bar.co.uk. Tube: Leicester Square.

The Hoist ★ A well-known leather dive with a dress code that changes per the night, it's not for the female or the fainthearted. Or, on some nights, for the clothed.

Arches 47b and 47c, South Lambeth Road, SE1. ℂ **020/7735-9972.** www.thehoist.co.uk. Tube: Vauxhall.

Manbar ★★ Its owners seem keyed into the corniness of their bar's name, because their central artwork is even more camp: a steamy image of Prince Harry without a shirt on. When other bars close, patrons come to this contemporary multileveled space to close the deal.

79 Charing Cross Rd., WC1. ℂ **020/7434-2567.** www.manbarsoho.com. Closed Sun. Tube: Leicester Square.

Royal Vauxhall Tavern ★★★ In 2013, a biography revealed that Diana, Princess of Wales, once secretly attended this gay drag landmark dressed as a man. That gives you an idea of its heft in British culture. There are three shows a night, all alternative, all transgressive.

372 Kennington Lane, SE11. $\textcircled{C}$ **020/7820-1222.** www.rvt.org.uk. Tube: Vauxhall.

XXL London ★★★ London's biggest dance night for "bears" (for the uninitiated, those are beefy guys who would never dream of shaving their chests like the young "twinks" do), it's colossal beyond belief. Its arched-ceilinged dance floor—actually you're in vaults beneath a railway—get super sweaty, but that doesn't bother the thousands of assembled men, who strip off their shirts and grind on.

1 Invicta Plaza, South Bank, Blackfriars Road at Southwark Street, SE1. $\textcircled{C}$ **020/7403-4001.** £15. Sat Wed 10pm–3am. 10pm–6am. Tube: London Bridge.

WALKING TOURS OF LONDON

aying for a sightseeing tour seems smart in principle. You glimpse monuments, briefly, and you hear one or two eye-glazing facts about them as they whiz past. But no coach tour, no hokey sightseeing boat, goes at your speed. None convinces you the things you're seeing are quite real, allowing you to mull what's before you, or lets you breathe in the atmosphere. Get up close to London. Don't pass it. Touch it—so that it can touch you.

WALKING TOUR 1: WESTMINSTER, WHITEHALL & TRAFALGAR SQUARE

START:	**Westminster Tube station**
FINISH:	**Trafalgar Square**
TIME:	**Allow 60 minutes, not including time spent in attractions**
BEST TIME:	**Be at the starting line just before noon to hear Big Ben deliver its longest chime of the day**
WORST TIME:	**After working hours, when energy drains out of the area**

When most people hear the word "London," this is the area they picture: the Houses of Parliament, the wash of the Thames, the gong of Big Ben, and the Georgian facade of Number 10 Downing Street. Kings and queens, prime ministers and executioners, despots and assassins—this is where they converged to shape a millennium of events, at the command center for England and the British Empire. History buffs, lace up.

---

1 Westminster Tube Station

The best train to take here is the Jubilee Line, which was added at great expense in 1999. The station's concrete-grey, 36m-deep (118-ft.) cavern, ascended by escalators from the Jubilee's platforms, is one of the city's finest new spaces, providing a modern-day analog to the majestic space of Westminster Abbey nearby. Portcullis House, where many MPs (Members of Parliament) keep offices, is overhead.

Walking Tour 1: Westminster, Whitehall & Trafalgar Square

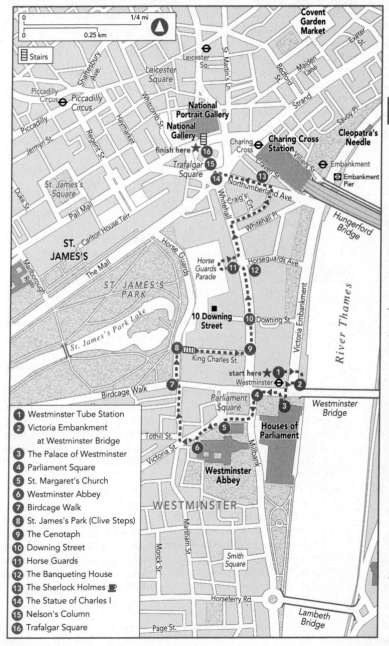

Covent Garden Market

Exeter St.

Leicester Sq.

St. Martin's Ln.

Bedford St.

Maiden Lane

Strand

Savoy Pl.

Leicester Square

Piccadilly Circus

Piccadilly Circus

Whitcomb St.

National Portrait Gallery

National Gallery

Charing Cross

Charing Cross Station

Cleopatra's Needle

Piccadilly

Haymarket

finish here ★ 16

Embankment

Embankment Pier

Jermyn St.

Regent St.

15

Trafalgar Square

14

Charing Cross

Villiers St.

ST. JAMES'S Square

Duke St.

Pall Mall

Carlton House Terr.

13

Northumberland Ave.

Craig's Ct.

Whitehall Pl.

Hungerford Bridge

Whitehall

ST. JAMES'S

Marlborough Rd.

The Mall

Horse Guards

Horse Guards Parade

11

12

Horseguards Ave.

Victoria Embankment

River Thames

ST. JAMES'S PARK

St. James's Park Lake

10 Downing Street

10 Downing St.

Stairs

9

King Charles St.

8

7

Birdcage Walk

start here ★ 1

Westminster 2

Westminster Bridge

Parliament Square

4

Tothill St.

5

3

Houses of Parliament

Millbank

Victoria St.

6

Westminster Bridge

0   1/4 mi
0   0.25 km

Stairs

Westminster Abbey

WESTMINSTER

Marsham St.

Monck St.

Smith Square

Horseferry Rd.

Page St.

Lambeth Bridge

1 Westminster Tube Station
2 Victoria Embankment at Westminster Bridge
3 The Palace of Westminster
4 Parliament Square
5 St. Margaret's Church
6 Westminster Abbey
7 Birdcage Walk
8 St. James's Park (Clive Steps)
9 The Cenotaph
10 Downing Street
11 Horse Guards
12 The Banqueting House
13 The Sherlock Holmes ☕
14 The Statue of Charles I
15 Nelson's Column
16 Trafalgar Square

2 Victoria Embankment at Westminster Bridge

Once you're outside, you'll see the River Thames. If you stood here in 1858, in the midst of what came to be known as The Great Stink, you'd have choked on the fumes rising from the fetid effluvia floating in the river below. Until then, the city had no sewers to speak of—only pipes that dumped into the water. The solution was the Victoria Embankment, a daring engineering project, completed in 1870, that saved engineers from having to dig up the whole city. They simply built a new riverbank, laid sewers along it, paired that with new Underground railway tracks, and topped the unattractive additions with a garden and a road. Destructive, but effective—how Victorian.

Today, the embankments' benches are raised to allow a good view of the water and it's dotted with triumphant statuary like Boudicca in her bladed chariot, which you can also see from here. This tribal queen rose up against the Romans; she failed politically but as you see, succeeded aesthetically.

The London Eye, spinning before you, had a tricky birth in 1999; it was constructed lying flat over the river, resting on pontoons, and then it was laboriously hoisted upright and into place. The mock-Baroque building behind it is County Hall—it looks old, but it only dates to the early 20th century, and was once the seat of the London city government.

At the bridge's opposite landing, you can see the South Bank Lion. Weighing 14 tons, 3.6m (12 ft.) tall, and eager-eyed and floppy-pawed as a puppy, he was carved in 1837 by the Coade Stone Factory, which once stood where County Hall stands today. Made of a durable, synthetic ceramic stone formulated by a mother-daughter team, the lion stood proudly for over a century, painted red, atop the Red Lion Brewery that was located past the London Eye. Blitz bomb damage destroyed his roost, but at the request of King George VI, he was saved and placed just feet from his birthplace.

Go back into Westminster station, head down the corridor, and turn left before the set of four stairs. Leave the station via Exit 3, marked Houses of Parliament.

3 The Palace of Westminster

You're now standing under the iconic Elizabeth Tower of the Houses of Parliament, once called St Stephen's Tower but renamed in 2012 in honor of QE2's Diamond Jubilee. This is as close as you can get to it, so have a good look at the assorted crowns, kings, and crests carved into the facade. These buildings may look like they're from the Gothic period, but in fact they date to 1859, when they rose from the ashes of the old Parliament House, destroyed by a nightmarish fire in 1834. Big Ben, the name of the largest of four bells inside (2.7m/9 ft. in diameter, 13 tons), was named for the portly commissioner of works who oversaw its installation. There's actually a bigger bell in town: Great Paul at St. Paul's is 2 tons heavier. Each side of the Clock Tower's four faces is 6.9m (23 ft.) long. Since 1923, the very earliest days of wireless, BBC has broadcast the 16-note prelude (called "Westminster Quarters" and replicated in doorbells around the world) of Big Ben before its news summaries. Thanks to a crack that developed in the 1860s, the bell is now slightly off from its original note: E above middle C, but you'd need perfect pitch to tell.

This plot of land has been used by royals since 1050, when Edward the Confessor built a palace here, away from the hubbub of the walled city. Kings ceased living on this block as of Henry VIII, when nearby Whitehall became his main London pad, followed by St. James's and currently, Buckingham—but Parliament's land is nationally owned, so technically it meets in Westminster Palace.

Head away from the river to:

4 Parliament Square

The heavy metal bars on the spiked fence that distances you from this building are not there out of mere paranoia; as far back as the thwarted Gunpowder Plot of 1605, the Houses of Parliament have been a target for would-be revolutionaries. Prime Minister Spencer Perceval was fatally shot on the steps of the House of Commons by a former convict on May 11, 1812, and in the Blitz, the buildings were smashed on more than a dozen occasions, including one (May 10, 1941) that caused the near-total destruction of the House of Commons.

The section of the Houses that juts into the yards, behind the statue of Oliver Cromwell, is Westminster Hall, from 1097, one of the only survivors from the 1834 fire. Charles I, Sir Thomas More, and Guy Fawkes were all condemned to death in the Hall.

Turn left and walk in front of the Houses of Parliament. Use the first crosswalk to your right, heading toward the church. At the far side of the church, enter the gate to see:

5 St. Margaret's Church

The little side church by Westminster Abbey (p. 101), the one with the four sundials on its tower, is the Church of Saint Margaret, dating to the early 1500s and much changed over the years. Sir Walter Raleigh, who was executed outside the Palace of Westminster, is buried inside, and both the poet Milton and Winston Churchill married their wives here.

You can see the statues of Parliament Square better from here. Probably the most famous one is that of American president Abraham Lincoln, at the western end; it's a copy of one in Chicago by Augustus Saint-Gaudens. The statue of Winston Churchill received a temporary Mohawk made of grassy turf during the anticapitalist protests of 2000. This square has always attracted well-intentioned screw-ups: In 1868, the world's first traffic light was erected here. Gas powered, it blew up.

Follow the footpath to the front of:

6 Westminster Abbey

The lawn beside the abbey—yes, the one you just walked across—is in fact a disused graveyard. In a city this old, you simply can't avoid treading on final resting places. There are an unknown number of plague pits scattered through the city, into which thousands of victims were hastily dumped to avoid the spread of disease, and several city parks likely had the germ of their beginnings, so to speak, as potter's fields—group graves for paupers.

Although most of the abbey is in the Early English style, the stern western towers above you now were the 18th-century work of Nicholas Hawksmoor, a protégé of Christopher Wren. Hawksmoor's designs are famous for emphasizing the forbidding, angry side of God. Some critics accuse him of using architecture to frighten people into piety. Most of the time the people who use this main entrance in an official capacity do so in a crown, a gown, or a coffin. If you peer down Broad Sanctuary, which becomes Victoria Street, you can see the Italianate tower of Westminster Cathedral, the primary cathedral of England. Good news, Catholics: The English don't execute you anymore!

Cross the street to your right (Broad Sanctuary), and cross again. You should be a block west of Parliament Square on Storey's Gate now. Walk straight until you find yourself at the corner of St. James's Park. You're at:

7 Birdcage Walk

You've just walked past a variety of European Union offices; the proximity to the Houses of Parliament has appealed to paper-pushers for centuries. The military has a presence here, too. The road that heads to the left is Birdcage Walk, which leads to the front of Buckingham Palace. Halfway down, you'll find the Wellington Barracks, the headquarters of the Guards Division, where a battalion of one of the Queen's five regiments of foot guards (Grenadier, Coldstream, Scots, Irish, and Welsh) bunks down. There's also a small, curio-packed Guards Museum (✆ 020/7414-3271; daily 10am–4pm, £5), where you learn that their tall "busby" helmets are made of Canadian brown bearskin. Who knew?

Storey's Gate, which you just walked, was named for the keeper of Charles II's aviary. Birdcage Walk, the street you have now encountered, was named after a royal aviary that was in St. James's Park; until 1928, only the Hereditary Royal Falconer was permitted to drive on Birdcage Walk. The park continues its tradition of hosting bird menageries; the pond is a haven for ducks and geese, and a small flock of pelicans has been in residence since the 1600s.

Cross the street and walk one block, passing the Treasury Building on your right, until you reach Clive Steps at King Charles Street on the right. Peek into:

8 St. James's Park

See if you can spot the lake in the park. The body of water was originally a formal canal belonging to St. James's Palace, the official royal residence from the burning of Whitehall in 1698 to the time Victoria moved into Buckingham Palace in 1837. The old canal was prim and straight in the French style and outfitted with gondolas, a gift of the Doge of Venice. In winter, Samuel Pepys wrote in the 1600s, it would freeze over, and people would frolic upon it using skates made of bone. It was later sculpted into something calculated to appear more random and thus more English. St. James's Palace, which is not open to the public (except for Clarence House, in summers, p. 104), is located on the north (far) side of the park. You might be able to make out a rustic-looking shack just inside the park. That's Duck Island Cottage, built in 1840 as a dwelling for the bird keeper. Not shabby for a servant's quarters.

You'd think that if London were under attack from flying bombers that you'd be much safer if you were a little farther from the Houses of Parliament. Yet in the basement of the sturdy 1907 Treasury Building, Britain's leaders orchestrated their country's "finest hour." Unbeknownst to the world, it was the hideout of Winston Churchill and his cabinet. Famously, but hardly wisely, that daredevil Churchill went onto the roof of the building so he could watch one of Goering's air raids slam the city. The cellar, preserved down to its typing pool and pushpins, is now the Churchill War Rooms and a superlative museum paying homage to the bulldoggy prime minister (p. 99).

Who is Robert Clive, the cutlass-wielding subject of this statue on the steps? He was the general who helped the East India Company conquer India and Bengal, partly through a series of underhanded bribes, thus delivering the region into the control of the British Empire for nearly 2 centuries. Don't be too hard on him; the opium-addicted fellow committed suicide by stabbing himself with a penknife.

Walk down King Charles Street and through the arches at the end. You are now on Parliament Street. Look into the center of it. The somber stone column in the traffic island is:

9 The Cenotaph

The Cenotaph (from the Greek words for "empty" and "tomb") is a simple but elegiac memorial to those killed in the two World Wars. A 1919 plaster parade prop that was made permanent in stone by Edwin Lutyens the next year, it was executed with inconceivable restraint when you consider that nearly a million British subjects died in the Great War alone. Its inscription to the "Glorious Dead," coined by Rudyard Kipling, is repeated on other memorials in Commonwealth nations; the Cenotaphs in Auckland, New Zealand, and in London, Canada, are replicas. Uniformed servicemen and -women will always salute it as they pass, and on the Sunday closest to November 11, Britain's Remembrance Day, the sovereign lays the first wreath while other members of the Royal Family observe from the balcony of the Foreign Office. You may see flowers around it, or possibly silk poppies (red flowers with black centers), the national symbol of remembrance.

Walk left up Parliament Street, which becomes Whitehall. In about 30m (98 ft.) on the left, you reach a black fence with glass lanterns. Look inside the gates. This is:

10 Downing Street

On the right, by the tree and tough to make out, is Number 10, the official home of the prime minister. It's famous for its lion's head knocker—although to be frank, if you have to knock, you aren't welcome. Once, you could walk around in there, but Margaret Thatcher made many enemies, so you'll have to make do with peering down the lane. Such security was a long time coming. In 1842, a lunatic shot and killed the secretary to the prime minister, mistaking him for the big man; and in 1912, suffragette Emmeline Pankhurst and friends pelted the house with stones, breaking four windows, in one of many acts of civil disobedience in the fight for voting rights for women. If sentries prevent you from approaching, then the prime minister might be on the move. Prepare for the black gates to burst open, spew forth an armada of cars, and watch the prime minister's Jaguar blast onto Whitehall as if he's just robbed a bank.

The lane was laid out by George Downing, the second man to graduate from Harvard University in America and by all accounts a shady individual, a turncoat, and a slumlord. He's one of history's great scoundrels; his underhanded dealings resulted in Dutch-held Manhattan being swiped by the British and the slave trade multiplying in the Colonies. Strange that the most important street in British politics should bear his name.

Downing built Number 10 (then, Number 5) as part of a row of terraced houses in the late 1600s, fully intending for it to fall apart after a few years (instead of actually laying bricks, he just painted on lines with mortar). Yet George II had his eye on the house, and he kicked out a man named Mr. Chicken—further information about him, tantalizingly, is lost to the mists of time—to give it as a gift to the first prime minister, Robert Walpole, in 1730. Walpole insisted that the house be used by future First Lords of the Treasury, his official capacity. He also connected it to a grand home behind it on Horse Guards, now nicknamed The House at the Back—this deceptive Georgian facade actually conceals 160 rooms. Number 10 is also connected with numbers 11 and 12, and it's even linked to Buckingham Palace and Q-Whitehall, a sprawling war bunker, by long underground tunnels. Many prime ministers elected to live in their own homes, using Number 10 for meetings, but not William Pitt, who moved in upon becoming prime minister at the virtually pubescent age of 24 in 1783. He lived here for more than 20 years, longer than any other prime minister, until his death at 46. Whitehall became a slum in the mid-1800s, and the house fell out of fashion, but then it served as the nerve center for the two World Wars and became indispensable to the British spirit. You can see the original front door, now replaced by a stronger one, on display at the Churchill Museum at the Cabinet War Rooms (p. 99), two stops back.

A little up Whitehall from Downing Street, look for the bronze monument to "The Women of World War II," which depicts no women, but rather their uniforms and hats, which hang on pegs as if they've been put away after a job well done. The implication of this 6.6m-tall (22-ft.) tableau is, of course, that the women went back to the kitchen after briefly filling a more robust societal role. This sly bit of statuary-as-commentary was unveiled by the Queen in 2005. Some 80% of the cost of the memorial was raised by a Baroness who won money on ITV's *Who Wants to Be a Millionaire?*.

Continue up Whitehall, past the monumental government buildings. In about 60m (200 ft.), you will reach another black gate broken by two stone guardhouses. Head inside the yard to view:

11 Horse Guards

Built in the Palladian style between 1750 and 1758 on a former jousting field of Whitehall Palace, the Horse Guards is the official (but little-used) entrance to the grounds of St. James's Palace and Buckingham Palace. Two mounted cavalry troops are posted in the guardhouses every day from 10am to 4pm, and they're changed hourly. At 11am daily and 10am Sundays, the guard on duty is relieved by a dozen men who march in from The Mall behind, accompanied (when the Queen is in town) by a trumpeter, a standard bearer, and an officer. Don't try to crack up guards with your shenanigans. You'll look boorish and rude—and they still won't react.

If you think the clock tower arch looks small, you're right. Its designer made it that way so that its proportions would match the rest of the building. Walk through the clock tower arch to reach the graveled Horse Guards Parade, the city's largest non-park gathering space, which you may recognize as the setting for volleyball during the Olympic Games.

Return from the yard to Whitehall. Across the street you'll see:

12 The Banqueting House

Built by Inigo Jones, this is not a home but it is the last remaining portion of the great Whitehall Palace. Inside is a bombastic ceiling by Rubens depicting the king as a god. That vainglorious posture, and the king's grabs for more power, led to the gory event that happened on this spot on January 30, 1649. If you were standing here then, you would have been in the crowd that watched King Charles I mount the scaffold (wearing two shirts so that he wouldn't shiver—he was no true god, after all), place his head on the block, and be decapitated, handing the reins of the country to a military dictatorship led by Oliver Cromwell. When the executioner held the head aloft, one witness said there was a queasy silence, followed by "such a groan by the thousands then present, as I never heard before and I desire I may never hear again." Charles I was buried privately at Windsor, not at Westminster Abbey, to avoid more unpleasant scenes. If you want to see what poor Charles looked like, hang on for the next stop. The regicide was somewhat for naught; by 1660, the country grew weary of its leadership and Charles I's son, the hedonistic spendthrift Charles II, was back on daddy's throne. In revenge, the second Charles chose the Banqueting House as the site for his restoration party, and then had the nerve to show up late. England was royal again—and how.

Continue up Whitehall. Take the next right, Great Scotland Yard, and then cross Northumberland Avenue, veer slightly left, and head into Craven Passage.

13 The Sherlock Holmes 🍺

Time for a pint and maybe some traditional English pub grub. The Sherlock Holmes (10-11 Northumberland St.), In 1957, a collection of Arthur Conan Doyle memorabilia was assembled as a tourist attraction for the huge Festival of Britain that gave London the Southbank Centre, and it became the centerpiece of this pub. It's nowhere near 221B Baker Street, but it has a roof garden and a terrace.

Return to Northumberland Avenue and turn right. When you reach Trafalgar Square, cross the street so you're in the oval traffic island.

14 Statue of Charles I

That this bronze statue stands here is a miracle. It's of Charles I, pre-headectomy, and is a precious Carolinian original from 1633. When the king was beheaded, the Royal Family was deposed (permanently, so people thought), and their riches were melted down for profit. The owner of this statue was commanded to destroy it, but he was clever enough to bury it instead. After the Restoration, it was dug up and placed here, in about 1675. That was even before Trafalgar Square existed (the zone was, as an equestrian statue suggests, used as stables). Charles wasn't a tall man, and boosting him with a horse went some way toward making the luckless fellow seem imposing. Someone stole his sword in 1867, and he went into hiding again during The Blitz, but otherwise, this is one of the oldest things in this part of London that remains in its original place. Its pedestal, unloved and weathered, could use a Restoration too.

This is a good spot, free of traffic and obstructions, to survey your surroundings and take some photos. Look back down Whitehall, from where you just came, and you'll see Big Ben's tower. To the right, the vista through Admiralty

Arch concludes in the distance with the grand Victoria Memorial at Buckingham Palace. Important buildings for two Commonwealth nations stand astride Trafalgar Square: Canada House to the left (west) and South Africa House to the right (east; its country's name is inscribed in Afrikaans as Suid-Afrika).

Cross again so that you're on the south side of:

15 Nelson's Column & Trafalgar Square

Not long after Charles's statue lost its original sword, lightning struck Lord Nelson, who is exposed at the top of his column, and damaged his left arm. The city finally got around to eliminating the bronze bands that held him together in 2006, using the same Craigleith sandstone with which he was constructed in 1843. Since the quarry had closed in the 1940s, craftsmen had to find stone left over from the restoration of a school in Edinburgh. During the work, surveying revealed that the monument is actually 4.8m (16 ft.) shorter than guidebooks have been claiming—it's 51m (167 ft.), not 56m (184 ft.), from the street to the crown of his hat. The man himself is 32m (105 ft.) tall. Why is Nelson so revered? The Admiral sacrificed his life in 1805 to defeat Napoleon Bonaparte's naval aspirations, which secured Britain's dominance over the oceans—and thus pumped untold wealth into London. The column's base is lined with four bronze reliefs that were said to be cast using metal from French cannon captured at the battle that each one depicts. All is guarded by four reclining lions (1867), the mascots of the square.

In the southeast corner, you'll see a stone booth big enough for a single person; that's the city's smallest police station, built in 1926. Once a closet for a phone that was used to summon backup, now it's used mostly to store chemicals for the fountains.

Lutyens, who did the Cenotaph, also designed the two fountains (from 1845 originals), which were ostensibly for beautification but conveniently prevented citizens from protesting in numbers. Trafalgar Square has long been the setting for demonstrations that turned from complaint to unrest, such as infamous riots over poll taxes and unemployment. The English gather here for happy things, too, as they did for the announcement of V-E Day (May 8, 1945), and as they still do for free summer performances.

You may have heard about Trafalgar's Square's famous pigeons. So where are they? Banished for overactive excretion. Until the early 1990s, the square swarmed with them—the fluttering flock was estimated to peak at 35,000--and vendors made a living from selling bird feed to tourists. Eventually, the GLC, London's government, grew tired of shoveling streaky poo off the statues and decided to return the square to its original function as a great public space. They began feeding the pigeons themselves first thing in the morning, and then hired a team of six hawks, tended by a leather-gloved keeper, to patrol the square. The flock, which now number as low as 400, quickly learned to chow down and then clear out for the day; anyone who feeds the birds is subject to a £500 fine.

Head to the other side of the fountains to:

16 North Trafalgar Square

At night when landmarks are picked out by lights, the views down Whitehall are sublime. Most of the statues dotting the square are of forgotten military and noble men; James II is finely crafted, but he looks ridiculous in those Roman robes. The northwestern plinth of Trafalgar Square was designed for an equestrian statue of its own, but money ran out and it stood empty from 1841. More than 150 years later, the naked spot was named The Fourth Plinth and filled by works commissioned by a subversive panel of top artists. Sculptures show for 12 to 18 months, and they get he city talking. Marc Quinn's marble *Alison Lapper Pregnant* depicted a snow-white, nude woman born with limb deformities and heavy with child. Until early 2015, it's Katharina Fritsch's two-story, ultramarine rooster, *Cock*, a sly send-up of the pompous military iconography elsewhere in the square.

Along the north terrace, by the Café on the Square, look for the Imperial Standards of Length, which were set into the wall in 1876 and moved in 2003 when the central stairs were installed. They are the literal yardsticks against which all other British yardsticks are measured, showing inches, feet, and yards, plus mostly obsolete measures such as links, chains, perches, and poles.

And now, reward yourself with a visit to the loo, left of the stairs, and a spot of tea in the cafe. Or, if you crave some more substantial victuals, head over to the street east of the square to St. Martin-in-the-Fields church, finished in 1724. Its combination of spire and classical portico were controversial at the time, but today, it pleases people of all persuasions with its excellent Café in the Crypt (p. 62).

WALKING TOUR 2: ST. PAUL'S & SOUTHWARK

START:	**St. Paul's Tube station**
FINISH:	**The George Inn, near London Bridge Tube station**
TIME:	**Two hours, not including restaurant breaks or attractions**
BEST TIMES:	**Weekend days in good weather, when the area is abuzz; Borough Market is most vital on Thursday to Saturdays**
WORST TIMES:	**After dark, when cobbled, medieval streets are too dark to see well**

It was the best of advertisements, it was the worst of advertisements. Charles Dickens' novels, largely social protests wearing the cloak of entertainment, made readers feel like they had traveled to London when they never left their own armchairs. Trouble is, the city that Dickens has primed visitors to expect—the foggy, coal-smudged metropolis teeming with pickpockets and virtuous orphans—is nowhere to be found. Partly thanks to Dickens' work, London reformed itself. On this tour, you'll explore what's left of its darker side—from the libertine London of Shakespeare's day to the desperate one Dickens sought to solve with his pen. Along the way, you'll enjoy gourmet food and a beer on the Thames, which conceals a body count of its own.

1 St. Paul's Tube Station

If you just took the Central Line here, you rode what was once called the Central Railway. In the first 75 years of the Underground, train lines were independently owned, and separate tickets were required each time a passenger changed trains. Fares were cumbersome, calculated according to the distance traveled and the

Walking Tour 2: St. Paul's & Southwark

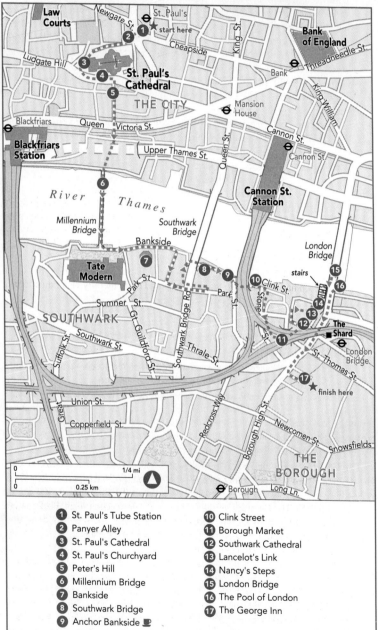

1 St. Paul's Tube Station
2 Panyer Alley
3 St. Paul's Cathedral
4 St. Paul's Churchyard
5 Peter's Hill
6 Millennium Bridge
7 Bankside
8 Southwark Bridge
9 Anchor Bankside

10 Clink Street
11 Borough Market
12 Southwark Cathedral
13 Lancelot's Link
14 Nancy's Steps
15 London Bridge
16 The Pool of London
17 The George Inn

class of carriage chosen. When the Central Railway held its grand opening in 1900, in the presence of American wit Mark Twain (who lived in London at the time), it soared above its competitors by dint of several innovations, the most important of which was that anyone could ride as far as they wanted on a flat fare. The so-called "Twopenny Tube," which had one class of carriage like today's Tube trains, was a sensation. Gilbert and Sullivan, swept along, amended a line in their operetta *Patience* from a reference to the threepenny bus to "the very delectable, highly respectable Twopenny Tube." The Central Railway helped democratize public transit and accelerated expansion into the suburbs—even if authorities eventually went back to the old format of charging passengers by distance. The St. Paul's station opened on July 30, 1900, as Post Office station— the city's main Post Office was then across the street (hence the name of Postman's Park, p. 120, just north).

Exit the St. Paul's Underground station and turn left, towards:

2 Panyer Alley

Panyer Alley, where you're standing, was named for the basketmakers, or panyers, who once traded here. Look for a plaque on the wall depicting a child sitting on a basket. This plaque, the so-called Panyer Stone, is dated "August the 27, 1688," and reads, "When you have sought / the citty round / yet still this is / the highest ground." The artists behind this stone surely knew that Ludgate is not the highest point in The City; that's Cornhill, which is about 30cm (12 in.) higher. But the sign has been here so long that it would quite literally be a crime to take it down.

Head left, toward St. Paul's, and make a right through the pedestrian alley, Paternoster Row, to Paternoster Square. Go through the ornate arch at the left:

3 St. Paul's Cathedral

The area you've just walked through, Paternoster Row, ranks among the most sacred in London. There have been major houses of worship on the plot of St. Paul's as far back as 604, and for centuries, these narrow surrounding streets have teemed with ecclesiastical scribes and clergy, as well as with untold hordes of desperate supplicants desperate for a handout from the merciful church. By the 1800s, Paternoster Row was known as the center of literary London, first for its publishers—who replaced the scribes—and later for its book market. Yet what you'll see today is modern. Even its 23m-tall (75-ft.) column was created only a few years ago to appear older than it is. Why would planners permit the wholesale demolition of such a rich heritage? They didn't. This was Ground Zero of the Blitz in 1940. The Germans, recognizing that the destruction of St. Paul's would demoralize the nation, focused their power on it, and the spillover devastated everything around it. Every firefighter was called to the cathedral, saving it at the expense of just about everything else.

The stone archway that you passed through, however, is a true antique, although it didn't originally stand here. It's Temple Gate, one of eight ancient gateways to The City of London, which stood where Strand becomes Fleet Street from 1672. Charles Dickens described it in *Bleak House* as "a leaden-headed old obstruction." It was dismantled in 1878 and was destined for a dump somewhere when a visionary stepped in and brought the stones home. After spending more than a century in the hinterland of his family's Hertfordshire estate, the gate, possibly designed by Christopher Wren, was restored and re-erected here in November 2004. The seven other gates, including Aldgate and Moorgate, were all lost.

A statue of Queen Anne, who ruled England when St. Paul's was completed, looks down Ludgate Hill. In attendance are ladies symbolizing England, France, Ireland, and North America, which she considered her subjects. The statue is an 1886 copy of the 1712 original, which (like Temple Gate once did) now resides, in scabby condition, in the countryside.

Herbert Mason's iconic photograph of St. Paul's dome, snapped during the mighty conflagration that engulfed London after air raids on December 29th and 30th, 1940, was taken from Ludgate Hill. Next time you see that picture, note that it's lit by firelight.

Skirt the cathedral along the busy street called:

4 St. Paul's Churchyard

At the crossing, go over the street. Now's a good time to duck into The City of London Information Centre (Mon–Sat 9:30am–5:30pm, Sun 10am–4pm), located inside the wing-roofed building, and stock up on free tourist brochures and timetables.

If you don't need information, turn left. If you do use the office, when you come out again, turn right. After the patch of grass, turn right again. You can see down Peter's Hill to a white pedestrian bridge over the river. Stroll down:

5 Peter's Hill

On the right is the Firefighters National Memorial, which depicts a young man gesturing wildly toward St. Paul's as two others grapple desperately with a hose. It's impossible to exaggerate the devastation caused by the Blitz, both in property and in lives. The superheated firestorms created damage greater in area than those of the Great Fire of 1666. More than 20,000 people were killed, and 1,400,000 left homeless. The names of some 1,000 victims, all volunteer firefighters defeated by the wild blaze and collapsing buildings, are inscribed on the octagonal base. Winston Churchill dubbed this monument "The Heroes with Grimy Faces." For their families, the survival of St. Paul's Cathedral amidst utter devastation remains a testament to their sacrifice. Keep going toward the river.

Go onto the:

6 Millennium Bridge

You're now on the steel Millennium Bridge, the central city's first new crossing over the Thames since the Tower Bridge in 1894. Its design, which features side-located suspension cables that sag about six times shallower than a conventional suspension bridge's supports do, was a little too advanced for its own good. When the bridge opened in 2000, it was discovered that the shifting weight of pedestrians caused it to sway, and people had to grasp the rails for support. (At the start of *Harry Potter and the Half-Blood Prince*, Death Eaters attack the bridge and make it wobble—that was an inside joke for Londoners.) Engineers closed the 325m (1066-ft.) span, poured in another £5.2 million to solve the issue, and reopened it in 2002. Now locals love it because it has transformed accessibility to the river's southern bank, and they're planning more foot crossings. It's still not perfect—it's plagued by joggers with little regard for idle strollers—but crossing the river here, in view of many of the city's landmarks, young and old, makes for some stirring photos.

Straight ahead is the monumental Tate Modern (p. 114), signaled by its factory-like "campanile" smokestack, which from 1952 to 1981 belched exhaust from the Bankside Power Station. Energy has been a fundamental part of the district's character for generations. The power station replaced an earlier one that dusted everything near it with a coating of soot, and that plant, too, supplanted a foul gasworks. Before that, the district was the domain of a legion of coal merchants who shuttled their filthy wares around town in shallow boats. These "lightermen" worked from docks that lined the entire southern shore, where land was cheaper than it was in The City on the northern side. The building you see before you is a direct descendant of the way of life that prevailed on the bank in the 1700s.

How deep is the Thames? The river fluctuates greatly with tides (so it's dangerous for swimming), but depending on when you measure around here, it's generally 8.9m (29 ft.) deep at highest tide and 1.8m (6 ft.) at low tide. The Thames' moodiness is the main reason Southwark, the side of the river where the Tate Modern sits, was written off for so many centuries. Until medieval times, the low-lying southern bank was boggy and mostly uninhabitable, so was instead thought of as part of Surrey, the county south of London. Londoners made use of the waterlogged land by turning it into gardens for secret trysts and fish farms (the Pike Garden, or Pye Garden, stood pretty much in front of you around the Tate's eastern flank), but it wasn't until the latter part of the 1700s that people figured out how to drain the water and settle the area fully. Southwark was where you went for a rowdy time—that is, until the Puritans quashed the fun in 1642.

Before you completely cross the river, turn back for a stupendous view of St. Paul's dome symmetrically rising from the center of the bridge.

Once you're on the opposite bank, with the river in front of you, turn right. Stand midway between the cluster of houses and the building with the thatched roof. You're on:

7 Bankside

This river promenade also continues west, past the Tate Modern, to the London Eye and the Houses of Parliament. When Hugh Grant told Andie MacDowell he loved her by way of David Cassidy in *Four Weddings and a Funeral,* he did it farther along this walkway by the National Film Theatre. There's no better place to stroll, people-watch, and appreciate the sweep of the city.

As late as the 1960s, the path you're on, which at this place was called Bankside, was a vehicular street bearing two-way traffic, as it had been since the 1600s. Each building on the street owned rights to the docks or water-stairs on the river opposite it, so tenants were usually people who needed access to the water, such as ferrymen or sailors. The four-story, white house at the left of the blind Cardinal Cap Alley, number 49, was built around 1710 on the foundations of a pub, the Cardinal's Cap, which itself went up in 1547 to entertain the people who came to Southwark to carouse. Number 49 was home to successive generations of coal merchants, but not, as its plaque purports, to Sir Christopher Wren as he built St. Paul's. Wren did live nearby, but in a building that was torn down when the power station needed land—this plaque, which hung on that vanished home, was appropriated by a D.I.Y. revisionist in the mid–20th century. Number 49 has received its own biography, *The House by the Thames* by Gillian Tindall.

To the left is Shakespeare's Globe theater, which made a premature exit in its own era, only to be rebuilt in ours. The circular Globe's stage is even at the same compass point as the 1599 original's (p. 114).

Southwark may be famous for Shakespeare, but interestingly, the city's theatrical life was only centered here from about 1587 to 1642, when it was illegal to operate a theater in The City proper. Once the laws relaxed, the entertainment venues moved back into town, where they've been ever since.

Southwark was the Tudor version of a multiplex, and the biggest blockbuster was bear-baiting—the spectacle of vicious dogs let loose upon tethered bears. Even Henry VIII and Elizabeth I were huge fans; he had a bear pit installed at Whitehall Palace, and she barred Parliament from banning the pursuit on Sundays. One short block past the Globe is a lane called Bear Gardens. Three quarters of the way down, you'll find a small courtyard. That's the former location of the Davies Amphitheatre, one of the most popular bear pits. Samuel Pepys wrote in his diary in 1666 of attending one such slaughter where he "saw some good sport of the bull's tossing the dogs—one into the very boxes. But it is a very rude and nasty pleasure."

Under a modern office building in the next street, Rose Alley, lie the foundations of another theater known to have premiered plays by Shakespeare, the Rose (p. 114). It lasted from 1587 to about 1606. The Swan stood nearby, too, although we may never find the footprint. The Rose's footprint gave us vital clues about what Elizabethan theaters looked like—architects also studied sketches made of it by a Dutch tourist in 1596. (Are you sketching your trip?)

Historians think they know where the original Globe stood. If you'd like to see it, head down Bear Gardens one block to Park Street, turn left and go under the bridge, and just after it, past the buildings on the right, you'll find a semicircular arc of stones. Not very suggestive, is it? In 1949, it was even drearier. It lay behind the locked gate of the decrepit Anchor Brewery, and when American actor Sam Wanamaker (father of Zoë, who played Madam Hooch in the Harry Potter movies) dropped by to pay pilgrimage, the indignity of the meager plaque (still there) so enraged him that he resolved to rebuild the Globe as a living home for England's great theatrical tradition. Which is what came to pass, albeit 4 years after his 1993 death.

Retrace your steps to the riverside. On the water at Bear Gardens, look for a stone seat embedded in the wall of Riverside House. It's said to be the last remaining Wherryman's Seat, dozens of which once lined the Thames. Boatmen, the taxi drivers of their day, would lounge in these perches—this one is 15th century—until someone came along and hired them for a trip across the water. Ferrymen would also court business by shouting destinations to theatergoers after their plays: "Eastward ho!" or "Westward ho!"

Continue along the river, keeping it to your left. You'll go through a pedestrian tunnel under:

8 Southwark Bridge

On the walls of the tunnel, you'll see illustrations of skaters and revelers at the bygone "Frost Fairs" that, starting in 1564, were regularly held on the icy

Thames. No matter how many winters you spend in London, you'll never see the Thames freeze over. But back then, they had the London Bridge, a few hundred yards downstream. Its 19 arches were so narrow, and its supports so thick, that the river's flow became sluggish, allowing water (and the outhouse filth that churned within it) to freeze. By contrast, during outgoing tides the rush was so fierce that boats capsized and passengers (few of whom knew how to swim, given the filth) drowned. When the bridge was dismantled in 1814, the Frost Fairs melted into history.

Walk past the two modern buildings and take a look underneath Southwark Bridge where it meets the shore. You can still discern the remains of some water-stairs, dating to before the construction of the first bridge here in 1819. In 1912, this bridge's central 72m (236-ft.) span was the largest ever attempted in cast iron. The drab hunk of a building to your right is the headquarters of the *Financial Times*.

9 The Anchor 🍺

Few pubs are more idyllic than the Anchor (p. 78), where Bankside meets the railway via-duct. The riverside patio is open in good weather; otherwise, the interior is charming. This pub was once controlled, as nearly all pubs once were, by a brewery; it was Barclay Perkins, located just behind it from 1790 until about 1980. Even before that, it was a fixture; in 1666, Samuel Pepys watched the Great Fire rage from here before coming to his senses and hur-rying across the river to rescue his possessions from his home in Seething Lane, near the Tower of London. In the 1950s, the Anchor was considered a slum and nearly went.

After the Anchor, the path jogs inland. Take the first left onto:

10 Clink Street

Pass under the railway arch. In a few moments, you've gone from Elizabethan Southwark (theaters, bear-baiting) to Georgian Southwark (coal merchants, breweries). Now you're in Victorian Southwark, a claustrophobic underworld teeming with fetid-smelling industry and river rats. You can almost hear the reverberations on this narrow wharfside street. You might even call the sensation Dickensian, and you wouldn't be wrong, since when the writer was 12 years old, his father was thrown into a debtor's prison near where you're standing, off the Borough High Street.

Prisons were something of a cottage industry for the area; the Clink Street Prison stood here from 1127, when the Bishop of Winchester built it as a lockup for his Winchester Palace, until 1780, when the anti-Catholic Gordon riots saw the dismal hole destroyed. Although The Clink gave its name as slang to all pris-ons that came after it, no one knows for sure how it got the name itself—Flemish or Middle English words for latch are likely the origin. Suffice to say it was awful. And so is the museum here that purports to tell its story.

In the 1800s, warehousing goods instead of people became this street's stock-in-trade. All around, you'll see hints of the street's past maritime uses, from wooden loft doors to cranes used to hoist crates into upper floors. Today, these spaces house media companies and architects. During the week, you'll see them in their fashionable clothes, staggering across the cobbles in their Italian shoes on their way to mid-afternoon cocktails.

The latter Bishops of Winchester were not nice guys. Henry II (1133–1189) gave them control of this neighborhood, and because it was outside of the jurisdiction of the city, they could pretty much get away with whatever they wanted to. Principally, they cultivated countless brothels and skimmed the profits for themselves—which is how Southwark got its rap as a den of vice. Anyone who annoyed them (heretics, troublemakers) wound up in the Clink, where no one was likely to find them again. Continue down Clink Street. By the building with the rounded grid of windows, you'll see all that's left of the Bishops' palace. This unique geometric rose window, dating to the 1300s when it lit the great hall, was forgotten behind a wall until a warehouse fire exposed it again. Double back to Stoney Street.

Turn down Stoney Street and walk under the railway arch. Just past it, on your left, you'll see:

11 Borough Market

Stop at the frilly grey portico.

The mood of the neighborhood has changed drastically again. To your left, behind the portico, is Borough Market, a fantasy for the tongue (described in gastronomic detail on p. 71) and the oldest fruit and vegetable market in the city. A market has been held around here since A.D. 43, when Roman soldiers noted passing a market on their way to sack The City. More reliable records date it to 1014, when it served the denizens on the old London Bridge, the city's only river crossing, The cream-grey portico is not original to this place; it's the cast iron Flower Hall of Covent Garden, rescued when the Royal Opera House was renovated in 2003. If it seems to blend seamlessly, it's because it was made around the same time as the rest of the Borough Market structure (1859–60).

The Market is best known for gourmet supplies. Park Street, which runs into Stoney Street, looks as quaint as a movie-set version of old England; in fact, it was used in *Harry Potter and the Prisoner of Azkaban*. The Market itself has appeared in films including *Howard's End* and *Bridget Jones's Diary*. The city's first railway, a 6.4km (4-mile) run to Greenwich, plowed its route .8km (half-mile) east of here in 1836. Even after tunneling technology improved, railway tycoons thought nothing of barricading thriving neighborhoods with massive brick viaducts, cutting them off from each other and creating slums. On your tour, you have crossed under a number of railway viaducts built that way, and shortly, you'll see how narrowly one of England's most historic churches averted its own destruction.

Cross the next street and enter the brick arch marked Green Market. Head straight into the grounds of:

12 Southwark Cathedral

(If for some reason the Green Market arch is closed, turn left down Bedale Street—it's not marked—until you see a church appear on your right.)

Before you stands the oldest Gothic church in the city, and the oldest building in Southwark. You'll see its tower appear in every old drawing of the city. In Roman times, it was the site of a villa. Its Christian chapter was begun by the daughter of a ferryman in the 7th century; it was rebuilt in the 850s and again 300 years later. There were once a monastery and a chapel in this yard, where office workers now lunch on gourmet items from Borough Market, but those came and went, too. Southwark teemed with the poor, with factory workers, and with grubby rivermen. One such blue-collar child was John Harvard, one of nine kids of a man who owned a tavern and butcher shop just northeast of here. John was baptized in this church in the early 1600s but when he grew up, he fled this slum for the Massachusetts Bay Colony, where Harvard University was later named for him. In time this place was limping along as a humble parish church called St. Saviour's and it dissolved into dilapidation. The re-routing of London Bridge Road sheared away several small chapels, and in 1863, the rumbling railway forced its way alongside the yard. But by 1905, its fortunes reversed when it was elevated to a cathedral, and now it's so well cared for it's hard to discern its true age and sordid past.

The cathedral's entrance is to the left. Go straight across the sanctuary, through the glass doors, up a short flight of stairs, and to the end of the glass-roofed corridor, which traces the line of an alley that was called:

13 Lancelot's Link

Nelson Mandela opened this building in 2001. Have a look at the display, which preserves surprising discoveries made in this small area during a 1999 renovation. Look down into the well on the far right, and you'll see the original paving stones from the Roman road that cut through this space in the 1st century. You crossed over this same road several times already today; you were standing above it when you entered Borough Market. Other relics, piled on top of each other, include a stone coffin, probably from the 1200s, with a carved slot for the head, and a kiln from the 1600s, soot marks intact—bits of the Delftware it made have been found as far away as Williamsburg, Virginia.

The cathedral has some beautiful painted monuments, including one of England's oldest wooden effigies (1280). Shakespeare's brother Edmond was buried here in 1607, as was Philip Henslowe, who built the Rose, in an unmarked grave. Other worthwhile sights include Edwardian stained glass tributes to the Bard's plays, the Harvard Chapel with masonry from the Norman period, and some of the original ceiling bosses, carved in 1469 and saved when things got bad. How bad? During Elizabeth I's reign, the retro-choir (the part behind the altar) was walled off and rented to a baker. Later on, vestrymen discovered the baker was also raising swine in there.

Back down the corridor, exit. Go through the yard into the lane (it's Montague Close; the Thames is in front of you). Turn right, and before the overpass, look left for:

14 Nancy's Steps

These are popularly held to be the location, in the Dickens novel *Oliver Twist*, where Noah Claypool eavesdrops on a conversation that leads to Nancy's murder by Bill Sykes. In the book, those steps faced the Thames, but these steps are indeed a rare surviving remnant of the same New London Bridge, built here in 1821 as a replacement for the 600-year-old, overcrowded London Bridge. The steps that Dickens wrote about were sold in 1968 to an American oilman who had most of the bridge shipped, stone by stone, to Lake Havasu, Arizona, where it remains today. These steps were left behind and attached to this featureless 1973 replacement.

Just so you know, the existing London Bridge was not the source of the nursery rhyme "London Bridge is Falling Down"—that either referred to the burning of a wooden version in 1013, during a skirmish between Danes and Norwegians; or to Henry III's "fair lady" Queen Eleanor, who skimmed the tolls of the medieval bridge for her own purse, leaving its maintenance in a parlous state.

Climb the stairs to the road above. You're now on:

15 London Bridge

At the top of the stairs, you'll see a pedestal topped by a dragon, the symbol of the city, holding London's crest. You'll see these dragons at several of the city's medieval borders. About 30m (98 ft.) east of here, under modern buildings, is where you would have entered the Stone Gateway, the entry to the disaster-prone medieval London Bridge. For more than 3 centuries, tar-dipped heads of executed criminals were impaled on pikes and stuck atop the Gateway as a vivid warning to would-be ne'er-do-wells.

Turn to the right to use the crosswalk. Go to the opposite side of the street and walk onto London Bridge, over the river. Don't cross the river—just enjoy the view of the:

16 Pool of London

This section of the Thames between London Bridge and the Tower Bridge is known as the Pool of London. It may be quiet now, but for nearly 2,000 years, it was the heart of international trade. So many goods passed through here that warehouses along the southern bank became known as "London's Larder." Ships finally became so large that they had to unload downstream, closer to the sea. The section of river in front of you, parallel to this bridge, is where the medieval London Bridge stood.

Across the river from the Tower, you'll just make out an egg-shaped glass building. That's City Hall (2002), designed by Norman Foster (who also did the Millennium Bridge) to be ergonomic, with a huge spiral staircase curling around its atrium and "smart" windows that open on hot days. Just like a politician, it has no edge and you can't tell if it's coming or going. Former London mayor Ken Livingstone, a man not known for tact or restraint, called it "a glass testicle." Anyone can have a ball in its public spaces from 8:30am to 5:30pm, weekdays (www.london.gov.uk).

Turn around and follow London Bridge inland, keeping on the left side of the road. This street becomes Borough High Street. You will pass under a railway arch. Just after you pass Southwark Street forking off to the right, look for "The George" sign. It marks:

17 The George Inn

Because the London Bridge was the only crossing to the city from the south for so many centuries, this area became the equivalent of a train depot, and it was dotted with inns, stables, coach yards, and pubs. Everyone going to or coming from southern England or Europe stopped here, often spending the night before pushing into the shoulder-to-shoulder crowds of London Bridge. If you've ever read *The Canterbury Tales,* you'll recall that in 1386, the pilgrims began their journey to the shrine of Thomas a Becket from the Tabard Inn. Until 1873, that was located a short walk farther down Borough High Street, on the left. The George, described on p. 79, is the last survivor from this bustling coaching era. Although the wooden building, which once encircled the entire yard, dates to 1677, the inn was here for at least another 130 years before that, if not longer. We know it was typical of the time because John Stow, in *A Survey of London* (1598), termed it "a common hostelry for travelers." A drink here makes a fitting end to your journey through time. Look up and you'll see the jagged glass spire of The Shard (p. 116), Europe's tallest building, peering down at you as you sit where people have lifted beer for nearly half a millennium.

WALKING TOUR 3: SHOPPING, SOHO & GIMME SHELTER

START:	**Oxford Circus Tube station**
FINISH:	**Goodge Street Tube station**
TIME:	**Two hours, not including shopping or restaurant breaks**
BEST TIMES:	**Weekdays, when Berwick Street's market is on and Oxford Street is slightly less crowded**
WORST TIMES:	**After dark, when stores and markets close**

All churched out? London is more than stories about dead queens and bloody uprisings. It's always been cosmopolitan, too, and the flash point for trends that ripple out to the rest of the world. Songs first sung at the clubs of Soho soon caused toes to tap on the other side of the planet, and fashion trends born on Carnaby Street remain internationally iconic 40 years later. Bring along your credit cards as we roam some of the city's best shopping streets and touch upon a few leftovers from London's recent past, including forgotten air-raid shelters and the settings for some good, old-fashioned sexual scandals. This is the London you found out about from the radio and the runways, not from your social studies teacher.

1 Oxford Circus

Leave the Tube station using Exit 2. Position yourself out of the fray.

You are in the thick of the mile-long Regent Street, which to the right is punctuated by the witches-hat steeple of All Souls Church and to the left curves toward Piccadilly Circus. When the Prince Regent, later George IV, was planning his new pet project, Regent's Park, he decided he also wanted a road to connect his house to it. He chose this particular location because, in his mind, it would provide a suitable demarcation line between the gentry of Mayfair, to the west, and the rabble of the traders who lived in Soho, to the east. George tapped John Nash to do the job, completed in 1825. Originally, the sidewalks were covered by stone colonnades, but when those attracted prostitutes, they were removed, and most of the original buildings were later rebuilt—the only Nash original is now All Souls. Even if most of the facades you see now mask more modern buildings,

Walking Tour 3: Shopping, Soho & Gimme Shelter

1 Oxford Circus
2 Marks & Spencer
3 Great Marlborough Street
   Magistrate's Court
4 Foubert's Court
5 Carnaby Street
6 Kingly Court
7 Berwick Street
8 The John Snow ☕
9 Berwick Street Market
10 Brewer Street
11 Old Compton Street
12 Frith Street
13 Soho Square
14 St. Giles Circus
15 Tottenham Court Road
16 The Goodge Street Deep Level Shelter
17 Goodge Street Tube Station

few streets in London impart such a sweeping, uplifting feeling, though few are also as congested with the hoi polloi George would have spurned.

The other avenue intersecting before you is Oxford Street, following the same line as a Roman road. George's class-centered definition of the landscape has more or less held: The exclusive shops of Oxford Street still lie west of Regent Street, and the downmarket stores tend to be east of it. Having a presence on Oxford Street is considered crucial for brands with mass appeal.

Head right, east on Oxford Street. You will pass Argyll Street on the right. When you pass Ramillies Street, prepare to stop in front of:

2 Marks & Spencer

London has a love-hate relationship with Oxford Street. People come here to shop by the thousands, but they often despair of the crush of the experience. Charles Dickens, Jr., described the street thusly in 1888: "It ought to be the finest thoroughfare in the world. As a matter of fact it is not by any means, and though it is, like all the other thoroughfares, improving, it still contains many houses which even in a third-rate street would be considered mean." We're only going to walk down a sample of Oxford Street. It's usually so crowded, it's all you can probably handle if you're keeping one eye on this book.

Marks & Spencer (p. 151), or M&S, dates to 1894 and is the favored British department store for staples. Perhaps proof of its appeal is that the chain can afford to run two giant frontages on Oxford Street; its flagship store is remarkably near here, between Bond Street and Marble Arch Tube stations. Its Food Halls (at this store, in the cellar) are well known as an ideal place to pick up prepared foods, sandwiches, and inexpensive but well-selected wines.

Turn right at Poland Street, walk 1 block, and turn right again onto Great Marlborough Street. Soon on your right, at 19-21, you'll see a stout white building. That's the:

3 Great Marlborough Street Magistrate's Court

Charles Dickens worked here as a reporter just before hitting it big as a novelist, and a variety of other big names appeared before the judges here, including the Marquess of Queensbury (defending himself from Oscar Wilde's libel charge). When this neighborhood turned bohemian in the Swinging '60s, it began trying a string of drug charges against the likes of Mick Jagger, Johnny Rotten, Keith Richards, Francis Bacon, and, curiously (and coming full circle), the guy who wrote the musical *Oliver!*, Lionel Bart. It's now a luxury hotel, but I suggest you go inside briefly, because much of the old judicial fittings were left intact. You can have a cocktail in one of the old jail cells—now converted into private booths—or even peek into Silk, a restaurant slotted into the authoritative Number One court, which still has its witness stand, bench, wood paneling, and vaulted glass ceiling.

Beyond the Courthouse Hotel on the left, you'll see a Tudor-style building of black beams and white plaster. This is Liberty (p. 150), famous for its haute fabrics. It's also famous for its building—it was made in 1924 using wood recycled from junked ships.

Great Marlborough Street runs into Regent Street. Turn left there and walk the short distance to:

4 Foubert's Court

Times have been better on Regent Street. Walmart–style box stores in the suburbs have put the screws on the destination shops of the city, and this avenue has seen a few long-termers lose their sizzle. Dickins & Jones, a department store at the corner you just turned, closed its doors in early 2006 after nearly 170 years of history, and the same old shopping mall brands are moving in.

Two doors farther from Foubert's Court, though, at 188-196, is a well-loved holdover from the street's glory days. It's Hamleys (p. 160), one of the largest toy stores in the world. Some 5 million customers pour through its doors every year, but since the sales force is famous for putting on a non-stop show on every floor, it's understandable if many of those customers come to gawp and not to buy. If you go into Hamleys, when and if you come out again, turn right and go back to Foubert's Court.

Walk down the very short Foubert's Court for one block; you'll see "Carnaby" on a metal arch. Go under it and head 1 block. Go right, and now you'll see a larger arch on:

5 Carnaby Street

Yes, those obnoxious arches proclaim your location with a self-promotion that proves this street is no longer the super-cool, forward-trending street of the kids in the know. It's more of a mall with an edge. The days of Swinging London, when men could cruise from store to store trying on hip-hugging black trousers and frilly shirts, are behind it. *Time* magazine spilled the secret of Carnaby Street in 1966, and by the 1970s, it was pedestrianized as a shopping street, making hipness a matter of retrospect.

Just after you cross Ganton Street, where Broadwick Street hits Carnaby Street, duck into the passageway on the right:

6 Kingly Court

Clever entrepreneurs capitalize Carnaby Street's mod rep with this development, a retail experiment in a former timber warehouse. A few niche chains are present, but the stores here are mostly boutiques pushing young designers.

Slip out the back door of Kingly Court, opposite its front door, and hang a left on Kingly Street. Three doors in, at number 8, is Drop Dead, which sells ironic '90s fashions. In the 1960s, it was the Bag 'O Nails pub, where future Wings-mates Paul McCartney and Linda Eastman first clapped eyes on each other. The pub was also where Fleetwood Mac's John McVie proposed to Christine.

Return to Kingy Court. Retrace your steps out of it, cross Carnaby Street, and head down Broadwick Street. You'll stop around:

7 Berwick Street

A hundred and sixty years ago, this block was a foul slum. French, Greek, and Italian immigrants fled hard times and revolutions by cramming into these tight streets, and by the 1850s, cholera was storming through the overstuffed city. An 1854 outbreak killed 500 people in barely 10 days. Common wisdom at the time held that the disease was spread through the air—a reasonable conclusion, given how terrible the sewage-smeared city smelled—but a local anesthetist, John Snow, suspected polluted water was the cause. He got permission to inspect the public pump at Broad Street, now Broadwick Street (it's on the sidewalk in the block before Berwick Street) and he found that it was being contaminated with sewage leaking from Number 40 nearby, proving his theory. The saga was recently retold in the book *The Ghost Map* by Steven Johnson.

When you reach Berwick Street, look left. Think of this location as the modern-day Abbey Road. It's where, in 1995, Oasis photographed the cover of *(What's the Story) Morning Glory,* one of the seminal CDs of the age. The photographer shot from farther down the street, aiming south, toward where you're standing. (Noel Gallagher, with characteristic eloquence, said he thought the album cover was "s**t.")

And here's another slice of rock history: One miniblock farther down Broadwick Street at number 7, the corner shop covered in striking rust-colored tiles (now Sounds of the Universe record store, a local landmark), was the Bricklayers Arms pub. Brian Jones auditioned The Rolling Stones here in 1962, and they held formative rehearsals upstairs. Across the road at number 6 is Agent Provocateur, a noted lingerie shop. The word "Soho" is probably derived from a hunting cry used when this area was parkland—it's nice to see that some folks around here are still on the hunt.

8 John Snow Pub ☕

So grateful were Dr. Snow's neighbors that they renamed their pub for him, albeit a century later. It stands at number 39, at Lexington Street, on the site of his practice. Raise a pint in his honor here, as we read the words of Dr. Snow himself: "I feel it my duty to endeavor to convince you of the physical evils sustained to your health by using intoxicating liquors even in the greatest moderation." (Oops.)

Turn south on Berwick Street. Walk down it to:

9 Berwick Street Market

This is the last great market in the center of the city, and it has been in operation since the 1840s, although vestry records indicate some illicit trading was going on as far back as 1778. London's first publicly available grapefruit was sold here in 1890. Buy a snack here; these hard-working vendors, many of whom speak fluent Cockney, could use your support. They have been known to cut deals on perishables in late afternoon.

Pass over Peter Street and under Maurice House, going under the crossover and winding up on:

10 Brewer Street

From the late 1700s to the 1950s, it was impossible for a single gentleman to pass unpropositioned through Soho. A 1959 act chased the open salesmanship indoors, to be replaced by drinking joints where men could buy lap time with a lady, and by the 1970s, even those were forced to seek a lower profile. By law, today's displays are not permitted titillate, complying with the British reputation (inaccurate in my book) for sexual modesty.

It was in this fleshly carnival that Laura Henderson bought a theatre at Great Windmill and Archer streets and got around indecency laws by ensuring that the performers in her naughty entertainment, the Revudeville, never moved a muscle. Famously, the Windmill never closed, not even during the Blitz. You might have seen it in the film *Mrs Henderson Presents.*

Go left to Wardour Street, make a right and then a quick left. You'll be at the head of:

11 Old Compton Street

First, note the church of St. Anne's, a few yards farther down Wardour Street, on the left. It was built in 1685, possibly by Wren (then again, which ones weren't?), but everything save the clock tower was creamed by the Germans.

Walk down Old Compton Street, Soho's de facto main street, which is busy round the clock and a center of gay life. Number 54 is the Admiral Duncan. Dylan Thomas once drank there (then again, where didn't he?), it was here, in 1999, that Nazi sympathizer David Copeland planted a bomb stuffed with 500 nails. It killed three people and injured many more. Copeland, an obvious madman, also bombed the South Asian population of Brick Lane and blacks in Brixton, but his only fatalities were here.

On the corner of Dean Street, look right. Down the block on the left, at number 49, is the French House, more commonly called the French Pub. During World War II, it was the drinking haunt of Charles de Gaulle, and it was where the exiled leader formed the Free French government and army. The street beyond the French House is Shaftesbury Avenue, the famous theatrical thoroughfare; many of the side streets between Old Compton and Shaftesbury contain the stage doors for the major playhouses, where famous actors report to work. Now look left, north up Dean Street. In the attic of number 28, Karl Marx dwelled in abject poverty with his wife and several kids, but no running water or toilet. Three of his kids died while he was in residence in Soho in the early 1850s. No wonder he thought communism would be better.

Turn left at:

12 Frith Street

Bar Italia, the stylish cafe at number 22, is a nightlife landmark of its own (p. 61). But history doesn't stop at the ground floor. Upstairs is where, in 1925, John Logie Baird privately tested a homemade invention he called "noctovision," using a local office boy as a test subject. The next year, he unveiled an improved model for the science nerds of the Royal Institution upstairs in this building. Baird's system, which used a spinning disc, was eventually discarded, but it debuted ahead of American Philo T. Farnsworth's more famous electronic version. Within a decade, the BBC was broadcasting "television"—its new name—regularly. In the 1940s, Baird invented the first color picture tube.

Walk up three doors. For ten months starting in September 1764, the 8-year-old Mozart lived with his father and sister at a house located at number 20 (the building was replaced in 1858). While he was in London, the prodigy amused King George III with his abilities, wrote his first two symphonies, and befriended fellow composer Bach. Music history of another kind happened at number 47, which in 1969 hosted the first public performance of The Who's *Tommy*, then Jimi Hendrix's last one, in 1970.

Use the gate to head into:

13 Soho Square

Laid out in 1681, Soho Square was, early on, fashionable and mansion-lined. Later it became the center of the ambassadorial and scientific cliques. Sir Joseph Banks, who made his name collecting exotic specimens as a tagalong on Captain Cook's voyages, moved here in 1777. These days, Soho is a center for the music and film industries.

In the center of the square, which is technically a private garden even though it's been open to the public for half a century, is a cottage you'd swear was Tudor in origin. In fact, it's an 1895 pastiche made to hide an electrical transformer. Beneath the lawns lie empty air-raid shelters.

Exit the opposite side of the square and go straight down Soho Street. You'll soon hit Oxford Street again. Turn right and head for the next major intersection, officially called:

14 St. Giles Circus

Look across the next major street, and you'll see the 35-story Centre Point development. Built in 1964 with heavy government concessions, it was kept empty for years by its unscrupulous owner, partly to hold out for astronomical rents and partly because doing so would get him off the tax hook, even as the city struggled through a homeless crisis. The charity Centrepoint, which started in the basement of St. Anne's church in Soho and grew into a force in housing issues, derisively took its name from the waste. Still, it's indisputably one of the landmarks of the skyline.

The area around the Tube station, which contains some tile mosaics by the great artist Eduardo Paolozzi, is under construction as part of the mammoth Crossrail project, a deep-level train line slated to open in 2018.

Turn left and head up:

15 Tottenham Court Road

Fans of Andrew Lloyd Webber (anyone?), or at least of T. S. Eliot, will recall that this is the "grimy road" roamed by Grizabella, the "glamour cat" who sings "Memory."

On the first corner, the Dominion Theatre was where, in 1957, Bill Haley and the Comets were the first American rock act to play Britain. Five minutes ahead, on your left, you will see Goodge Street, whose pubs and charity shops are frequented by students who attend the several universities in this area.

Duck into Chenies Street, on your right. At the curving side alley of North Circle, look for the striped, rounded buildings. That's:

16 The Goodge Street Deep Level Shelter

In 1939, planners decided to build an express train line beneath the existing Northern Line platforms of Goodge Street. War intervened. In 1942, the unfinished tunnel was allocated to the Americans, and it was under the ground here where General (later President) Dwight D. Eisenhower orchestrated D-Day and announced it to the world, in 1944. There were eight deep-level shelters, and five were open to bomb-shocked civilians; this is one of the most central and best kept. It retains its ground-level entry blocks, one pillbox and one octagonal, connected by a brick building—thousands of Londoners pass them daily but don't know their original purpose. Since the Cold War, the onetime shelters, now innocuously painted grey with blue stripes, have been used for storage.

Double back onto Tottenham Court Road. Across the street will be:

17 Goodge Street Tube Station

Before you end your tour at the Tube station opposite, turn right. The Goodge Street Deep Level Shelter could originally be accessed from a second point on the west of Tottenham Court Road opposite Torrington Place; some brick-and-concrete structures and vents linger. Goodge Street Underground station, opened in 1907 and still sporting much of its original tile work, is one of the few in the system that uses elevators, not escalators. You can always use the 136 steps, too—that is, if you have the juice after your walking tour.

DAY TRIPS FROM LONDON

You've flown all the way to England. It would be a shame to miss seeing some of the sights that make it special—the rolling countryside, the stately mansions cradled by ancient trees, the ageless villages built alongside slow-flowing rivers. You can't get these things in London, but you can sample them in nearby places that have played an integral role in the development and culture of London life. An excursion enriches you with two experiences for the price of one: You'll taste everyday English life while you immerse yourself in world-famous landmarks.

Britain has comprehensive transport, but it's not quick as mercury. Because of traffic and a dearth of superhighways, you can expect a 48km (30-mile) trip to take an hour, so a spot that's 129km to 161km (80–100 miles) each way, such as Stonehenge or Bath, will require you to rise at dawn if you want to buy yourself much touring time at all. Going by bus is often less expensive than by rail, but the inefficient journey will involve narrow roads.

The tourist offices listed will be able, for a fee (£4–£5, plus 10% of the room rate), to hook you up with a bed for the night, should you decide that you'd rather not trek back to London right away. You can find lots more information at **Visit England** (www.visitengland.com) and **Visit Britain** (www.visitbritain.com).

WINDSOR & ETON

Buckingham Palace is a mere *pied a'terre*. The Queen actually prefers this great castle, which dominates the skyline of town like a cloud of stone. Windsor Castle (32km/20 miles west of London) has been the home of the Royal Family for some 900 years, far longer than anything in London. Queen Victoria is buried in the back yard (although they don't phrase it quite that way). Despite the inevitable crowds, this is unmissable.

Essentials

GETTING THERE The price difference between transport options is negligible. Riding the rails is quicker, so it's got the edge. **Trains** (ℂ **08457/48-49-50;** www.nationalrail.co.uk; 38–56 min.; £11.10) go directly from Waterloo station to Windsor & Eton Riverside or from Paddington to Windsor & Eton Central with a change at Slough. Trains requiring no changes leave twice an hour, and trains requiring a change leave a little more frequently. Or take a coach by **Green Line** (℗ **0844/800-4411;** www. greenline.co.uk; 1 hr. 45 min.; £10 single) numbered 701 or 702 from Hyde Park Corner or the Colonnades Coach Station south of Victoria Station.

VISITOR INFORMATION   Royal Windsor (Old Booking Hall, Windsor Royal Shopping, Thames St.; ℗ **01753/74-39-00;** www.windsor.gov.uk). From there, Blue Badge guides give **walking tours** (http://shop.windsor.gov.uk; ℗ **01753/743909;** March to September, Sat at 11:30am, Sun at 2:30pm; £7 adult, £5 senior/student).

TOURS   The most appealing way to see the area is by **boat,** which departs from Windsor Promenade, Barry Avenue, for a 40-minute round-trip with fine views of the castle. The cost is £5.70 for adults, £2.85 for children. Tours are operated by **French Brothers,** Clewer Boathouse, Clewer Court Rd., Windsor (℗ **01753/851-900;** www. frenchbrothers.co.uk). Two-hour trips cost £9 for adults and £4.50 for children.

Exploring Windsor

Two miles from town, **Legoland Windsor** (℗ **0871/222-2001**; www.legoland.co.uk; open March to October; £34 adult, £29 kids) has top-notch rides catering to small children and some impressive Lego constructions. Shuttles go from the Theatre Royal. The tourist office sells discounted tickets for late afternoon entry.

Windsor Castle   You may have had your fill of palaces in London proper, but you haven't seen the best. A fortress and a royal home for more than 900 years, it was expanded by each successive monarch who dwelled in it—more battlements for the warlike ones, more finery for the aesthetes. The resulting sprawl, which dominates the town from nearly every angle, is the Queen's favorite residence—she spends lots of time here—and its history is richer than that of Buckingham Palace.

The castle's **State Apartments** are sumptuous enough to be daunting, and a tour through them, available unless there's a state visit, includes entrance to some mind-bogglingly historic rooms. Around a million people file through every year, so sharpen your elbows, and there are no cafés, so eat first. **St. George's Chapel** (closed Sun), a delicately vaulted Gothic spectacle opened by Henry VIII, is his final resting place and that of nine more monarchs, including Elizabeth II's father (George VI). EII's mother (the Queen Mum), and sister (Princess Margaret) are with him in a side chapel and it's safe to assume that this is where she will wind up one day, too. The palace also has a cache of priceless furniture (some of it solid silver), paintings, ephemera (look for the bullet that killed Lord Nelson, sealed in a locket) and weaponry, all of which, frustratingly, the audio guide, signage, and £5 souvenir book do little to describe, so the only recourse is to pepper staff with questions. In 1992, one-fifth of the castle area was engulfed by an accidental fire; the Queen recounted her despair over that, plus the breakup of two of her children's marriages, in her now-famous "annus horribilus" Christmas speech to the nation, and much effort and funding went into putting everything back to the way it was before. In fact, the Queen originally opened Buckingham Palace to visitors to fund the restoration. **St. George's Hall,** one of the repaired areas, is the Queen's chosen room for banquets. Kids love **Queen Mary's Doll's House,** an preposterously extravagant toy built for the allegedly grown-up Queen Mary in the 1920s with working electricity, elevators, plumbing, specially written library books, and other details so extravagant they're borderline offensive. From October to March, the tour also includes the **Semi-State Rooms,** George IV's private area, considered by many to be among the best-preserved Georgian interiors in England. In August and September, you can climb the **Round Tower** for views, and sometimes in January and midsummer, the castle's ancient **Great Kitchen** is open. There's also a **Changing the Guard** ceremony at 11am (Mon–Sat, but alternate days August–March; check the website).

The Castle is the superstar here, but supporting roles are played by the succinctly named **Great Park** adjoining it; the 4.8km (3-mile), pin-straight **Long Walk** that culminates with an equestrian statue of George III. **Frogmore**, open a pitiful few days in August, is the house where Victoria and Albert share their mausoleum. Just south of the castle is the **Guildhall**, where Prince Charles and Camilla Parker-Bowles had a quiet civil marriage in April 2005; it's no St. Paul's, where in 1981 Charles wed his first wife, what's-her-name, but it is also the work of Christopher Wren (note its delicate arches). The building was apparently designed without the center columns, which made councilors nervous; Wren threw up some columns but left them an inch shy of the ceiling, just to prove that his architecture was sound.

Castle Hill. ✆ **020/7766-7304.** www.royalcollection.org.uk. Admission £18 adults, £16 students and seniors, £11 children 5–16, free 4 and under, £46.50 family of 5 (2 adults and 3 children 16 and under). Daily Mar–Oct 9:45am–5:15pm, last admission 4pm; Nov–Feb 9:45am–4:15pm, last admission 3pm. Closed for periods in Apr, June, and Dec, when the royal family is in residence. National rail: Windsor Central or Windsor & Eton Riverside.

Eton College   A 15-minute walk over a footbridge on the Thames (narrow at this western remove), you're in a world of snooty stationers and haberdashers. Eton is probably the most exclusive boys' school on Earth. Princes Harry and William are alums, known as Old Etonians, as are kings and princes from around the world. There's a museum in its wine cellars—and the fact this school has a wine cellar tells you what kind of rich these kids are. Be nice to them. They're tomorrow's dictators.

Keats Lane, Eton, Windsor. ✆ **01753/671-177.** www.etoncollege.com. Admission £7.50 adults, £6.50 children 8–13. 1 hr. tours March-October at 2pmand 3:15pm, with some blackout days during school term; check the website's schedule.

Saving on Your Excursion's Rail Ticket

Train fares listed in this section are provided as a guideline; National Rail pricing schemes are complicated and unpredictable. The good news is that for all of the destinations served by trains, if you return to London on the same day that you leave it, you can pay just a little more than the price of the usual one-way (single) ticket. Rail clerks may call this kind of a deal a "day return." More tips:

- Tickets tend to be most costly on Fridays, when Londoners head out of town.

- You can find incredible deals (up to 70% off) if you happen to be among the first customers to get tickets for a given departure. Book starting 12 weeks out.

- Prices are highest for "open" tickets with no restrictions, so always spring for the discounted restricted fare, since you probably won't need to change your plans.

The Drury House   Touristy pub-style outfits run by companies cluster by the castle entrance, all of them serving fish and chips for around £10, but this creaky and potentially haunted wooden building is the most interesting. It's where Charles II is said to have stashed his mistress ("Rumored," the waitress cautions) for easy access to his chambers via a tunnel, now sealed off. Family-run, it serves a gamut of British food from breakfast to cream tea to club sandwiches.

4 Church St. ☎ **01753/863734**. www.druryhouse.co.uk. Daily 9:30am to 11pm. Mains £7 to £10.

BATH

Easily roamed on foot, Bath, about 161km (100 miles) west of London, is revered as a splendid example of Georgian architecture—to tourists, Bath is resolutely stuck in that past. The pleasing sandstone hue of its buildings set against the slate-grey British sky, the assiduously planned symmetry of its streets, the illusion that Jane Austen (who lived here from 1800–1805) is taking tea within one of its 18th-century Palladian town houses—Bath's magic comes from its consistent and regal design. No wonder the upper crust of the 1700s found it so fashionable, and no wonder their descendants have not dared to alter it. And no wonder UNESCO inscribed it as a World Heritage Site—a rarity for an entire city.

Essentials

GETTING THERE   **Trains** (☎ 08457/48-49-50; www.nationalrail.co.uk; 90 minutes, twice an hour; £15.50 with advance purchase) leave from Paddington and let off in Bath Spa, an ugly section of town about 5 minutes' walk from the good stuff. Because buses take twice as long, I don't recommend National Express (☎ 08705/80-80-80; www.nationalexpress.com; 3 hr.; £7 single).

VISITOR INFORMATION   **Visit Bath/Bath Tourist Information Centre** (Abbey Chambers, Abbey Churchyard; ☎ **090/6711-2000,** from overseas ☎ 011-44-844-847-5257; www.visitbath.co.uk).

TOURS   The Mayor's office provides professionally guided free 2-hour **Walking Tours of Bath** (Sun–Fri 10:30am and 2pm; Sat 10:30am. May–Sept also Tues and Fri 7pm). Meet outside the Abbey Churchyard entrance to the Pump Room.

Exploring Bath

Begin your tour of Georgian Bath at **Queen Square** for some of the famous streets laid out by John Wood the Elder (1704–54). Walk up to the **Circus**, three Palladian crescents arranged in a circle, with 524 different carved emblems above the doors. His son designed the **Royal Crescent**, an elegant half-moon row of town houses. Robert Adam put up **Pulteney Bridge,** a shop-lined crossing of the River Avon, in 1773, just as a similar bridge in the same medieval style, London Bridge, was crumbling.

Roman Baths   The Romans were the first to recognize the tourism potential of the natural hot springs, which bubble at a rate of 250,000 gallons a day. These steamy facilities were discovered in the late 1800s, and the restoration and accompanying museum are excellent. The Victorians mounted a proud colonnade around the excavation, and water has long been drawn in the adjoining Pump Room; you can drink a glass of the sulfuric stuff if you like, or settle down for a pricey lunch in neoclassical style. It's been the done thing in Bath since your great-great-great-grandma was in bloomers.

Bath Abbey Church Yard, Stall St. © **01225/477785.** www.romanbaths.co.uk. £13 adults, £11 seniors/students, £8.50 kids 6–16. Daily 9am–10m Jul–Aug; 9am–6pm Sep–Oct and Mar–Jun; 9:30am–5:30pm Nov–Feb. Last admission 1 hr. before closing. Closed Dec 25–26.

No. 1 Royal Crescent
First-time visitors are blown away by the sweep and elegance of The Royal Crescent, a dazzling 30-house development that took some 7 years to complete, from 1767 to 1775. Its first house, which recently absorbed the old servant's quarters in a massive restoration that religiously presents daily life in those days, is worth a swing-by if you want the full Regency effect.

1 Royal Crescent. © **01225/428126.** www.no1royalcrescent.org.uk. £8.50 adults, £6.50 students and seniors, £3.50 children 5–16, family ticket £17. Tues–Sat Tues–Sun 10:30am–5:30pm, Mon noon–5:30pm (last admission 1 hr. before closing).

Fashion Museum & Assembly Rooms
The grand **Assembly Rooms,** designed by the younger John Wood and completed in 1771, once played host to dances, recitals, and tea parties. Damaged in World War II, the elegant rooms have been gloriously restored and look much as they did when Jane Austen and Thomas Gainsborough attended society events here. Housed in the same building, the **Fashion Museum** offers audio tours through the history of fashion from the 16th century to the present day. Exhibits change every 6 months. There's also a "Corsets and Crinolines" display where enthusiastic visitors can experience the masochism of period garments.

Bennett St. © **01225/477789.** www.fashionmuseum.co.uk. Admission (includes audio tour) £7.75 adults, £7 students and seniors, £5.75 children 6–16, £22 family ticket, free for children 5 and under. Nov–Feb daily 10:30am–4pm; Mar–Oct daily 10:30am–5pm. Closed Dec 25–26.

Jane Austen Centre
This small homage to Britain's favorite 19th-century writer isn't in her house, but Miss Austen did live down the street (at no. 25) for a few months in 1805. Exhibits and a video convey a sense of what life was like when Austen lived

---

Taking Tea in Bath

Yes, it's super touristy—just go with it. The Regency stiffness of Bath is bound to give you a craving for that quintessentially English tradition of afternoon tea, served with jam, clotted cream, and scones. Try the **Pump Room** at the Roman Baths (p. 212), which serves "Bath buns" (sweet buns sprinkled with sugar), or **Sally Lunn's** at 4 North Parade Passage (www.sallylunns.co.uk; © **01225/461634**), which makes such a big deal of its light Sally Lunn buns you'd swear you'd even heard of them before, which you haven't. The latter's building itself is one of the oldest in Bath, dating from 1482, and shows little hint of any changes with its crooked floors and low ceilings. For £6.25 to £12, you can sample a range of cream teas, which include toasted and buttered buns served with strawberry jam and clotted cream. The **Regency Tea Rooms** at the Jane Austen Centre offers "Tea with Mr Darcy" sets (yes, I know . . .) for £15 to £28 for two, and basic cream tea sets from £7.40.

in Bath between 1801 and 1806. Ladies can also learn the esoteric skill of using a fan to attract an admirer. Wholesome, corny fun. The tearoom is worth a visit (see "Taking Tea in Bath," p. 213).

40 Gay St. ℂ **01225/443000.** www.janeausten.co.uk. Daily 9:45am–5:30pm Apr–Oct. 11am–4:30pm Nov–Mar. Allow at least 45 min. £8 adults, £7 students and over-65s, £6 children 6 to 15, £22 family.

OXFORD

Whereas the face of London, 92km (57 miles) east, has been forcibly reshaped by the pressures of war, disaster, and commerce, Oxford was made stronger by them. When plague killed townspeople, the colleges snapped up their houses, and when the Reformation cleaned out the churches, the colleges took their land, too. Academies used the extra space to carve out some of the most beautiful college buildings in the world. Here, the reverence for education borders on the ecclesiastical. Yet Oxford is no cloister; it's a decidedly modern city—thriving, sophisticated, and busy.

Essentials

GETTING THERE   The least expensive, easiest method is by coach, since companies compete for students with regular buses rolling round the clock. The **Oxford Tube** (ℂ **01865/772250;** www.oxfordtube.com; 100 min. with no traffic; £14 adult, £11 seniors/students, £7 under 16, same-day or next-day return £17/£13/£8) bus leaves every 12 to 20 minutes at all hours. It picks passengers up near the Tube stations at Marble Arch, Victoria, Notting Hill Gate, and Shepherd's Bush. Give rush hours wide berth. **Trains** (ℂ **08457/48-49-50;** www.nationalrail.co.uk; 1 hr.; from £13 single with advance purchase) go from Paddington station to Oxford, sometimes via Reading.

VISITOR INFORMATION   In addition to selling (yes, selling—not giving) maps and guides, **The Oxford Information Centre** (15-16 Broad St.; ℂ **01865/252037;** www.visitoxford.org) offers daily walking tours using accredited guides. You can download free maps of the city from Visit Britain (www.visitbritain.com).

TOURS   The Information Centre offers excellent **theme tours** such as "Pottering in Harry's Footsteps," "C.S. Lewis and J.R.R. Tolkien," and "Stained Glass." **Oxford River Cruises** (ℂ **0845/226-9396;** www.oxfordrivercruises.com) runs several boat tours along the River Thames; the tranquil 50-min River Experience (cheaper online: £9 adults, £6 children 15 and under) is popular.

Exploring Oxford

Wandering the Oxford's cobbled streets and ducking into its colleges to soak up their abject loveliness makes for a happy afternoon, particularly for fans of architecture. Many of the most iconic building clusters in this city of 140,000 (30,000 of whom are students) are collected together in the center of town, and they were built to house the university's nerve center. Oxford, like Cambridge, is comprised of individual colleges that feed off a central university system. Each of the 39 colleges has its own campus, tradition, character, and disciplines, although many close their grassy inner sanctums to visitors. During the school term (mid-Jan to mid-March, late April to mid-June, Oct to early Dec), some university buildings required for study (libraries, residence halls) are closed, or they only open on Saturdays. At all times of year, watch out for zooming bicyclists; an unwritten law appears to grant them ownership of the city.

To get the most out of Oxford, poke around, looking both inside cloisters and above rooftops. The doors between the inner and outer quadrangles of **Balliol College** (Broad St. and St. Giles; ✆ 01865/27-77-77; www.balliol.ox.ac.uk) still bear scorch marks from where Bloody Mary burned two Protestants alive for refusing to recant. Viewpoints are popular attractions here: The 22m (72-ft.), rectangular **Carfax Tower** (Carfax; ✆ 01865/790522; £2.30 adult, £1.20 children; Apr–Sept 10am–5:30pm, Oct–Mar 10am–4:30pm), the last remaining chunk of the 13th-century St. Martin's Church, has only 99 steps so it's not too taxing, which may be why it's a well-known suicide spot. It's located by the crossroads of the city center. Other popular panoramas are from the octagonal cupola above Sir Christopher Wren's **Sheldonian Theatre** (Broad St.; ✆ 01865/277299; www.sheldon.ox.ac.uk; £2.50; Mon–Sat 10am–12:30pm and 2–4:30pm, closes 3:30 Nov–Feb). Perhaps the top view is from the **University Church of St. Mary the Virgin** (✆ 01865/279113; www.university-church.ox.ac.uk; £4; daily 9am–5pm, 6pm closing July–Aug).

Bodleian Library The main research library in town that made its name in research, "the Bod" opened in 1602 and has been burrowing under the streets of Oxford, trying to find new places to store its multiplying collection (11 million tomes and counting), ever since. The round **Radcliffe Camera** ("Rad Cam"; open via guided tours at the Bodleian) was built in the 1740s to house scientific books. It stands on the north side of Radcliffe Square.

Catte St. ✆ **01865/277182.** www.bodleian.ox.ac.uk. Admission £1, Divinity School only; £7 (standard tour) or £5 for mini-tour (30 min); £13 (extended tour). Mon–Fri 9am–5pm; Sat 9am–4:30pm; Sun 11am–5pm. Closed Dec 24–Jan 3. Call to confirm specific tour times.

Magdelen College Pronounced "Maudlin," is one of the largest and most peaceful colleges here; its tower is the city's highest point, and its chapel is carved with breathtaking detail. Its site has a virtual tour to prep you on your explorations. U.S. Supreme Court justice Stephen Breyer attended.

High St. ✆ **01865/276000.** www.magd.ox.ac.uk. £5 adults, £4 seniors, students, and children. Jul–Sep daily noon–7pm; Oct–Jun daily 1–6pm or dusk (whichever is the earlier). Closed Dec 21-Dec 31.

Christ Church The largest, most beautiful, and the most popular college to visit looms large in children's literature; it was copied for Hogwarts School in the Harry Potter films, and it was where Lewis Carroll (aka mathematician Charles Dodgson) befriended the little girl for whom he wrote *Alice in Wonderland.* The college chapel, which dates from the 12th century, also serves as Oxford Cathedral for the local diocese; and bowler-hatted "custodians" still patrol the pristine lawns. Its Meadow, still grazed by cattle, is a delightful place to watch punters on the rivers Isis and Cherwell. Just being here makes you feel smarter.

St. Aldate's. ✆ **01865/276150.** www.chch.ox.ac.uk. £8.50 adults, £7 students, seniors/children 5–17, free 4 and under. Mon–Sat 9am–5pm; Sun 2–5pm. Last admission 4:30pm. Closed Christmas Day.

The Ashmolean Museum Offering more than just a pretty facade, it was founded way back in 1683, literally before anyone knew what the word "museum"

Punting on the River Cherwell is an essential if slightly eccentric Oxford pastime. At the **Cherwell Boathouse,** Bardwell Rd. (✆ **01865/515978;** www. cherwellboathouse.co.uk), you can rent a punt (a flat-bottomed boat maneuvered by a long pole and a small oar) for £14 (weekdays) to £17 (weekends) per hour. **Magdalen Bridge Boathouse,** the Old Horse Ford, High St. (✆ **01865/202643;** www.oxfordpunting. co.uk), charges £18 (weekdays) to £20 (weekends) per hour. Punts are available from mid-March to mid-October, daily from 10am until dusk.

actually meant. It houses an important hodgepodge of antiquities and art on par with (but on a smaller scale than) the British Museum, including a lantern carried by Guy Fawkes during the foiled Gunpowder Plot; the Anglo-Saxon Alfred Jewel of gold, enamel, and rock crystal; a Stradivarius violin; and assorted Old Masters paintings. Oh, and you know, minor stuff by Raphael and Michelangelo.

Beaumont St. at St. Giles. ✆ **01865/278002.** www.ashmolean.org. Free admission. Tues–Sun 10am–6pm. Closed Dec 24–26.

The Pitt Rivers Museum In an imposing 1886 cast-iron cathedral-like building not unlike a railway station, oft-freakish blend of folk art and anthropology—think shrunken heads and bundles of poisoned arrows brought back by British explorers over hundreds of years. It is, to use an academic term, totally gnarly.

Parks Rd. ✆ **01865/270-927**. www.prm.ox.ac.uk. Free. Tues–Sun 10am–4:30pm, Mon noon–4:30pm.

Blenheim Palace Within 30 minutes, the half-hourly S3 bus from the train station or Gloucester Green whisks visitors to Hensington Road, Woodstock, and the gates of the birthplace of Winston Churchill, now a UNESCO World Heritage site. The British rarely remind you that their oh-so-English savior was, in fact, half American; like Lady Cora on *Downton Abbey*, his mom Jennie, who was from Brooklyn, married an English lord, and Winston was born here in 1874, several hundred years into the palace's history. A few decades later, the home was saved from financial ruin when the Duke of Marlborough married another American, a Vanderbilt; their descendants still live here for part of the year. Tours of the grounds, landscaped by Capability Brown, and the state rooms, which are in excellent nick, take about three hours.

Hensington Road, Woodstock, Oxfordshire. ✆ **01993/810-530**. www.blenheimpalace.com. Daily 10:30am–5:30pm. Palace and grounds tickets £22 adults, £17.50 senior/student, £12 child.

CAMBRIDGE

Oxford is a city in its own right, but Cambridge, in the marshes 79km (49 miles) northeast of London, would barely have a pulse without its university. That makes Cambridge manageable. It feels in some ways like a typical English town, with a daily market for crafts and food on its central square, Market Hill. Its best rewards come when you wander through randomly chosen iron gates or along a river path—that's when the inviting little town really opens up.

Essentials

GETTING THERE Nonstop **coaches** from National Express (℡ 08705/80-80-80; www.nationalexpress.com; 2 hr. 30 min.; £7 single) leave hourly from Victoria Coach station; don't get off at Trumpington, but wait for the city center stop. There are **trains** from Liverpool Street or King's Cross, but be warned that Cambridge's station is several miles from the city center, so you will need to bike or call a taxi once you arrive; coaches are the smarter way to travel. If you insist, though, the ones run by One Railway (℡ 08457/48-49-50; www.nationalrail.co.uk; 45–90 min.; £19) take 90 minutes, but the First Capital Connect trains take half that time and leave twice an hour.

VISITOR INFORMATION **Cambridge Visitor Information Centre** (The Old Library, Wheeler St.; ℡ 08712/26-80-06, from overseas ℡ 011-44-1223/464-732; www.visitcambridge.org) sells maps and guides but won't dispense them for free. Cambridge also sells hour-long walking tours on downloadable MP3s (www.tourist-tracks.com; £5 for two). You can download free maps of the city from Visit Britain (www.visitbritain.com).

TOURS The **Cambridge Tourist Information Centre** (see Visitor Information) has several 2-hour walking tours of the city, from £6 to £16 for adults, and up to £7.50 for children under 12. Book tours at www.visitcambridge.org/official-tours (℡ **01223/457-574**).

Exploring Cambridge

Like Oxford, Cambridge's calling card is the elaborate and ancient architecture of its colleges. Unlike in Oxford, it's easy to venture into the cloistered grounds of many of Cambridge's colleges (the oldest was founded in 1286 after a squabble in Oxford necessitated the establishment of a second educational capital), though doing so usually requires a few quid. Mill Lane leads to the River Cam, where you can rent a punting boat for £6 or sit at The Mill pub overlooking the water. (The punting alone will set you apart as a tourist, but if you want to look like a tourist savvy to Cambridge traditions, punt from the back of the boat. In Oxford, they punt from the front.) The meadows along the Cam are known as **The Backs,** and they make for idyllic walks.

The head of Oliver Cromwell, which was impaled outside Westminster Hall in London as a warning against regicide (albeit 3 years after the man died of natural causes), was finally buried within an antechapel (not open to visitors) at Sidney Sussex College in 1960. It's in an unmarked grave to keep pranksters from pinching the much-abused thing. That's Cambridge in a nutshell: It has many secrets, but since it's still a working university town, marvels won't be handed to you. You have to wander, wonder, and ask questions. Colleges aren't open, and street life is at a minimum, outside of term (mid-Jan to mid-Mar, late Apr to mid-June, Oct to early Dec).

King's College Chapel For some reason, the marauding Puritans neglected to smash the 16th-century stained glass windows of its Chapel—they probably thought they were just as divine as you will. The chapel's fanned and vaulted ceiling, a work of craftsmanship that stuns even those who care little for such things, was completed at the behest of Henry VII. Its famous choristers sing at services during term time.

King's Parade. ℡ **01223/331212.** www.kings.cam.ac.uk. Adults £7.50, students, seniors £5, children 11 and under free. Mon–Fri 9:45am–3:30pm; Sat 9:30am–3:15pm, Sun 1:15–2:30pm.

Pembroke College   The third-oldest college in town is one of the best, distinguished by the oldest gatehouse in Cambridge and by a chapel with an ornate plaster ceiling, which was the first completed work by Christopher Wren (after finishing, the man seemed never to rest again). Unlike many of the colleges, Pembroke never charges visitors to poke around its common areas.

Trumpington Street. ✆ **01223/33-81-00**. www.pem.cam.ac.uk. Free. 2pm–5pm.

Trinity College   Trinity is the largest and most endowed of Cambridge's 31 colleges. Sir Isaac Newton first calculated the speed of sound here, at Neville's Court, and Lord Byron used to bathe naked in the Great Court's fountain with his pet bear. The University forbade students from having dogs, but there was no rule against bears. In *Chariots of Fire*, sprinters tried to get around the .8-hectare (2-acre) yard in the time it took for its clock to strike 12. Your attempts will not be appreciated.

Trinity St. ✆ **01223/338400**. www.trin.cam.ac.uk. Free. The Wren Library: Mon–Fri noon–2pm, Sat 10:30am–12:30pm. Various other areas are open at different times; inquire at the porter's lodge.

Queen's College   Founded by the wife of Henry VI and the wife of Edward IV, the college dates from 1448 and is regarded as the most beautiful of Cambridge's colleges. Entry and exit is by the old porter's lodge in Queens' Lane. Tourists are often told that the wooden **Mathematical Bridge** (1749) spanning the Cam behind it (see it from Silver Street) was constructed using no nails, and when curious students disassembled it to figure out how, they couldn't put it back together without using screws. The college is curiously defensive about the accusation, saying that anyone who believes this story "cannot have a serious grasp on reality."

Silver St. ✆ **01223/335511**. www.quns.cam.ac.uk. Daily Jun–Sep & Nov–May 10am–4:30pm; Oct Mon–Fri 2–4:30pm & 10am–4:30pm Sat–Sun. (Closed late May–late June for exams). Admission £2.50, free 11 and under, late June–early Oct 10am–4:30pm; free admission Nov–May.

Fitzwilliam Museum   Cambridge's most storied attraction is a first-rate neoclassical building full of examples of applied arts and Old Masters that a city ten times Cambridge's size (of 108,000) would covet. If a colonial Englishman could carry it home it on ship, it's here: precious antiquities from Rome, Greece, Egypt, Asia, and paintings by every famous name under the European sun.

Trumpington St., near Peterhouse. ✆ **01223/332900**. www.fitzmuseum.cam.ac.uk. Free admission; donations appreciated. Tues–Sat 10am–5pm; Sun noon–5pm. Closed Mondays, Good Friday, Dec 24–26 & 31 and Jan 1. Saturday guided tours at 2:30pm £6.

STONEHENGE & SALISBURY

To some, Stonehenge is a circle of rocks. If it's raining, it's a damned circle of rocks. But people still ask to go, and if that's their dream, then they should do it. Just understand that you may not get it, even though the inadequate visitor center has a few bits about ancient practices and theories on how Stonehenge's arrangement may have evolved over time.

Essentials

GETTING THERE   Trains don't go directly to Stonehenge; the nearest station is in Salisbury, nearly 16km (10 miles) south. So the easiest way to get here is to drive. The

THE TRADE-OFF WITH escorted tours

Arranging your own day trips using public transportation will almost always be the most cost-effective method, but there are cogent reasons for choosing a guided coach tour. It's simply quicker to allow someone else to drive you around, making sure you cram a laundry list of major sites into a short time span, and consuming spoon-fed nuggets of information about each place. What you learn won't have much depth, but at least you'll have been.

Problem is, you'll have paid a pretty penny for it: Most tours cost at least £70 a day, not including food. You get a richer experience (and one that doesn't have you idling in traffic and trooping into gift shops all day), when you do it yourself. But some people desperately want to soak up as many sights as they can, even if it means they skim the surface. For them, here are the major

players in the coach-tour biz, sold aggressively through the concierges at expensive hotels (who love getting the commissions):

○ **Evan Evans Tours** (in the U.K. ℰ 020/7950-1777, in the U.S. ℰ 800/422-9022; www.evan evans.co.uk)

○ Gray Line's **Golden Tours** (in the U.K. ℰ 084/4880-6981, in the U.S. ℰ 800/548-7083; www.gold entours.co.uk)

○ **Premium Tours** (ℰ 020/7713-1311. www.premiumtours.co.uk)

Better yet are the more affordable **London Walks** (ℰ 020/7624-3978; www. walks.com), which run frequent "Great Escapes!" for just £16. These use public transportation and don't include admission fees, but you'll have a local guide every step of the way to show you how it's all done.

---

rocks are located 3.2km (2 miles) west of Amesbury in Wiltshire on the junction of A303 and A344/360. Or take a half-hourly **train** (ℰ 08457/48-49-50; www.national-rail.co.uk; 90 min.; £35 single with advance purchase) from Waterloo station to Salisbury station. There used to be a cheap public bus to the rocks from there, but it says a lot about the values of the local tourism authorities that they replaced that route entirely with the expensive Stonehenge Tour Bus by **Wilts & Dorset Buses** (ℰ 01722/33-68-55; www.thestonehengetour.info; 30 min.; round-trip £12 adult, £8 children), which leaves seven times a day between 10am and 4pm from Salisbury station. A few extra buses are tossed in during the summer; check its website for updated schedules.

VISITOR INFORMATION   Salisbury and Stonehenge (Fish Row, Salisbury; ℰ 01722/342-860; www.visitwiltshire.co.uk).

TOURS   You can easily see Salisbury on foot, either on your own or by taking a guided daytime or evening walk run by **Salisbury City Guides** (ℰ 07873/212-941; www.salisburycityguides.co.uk). Tickets are £4 for adults and £2 for children.

Exploring Stonehenge & Salisbury

Stonehenge   Construction began about 5,000 years ago, and the first recorded day trips to the megalith were in 1562. Arranged in such a way that it aligns with the rising of the sun during the midsummer solstice, this Neolithic circle of stones is certainly

Britain's most important ancient wonder, it's a UNESCO World Heritage Site (together with Avebury, a far less interesting, but still important, line of rocks 39km/24 miles north). Whether its builders, who remain anonymous, worshiped the sun or merely appreciated astronomy is only the beginning of the mystery. We also can only make educated guesses as to how these prehistoric people, using only rudimentary tools, managed to hoist these slabs from Wales to here, and then into place. Even if you don't salivate over such long-ago feats of ingenuity, the distinctive profile of the stones, surrounded by empty plains, "henge" earthworks, and hundreds of lumpen burial mounds, will surely be iconic.

You're not allowed to walk amongst the rocks the way visitors once were; you have to stick to a footpath that curves near the circle but keeps the formation at a safe distance, good for pretty photographs but bad for curiosity. Most tourists like you and me are being kept at arm's length (exception: Clark Griswold, who managed to topple them like dominoes in *National Lampoon's European Vacation*), but you can apply in advance for a 1-hour pass to stroll among the rocks, timed just before or after the site closes to the public for the day. These passes are never given for Tuesday or Wednesday mornings, and October through February is usually blocked off, too, and slots must be applied for in writing. The forms at the English Heritage website. The limited experience (a disappointment for many who trudge 129km/80 miles west of London to have it) is why few people see Stonehenge without passing through Bath on the same day. That itinerary is offered by coach tours; putting it together yourself with trains and buses is not ideal because the connections chew up too much time. Salisbury is doable, though, since trains headed there connect with a bus (see "How to Get There," below). Alternatively, climb **Amesbury Hill,** clearly visible 1½ miles up the A303. From here, you'll get a free panoramic view.

At the junction of A303 and A344. ⓒ **08703/331181.** www.english-heritage.org.uk/stonehenge. £8 adults, £7.20 students and seniors, £4.80 children 5–15, £21 family ticket. Daily. June–Aug 9am–7pm; Mar 16–May and Sept–Oct 15 9:30am–6pm; Oct 16–Mar 15 9:30am–4pm. If you're driving, head north on Castle Rd. from the center of Salisbury on to the A345 to Amesbury, and then the A303 to Exeter. You'll see signs for Stonehenge, leading you up the A344 to the right. It's 2 miles west of Amesbury.

Salisbury Cathedral Built with uncommon efficiency between 1220 and 1258 and barely touched since, this early English Gothic masterpiece is considered by many to be the most breathtaking church in the world. After you've seen it, and lost yourself in gazing at it and sighing, the rest of your time in Salisbury will be contentedly spent walking medieval streets, which were laid in a loose grid and give the city an airy character. The cathedral complex's octagonal Chapter House possesses one of the four surviving copies of the Magna Carta signed by King John in 1215. Two more are in London at the British Library (p. 89).

The Close. ⓒ **01722/555120.** www.salisburycathedral.org.uk. Suggested donation £6.50 adults, £5.50 students and seniors, £3 children 5–17, £15 family. Daily 9am–5pm; Chapter House closes 4:30pm (5:30pm Apr–Oct) and all morning Sun.

Old Sarum ★ Believed to have been an Iron Age fortification, Old Sarum was used again by the Saxons and flourished as a walled town into the Middle Ages. The Normans built a cathedral and a castle here; parts of this old cathedral were taken down to build the city of "New Sarum," later known as Salisbury, leaving behind dramatically sited remains with unforgettable views of Salisbury and rolling green hills, not to mention the opportunity to commune with grazing sheep.

2 miles north of Salisbury off A345 Castle Rd. ⓒ **01722/335398.** www.english-heritage.org.uk/oldsarum. Admission £3.90 adults, £3.50 seniors, £2.30 children 5–15. Daily Apr–June and Sept 10am–5pm; July–Aug 9am–6pm; Mar and Oct 10am–4pm; Nov–Jan 11am–3pm; Feb 11am–4pm. Bus: 5, 6, 7, 8, or 9, every 30 min. during the day, from Salisbury bus station.

STRATFORD-UPON-AVON

Stratford-upon-Avon, often described as a "chocolate box" of a town in the Heart of England, is too far away to make an ideal day trip unless you're willing to make some decisive sacrifices. Stratford-upon-Avon in Warwickshire, 144km (89 miles) northwest of London, is lily-white, touristy, and all about the Bard. If he touched it, or if his descendants did, you can bet it's being sold to tourists. The problem, besides heaving summer crowds, is that its biggest attraction, the highly respected **Royal Shakespeare Company** (Waterside; ⓒ **0844/800-1110;** www.rsc.org.uk), is hard to see on a day trip. The RSC has several venues where it presents as many as three shows a day. Unless you take the train on a matinee day, seeing a show requires an overnight stay. And matinees are frequently booked out by school trips and group tours; you'll need to book about 2 months ahead so you're not shut out. Even if you are, don't sweat it, because the RSC performs steadily in London, too.

For all the fragrant gardens and twee, humpbacked cottages, it's easy to forget that in Shakespeare's day, Stratford was a squalid, smelly market town. That's not to say that Stratford won't fulfill some stereotypes of a pretty English town. Stratford's popularity is enhanced by its nearness to the surrounding Cotswolds, which you simply won't be able to see comfortably on a day trip from London.

GETTING THERE Direct **trains** (ⓒ 08457/48-49-50; www.nationalrail.co.uk; 2hr., 15 min.; £9 with advance purchase) go from Marylebone station to Stratford-upon-Avon, trains from Euston take another 50 min. Make sure you don't buy a ticket for plain old "Stratford," or you won't leave London. Buses run by **National Express** (ⓒ 08717/81-81-78; www.nationalexpress.com; 3 hr., 15 min.; £6 single) take an hour longer, but cost less. Taking the first bus of the morning and the last bus back only gives you about 6 hours in town, which is do-able but won't enable you to see even a matinee.

VISITOR INFORMATION Stratford-upon-Avon Tourist Information Centre (Bridgefoot; ⓒ 0871/978-0841; www.shakespeare-country.co.uk).

Exploring Stratford-upon-Avon

Shakespeare's Birthplace It's thought to be the home where the playwright was born, but even if it wasn't—subsequent adoration of the writer has colored judgment—it's a good, if heavily restored, example of an upscale Elizabethan house. The locals didn't care for it much until P. T. Barnum tried to buy it and ship it, stone for stone, over to America, and suddenly, it became a national treasure. Admission there includes entry to two other historic homes, Hall's Croft and Nash's House, both associated with the Bard's descendants and valued mostly for their Tudor aesthetic.

Henley St. ⓒ **01789/20-40-16**. www.shakespeare.org.uk. £15 adults, £9 children, £14 seniors; Spring through autumn, Mon–Sat 9am–5pm, winter 10am–4pm, slightly extended hours in summer.

Anne Hathaway's Cottage   A mile northwest of town, the picturesque thatched home with a quintessential English garden, is where the playwright's wife (not Fantine) lived before she married him, and it dates to the 1400s. You can reach the cottage, a rare window into life 500 years ago, along a public footpath from town.

Cottage Lane, Shottery. ℂ **01789/29-21-00**. www.shakespeare.org.uk. £9 adults, £5 children, £8 seniors/students. Spring through autumn, Mon–Sat 9am–5pm, winter 10am–4pm, slightly extended hours in summer.

PLANNING YOUR TRIP TO LONDON

First of all, relax. Getting to London isn't as tricky as it used to be. Finding airfare was once the most daunting part, but thanks to the emergence of Web booking, now it's not much harder than finding a cross-country flight. Being ready for the rest (money, electricity, packing) is simply a matter of having the facts.

GETTING THERE

By Plane

FROM THE AIRPORT

Transatlantic flights almost always land at Heathrow, Europe's busiest international airport (17 miles west), or Gatwick, perhaps the most dissed (31 miles south). With a few minor exceptions, the other three airports, Stansted (37 miles northeast), Luton (34 miles northwest), and London City (in London's Docklands area) serve flights from Europe, and they're where cut-rate flyers and executive jets tend to go. Rail service doesn't start until around 5am. So don't book flights that depart at 6am unless you're prepared to a) grab a £80 hotel room near the airport or b) splash out on a taxi.

Happily, getting to and from all of the airports is easy and clear. Every airport offers some kind of rail connection to the central city, and it's the smart way to go. Tickets can be bought at windows in the arrivals halls, at machines, or online, where you get a discount. You'll rarely have to wait more than 20 minutes for the next train.

Airport Transportation Options

The comfy, business-class-level **Heathrow Express** (© 08456/00-15-15; www.heathrowexpress.com) zooms to Paddington station every 15 minutes in 15 minutes. First Class is a waste of money; Express Saver, the cheapest option for purchase online or at vending machines, is plenty plush. The plain **Heathrow Connect** (© 084/5678-6975; www.heathrowconnect. com) is designed to give access to local stations, so it takes twice as long (almost 30 min.—still not long at all) and costs half as much. It uses commuter-style carriages and leaves every half-hour. Both trains arrive at Paddington, where you can hop the Tube system or a taxi (above Platform 12).

AIRPORT	COST/AVG. TIME USING NATIONAL RAIL	HOURS OF RAIL SERVICE
Heathrow (LHR), HeathrowAirport.com	Heathrow Express: £20 single, £34 return, kids 5 to 15 £8.20/£14*/ 15 minutes OR Heathrow Connect: £9.50 single/30-45 minutes	5:10am to 11:48pm
Gatwick (LGW), GatwickAirport.com	Gatwick Express: £19.90 single, £34.90 return (in person) £17.75/ £31.05 (online)/30 minutes *or* First Capital Connect: £9.50 single /£18 return/30 to 50 minutes	Four times hourly 5am to 11:45pm (to Gatwick) or 12:35am (from Gatwick)
Luton (LTN), www. London-Luton.co.uk	First Capital Connect: £15 single/£26 return including shuttle bus, 40 minutes	Six times hourly, 5am to midnight
Stansted (STN), StanstedAirport.com	£23.40 single, £32.80 return, kids 5 to 15 £11.70/£16.40/47 minutes	5:30am to 12:30am
London City (LCY), LondonCityAirport.com	N/A	DLR: 5:30am to midnight

*Online fare. Tickets £5 more if you wait to pay on board.

** As if you'd be daft enough to want a taxi after seeing those prices and times, you're more likely to find one by booking ahead. Check www.london-luton.co.uk and www.stanstedairport.com for a list of their latest approved taxi companies. Addison Lee (www.addisonlee.com) is an established minicab company.

Gatwick Express (℃ 084/5850-530; www.gatwickexpress.com) runs from Victoria station. On **First Capital Connect** (℃ 08456/76-47-00; www.firstcapitalconnect. co.uk), you can also get to Gatwick via Farringdon, St Pancras, or London Bridge stations in 30 to 50 minutes—service ends at 11:45pm.

Stansted Express (℃ 0845/600-7245; www.stanstedexpress.com) runs from Liverpool Street station. Luton and Gatwick have rail service from St. Pancras station, Blackfriars, Victoria, or London Bridge stations by **First Capital Connect** (℃ 0845/ 026-4700; www.firstcapitalconnect.co.uk; four times hourly). The correct stop is Luton Airport Parkway Station, which is linked by a 10-minute shuttle (5am–midnight) to the terminals.

City Airport is linked so expediently and affordably by the **Docklands Light Railway** that it doesn't support commuter rail or coach service.

Finding the Lowest Airfare

The central question is *when* are they? London is such a popular destination (it's served by more flights from the United States than any other European city) that plenty of airlines vie to carry you across—although the ones that are not American-run are usually of higher quality. If you're not redeeming frequent flier miles, there are five rules to finding bargains:

1. **Fly on Tuesday, Wednesday, or Saturday, when traffic is lightest.** Some airlines post calendars that show you when the best prices are.

RAIL SERVICE TO	COST/TIME USING TUBE OR DLR	COST/AVG. TIME FOR NATIONAL EXPRESS SHUTTLE SERVICE TO CENTRAL LONDON	COST/AVG. TIME TO AIR-PORT BY TAXI
Paddington	£4.50/60 minutes on Piccadilly Line	£6 single, kids 11 to 16 £3, under 11 free, £8 return (www.nationalexpress.com)/ 50–70 minutes	£65–£85/ 70 minutes
Gatwick Express: Victoria; FCC: St. Pancras, Farringdon, Blackfriars, or London Bridge	N/A	£8 each way (www.national express.com)/90 minutes	£100/ 70 minutes
St. Pancras, Victoria, or London Bridge	N/A	From £10 (www.national express.com)/90 minutes	£100/ 80 minutes**
Liverpool Street	N/A	£8.50–10.50 single (www. nationalexpress.com)/ 60–100 minutes	£99/ 80 minutes**
N/A	£4.50/25 minutes on Docklands Light Railway	N/A	£25 to £40/20 to 40 minutes

2. **Depart after dinner.** This saves you from paying another hotel night, since you'll arrive in the morning. You're also likely to find lower fares, because business travelers like day flights.

3. **Go off-season.** London's weather isn't extreme, so there's really not a no-go month. November through March yield the lowest airfares and hotel rates, although the late December holidays and the last week of November (American Thanksgiving) can be busy, too. Summer prices (June–Sept) soar over a grand.

4. **Search for fares for or on a weekend.** Many major airlines post lower prices to fly then. You might also save money by booking your seat at 3am. That's because unpaid-for reservations are flushed out of the system at midnight, and prices often sink when the system becomes aware of an increase in supply.

5. **Don't buy last-minute.** Desperation bleeds wallets dry.

Hotwire's **TripStarter** tool (www.hotwire.com/tripstarter/index.jsp) tracks how much the airlines charge, and when. Also keep your eyes open for sales. Monitor airline newsletters, sale pages, and sites as **Frommers.com**, **SmarterTravel.com**, and **Airfarewatchdog.com**. **Yapta.com** can spit out an email when airfare drops.

Primary websites that collect quotes from a variety of sources (whether they be airlines or other websites) include **Ebookers.com**, **Expedia.com**, **Kayak.com**, **Lessno.com**, **Mobissimo.com**, **Momondo.com**, **Orbitz.com**, and **Travelocity.com.** Always canvas multiple sites, because each has odd gaps in its coverage because of the way they obtain their quotes. Then compare your best price with what the airline is offering, because that price might be lowest of all. Some sites have small booking fees of $5 to $10, and many force you to accept non-refundable tickets for the cheapest prices. If you're hitting a wall, search for transatlantic itineraries that allow for one or two stops, since routes that include stops in Reykjavik or Frankfurt (on Icelandair or Lufthansa, say) can produce hidden bargains. No matter which airline you go with, prepare yourself for added taxes and fees, which are usually $500 or higher round-trip from the USA—London's airport fees are noxious.

Most times of year, the least expensive way to reach London is with an **air-hotel package** (p. 38), which combines discounted airfare with discounted nights in a hotel. Most air-hotel deals will allow you to fly back days after your hotel allotment runs out, and at no extra charge. Keep in mind that solo travelers always pay a little more, typically $200.

If you despise flying, one ocean liner still makes a 7-day trip between New York City and Southampton, which connects by rail to London in an hour. That's the *Queen Mary 2* (📞 **800/728-6273**; www.cunard.com), intermittently scheduled. Fares start around $900 per person, including all your food.

By Bus

The least expensive way to get from city to city in Britain (but not the fastest—that's usually the train) is via coach, and because the country's not very big, it rarely takes more than a few hours to reach anyplace. Some lifelong Londoners have never ventured as near as Scotland because they find the journey—around 5 hours—too cumbersome. **National Express** (📞 **08717/818-8178**; www.nationalexpress.com) is a major carrier with scads of departures, but the best-priced is **Megabus** (📞 **090/0160-0900** or 📞 **0871/266-3333**; www.megabus.com), which serves more than 60 cities across Europe, and charges as little as £1.50 for early bookings, although £19 to £45 for Edinburgh is a more typical rate. It accepts bookings 2 months ahead; book online to avoid phone fees. Both coach services depart from Victoria Coach Station, located very near Victoria railway station.

What's the best place to hear about inexpensive ground tours? Hostels. Drop into one; most of their lobbies are papered with brochures. Don't neglect their bulletin boards, either, since you may catch wind of a shared-ride situation that'll often cost you no more than your share of the gasoline (in Britain, *petrol*).

A few coach companies also travel to Europe, usually crossing the Channel with a ferry. Because of the pressure put on the market by mushrooming no-frills airlines, rates are extremely low. You'll pay as little as £21 one-way to Paris via **Eurolines** (📞 **08717/81-81-78**; www.eurolines.co.uk; 8–10 hours each way). Brussels or Amsterdam are £25 with a 7-day advance purchase. The trade-off: It can take all day, sunrise to sunset, to reach Paris by this method.

Young, social adventurers should investigate **Busabout** (📞 **8450/267-514**; www.busabout.com), a coach system that follows set loops from London to France and Spain, Austria, Belgium, Italy, Switzerland, and Germany and the Czech Republic. Passengers can hop on and hop off as they please. Some other companies arrange full-on organized tours of Europe's greatest hits—but never for less than you could do independently; choose one only because you'd enjoy having company: **Contiki** (📞 **866/266-8454**; www.contiki.com) is geared toward a party-hearty under-35 crowd, **Tucan Travel Adventure Tours** (📞 **855/444-9110**; www.tucantravel.com) is for social scrimpers, and **Fanatics** (📞 **020/7240-3233**; www.thefanatics.com) is for followers of organized sports.

By Car

Don't. Roads are clogged. In bad traffic, a trip from Heathrow to even the western fringe of London can take 2 hours. And once you're in the city, just about every technology is deployed against you (see "Getting Around" below). Cameras will catch and ticket your honest driving errors. I heartily beseech you to choose rail over road. Many North Americans think of cars as the default transportation mode, but not in London. Chauffeured rides of any kind are considered a luxury service, and are priced accordingly.

Pay more and take longer than you must to get in from the airport? If you insist. The cheapest coach and van services for each airport are listed in the chart, and they all drop you off at standardized stops such as major train stations. For Gatwick, Stansted, and Luton, in addition to the usual National Express coach options, there's the no-frills **easyBus** (www.easybus.co.uk). Unless you book far in advance, it may not beat the National Express prices.

If you insist upon wheels, reserving ahead from home yields the best prices. Try to return your car outside the congestion-charge zone to avoid charges and aggravation. You will find similar rates among **Nova Car Hire** (www.novacarhire.com), **Auto Europe** (www.autoeurope.com), **Europe By Car** (www.ebctravel.com), **Europcar** (www.europcar.com), and **Holiday Autos** (www.holidayautos.com). Also check the major names like Avis, Hertz, and Budget, in case they can do better. Air conditioning, something you won't need, adds about £5 to the daily bill. Fuel, or "petrol," is even more expensive than at home, and although most rentals include unlimited mileage, make sure yours does. Also note, many rental cars are stick shift models.

By Train

The original railway builders plowed their stations to every town of size, making it easy to see the highlights of the United Kingdom without getting near a car. While the British whine about the declining quality of the service, Americans, Canadians, and Australians will be blown away by the speed (and the cost, if they don't book ahead) of the system. Find tickets to all destinations through **National Rail** (© 08457/48-49-50; www.nationalrail.co.uk). Make every effort to book as far ahead as possible, since early-bird bookings can yield some marvelous deals, such as £26 for a 4-hour trip to Scotland (£125 last-minute is common). When searching for tickets, always search for trips going or coming from all London stations, not just the ones leaving from the station nearest your hotel, because different destinations emanate from different London stations. Unfortunately, not every train company website accepts international credit cards. You may have to phone or use **TheTrainLine.com**.

Tickets bought reasonably in advance will still be cheaper than what you'd pay for the same trips on a **BritRail pass** (© 866/938-7245 in North America; www.britrail.com) and few tourists ride the rails with the near-daily regularity and long distances that would make a pass pay for itself. You can get timetables on its site, too. Check prices against the U.S. seller **Rail Europe** (© 800/361-7245; www.raileurope.com) because its quotes may vary.

For trips to northwestern Europe, the train is more dignified, since it doesn't require juggling luggage, enduring airport waiting rooms, and folding yourself into puny airline seats. Unlike taking a flight, you won't need to set aside extra hours and pounds to get to and from airports; train stations are in the middle of town. We're living in marvelous times: Thanks to the 1994 opening of the Channel Tunnel, you can reach Paris in an incredible 2 hours and 15 minutes from London. You can literally ride both the Tube and the Métro before lunch. In fact, you can ride both a black taxi and Space Mountain before lunch, since the Eurostar train alights in the middle of Disneyland Resort, just east of Paris. Eurostar links London's St. Pancras station with Paris, Brussels, Lille, and Calais, and from there, you can go just about anywhere using other trains.

Book via **Eurostar** (*©* **08432/186-186** in the U.K. or +44 1233/61-75-75; www. eurostar.co.uk; phone bookings are £4 more) itself or the U.S.-based **Rail Europe** (*©* **800/361-7245** in North America; www.raileurope.com), which also sells European rail passes. Check both sites, since prices can differ, but do it early, because rates boom as availability decreases. Pay attention to the special offers on Eurostar's site; using them, prices go as low as £69 round-trip in summer. **Seat61.com** has up-to-date tips for booking European train travel.

By Boat

No ferry to Europe sails from London. For those, you'll have to get down to the Southern coastal towns of Folkestone and Dover (for France), or Portsmouth (for Spain). Unless you have your own car, it's hard to use the ports of the France-destined lines; most people take them in conjunction with a coach trip booked from London. Some of the bigger players, many sailing the Channel more than a dozen times daily (advance purchase from £35 each way with a car and including taxes, 150 min.), are **Seafrance** (*©* **0844/2482-100;** www.seafrance.com) and **P&O Ferries** (*©* **08716/64-21-21;** www.poferries.com). P&O Ferries does the Netherlands, too. Portsmouth, a harbor on the Southern English coast, is the country's primary ferry port (mostly to France, but a few to Spain); obtain contacts for the latest operators at its website, www.portsmouth-port.co.uk. Given the proliferation of low-cost airlines, ferry travel has become an outdated and time-consuming way to travel, and it's mostly used by people who need to transfer cars.

GETTING AROUND

By Public Transportation

There are three practical methods for taming London's sprawl: by Tube (historic and enchanting, but expensive); by bus (less expensive and less glamorous, but more edifying and often quicker); and by foot (the best method, but not always possible). Taxis are overpriced, and driving your own car is lunacy.

The Underground

More culture shock: It's not called a "subway." In England, when you see a sign for a "subway," the word just signifies a foot passageway under a busy street.

Instead, Londoners call their 402km (249-mile) metro system the Underground, its official name, or just as commonly, "the Tube." Its elegant, distinctive logo—a red "roundel" bisected by a blue bar—debuted in 1913 as one of the world's first corporate symbols, and it remains one of the city's most ubiquitous sights.

There's no older system on Earth—London's Metropolitan Railway got there first, which took no small leap of imagination and engineering. The first section, running from Paddington to Farringdon, opened in 1863. That was 33 years ahead of the next European city (Budapest), 34 years before Boston, and 41 years before New York—indeed, the original snippet that opened in 1863 is still in use today. The Tube is an attraction unto itself. It's fun to seek out vestiges of the early system (1907 tilework on the Piccadilly Line; the fake house facades built at 23-24 Leinster Gardens to hide exposed tracks; abandoned stations like the one at Strand and Surrey St.). If such "urban archaeology" fascinates you, visit the London Transport Museum in Covent Garden (p. 92), one of the city's family-friendly highlights. The Tube is also much more dignified than most American systems. In fact, its seating is upholstered. That's because the British know how to take care of nice things.

OPERATING SCHEDULE

The Tube shuts down nightly, mostly to maintain tracks. Although exact times for first and final trains are posted in each station (using the simple 24-hr. clock), based on when they arrive in Central London, the Tube generally operates Monday to Saturdays from 5:30am (0530) to just after midnight (0000), and Sundays 7am (0700) to 11:30pm (2330). If you plan to take the train near the starting or ending times, always check the schedule beforehand.

What happens if you miss the last train? Don't worry—you're not stranded, although your trip may take longer or cost more. Just turn to the city's network of Night Bus routes (p. 233). Or, as a last resort, take a taxi (p. 234).

HOW THE TUBE WORKS

There are 13 named lines on the Tube network, plus the Docklands Light Railway (DLR) serving East London and a tram line in South London, which together serve nearly 300 stations. On an average visit, you'll become familiar with a dozen or so stations. Lines are color-coded: the Piccadilly is a peacock purple, the Bakerloo could be considered Sherlock Holmes brown, and so on.

Navigating is mostly foolproof. Look for signs pointing to the color and name of the line you want. Pretty soon, more signs separate you according to the direction you want to go in, based on the Tube map. So if you know the name/color of the line you want, as well as the direction of your destination, the signs will march you, cattlelike, to the platform you need.

If you need to change trains (and you will), the follow-the-signs method repeats until it's time to look for the "Way Out," which is Undergroundese for "Exit." You'll shuffle through warrens of ancient cylindrical tunnels, many of them faced in custard-yellow tiles and overly full of commuters, and you'll scale alpine escalators lined with ads. Stand to the right on those.

One of the groovier things about the Underground is the electronic displays on platforms that tell you how long it'll be until the next train. Knowing how long you'll have to wait takes some frustration out of a commute. A 24-hour information service is also available at (C) **0343/222-1234.** The best resource is the TfL Journey Planner, online at **www.tfl.gov.uk/journeyplanner**. For specific journey information on-the-move, text your start-point and end-point—as full postcodes, or station or stop names, in the format "A to B"—to (C) **60835.** TfL will fire off a text with the quickest route and scheduled times.

The most confusing lines for tourists are the Northern Line (black on the maps), and the District Line (green). Owing mostly to the petty backbiting of the Victorians who

frustrations OF THE TUBE

The Tube lists everything about itself in exhaustive detail at www.tfl.gov.uk, which contains more maps, planners, and FAQs than a normal person can use. As endearing as the Tube is, it is not perfect. Be prepared for a few things:

1. **Stairs.** Most stations are as intricate as anthills. Passengers are forever being corralled sadistically up staircases, around platforms, down more staircases, and through still more staircases. The Victorians must have had some sexy legs. Yours might hurt. Even stations equipped with extremely long escalators (Angel has the longest one in the system—59m/194 ft.) perversely require passengers to climb a final flight to reach the street. So if you bring luggage into the Tube, be able to hoist your stuff for at least 15 stairs at a time. (This is where backpacks make sense.) For a list of which station are accessible, contact **Transport for London Access & Mobility** (© 020/7941-4600; www.tfl.gov.uk).

2. **Delays.** When you enter a station, look for a sign with the names and colors of the Tube lines on it. Beside each line, you'll see a status bar reading "Good service," "Severe delays," or the like. Trust this sign—it's updated by staff every 10 minutes and lines close without warning. If you note "Minor delays," don't worry.

3. **Heat.** Especially in the summer, the network can be stuffy and hot. During a heat wave in July 2013, health advisories were issued. AC is slowly being added.

4. **Tough weekends.** London's system was experimental, so it was built on the cheap, which means each line gets only one set of tracks per direction, unlike modern systems, which generally have two sets in each direction. When tracks need maintenance, everything shuts down. Weekends, by and large, are when this happens, and never one goes by when there isn't a list of roving closures to contend with. Check in the ticket hall to see what's out of commission.

built these lines as individual businesses, they split and take several paths. You can handle it. Platform placards and signs on the front of the trains tell you what you're in for before you board, and you won't get too far off course if you mess up. If you ride the DLR (and you should—it provides a lovely rooftop-level glide through the brickwork of the old East End and the monolithic towers of Canary Wharf), those lines split variously, too, but there are lots of chances to rectify mistakes.

On the DLR and commuter trains, carriages that go to outdoor stations may not automatically open to let cold air in. If the carriage door doesn't open on its own, push the illuminated button and it will.

Visit the **London Underground's website** (www.tfl.gov.uk/tube/maps) and download the free "London Rail and Tube Services map." On it, all the stations and zones in both networks will conveniently appear on the same page. (Buses are on a separate map.) The site also has terrific simplified bus maps that show you routes from any neighborhood. Plug in your hotel's address before you go.

FARES

London Underground (**tfl.gov.uk/tickets**) gives 1.1 billion rides a year—and seemingly every passenger pays a different fare. Rates go up every January (these rates were current at press time and will give you a sense of proportion). The LU system is so complicated that it must have been engineered to bewilder travelers into paying more than they have to. But it can be boiled down like this:

Start with the concept of zones. The center of town—basically everything the Circle Line envelops, plus a wee bit of padding—is zone 1. Heading outside of town, in a concentric pattern like a target, come zones 2 through 6. Most tourists stick to zones 1 and 2; very few popular sights are outside those (Wimbledon, Hampton Court, and Kew being the main exceptions). Your fare is calculated by how many zones you go through, and the lower the zone number, the less you pay. If a station appears to straddle zones, you'll pay the cheaper zone's price. One-way tickets are called "singles" and round-trips are "return."

If you are paying with a credit card, **do not use a vending machine**. They only accept European-style chip-and-PIN cards. If you have a magnetic-stripe card (most North Americans do), go to the live human at the ticket window.

Important: Keep your ticket handy because you'll need it to get back out through the turnstiles. If you can't find it, you'll have to fork over the maximum rate. If you don't go through turnstiles, you must remember to touch your Oyster card (if you have one; see below) to a yellow reader dot both before you board *and* after you get off—that's the part people always forget. Inspectors regularly check passengers' tickets and they won't hesitate to fine you.

Astonishingly, **kids under 11 travel for free** when accompanied by an adult. Adults must buy their own ticket and then ask the staff to wave Junior through the entry gate. Kids 11 to 16 can travel with an adult for £1 all day after 9:30am with a Child Day Travelcard. Ask an agent about the going discounts for kids.

There are essentially three ways for adults to pay for a trip, which they can do at automated machines or at staffed ticket windows.

1. **Per ride.** Only fools (or tourists) buy per ride. Why? Here's some perspective: It costs about $7,920 in winter to fly the 3,500 miles from London to New York City in First Class on British Airways, or about $2.28 per mile. But to travel a mile in zone 1 on the Underground, the cash fare stands at £4.50, or about $6.90. So it costs three times as much to go a mile on the Tube than it does to go a mile in transatlantic First Class. Buses aren't much better: £2.40 a ride in cash. For short trips, sharing a cab costs just as much. On to option B.

2. **Via Travelcard.** This is a set-price, unlimited pass for 1 or 7 days on the Tube, bus, and the DLR. One-day passes are paper but week-long ones are loaded onto an Oyster card (see below). For 1-day cards for zones 1 and 2, the location of the majority of stuff you'll see, there are "Off-Peak" Travelcards good after 9:30am (£7.30); they're still valid for the evening rush. "Day Anytime" Travelcards with no morning restrictions are £8.80. The pass also covers buses and stations on the Overground and National Rail railway network in those zones, which cover swaths of London that the Tube doesn't. If you find you have to pop into a zone that isn't covered by your card, buy an extension from the ticket window before starting your journey; it's usually £1.50 to £2 more. **7-Day Travelcards** cost adults £30.40 for travel anytime in zones 1 and 2. For more Travelcard prices, visit **www.tfl.gov. uk/tickets**.

3. **Via Oyster Pay As You Go (PAYG).** This credit card–size pass, which you just rub on a yellow dot at the turnstiles, offers the lowest fares and fills the gap between 1-day and 1-week Travelcards. It is encoded with what you've paid and won't get erased if you keep it beside your mobile phone. No matter how many times you ride the Tube (debited at £2.10 in zone 1 after 9:30am—that's a lot better than the £4.50 cash fare!) and bus (debited as £1.40, or £1 cheaper than paying cash), the maximum taken off your card in a single day will always be a little less than what an equivalent Day Travelcard would cost. So, heavy use will always peak at £8.40 for anytime travel in zones 1 and 2, versus £8.80 if you'd bought an equivalent Travelcard. But getting an Oyster usually requires a £5 deposit, so before you skip town, drop by any Tube ticket office (there's also a desk at Heathrow; I.D. may be requested), where you can get a refund of your unused money long as there's less than £10 value left on your card. You may buy an Oyster card before your trip and have it sent to you, but that's a waste of time and shipping costs since you can just get it at the first Tube stop you visit. Confused? Use www.tfl.gov.uk or call ✆ **0343/222-1234**.

No matter which method you choose, the Tube's an expensive proposition. It may be most econmical to get an Oyster PAYG and then do everything you can to plan days during which you don't have to take it at all. A significant aspect of that strategy is choosing a hotel that's within walking distance of lots of the things you want to do. Fortunately, that's not hard to do because the city's very walkable. Trains go so slowly (34kmph/21 mph is the *average* and has been for over 100 years); you can watch the tunnel walls creep by, and in the center of town, stations are remarkably close together. In fact, if your journey is only two or three stations, you can often walk the distance in the same amount of time.

NATIONAL RAIL

These are the lines that aren't operated by the Underground. These lines are covered by Travelcards and Oyster PAYG as long as you stay in the zone system. The major London terminals have information desks if you're unsure about Oyster's validity on any journey. National Rail stations are only marginally less convenient than Tube stops since trains are regular.

There are many termini, but you don't have to hunt for by trial and error. Call the 24-hour operators at **National Rail Enquiries** (www.nationalrail.co.uk; ✆ **08457/48-49-50**). You can't book there, but it will tell you where you can. Alternatively, each station posts timetables. Schedules are listed by destination; find the place you're going, and the departures will be listed in 24-hour time.

National Rail stations (not Eurostar or the Underground) accept discount cards for certain folks. Each card requires proof of eligibility (passport, ISIC student ID), but since they can be used for trips to distant cities, they pay for themselves quickly if you're doing lots of rail-riding. Get them at rail stations:

○ The **Senior Railcard** (www.senior-railcard.co.uk, £30 a year): Discounts of about 33% for those 60 or over.

○ The **16-25 Railcard** (www.16-25railcard.co.uk, £30 a year): Discounts of 33% for those 16 to 25, plus full-time students of any age. It requires a passport-size photo, which may be uploaded from a computer. If you're applying in the U.K., bring a passport photo for that purpose.

• The **Family & Friends Railcard** (www.family-railcard.co.uk, £30 a year) is for at least one adult and one child aged 5 to 15, with a maximum of three adults and four kids on one ticket; at least one child must travel at all times. It awards adults 33% off and kids 60% off. But know that two kids under the age of five can travel with an adult for free at all times, even without this card.

BUS

The buses in your city may not come often, but London's are frequent (every 5 min. or so on weekdays), plentiful (some 100 routes in central London and 700 in the wider city), and surprisingly fast (many operate in dedicated bus lanes). Let's admit it: Sitting on the second level of a candy-apple red double-decker, watching the big landmarks roll past, is one of London's priceless pleasures. Best of all, the bus is cheaper than the Tube. The 1-day Oyster PAYG price cap for bus-only travel is £4.40, no matter the zone. Single trips cost £2.40 in cash. Travelcards and Oysters yield the best fares (per-trip £1.40). If you can't find an automated ticket machine, duck into the nearest Tube station and buy them from the cashier there.

Some shelters have automated ticket machines (cash only, and don't expect change), but all have easy-to-read maps of that tell you where to catch the bus going in your direction. Many shelters even have electronic boards that approximate the arrival time of the next bus. Board by the driver, who operates the ticket machine, and get off via the door at the middle. An automated voice announces every stop. Press one of the yellow buttons on the handrails to request a halt at the next one.

Routes that start with N are Night Buses, which tote the clubbers home after the Tube stops; many connect tediously in Trafalgar Square, so pee before setting off. Bus passes and Travelcards expire at 4:30am the day after you buy them, so if you have one for the day, you shouldn't have to pony up money that night to get home. TfL 24-hour information: ✆ 0343/222-1234.

FERRY

One of the happy outcomes of the Olympics was a revitalization of London's river ferry services, which are now one of the most pleasurable ways to get around. The

RED-LETTER double-deckers

A few routes are truly world-class, linking legendary sights. With routes like these, you won't need to splurge on those tedious hop-on, hop-off tour buses:

• The **15 bus,** which crosses the city northwest to southeast, takes in Paddington, Oxford Street, Piccadilly Circus, Trafalgar Square, Fleet Street, St. Paul's, and the Tower of London. And it's on an antique Routemaster.

• The **10** passes Royal Albert Hall, Kensington Gardens, Knightsbridge (a block north of Harrods), Hyde Park Corner, Marble Arch, Oxford Street, Goodge Street (for the British Museum), and King's Cross Station.

• The **159** links Paddington, Oxford Circus, Trafalgar Square, and Westminster.

• The **RV1** hits Covent Garden, Waterloo, the Tate Modern, and as a bonus, you get to ride over the Tower Bridge to the Tower of London.

boats cover a surprising amount of terrain quickly, with 16 stops, including right outside the London Eye, the Tate Modern, the Tower of London, Greenwich, and the O_2 dome, among others. Getting from Greenwich to Embankment takes all of 45 idyllic minutes. You can go right under the famous Tower Bridge—and because it's intended for commuters, it's at a fraction of the price of a tourist boat.

Fares depend in how far you're going, but for a trip from Westminster to Greenwich, expect a one-way fare of £7.50. You will always save money if you buy a return trip instead of two one-ways (say, £7.80 round-trip instead of £12.80 for two singles). **Thames Clippers** (© **020/7930-2062;** www.thamesclippers.com; generally 9am–9pm) fast catamarans go every 20 minutes during the day. Passes that allow you to take as many trips as you want on a single day are called River Roamer passes, and they cost £8 for adults and £4 for kids (these tickets stop short of Greenwich). Unfortunately, fares are not covered by your Oyster card, although those with Travelcards loaded into their Oyster cards can score discounts of about £2.80 for adults and £1.40 for kids on a Day Roamer pass. Two adults and two kids can all use the same Roamer ticket for £18.

CYCLE

Scattered throughout town, you'll see a fun addition to London's street furniture: racks of identical blue bikes in racks. Guess what? They're yours to borrow! They are officially called **Barclays Cycle Hire**, but Londoners call them **Boris Bikes**, after the blustery mayor who brought them here.

It works like this: You choose one and pull it out of the rack by lifting the seat. You ride it to any other docking station in the city with a free space, and you park it by slotting the front wheel in until a green light appears on the dock. When you're ready to ride somewhere else, just get another bike. You buy the right to borrow a bike for £2 a day or £10 a week (payments are on your credit card) at the pylon standing above any rack and from there, you have 30 free minutes every time you pull a bike out of the rack. Go past that, and you start paying: £1 for up to hour, £4, for up to 90 minutes, £6 for 2 hours, and so forth. The idea is for you to use the bikes in place of public transport, not to keep it with you all day. If you think your trip will take more than a half hour, just stop off at another rack, select a new bike after a 5-minute wait, and the clock restarts. You can do that as many times as you want, but you are required to follow the same traffic rules that cars do.

Locations of nearby docks are on every pylon, use the free apps **Barclays Bikes** (© **0845/026-3630;** http://tfl.gov.uk/barclayscyclehire) or **Spotcycle** (www.spotcycle.net). Interestingly, it's been reported this is the only part of Transport for London that makes a profit. Now one in four Londoners commutes to work on a bike.

TAXI

Even Londoners think taxis are crazy expensive. It's not the fault of the cabbies. They're the best in the world. Before they're given their wheels, every London taxi driver (there are some 24,000 of them) must go through a grueling training period so comprehensive that it's dubbed, simply, "The Knowledge." On Sundays, you'll see trainees zipping around on mopeds with clipboards affixed above their dashboards. Cabbies arrive inculcated with directions to every alley, mews, avenue, shortcut, and square in the city, and if they don't know, they'll find the answer so discreetly you won't catch the gaffe. And then there are those adorable vehicles: bulbous as Depression Era jalopies, roomy as a studio apartment, yet able to do complete U-turns within a single lane of traffic.

But for this admittedly peerless carriage, you'll pay a £2.40 minimum. Trips of up to 1.6km (1 mile) cost £5.60 to £8.80 during working hours; 3.2km (2-mile) trips are £8.60 to £13.80; 6.4km (4-mile) trips are £14 to £22; and trips of around 9.6km (6 miles) hit you for a painful £23 to £29. Rates rise when you're most likely to need a taxi: by about 10% from 8pm to 10pm, and roughly another 20% from 10pm until dawn. Mercifully, there is no charge for extra passengers or for luggage. It has become customary to tip 10%, but most people just round up to the nearest pound. Some taxis accept credit cards plus a 12.5% surcharge, but mostly, they are a cash-only concern.

Taxis are often called "black cabs," although in fact 12 colors are registered, including "thistle blue" and "nightfire red." If you need to call a cab, **One Number** (© **087/ 1871-8710**) pools all the companies, with a surcharge of £2.

Minicabs, which are hire cars that operate separately from the traditional black cab system, should be hailed with care. Don't accept a ride from one that approaches you. Insead, use the free Cabwise app, text CAB to 60835, or go to www.tfl.gov.uk/ cabwise, to hail the nearest one.

RENTING A CAR

Are you insane? Rare is the local who drives in central London, where there's a mandatory daily "congestion charge" of £8 (don't believe me? See **www.cclondon.com**), and where parking fees are several times that. Streets were cramped even when people rode horses and haven't improved, plus they're dogged with one-way rules and police cameras will ticket you for even honest errors, which you'll make since you're visiting. You'll go crazy and broke, so why do it?

WHEN TO GO

CLIMATE It's always time to visit London. Even though it's approximately at the same latitude of Edmonton, Alberta, weather patterns keep the environment from being extreme in any way. It gets cold in the winter, but rarely snowed in. It gets warm in the summer, but rarely blisteringly so (in fact, most buildings don't even have air-conditioning). The winter months are generally more humid than the summer ones, but experience only slightly more rain.

The principal art season (for theatre, concerts, art shows) falls between September and May, leaving the summer months for festivals and park-going. A few royal attractions, such as the state rooms of Buckingham Palace, are only open in the summer when the Queen decamps to Scotland. In summer, when the weather is warmest, the sun sets after 10pm, and half of Europe takes its annual holiday, the airfares are higher, as are hotel rates, and the queues for most of the tourist attractions, such as the London Eye and the Tower of London, might make you wish you'd come in March. For decent prices and lighter crowds, go in spring or fall—April and October seem to have the best confluence of mild weather, pretty plantings, and tolerable crowds. Prices are lowest in mid-winter, but a number of minor sights, such as historic houses, sometimes close from November to March, and the biggest annual events take place during the warmer months.

London's Average Daytime Temperatures & Rainfall

	JAN	FEB	MAR	APR	MAY	JUNE	JULY	AUG	SEPT	OCT	NOV	DEC
Temp. (°F)	39	39	43	46	52	58	62	62	57	51	44	42
Temp. (°C)	3	3	6	7	11	14	16	16	13	10	6	5
Rainfall (in.)	3.1	2	2.4	2.1	2.2	2.2	1.8	2.2	2.7	2.9	3.1	3.1
Rainfall (mm)	49	39	40	43	47	52	59	57	56	62	59	53

London's Public Holidays

England observes **eight public holidays** (also known as "bank holidays"): New Year's Day (January 1); Good Friday and Easter Monday (usually April); May Bank Holiday (first Monday in May); Spring Bank Holiday (usually last Monday in May, but occasionally the first in June); August Bank Holiday (last Monday in August); Christmas Day (December 25); Boxing Day (December 26). If a date falls on a weekend, the holiday rolls over to the following Monday.

London's Calendar of Events

Special events are an integral part of London's calendar, and many regular happenings draw tourists from around the world. Find even more events at London's **city website** (www.london.gov.uk/get-involved/events), at the **official tourism site** (www.visitlondon.com), the blog **Londonist** (www.londonist.com), and *Time Out* magazine (www.timeout.com/london).

JANUARY

London New Year's Day Parade. As many as 10,000 dancers, acrobats, musicians, and performers (heavy on the marching bands) promenade from Parliament Square to Piccadilly for 500,000 spectators and TV audiences. ℂ **020/3275-0190.** www.londonparade.co.uk. January 1.

Chinese New Year Festival. In conjunction with the Chinese New Year, the streets around Leicester Square come alive with dragon and lion dances, children's parades, performances, screenings, and fireworks displays. ℂ **020/7333-8118.** www.chinatownlondon.org.

Get into London Theatre. Theatre gets a jolt of new audiences during this promotional period during which producers get together to sell some 75,000 tickets at big discounts. www.getintolondontheatre.co.uk. Early January to February.

London International Mime Festival. Not just for silent clowns, but also for funky puppets and Blue Man–style tomfoolery, it's held around town in mid-January. ✆ **020/7637-5661**. www.mimelondon.com.

Imagine Children's Literature Festival. U.K.'s kids' lit has spanned Potter, Beatrix to Potter, Harry, and its best contemporary children's writers, storytellers, and illustrators enrapture young audiences with readings, discussions, and workshops. ✆ **020/7960-4200**. www.southbankcentre.co.uk/imagine-childrens-festival. 2 weeks in mid-February.

London Fashion Week. Collections are unveiled for press and buyers at a biannual fashion festival also held in September. It's tough to get a runway show ticket, but there's a raft of slick events and parties across the city. www.londonfashionweek.co.uk. Mid-February and mid-September.

St. Patrick's Day Festival. When you're this close to Dublin and you consider England's long rivalry with the Emerald Isle, you can expect lots of raging Irish pride—parades, music, cultural village, and food stalls around Trafalgar Square, where the fountains gush green. The city also sponsors concerts and craft fairs promoting Irish culture and heritage. It's not just about drinking—it just looks that way. ✆ **020/7983-4000**. www.london.gov.uk.

BADA Antiques & Fine Art Fair. Sponsored in mid- to late March by the British Antique Dealers' Association, it's considered to be the best in Britain for such collectors. Some 100 exhibitors move into a mighty tent in Duke of York's Square, in Chelsea, for the 7-day sales event. Don't expect a bargain. ✆ **020/7589-6108**. www.bada-antiques-fair.co.uk.

Oxford and Cambridge Boat Race. Taking place in late March or early April, the popular annual event (since 1829) held on the Thames in Hammersmith takes less than a half-hour, but the after-party rollicks into the night and the good-natured rivalry is undying. www.theboatrace.org.

London Marathon. Although it draws some 35,000 runners, the Marathon is also a kick for spectators, so hotels tend to fill up ahead of it. The starter pistol fires in Greenwich, and the home stretch is along Birdcage Walk near Buckingham Palace. If you want to run, apply by the previous October. www.virginlondonmarathon.com. Sunday in mid-April.

Regent's Park Open Air Theatre. Forget stuffy auditoriums. There's little shelter from sudden downpours, but in good weather the repertoire of high drama, musicals, and Shakespeare sparkles under a canopy of blue skies, towering trees, and natural beauty. ✆ **0844/826-4242**. www.openairtheatre.org. Tube: Regent's Park or Baker St. Mid-May to September.

Chelsea Flower Show. The Royal Horticultural Society, which calls itself a "leading gardening charity dedicated to advancing horticulture and promoting good gardening" (don't you just *love* the English?), mounts this esteemed show for 5 days in late May on the grounds of the Royal Hospital in Chelsea. The plants, all raised by champion green thumbs, are sold to attendees on the final day, but sadly, foreigners aren't usually able to get their plants past Customs. Tickets go on sale in November for this lilypalooza, and they're snapped up quickly. The event is so celebrated that it is covered on nightly prime-time TV. Really. ✆ **0845/260-5000**. www.rhs.org.uk.

Beating Retreat. Drum corps, pipes, and plenty of bugle calls: This anachronistic twilight ceremony, held for two evenings in early June at Horse Guards Parade by St. James's Park, involves the salute of the Queen (or another member of the royal

10

family) and the appearance of many red-clad marchers. Scholars trace its origins to 1554—so for tradition's sake, it's deeply meaningful. It's the nearest relative to the better-known Trooping the Colour, but without the crowds. Reserve ahead. ✆ **020/7839-5323.**

Hampton Court Palace Festival. High-end niche names (Rufus Wainwright, Van Morrison, Russell Watson) perform early in the month in a temporary theater on palace grounds. Tickets are around £50. ✆ **084/4412-2954.** www.hamptoncourtpalacefestival.com.

The Royal Academy Summer Exhibition. Artists have been in a frenzy to win entry to this blind competition for nearly 250 years. Paintings, sculpture, drawings, architecture—if you can dream it, you can enter it, and if you're one of the most talented, your piece is anointed as the best that year. The show is what the Royal Academy is known for, and although it's not envelope-pushing, it's a seminal event in British art culture and shouldn't be missed if you're in town. www.royalacademy.org.uk.

Trooping the Colour. Never mind that the Queen was born in April. This is her birthday party, and as a present, she gets the same thing every year: soldiers with big hats. Gee, thanks. A sea of redcoats and cavalry swarm over Horse Guards Parade, 41 guns salute, and a flight of Royal Air Force jets slam through the sky overhead. The Queen herself leads the charge, waving politely to her subjects before they lose themselves in a hearty display of marching band prowess. After such extravagant displays of pomp, no doubt is left that the colour has been truly trooped. Held in mid-June, it starts at 10am. If you want grandstand seats instead of standing in the free-for-all along the route, where you'll only get a fast glimpse of passing royalty, send a request by February to Brigade Major, Headquarters Household Division, Horse Guards, Whitehall, London, SW1A 2AX, United Kingdom. SASEs are required, so include an International Reply Coupon from your post office so that your return postage is paid. Otherwise, check out the Beating Retreat for a similar, if less elaborate, experience. ✆ **020/7414-2479.** www.royal.gov.uk.

Taste of London Festival. For 4 days in mid-June, the city's top chefs and the region's finest farmers convene in Regent's Park for a belly-stuffing. ✆ **087/1230-5581**.

Pride London. A signature event on the world's LGBT calendar, in a good year London Pride can pull some 825,000 revelers, many of them heterosexual, with a buoyant roster of concerts and performances by famous names plus a parade (the U.K.'s largest) in the center of the city. The gay pride week, co-sponsored by the Mayor's office also makes for an excellent excuse for some blowout dance parties. Late June or early July. www.londoncommunitypride.org.

Wimbledon Championships. Why watch on television yet again? Check p. 136 for how to be one of the 500,000 to witness it in person. Late June to early July. ✆ **020/8971-2473.** www.wimbledon.org.

Hard Rock Calling. Tickets are steep (around £70), but the lineup for this 2-day concert at the former Olympic Park is A-list; names have included Eric Clapton, The Police, Bon Jovi, and Bruce Springsteen. www.hardrockcalling.co.uk.

Greenwich and Docklands International Festival. An ambitious program of free theatrical and musical pieces, many of them developed by artists expressly for the spaces they're performed in. It's held in late June. ✆ **020/8305-1818**. www.festival.org.

City of London Festival. Traditional and high-minded classical music concerts are held toward the end of the month in some of The City's oldest buildings. ✆ **0845/120-7502.** www.colf.org.

Meltdown. A compendium of hip prestige arts held at the end of June at the Southbank Centre, curated each year by a notable such as Patti Smith, David Bowie, and Yoko Ono. ✆ **020/7960-4200**. www.southbankcentre.co.uk/meltdown.

BBC Promenade Concerts. The biggest classical music festival of the year, held primarily at the Royal Albert Hall, "the Proms" consists of orchestral concerts for every taste. Seats start at £6. ☎ **020/7589-8212.** www.bbc.co.uk/proms.

Lovebox. The weekend-long music marathon held in Queen Victoria Park in northeast London mixes newcomers with giants of sound, including (in 2013) Azealia Banks, Disclosure, Jurassic 5, and Goldfrapp. The crowd is young and fun, starting with nitrous-huffing kids on Friday and morphing into a de facto gay pride day by Sunday. www.mamacolive.com/lovebox.

Virgin Active London Triathlon. Some 13,000 participants cycle through the City from Westminster, sprint around the ExCeL center in Docklands, and swim in Royal Victoria Dock in this annual late July event. Sir Richard Branson attends. ☎ **020/8233-5900.** www.thelondontriathlon.co.uk.

Yahoo! Wireless Festival. Held al fresco in Queen Elizabeth Olympic Park for 3 days in mid-July, it books the best names in the biz. In 2013, those included Justin Timberlake, Jay-Z, and Snoop Dogg. www.wirelessfestival.co.uk.

The Lambeth Country Show. A free, old-fashioned farm show overtakes Brixton's Brockwell Park (for a single weekend in July, anyway) with farm animals, jam-making contests, a fun fair, tractor demonstrations, and Punch and Judy puppet shows. Very English stuff. ☎ **020/7926-7085.** www.lambeth.gov.uk/Country-Show.

AUGUST

Notting Hill Carnival. In August 1958, roving bands of white racists combed the slums of Notting Hill in search of Caribbean-owned businesses to destroy. Resulting community outrage and newly rediscovered cultural pride led to the formation of a new festival, which today is Europe's largest street parade, a powerhouse smorgasbord of cultures spanning the rest of the Caribbean as well as Eastern Europe, South America, and the Indian subcontinent. It attracts some 2 million people during the August Bank Holiday weekend, which includes the last Monday in August. Sunday is kids' day, with scrubbed-down events and activities, but on Monday, the adults take over, costumes get skimpy, floats weave through small streets, and rowdy hordes celebrate into the wee hours. www.nottinghillcarnival.biz.

Great British Beer Festival. Just like it sounds: More than 800 British ales and ciders are available to try at London Olympia—after all those tastings, you'll be relieved to learn the Tube is within easy reach. It runs 5 days. ☎ **0844/412-4640.** www.gbbf.org.uk.

SEPTEMBER

The Great River Race. Always over too soon, the Race is the aquatic version of the London Marathon, with rowers vying to beat out 300 other vessels—Chinese dragon boats, Canadian canoes, Viking longboats, and even Hawaiian outriggers—on a morning jaunt upriver from the Docklands to Richmond. It's held on a Saturday in mid-September. ☎ **020/8398-8141.** www.greatriverrace.co.uk.

The Mayor's Thames Festival. In conjunction with the Great River Race, nearly half a million souls attend London's largest free open-air arts festival, which includes more than 250 stalls selling food and crafts (Southwark Bridge is closed for a giant feast), a flotilla of working river boats, circus performers, and antique fireboats, tugs, and sailboats. Sunday sees the Night Carnival, a lavish procession of thousands of lantern-bearing musicians and dancers crawling along the water. Everything is topped off with barge-launched fireworks. It takes place over 10 days. ☎ **020/7928.8998.** www.thamesfestival.org.

Open House London. More than 600 buildings, all of them deemed important but normally closed to the public, yawn wide for free tours on a single, hotly anticipated weekend in mid-September. Past participants have included the skyscraper headquarters of Lloyd's and Swiss Re (officially "30 St. Mary Axe" but usually called "The

Gherkin") and the Mansion House (official residence of the Lord Mayor, completed in 1752). The list of open buildings comes out in August, and some require timed tickets, but for most the line forms at dawn. Open House also organizes year-round walking tours. ℭ **020/3006-7008**. www.open houselondon.org.

London Fashion Weekend. It's got nothing on its kin in New York or Milan, but here, pop-up shops from more than 100 designers are put on sale at deeply discounted prices in the hopes they'll build style buzz. www. londonfashionweekend.co.uk.

OCTOBER

Frieze Art Fair. More than 175 galleries vie for big money from collectors in a colossal 4-day tent show in Regent's Park. It has become influential in the contemporary art world. ℭ **0871/230-3452**. www.friezeartfair. com.

Diwali. One advantage of visiting a multicultural city like London is that it affords you the chance to sample major international holidays in an English-speaking environment. One such treat is Diwali, the Indian "festival of light," when Trafalgar Square is transformed with lights, floating lanterns, massive models of the elephant god Ganesh, music, dance, and DJs. It's free and held in mid- to late October.

BFI London Film Festival. An important stop on the cinema circuit, this event, sponsored by the British Film Institute, is geared toward media exposure, but there are plenty of tickets for the public, too. ℭ **020/7928-3232**. www.bfi.org.uk/lff.

Dance Umbrella. One of the world's best dance festivals, with plenty of standing-room seats for as little as £5; it peaks in late September. ℭ **020/7407-1200**. www.dance umbrella.co.uk.

NOVEMBER

Guy Fawkes Night. In 1605, silly old Guy Fawkes tried to assassinate James I and the entire Parliament by blowing them to smithereens in the Gunpowder Plot. Joke's on him: To this day, the Brits celebrate his failure by blowing up *him*. His effigy is thrown on bonfires across the country, fireworks displays rage in the autumn night sky, and more than a few tykes light their first sparklers in honor of the would-be assassin's gruesome execution. Although displays are scattered around town, including at Battersea Park and Alexandra Palace, get out of the city for the weekend nearest November 5, also called Bonfire Night, because the countryside is perfumed with the woody aroma of burning leaves on this holiday. Mount Primrose Hill or Hampstead Heath for a view of the fireworks going off around the city.

Lord Mayor's Show. What sounds like the world's dullest public access program is actually a delightfully pompous procession, abut 800 years old, involving some 140 charity floats and 6,000 participants (Pewterers! Basketweavers!) who parade round-trip from Mansion House in The City and head to the Royal Courts of Justice, on the Strand, all to ostensibly show off the newly elected Lord Mayor to the Queen or her representatives. The centerpiece is the preposterously carved and gilt Lord Mayor's Coach, built in 1757—a carriage so extravagant it makes Cinderella's ride look like a Toyota Corolla. That's a lot of hubbub for a city official whose role is essentially ceremonial; the Mayor of London (currently Boris Johnson) wields the true power. All that highfalutin strutting is followed by a good old-fashioned fireworks show over the Thames between the Blackfriars and Waterloo bridges. It's held on the second Saturday in November. www.lord mayorsshow.org.

London Jazz Festival. Some 165 mid-November events attract around 60,000 music fans. Many performances are free, and tickets are distributed by the venues. ℭ **020/7324-1880**. www.londonjazzfestival.org.uk.

Remembrance Sunday. Another chance to glimpse Her Royal Highness. She and the prime minister, as well as many royals, attend a ceremony at the Cenotaph, in the middle of Whitehall, to honor the war dead and wounded, of which Britain has borne more than its share. Those red flowers you'll see everywhere—red petals, black centers—are poppies, the symbol of remembrance in Britain. It takes place on the Sunday nearest November 11.

DECEMBER

Carols by Candlelight. Royal Albert Hall's annual evening of sing-along Christmas carols, readings from Dickens, and music by Handel, Bach, Mozart, and Corelli played by The Mozart Festival Orchestra—in period costume. (©) **020/7589-8212.** www.royal alberthall.com.

New Year's Eve Fireworks. As Big Ben strikes midnight, London rings in the New Year with fireworks over the Thames and the Eye. It's crowded, but the memory is worth it.

[FastFACTS] LONDON

Accessible Travel London can be hard going. It can't seem to strike the right balance between preserving old buildings and making sure they're accessible to all. With the laudable exception of the Docklands Light Railway, only a slim selection of Tube stations offer lifts, and those with plenty of escalators still require passengers to climb several flights of stairs. The situation is so scrambled, and positive changes so slow, that you'll need to do a bit of research. Your first stops should be **Visit London** (www.visitlondon.com/access) and **Transport for London** (www.tfl.gov.uk/accessguides). Many London hotels, museums, restaurants, buses, Tube stations, buses, taxis, and sightseeing attractions have dedicated wheelchair access, and persons with disabilities are often granted admission discounts. Generally speaking, the more expensive a hotel is, the more likely it is to be wheelchair accessible, but not always. For £2, iPhone users can download the LDN Access app (www.myukaccess.co.uk), which reviews the accessibility of hotels, restaurants, attractions, and more across the city. The website for **Nationwide Disabled Access Register** (www.directenquiries.com) tattles about the accessibility features of a wide range of facilities, from attractions to car renters.

Artsline (www.artsline.org.uk) distributes information about accessible entertainment venues, including which ones have infrared hearing devices for rental; it also welcomes calls. Blind or partially sighted travelers will find useful advice from the **Royal National Institute of Blind People** (© 0303/123-9999; www.rnib.org.uk). **Tourism for All** (© 084/5124-9971; www.tourismforall.org.uk) passes accessibility information to older travelers as well as to travelers with disabilities. The British agency **Can Be Done** (© 020/8907-2400; www.canbedone.co.uk) runs tours adapted to travelers with disabilities. **Wheelchair Travel** (© 01483/23-76-68; www.wheelchair-travel. co.uk) rents out self-drive and chauffeured chair-accessible vehicles (including ones with hand controls), provides day tours, and arranges city sightseeing in special vehicles.

Area Codes The country telephone code for Great Britain is **44.** The area code for London is **020.** The full telephone number is then usually 8-digits long. As a general rule, businesses and homes in central London have numbers beginning with a **7;** those from further out begin with an **8.** For more info, see "Telephones," later in this section.

ATMs/Banks See "Money" in this section.

Business Hours Offices are generally open weekdays between 9 or 10am and 5 or 6pm. Some remain open a few hours longer on Thursdays and Fridays. Saturday hours for stores are the same, and Sunday hours for stores are generally noon to 5 or 6pm. Banks are usually open from 9:30am to 4 or 5pm, with some larger branches open later on Thursdays or for a few hours on Saturday mornings.

Cellphones See "Mobile Phones," later in this section.

Crime See "Safety," later in this section.

Customs Rules about what you can carry into Britain are standard but ever-shifting, so get the latest restrictions from HM Revenue & Customs (© 011-44/2920-501-261; www.hmrc.gov.uk). Your own government is responsible for telling you what you can bring back home.

Doctors Ask your hotel first. Then try the G.P. (General Practitioner) finder at **www.nhsdirect.nhs.uk**. North American members of the **International Association for Medical Assistance to Travelers** (IAMAT; © **716/754-4883,** or 416/652-0137 in Canada; www.iamat.org) can consult that organization for lists of local approved doctors. *Note:* U.S. and Canadian visitors who become ill while they're in London are eligible only for free *emergency* care. For other treatment, including follow-up care, you'll pay. See "Insurance," below.

In any medical emergency, call © **999,** or 112. Less urgent? Call 111.

Drinking Laws Legal drinking age is 18. Children 15 and younger are allowed in pubs only if accompanied by a parent or guardian.

Although there are no open container laws, drinking on London's **public transport network** is forbidden and on-the-spot fines are issued to transgressors.

Driving Rules See "Getting Around," earlier in this chapter.

Electricity The current in Britain is 240 volts AC. Plugs have three squared pins. Foreign appliances operating on lower voltage (those from the U.S., Canada, and Australia use 110–120 volts AC) will require an adapter and possibly a voltage converter, although the range of capability will usually be printed on the plug. Many modern phone, chargers, and laptops can handle the stronger current with only an adapter. A few hotels, not many, provide a bathroom plug for a simple appliance such as a shaver.

Embassies & Consulates The **U.S. Embassy** is at 24 Grosvenor Sq., London W1 (© **020/7499-9000;** http://london.usembassy.gov; Tube: Bond Street or Marble Arch). Standard hours are Monday to Friday 8:30am to 5:30pm. Most non-emergency inquiries require an appointment.

The **High Commission of Canada,** 1 Grosvenor Square, London W1 (© **020/7258-6600;** www.canadain-ternational.gc.ca/united_kingdom-royaume_uni/index.aspx; Tube: Bond Street), handles passport and consular services for

Canadians. Hours are Mon, Wed, and Fri 8am to 10:30am.

The **Australian High Commission** is at Australia House, Strand, London WC2B 4LA (© **020/7379-4334;** www.uk.embassy.gov.au; Tube: Temple). Hours are Monday to Friday 9am to 5pm.

The **New Zealand High Commission** is at New Zealand House, 80 Haymarket (at Pall Mall), London SW1Y 4TQ (© **020/7930-8422;** www.nzembassy.com/uk; Tube: Charing Cross or Piccadilly Circus). Hours are Monday to Friday 9am to 5pm.

The **Irish Embassy** is at 17 Grosvenor Place, London SW1X 7HR (© **020/7235-2171;** www.embassyofireland.co.uk; Tube: Hyde Park Corner). Hours are Monday to Friday 9:30am to 5pm.

Emergencies The one-stop number for Britain is © **999**—that's for fire, police, and ambulances. It's free from any phone, even mobiles.

Family Travel Attractions cater to the family market. The kingly treatment starts, at many places, with the so-named **Family Ticket,** which grants a low price for parents and kids entering together. For any length of stay, you can rent baby equipment from **Chelsea Baby Hire,** 31 Osborne House, 414 Wimbledon Park Rd., SW19 6PW (© **07802/846-742;** www.chelseababyhire.com).

Babysitting: **Top Notch Nannies** (📞 020/7881-0893, 020/7824-8209; www.topnotchnannies.co.uk) normally brokers child-minders—usually Australians or Eastern Europeans—to wealthy London families, but it also runs a sideline, **Brilliant Babysitters,** which starts with a £12 booking fee then £10-15 an hour.

If you are a **divorced parent** with joint custody of your children, bring proof that you are entitled to take your kids out of the country; otherwise Immigration may give you a hard time.

Some resources that offer family-specific travel tips include the **Family Travel Network** (www.familytravelnetwork.com), online since 1995. **Travel with Your Kids** (www.travelwithyourkids.com) specializes in tips for international travel, and it also maintains a section just about London's finds. **The Family Travel Files** (www.thefamilytravelfiles.com) rounds up tour operators and packagers geared to families, but its suggestions aren't always the most economical or efficient. The weekly *Time Out* magazine also includes a section on kids' activities.

When it comes to baby supplies, pacifiers are called "dummies," diapers are "nappies," a crib is a "cot," and Band-Aids are "plasters".

Health   Traveling to London doesn't pose specific health risks. Common drugs are generally available over the counter and in large supermarkets, although visitors should note the generic rather than brand names of any medicines they rely on. Pack **prescription medications** in carry-on luggage and carry prescription medications in their original containers, with pharmacy labels—otherwise they may not pass airport security. Also bring copies of your prescriptions, just in case. Don't forget an extra pair of contact lenses or prescription glasses. The general-purpose painkiller known in North America as acetaminophen is called **paracetamol** in the U.K. If you don't feel well and you need the advice of a doctor or a nurse, the national health care system operates a free, 24-hour hotline: **National Health Service Direct** (📞 111; www.nhsdirect.co.uk). Citizens of many European countries are entitled to free health care while in Britain (see www.dh.gov.uk/travellers), but everyone else is not, although clinics have been known to treat tourists and then look the other way rather than embark upon the odyssey of paperwork required to bill them. Still, non-EU citizens should probably get health or travel insurance.

Hospitals   In the U.K., the ER is usually called A&E, or Accident and Emergency. If your need is urgent, dial 📞 **999** (it's free no matter where your phone is registered) rather than risk going to a medical center that doesn't offer A&E. You can search www.nhs.uk for the nearest A&E, or go to the 24-hour, walk-in A&E departments at **University College London Hospital,** 235 Euston Rd., London NW1 (📞 **020/3456-7890 or 0845/155-5000;** www.uclh.nhs.uk; Tube: Warren Street) and **St. Thomas' Hospital,** Westminster Bridge Rd., entrance on Lambeth Palace Rd., London SE1 (📞 **020/7188-7188;** www.guysandstthomas.nhs.uk; Tube: Westminster or Waterloo). **Soho NHS Walk-In Centre** (1 Frith St., W1; 📞 **020/7534-6500;** Tube: Tottenham Court Road) is a central clinic.

Insurance   U.K. nationals receive free medical treatment countrywide, but visitors from overseas only qualify automatically for free **emergency** care. **U.S. visitors** should note that most of your domestic health plans (including Medicare and Medicaid) do not provide coverage, and the ones that do often require you to pay for services upfront and reimburse you only after you return home. Among many options, you could try **MEDEX** (📞 800/732-5309; www.medexassist.com) or **Travel Assistance International** (📞 800/821-2828; www.travelassistance.com) for overseas medical insurance cover. **Canadians** should check with their provincial health plan offices or call **Health Canada** (📞 866/225-0709; www.

hc-sc.gc.ca) to find out the extent of their coverage and what documentation and receipts they must take home in case they are treated overseas. **E.U. nationals** (and nationals of E.E.A. countries and Switzerland) should note that reciprocal health agreements are in place to ensure they receive free medical care while in the U.K. However, it is essential that visitors from those countries carry a valid **European Health Identity Card** (EHIC).

So what else may you want to insure? You may want special coverage for **apartment stays,** especially if you've plunked down a deposit, and any **valuables,** since airlines are only required to pay up to $2,500 for lost luggage domestically, less for foreign travel.

If you do decide on insurance, compare policies at **InsureMyTrip.com** (✆ 800/487-4722). Or contact one of the following reputable companies: **Allianz** (✆ 866/884-3556; www.allianztravelinsurance.com); **CSA Travel Protection** (✆ 877/243-4135; www.csatravelprotection.com); **MEDEX** (✆ 800/732-5309; www.medexassist.com); **Travel Guard International** (✆ 800/826-4919; www.travelguard.com); **Travelex** (✆ 800/228-9792; www.travelex-insurance.com).

Internet & Wi-Fi Wi-Fi flows freely at many pubs, restaurants, museums, and nearly all hotels. Usually, you will have to fill in a browser page of information to activate it, but often, it's a data collection ploy and you can write dummy information. Virgin Media (www.virginmedia.com/wifi) provides Wi-Fi in many Tube stations but not between them. Visitors can buy passes for £2 (one day), £5 (one week), or £15 (one month). Savvy smartphone users will find it cheap and practical to switch off 3G altogether and use available Wi-Fi in combination with **Skype** (www.skype.com) for voice calls, **WhatsApp** (www.whatsapp.com) for texts, and **Voxer** (www.voxer.com) for voice messages. See Mobile Phones, below, for more.

Left Luggage Useful for taking those cheap European flights with steep luggage fees, **Left Baggage** (✆ 0800/077-4530; www.left-baggage.com) has locations at Heathrow, Gatwick and the big railway stations: £8.50 per item per 24 hours for up to a week, then £4.25 per item per day thereafter.

Legal Aid If you find yourself in trouble, contact your consulate or embassy (see "Embassies & Consulates," above). It can advise you of your rights and will usually provide a list of local attorneys (for which you'll have to pay if services are used), but they cannot interfere on your behalf in the English legal process. For questions about American citizens who are arrested abroad, including ways of getting money to them, telephone the **Citizens Emergency Center** of the Bureau of Consular Affairs in Washington, D.C. (✆ 202/501-4444).

LGBT Travelers Gay and lesbian people have equality and marriage rights. Public displays of affection are received with indifference in the center of the city, although in the outer suburbs couples should show more restraint. Gay bashings are rare enough to be newsworthy, but it's true that an element of society can, once full of ale, become belligerent. Particularly in parks at night, be aware of your surroundings and give wide berth to gaggles of drunken lads. This advice holds irrespective of your sexuality.

The **Turing Network** (www.turingnetwork.org.uk) lists gay and lesbian social events and festivals and is partnered with the **London Gay & Lesbian Switchboard** (✆ 0300/330-0630; www.llgs.org.uk), a counseling hotline. For nightlife planning, the best sources for information (among many less handy glossy lifestyle magazines) are the **Boyz** (www.boyz.co.uk), which publishes a day-by-day schedule on its website. The free **QX International** (www.qxmagazine.com) posts a downloadable version of its printed edition every week, so you can plot a course through the hotspots while you're still at home. Both publications are distributed for free at many gay bars. Also see p. 179.

Mail An airmail letter to anywhere outside Europe costs 88p for up to 10g (⅓ oz.) and generally takes 5 to 7 working days to arrive; postcards also require a 88p stamp. Within the E.U., letters or postcards under 20g (⅔ oz.) cost 88p. Within the U.K, First Class mail ought to arrive the following working day; Second Class mail takes around 3 days.

Medical Requirements Unless you're arriving from an area known to be suffering from an epidemic (particularly cholera or yellow fever), inoculations or vaccinations are not required for entry into the U.K.

Mobile Phones Apart from renting a phone (not recommend to the casual visitor), many tourists simply enable their international **roaming** feature. That works, but your provider will bleed you. You'll pay as much as $2 per minute, even if someone from home calls you, and data is a killer. Package plans tend to be stingy with time and data allowances.

There is a cheap solution. If you do have a quad- or tri-band phone that uses the GSM system, you can potentially hop into any mobile phone shop or newsstand and buy a cheap **pay-as-you-talk** phone number from a mobile phone store. You pay about £4 for a SIM card, which you stick in your phone, and then you buy vouchers to load your account with as much money as you think you'll use up (no refunds). That will give you a British number, which you can e-mail to everyone back home, that charges local rates (10p–40p per min.) and a deal on data that might allow 500MB in a month for about £5—much, much cheaper than roaming. Just call your provider before you leave home to "unlock" your phone (out-of-contract phones are better candidates) so that the British SIM card will function in it. That service is usually free. U.K. mobile providers with pay-as-you-talk deals, all comparable, include: **Vodafone** (www.vodafone.com), **O₂** (www.o2.co.uk), **Lebara** (www.lebara.co.uk), **T-Mobile** (www.t-mobile.co.uk), and **Virgin Mobile** (www.virginmobile.com). Even if you are not permitted to unlock your phone, you can use its Wi-Fi feature. Anytime you call a mobile phone in Britain, the fee will be bearably higher, although under the European system there is no fee to *receive* a call.

Money The British pound (£1), a small, chunky, gold-colored coin, is usually accepted in vending machines, so you can never have too many in your pocket. It's commonly called a "quid." Like money in America, Canada, and Australia, it's divided into 100 pennies (p)—the plural, "pence," is used to modify amounts over 1p. Pence come in 1p, 2p, 5p, 10p, 20p, and 50p denominations. Patterns on the obverse of the £1 and 50p coins periodically change to commemorate various areas or events. Sometimes you'll see large bull's-eye £2 coins, too. Bills come in £5, £10, £20, and £50. Now and then, you'll receive notes printed by the Royal Bank of Scotland; don't be troubled, since these are legal tender in London, too.

Currency rates fluctuate, so before departing consult a currency exchange website such as **www.oanda.com/currency/converter** to check up-to-the-minute rates. There's also a smartphone app available for pretty much any mobile device; see **www.oanda.com/mobile**.

All prices (including at most B&Bs but not at all hotels) are listed including tax, so what you see is what you pay. No guesstimating required.

When bringing up prices, always insert the word "pounds": For example, £2.50 would be uttered as "two pounds fifty" but not "two fifty."

Every visitor should have several sources for money, but cash is still king, as they say (Queen Elizabeth isn't jealous—her face is on all the money). The simple prescription is to pull cash from an ATM upon arrival; the rates are the cheapest there. Before leaving home, warn your bank and your credit card issuers that you intend to travel internationally so that the don't place a stop on your account when international charges start cropping up. You may also need to adjust your PIN, since English banks require 4-digit codes. If you know your PIN as a word, memorize the numerical equivalent. Most banks hit you with fees of a few pounds each time you withdraw cash. Your own bank may toss in a small fee of its own (another 2% or 3%, but ask ahead to see what its policy is), so gauge for yourself how much you feel comfortable withdrawing at a time to offset that fee. If you have an account with an international bank chain, ask whether using their machines during your visit will save on fees. Also ask your bank if it has reciprocal agreements for free withdrawals anywhere. One institution known to charge international usage fees that are below the industry standard is **Everbank** (✆ **888/ 882-3837;** www.everbank. com); another is **Charles Schwab** (✆ **866/855-9102;** www.schwab.com), which reimburses ATM fees. Be quick when using ATMs. Retrieve your card immediately from ATM slots; many machines suck them in within 10 to 15 seconds, for security. Should that happen, you'll have to petition the bank to have it returned to you.

Now that ATMs are common, traveler's checks are nearly dead. Using them, you run the risk of most places declining them. Creditors have come up with **traveler's check cards,** also called **prepaid cards,** which are essentially debit cards loaded with the amount of money you elect to put on them. They're not coded with your personal information, they work in ATMs, and should you lose one, you can get your cash back in a matter of hours. If you spend all the money on them, you can call a number or visit a website and reload the card using your bank account information. **Travelex Cash Passport** (✆ **877/465-0085** or ✆ 01733/501-370 in the U.K.; www.cashpassport. com; $2 per ATM transaction) works anywhere MasterCard does and can be loaded in British pounds, Euros, or American dollars; also try **NetSpend** (✆ **866/ 387-7363;** www.netspend. com; $1 per purchase, $5 per ATM transaction). That one costs $4.

Changing cash is also on the outs, and good riddance, since exchange rates are usurious. ATM withdrawals give the best better deals, so old-fashioned cambios are few and far between these days, although you'll still find a few upon landing at the airport and around Leicester Square and Piccadilly Circus. If you need to change money, take advantage of

the better rates offered by banks during regular banking hours (9:30am–4pm).

Credit cards are accepted nearly everywhere. However, **American Express** is accepted less widely. Bring a Visa or MasterCard; they are the chief cards. Most credit card issuers levy an annoying international transaction fee on top of your purchase; **Capital One** (✆ **800/955-7070;** www.capitalone.com) is one of the few that does not. Small vendors may charge a transaction fee (3% is the norm) as a way of defraying the cost of dealing with credit card companies. Try not to use credit cards to withdraw cash. You'll pay a currency exchange fee, and worse, you'll be charged interest from the moment your money leaves the slot.

Europeans use "chip and PIN" credit cards requiring a code number. Many vending machines **will not accept** swipe-only cards and may cause you to think you were declined. Travelex (see above) sells debit cards that work in chip-and-PIN readers. For swipe-only cards, clerks will always verify your signature, so make sure your card is signed. For security, restaurants will usually process your payment at your table with a radio device.

Newspapers & Magazines London offers more publications than one would think a city of its size could support. The broadsheets, ordered from left to right, politically speaking, are: *The Guardian, The Independent, The Daily Telegraph,* and *The Times.* The *Evening Standard* and the *Metro* are free. The salmon-colored *Financial Times* covers business. The tabloids are fluffier and more salacious, and they include *The Sun* (which has published photos of topless "Page Three Girls" since 1970), *The Mirror, Daily Star, The Daily Mail,* and *Daily Express;* few of those deliver news as most people would define the term. *Time Out* publishes a thorough weekly listing of events and entertainments; new issues go on sale Tuesdays. International publications such as *USA Today* are widely available. Other popular magazines include *Heat* (celebrity gossip), *Radio Times* (TV listings and celebrity interviews), *Hello!* and *OK!* (fawning celebrity spreads usually planted by publicity agents), and *NME* (music).

Packing   For your wallet's sake, pack sparingly! You've heard that before, but it's really true this time. It's not as easy as it used to be to wink your way through the weigh-in. In some cases, the conveyor belts at check-in are programmed to halt if they sense a bag over the limit.

British Airways, for example, grants coach passengers a puny **23kg (51 lb.).** If you exceed that, you will be smacked with a flat fee of £25 per flight. That only buys you another 9kg

(20 lb.), because bags over 32kg (71 lb.) will be rejected outright. When it comes to carry-ons ("hand baggage"), it's got to measure no more than 56cm long by 45cm wide by 25cm deep (22×18×10 in.). Some airlines, such as Virgin Atlantic, can be ruthless about making sure even your hand baggage weighs no more than 10kg (22 lb.). That's very little. If you're taking multiple airlines, stick to the tightest set of restrictions of the lot. Many airlines (even the no-frills) discount for booking baggage at least 24 hours early, and charge more at the airport.

If you need new luggage, Primark (p. 156) sells it for less than £20.

Keep prescription medications in their original, labeled containers for Customs even though they're unlikely to be inspected. If you require **syringes,** always carry a signed medical prescription.

Pare toiletries to essentials. You're not going to the Congo. You will find staples like toothpaste, contact lens solution, and deodorant everywhere—many pharmacies stock many of the same brands you have at home. Women should bring a minimum of make-up; the British don't tend to use very much themselves. Brits are also more likely to wear trousers than blue jeans. If you plan to go clubbing, pack some fashionable duds—Londoners aren't slouches when it comes to dressing up.

Speaking of that, don't wear a lot of tee-shirts with writing or logos; it marks you as a tourist.

You'll be most comfortable if you dress in clothing that layers well. Even in winter, London's air can be clammy, and dressing too warmly can become uncomfortable. No matter what the average temperature is (see the box on weather, p. 236), the air can grow cool after the sun sets, so plan for that, too. In the winter, a hat, scarf, and gloves are necessities. A compact umbrella is wise year-round, as is an outer coat that repels water, since you never know when you're going to find yourself out in one of those misty rains that makes the British Isles so lush and green.

Don't bring illegal drugs (duh), and also leave the pepper spray and mace at home; they're banned in the U.K.

Passports   To enter the United Kingdom, all U.S. citizens, Canadians, Australians, New Zealanders, and South Africans must have a passport valid through their length of stay. No visa is required. A passport will allow you to stay in the country for up to 6 months. The immigration officer may also want to see proof of your intention to return to your point of origin (usually a round-trip ticket) and of visible means of support while you're in Britain (credit cards work). If you're planning to fly from the United

States or Canada to the United Kingdom and then on to a country that requires a visa (India, for example), you should secure that visa before you arrive in Britain.

Pharmacies Every police station keeps a list of pharmacies that are open 24 hours. Also try **Zafash,** open 24 hours, 233-235 Old Brompton Rd., SW5; ℂ **020/7373 2798;** Tube: Earl's Court; and **Bliss,** open daily 9am to midnight, 5-6 Marble Arch, W1; ℂ **020/ 7723-6116;** Tube: Marble Arch. For nonemergency health advice, call NHS Direct at ℂ 111.

Police London has two official police forces: The City of London police (www. cityoflondon.police.uk) whose remit covers the "Square Mile" and its 8,600 residents; and the Metropolitan Police ("the Met"), which covers the rest of the capital and is split into separate borough commands for operational purposes. Opening hours for all the Met's local police stations are listed at **www.met. police.uk/local.** In a nonemergency, you can contact your local police station from anywhere by dialing ℂ **101.** Losses, thefts, and other criminal matters should be reported at the nearest police station immediately. You will be given a crime number, which your travel insurer will request if you make a claim against any losses. Always dial ℂ **999** or 112 if the matter is serious.

Safety Few places in London are unsafe. Some locals are made nervous by a few parts of the East End, but there's not much evidence of random violence to back that fear up. Neighborhoods that pessimistically might be called sketchy are usually distant from the Tube lines, and they only feel tense after dark, when shops close. London is like anyplace; simply be sensitive to who's around you and you'll do fine.

The biggest nuisance tourists might encounter—besides tipsy locals—is pickpockets. As chronicled in *Oliver Twist*, London, like all cities of size, is home to a skilled subspecies of crook eager to lift your valuables. Oxford Street and the Tube are the prime picking grounds. Simply be smart about where you put your cash and about who's pressing up against you.

Surveillance is the new British national pastime; there are more cameras per person than in any other country. Guns are banned—even on most police officers—so you don't often see the kind of violence taken for granted in the United States. Londoners cite increasing knife crime as a problem, but the victims are almost always young men who themselves carry knives. Some male tourists have gotten fleeced at some of the **"hostess bars"** in Soho. If you do suffer a lapse of judgment and

accept the barker's invitation to go into one, understand that if you might have cash exacted by lunkheaded yobs with tattooed fingers.

Should you find yourself on the business end of the legal system, you can get advice and referrals to lawyers from **Legal Services Commission** (ℂ **084/5345-4345;** www.legalservices. gov.uk). Victims of crime can receive volunteer legal guidance and emotional fortification from **Victim Support** (ℂ **0845/450-3936;** www.victimsupport.org.uk). In the unlikely event of a sexual assault, phone the **Rape Crisis Federation** (ℂ 0808/082-9999; www. rapecrisis.org.uk).

Senior Travel Don't hide your age! Seniors in England are usually classified as those aged 60 and over, and they're privy to all kinds of price breaks, from lower admission prices at museums to a third off rail tickets (but you first have to apply for the **Senior Railcard;** www.senior-railcard. co.uk). You may hear seniors being referred to as OAPs, which stands for Old Age Pensioners. That acronym is falling out of use, perhaps because it's rare to find a solvent pension fund anymore. Don't be offended if you're also referred to as a "geezer," though—in England, it's a compliment that means a fun-loving (if sometimes rowdy) bloke.

If you're over 50, you can join **AARP** (601 E Street NW, Washington, DC,

20049; ☎ **888/687-2277;** www.aarp.org), and wrangle discounts on hotels, airfare, and car rentals. The well-respected **Elderhostel** (☎ **800/454-5768;** www.elderhostel.org) runs many classes and programs in London designed to delve into literature, history, the arts, and music. Packages last from a week to a month and include airfare, lodging, and meals.

Smoking   Smoking is prohibited by law in any enclosed workplace, including museums, pubs, public transportation, and restaurants. If in doubt, ask permission.

Student Travel   Have ID ready to go, and always mention that you're a student, because it'll save you cash, including on trains to other cities. Attractions gladly offer discounts of around 25% for full-time students, but your high school or university ID may not cut it where clerks haven't heard of your school. Before leaving home, obtain a recognized ID such as the **International Student Identity Card** (ISIC; www.isic.org or www.myISIC.com). Those under 26 who are not in school can obtain an **International Youth Travel Card,** also through ISIC, which performs many of the same tricks as a student discount card.

Before buying airline tickets, those under 26 should consult a travel agency that specializes in the youth

market and is versed in its available discounts: **STA Travel** (☎ **800/781-4040;** www.statravel.com) is big.

Taxes   All goods prices in the U.K. are quoted inclusive of taxes. Since 2011 the national value-added tax (**VAT**) has stood at 20%. This is included in all hotel and restaurant bills, and in the price of most items you purchase.

If you are permanently resident outside the E.U., VAT on goods can be refunded if you shop at stores that participate in the **Retail Export Scheme**—look for the window sticker or ask the staff. See p. 162 for details. Information about the scheme is also posted online at **www.hmrc.gov.uk/vat/sectors/consumers/overseas-visitors.htm**.

Telephones   Directory assistance: ☎ **118-500** or www.bt.com. Local calls start with 020. The main toll-free prefixes are 0800, 0808, and 0500. Numbers starting with 07 are usually for mobile phones and will be charged at a higher rate. Numbers starting with 09 and are premium-rate calls that will usually be very expensive (around £1.50 per minute) and may not even work from abroad.

Many attractions, hotel companies, and services have cynically changed their standard phone numbers to profit-generating ones that charge for every minute you call them. Sometimes, these are not reachable from

outside the United Kingdom or Internet calling. If you find you cannot reach a number in this book, try from London, or use the website.

When dialing a number in this book from abroad, precede it with your country's international prefix (in the U.S. and Canada, it's 011), add the U.K.'s country code (44) and drop the first zero in the number. Many British companies are cheap and don't offer toll-free numbers. You often can't reach 0845, 0870, and 0871 numbers (charged at 10p a minute or less) from abroad, and when you can, you're charged more; if you have to call one from abroad, use the Web instead to get information. 0845 numbers are charged at a local rate; 0870 at the national rate. The 0845 prefix enables some companies to make a little money for every call received. As you can imagine, this profiteering leads to putting customers on hold.

To make an **international call** from Britain, dial the international access code (**00**), then the country code, then the area code, and finally the local number. If you call a toll-free number located back home, you'll still pay international rates for it.

The majority of London's rapidly vanishing **payphones** are operated by BT (British Telecom), and they are costly. The minimum charge is 60p (nothing under a 10p coin accepted, and phones don't give change), which buys a 30-minute call for local and national numbers. You can imagine how outrageous an international call would cost from the same machine. Some payphones accept credit cards at a premium: £1.20 to start and 20p per minute for local and domestic. Full charge breakdowns by country and call duration are at **British Telecom** (www.payphones.bt.com/publicpayphones). Stick to payphones on the street if you can, since phones at many pubs and hotels legally jigger their phones to charge at a higher rate.

Calling from a mobile phone, dial the full number including area code.

Phonecards are often the most economical method for both international and national calls. They are available in several values, and are reusable until the total value has expired. Cards can be purchased from newsstands and small retailers citywide, and offer call rates of a few pence per minute to English-speaking countries such as Australia and the United States.

Many hotels routinely add outrageous surcharges onto phone calls made from your room. It's usually much cheaper to purchase a phonecard.

Time London is generally 5 hours ahead of New York City and Toronto, 8 hours ahead of Los Angeles, 11 hours behind Auckland, and 9 hours behind Sydney. It is

1 hour behind western continental Europe.

Tipping It's less intense than in the United States, but it's gradually Americanizing. **Waiters** should receive 10% to 15% of the bill unless service is already included—always check the menu or bill for service charges because traditions are changing. At pubs, tipping isn't customary unless you receive table service. Fine hotels also usually levy a service charge, but at the finest ones, it may help your treatment to grease the staff with a pound here and there. Staff at B&Bs and family-run hotels don't expect tips. Bartenders and chambermaids need not be tipped.

There's no need to tip **taxicab drivers** but most people round up to the next £1, although a 10 to 15% tip is becoming increasingly standard.

Toilets London doesn't have enough of them. Washrooms can be found at any free museum in this guide, any department store, any pub or busy restaurant (though it's polite to buy something), and at Piccadilly Circus and Bank Tube stations. Train stations also have public toilets, some of which may cost 20p to 50p. Also keep an eye out for spray-cleaned, coin-operated (50p) Automatic Public Conveniences, or APCs.

VAT See "Taxes," above.

Visas No E.U. nationals require a visa to visit the

U.K. Visas are also not required for travelers from Australia, Canada, New Zealand, or the U.S. To be sure that hasn't changed, see **www.ukvisas.gov.uk/en/doineedvisa**. The usual permitted stay is 90 days or fewer for tourists, although some nationalities are granted stays of up to 6 months. If you plan to work or study, though, or if you're traveling on a passport from another country, you'll need to obtain the correct paperwork.

Visitor Information Three official information offices supported by British tax dollars are set up to help tourists—all for free. **Visit Britain** (www.visitbritain.com) is the bureau for the whole country; **Visit England** (www.visitengland.com) is for just England. But **Visit London** (www.visitlondon.com) possesses the bigger database by far. It doesn't offer a phone number, but it has a blog (blog.visitlondon.com) and a steady showing on Facebook and Twitter where responds to questions. When it books tickets for you, it makes money from commissions.

The Square Mile has its own leaflet-crammed visitor information center, the **City of London Information Centre** (✆ **020/7332-1456**) opposite the south side of St. Paul's Cathedral. Opening hours are Monday to Saturday 9:30am to 5:30pm, Sunday 10am to 4pm.